A NOTE ON THE AUTHOR

DAVID PLANTE is the author of the novels *The Ghost of Henry James*, *The Family* (nominated for the National Book Award), *The Woods*, *The Country*, *The Foreigner*, *The Native*, *The Accident*, *Annunciation* and *The Age of Terror*. He has published stories and profiles in the *New Yorker* and features in the *New York Times*, *Esquire* and *Vogue*. He lives in London; Lucca, Italy; and Athens, Greece.

Fiction

The Ghost of Henry James
Slides
Relatives
The Darkness of the Body
Figures in Bright Air
The Family
The Country
The Woods
The Catholic
The Native
The Accident
Annunciation
The Age of Terror
ABC

Non-fiction

Difficult Women: A Memoir of Three
American Ghosts
The Pure Lover

BECOMING A LONDONER

A Diary

DAVID PLANTE

B L O O M S B U R Y
LONDON · NEW DELHI · NEW YORK · SYDNEY

First published in Great Britain 2013

This paperback edition published 2014

Copyright © David Plante 2013

The moral right of the author has been asserted

All images ~~ ~ ~~~ ~~~ ~~~ ~~~ ~~ ~~~~ ~~~ ~~~ ~~ ~~~~~~~ ~~~ lited otherwise

E
m

Jers of
rtently
n.

A CIP catalogue record for this book is available from the British Library

ISBN 978 1 4088 4011 5

10 9 8 7 6 5 4 3 2 1

Typeset by Hewer Text UK Ltd, Edinburgh
Printed and bound in Great Britain by CPI Group (UK) Ltd, Croydon CR0 4YY

For Paul LeClerc

'You always get it wrong.'

Philip Roth to David Plante

Nikos Stangos and David Plante by Stephen Spender, San Andrea di Rovereto di Chiavari, 1968

Author's Note

I have kept a diary for over half a century. It is many millions of words long, and is stored in the Berg Collection of the New York Public Library. This present book is just over 165,000 words, and is roughly within the scope of the first twenty or so years of my life in London, 1966 to 1986, with events from later. The book consists of selections taken from my diary, all elaborated upon by memory and, too, made informative of people and places for publication, as I find footnotes distracting, though I do sometimes introduce a name and later give the person an identifying context. It is not uncommon for me to take an entire day, or even days, to complete one diary entry. The entries are not chronological – in fact, I have eliminated all but one date with the idea of forming something of a narrative which I hope forms into a world. The narrative continues beyond this book into what may be further books, allowing me in the present book to introduce someone who will, I hope, be more fully realized in the next book. I think of the title of Stephen Spender's World within World as appropriate to what I would like to do – appropriate in many ways, as he is himself a world within the world of this book. To make a book out of the diary has meant choosing what to put in and what to leave out, and though my impulse is to put everything in as the honest way (no doubt a more honest way would be to leave everything out), the book would bulge its covers. I have had to leave out worlds of experience in Italy, in Greece, in France, in Russia, in

New York, in, oh!, Tulsa, Oklahoma, worlds which occurred within the more circumscribed London world that I have concentrated on here. And within the London world I have concentrated on people I think most representative of the culture of that world. I came as a stranger to London and here was lucky enough to form relationships with people I could not have imagined meeting before I came to London. Ideally, I would have liked to start with the very first entry of my diary, June 1959, and only after having included the entries from then arrive at June 1966, this the only date stated in this book. Within the millions of words of my diary there are worlds within worlds, but this book accounts for a span (by no means all of it) of my continuing life in London, in which world capital my life continues to expand far beyond this book.

The entries from my diary featuring Francis Bacon were collated and published in the New Yorker; the entries featuring Harold Acton were expanded from diary entries for a portrait also published in the New Yorker; as for Steven Runciman, I used a tape to record his amazing elaborations on history, especially the history of a hubble-bubble, none of which I could have remembered, the resulting portrait also published in the New Yorker. The events featuring Philip Roth were first published in the New York Times Book Review.

Spelling and usage have sometimes changed into British from American over the years, so I note that I write 'honour' but kept 'gray'. I rather like this evidence of an American becoming British while remaining American as well.

From so many years past, I feel that the events recorded in here have nothing to do with me. I have no idea whom they have to do with, this young man dazed by a world around him that in itself has gone.

As for my continuing the diary now, as a diarist I remain who I was at least in this way: possessed by a diary that is in itself possessive, always anxious that much more has been left out than got (gotten?) in.

David Plante, June 2013

London

June 1966

As I was approaching from one end of the street the house where Nikos lives, 6 Wyndham Place, I saw him approaching from the other end. He was wearing a dark business suit and carrying a briefcase, returning from the office of the press attaché at the Greek Embassy.

Meeting me, he said, 'If you'd come a minute earlier, you would have rung and no one would have answered.'

'I'd have come back,' I said.

I followed close behind him as he opened doors with keys into his flat, so close I bumped into him when he paused just inside to turn to me to ask me, his face so near mine I could have leaned just a little forward and kissed him, if I'd like to go out or stay in to eat.

'I'd prefer to stay in,' I said.

'You like staying in?'

'I do.'

'So do I,' he said.

He said he'd change, and I, in the living room, looked around for something Greek, but saw nothing.

He came from his bedroom wearing grey slacks and a darker grey cardigan, and we had drinks before, he said, he'd prepare us something to eat.

He told me how much he likes America, how much he likes Americans, who were, he believed, the only people capable of true originality.

I asked him why he was living in London.

Because, he said, living in London he was not living in Athens. His job in the office of the press attaché was the only job he had been able to get that would allow him to leave Greece.

Why?

He would tell me later.

I said, 'I have a lot to learn about Greece.'

He showed me one of his poems, written in English. It was called 'Pure Reason', and it was a love poem, addressed to 'you'. The poem read almost as if it were arguing a philosophical idea with the person addressed, the terms of the argument as abstract as any philosophical argument. The philosophical idea is reasoning at its purest. What is remarkable about the poem is that, in conveying, as it does, intellectual purity, it conveys, more, emotional purity, and it centres the purity – intellectual and emotional and moral – in the person with whom the poet is so much in love. I had never read anything like it.

When I handed the poem back to him, he asked me if I would stay the night with him.

In his bed, he said to me, 'Even if you're worried that it would hurt me, you must always tell me, honestly, what you think, because, later, your dishonesty would hurt much more.'

I said, 'I'm not certain what I think.'

'About me?'

'About everything.'

————

I am staying with Öçi in his small flat in Swiss Cottage.

He is at work, at Heathrow Airport, where he welcomes and sorts out the problems of visitors using his languages, besides English, Turkish, Greek, Hungarian, Spanish, making him linguistically the most cosmopolitan person I know.

Seven years ago, the Öçi I came to London longing to be with is no longer the Öçi I now know. I was in love with him. I don't love him as I so loved him, but he is a friend.

It seems to me that the Öçi I loved is contained within a room, a moonlit room, in Spain, in a seaside town in Spain, we both in beds across the room from each other, talking. Never mind how we found ourselves in that room, in our separate beds across the room from each other, talking, but remember the smell of suntan lotion, remember the sensation of skin slightly burnt by the sun, remember that skin seemingly made rough by sea salt, remember lying naked in the midst of a tangled sheet, the erection of a nineteen-year-old who had never had sex bouncing against his stomach. We talked, we talked, I can't remember about what – perhaps my telling him that my holiday in Spain would soon come to an end and I would go to the Catholic University of Louvain, Belgium, for the academic year, emphasizing my regret that I would be leaving Spain, which would be leaving all that was promised in my having met him – and then silence between us. He got up from his bed and, naked, went to the open window and leaned out into the moonlight and breathed the fresh pre-dawn air, from where he turned to me and I held out my arms to him. Never, never had I known such a sensation, never, and I fell in love with Öçi for the wonder of that sensation.

A sensation I had to have again and again with him, because I felt that it was only with him that such a sensation was possible.

I went to Louvain, but longed for Öçi in Spain.

When he wrote that he would be in London for the winter holidays, I, possessed by my love, came to London.

He did not love me.

Leave this, from seven years ago, but remember that moonlit room.

When I told Öçi that I had met someone named Nikos Stangos, whom I liked, he said he would find out about this Nikos Stangos through his connections. He smiled his slow, sensual, ironical smile, and said he had many connections, in Turkey, in Greece, in Spain, even in Hungary if I was interested, and, of course, in London.

Later, Öçi told me he had made contact with a Greek who had met Nikos, and, as always with his slow, sensual, ironical smile, as if this was his attitude towards all the world, he said that he had heard that Nikos, working in the Press Office of the Greek Embassy, is 'acceptable.'

I tried to smile, saying, 'That's good to know.'

―――――

I rang Nikos at the Press Office of the Greek Embassy. He said he had thought of going, that evening, to a cello recital by Rostropovich at the Royal Festival Hall. Would I like to go with him? During the recital I was attentive to his attention to the music. As always, I felt that he was in a slight trance; it showed in his stillness, but also in what appeared to me a presence about him, as if his calm extended around his body.

After the recital, he was silent. I didn't know why he was so silent, but I, too, remained silent. Delicate as the calm was that appeared to extend all about him, I felt, within him, a solid gravity; it was as if that gravity caused the outward, trance-like calm by its inward pull. Silent, we crossed the Thames on the walkway over Hungerford Bridge. The trains to the side of the walkway made the bridge sway. In the middle, Nikos reached into a pocket of his jacket and took out a large copper penny, which he threw down into the grey-brown, swiftly moving river far below.

'What's that for?' I asked.

'For luck,' he said.

The evening was warm and light. We walked from the Embankment at Charing Cross up to Trafalgar Square, all the while silent.

In Trafalgar Square, he suggested we sit, and we walked among the people standing in groups to the far left corner, behind a great, gushing fountain, where there was no one else and we sat on a stone bench.

We wondered who, in history, had first thought of a water-gushing fountain. In ancient Greece, Nikos said, a fountain was usually a public spigot that water flowed from to fill jugs brought by women. Perhaps the ancient Romans first thought of a gushing fountain that had no use but to look at?

After a silence, Nikos said he had thought very carefully, and he wanted me, too, to think carefully, about what he was going to say. It was very, very important that I be totally honest.

He was in a love relationship with an older Englishman, who was in fact away, and Nikos decided that on the Englishman's return he would tell him their love relationship must come to an end. He had decided this on meeting me, but I must not think that this meant I should feel I had to return the feelings Nikos had for me. I was free, and I must always know that I am free. Then he asked me if I would live with him.

I placed my hands over my face and rocked back and forth.

I moved in with him the next day.

He is twenty-eight and I am twenty-six.

———

Öçi is offended that I should have left him to move in with Nikos. He sent me a sarcastic letter, denouncing me for my 'opportunism' in my 'affiliation with Mr. Stangos,' who I must think can offer me more than he, Öçi, can as a friend. I showed the letter to Nikos; he said that he would find out about Öçi among Greeks living in London (Öçi's mother is Greek from the Pontus in Turkey, his father Hungarian, and he grew up in Turkey), and when Nikos did he said that he had passed on a message to Öçi through the network of Greek connections (a network that Nikos does everything to stay out of) that he would like to meet Öçi, that we should all meet.

———

Nikos was eager to show me something he had received from Stephen Spender, in Washington, which is on his desk in the sitting room. 'Look,' he said, 'a reproduction of Andrea del Castagno's The Youthful David.'

He said he was not sure how he would tell Spender about me when Spender returned to London.

———

We should go for the weekend to Brighton, Nikos said, to see Francis King, who lives there. Francis has recently published a novel, called, I think, The Man on the Rock, about an Englishman falling in love with a Greek young man. With his pointed, pale face and large, gold-rimmed glasses, Francis King looks like someone who would work for the British Council, which he did do in Japan and in Greece. He spoke a little Greek with Nikos. He arranged a hotel for us. He said he was sorry, he had tried to put us into a hotel for queers, but it was full up. I was relieved that Nikos and I were not staying in a queer hotel. Our room had zebra-stripe wallpaper. We met Francis to go to a pub, and as we were entering I realized it was for queers, and everything in me drew back from going in with Nikos. He hung back with me and asked what was wrong. I said, 'I don't want to go in there with you.' He asked me, please, not to insist, and I went in.

As though he assumed Nikos would be amused, Francis recounted how, for a pack of cigarettes, he had had sex in Greece with a shepherd. Nikos smiled a small, tight smile, clearly holding back from this insult to Greece.

Later, alone, he told me how the long tradition of men from Northern Europe thinking that Greek boys were there for them to have sex with is part of the fantasy that these men have of ancient Greece continuing in the Greece of today, and the Greek boys are so in need of money that they comply.

He said he was glad I hadn't wanted us to go into that pub.

Why didn't I want to go into the pub? I wanted, and want, Nikos to have nothing to do with my past in America, in New York, where I failed, and failed most severely in relationships that I associate with being in the New York queer world. I want, here in London, in England, in Great Britain, to form a new life with Nikos, even though he is Greek and I am American, for we have both left our countries for new lives in this country.

I want us to be, as a couple, Nikos and David, which I think we could not be if we were Nikos and David in Athens, which city Nikos has left, or David and Nikos in New York, which city I have left.

We went to the pier and played at the slot machines, using up many big copper pennies. A penny animated a whole landscape in a glass case: a tiny train ran about a track, children's heads popped out of flowers, and, in the midst, a large, plastic tulip opened and out of it emerged a ballerina, en pointe, who turned round in jerks and then sank back into the tulip, which closed its petals over her.

For the fun of it, Nikos and I took photographs of ourselves together in an automatic booth.

In a junk shop, as if acquiring objects that would fix us in our domestic lives, Nikos and I bought two yellow ceramic pots, an art nouveau vase with purple irises, and four blue volumes of Master-pieces of British Art with a gold art nouveau design on the covers, the objective beginnings of our shared lives.

Nikos showed me a poem which Stephen Spender, who is now
resident poet at the Library of Congress in Washington, wrote for
him.

> When we talk, I imagine silence
> Beyond the intervalling words: a space
> Empty of all but ourselves there, face to face,
> Away from others, alone in the intense
> Light or dark, it would not matter which.
>
> But where a room envelopes us, one heart,
> Our bodies, locked together, prove apart
> Unless we change them back again to speech.
> Close to you here, looking at you, I see
> Beyond your eyes looking back, that second you
> Of whom the outward semblance is the image –
> The inward being where the name springs true.
> Today, left only with a name, I rage,
> Willing these lines – willing a name to be
> Flesh, on the blank unanswering page.

Nikos said he loved Stephen Spender very much.

———

Why Nikos left Greece, he told me, is history – the history of his
father having to leave Bulgaria, where his father's family had lived
since when the town, now Sosopol, was the ancient Greek town of
Apollonia; and his mother having to leave Constantinople, where
her family had been since Byzantium – had to leave because Greece
had invaded Bulgaria and Turkey to reclaim, after centuries, the
Hellenistic empire, known as the Big Idea, but Greece had been
defeated, and the agreement was, in the 1920s, an exchange of
populations in which all Greeks had to leave Bulgaria and Turkey
and all Bulgarians and Turks had to leave Greece. Nikos' parents
were refugees in Athens, and were treated as refugees, Nikos himself

always feeling that he was a foreigner in Greece, his accent not Athenian, and, his parents of the diaspora more cultured than native Greeks, more culturally and linguistically international.

He told me that if I meet Greeks who speak various languages, who are informed about art and literature and music, most likely they will have come from Constantinople or Alexandria, from both of which cities they were expelled.

The Exchange of Populations is called the Catastrophe.

'Catastrophe' is a word he often uses.

We are back from Yugoslavia, in 6 Wyndham Place. Coming back from our holiday together to his flat makes me feel I am no longer just staying with him, but living with him, so that his flat is my flat too.

In Venice, crossing the Piazza Grande, Nikos put his arm across my shoulders and said, 'Here in Italy, we can walk together like this.' We stayed in a cheap hotel behind the basilica.

The boat from Venice to Opatija stopped for a few hours at Pula. The little seaside town appeared to be all hard edges, with a roughness to it that was like the roughness of the khaki-green uniforms of the soldiers walking down a muddy road. Nikos and I went to the Museum of the Revolution in the ruins of the fortress on a promontory overlooking the town, a small, whitewashed museum with machine guns, yellowing posters and blown-up photographs of executions. We were the only ones there, all around us the summer sound of insects. The museum seemed to be falling apart. Nikos looked at everything carefully, even reverentially, and said, 'I feel so safe here.'

The boat took us to Rijeka, from where we took a taxi to Medveja, outside Opatija, and we found a hotel on the coast, a former mansion of Tito, where we had a small room with two very small beds. It rained a lot. Yugoslavia was not at all like Greece, as Nikos had supposed it would be, so there were no coffee houses to go to and sit out the rain. We stayed a lot in our room.

He had taken Stephen Spender's autobiography World within World for me to read. Often we read it together, both of us squeezed into one of the narrow beds.

This was a touchy period for us. We easily argued, easily became depressed about the rain or the bad food, but were also easily elated when the sun came out or when we were able to order a fresh fish for dinner. Whatever we did, whatever we said, whatever we read took on large proportions, the proportions of a relationship expanding and contracting and expanding again into some form of love. Reading passages from World within World to one another about Stephen Spender's relationship with Jimmy Younger, we were moved to tears.

And for me to read about people I had only ever fantasized about – W. H. Auden, Christopher Isherwood, and the inner world of the fantastic Bloomsbury group which included Virginia Woolf and Leonard Woolf and Vita Sackville-West and Vanessa Bell and Duncan Grant and Lytton Strachey and Lady Ottoline Morrell and T. S. Eliot and E. M. Forster, all of whom Spender in fact knew – was to open up that world, that entirely English world, in which I fantasize having a place, even if that world no longer exists in itself. It exists in the witness of Stephen Spender.

And this is my overwhelming fantasy of England: that it is a country of absolute respect for differences in each and every one, all the more so for the startling originality of each and every one, this respect made possible because they all knew one another, all of them, and they all knew that they had created in their work a new awareness that was English, whatever the Englishness of the awareness could be.

I fantasize myself, say, at High Table at King's College Cambridge, with Maynard Keynes presiding, I at one side of him and at the other Rupert Brooke; and after there would be wine in Maynard Keynes' rooms with Dadie Rylands and Virginia Woolf and E. M. Forster, talking about – well, talking about everyone that they knew, talking about them, however critically, with a sense that they made up a world. And they did make up a world, and they knew that the world was English. And they all slept with one another!

But, I have to remind myself, this is my overwhelming fantasy, and I have no idea if it has anything at all to do with England.

When we were lying together in the sun on the rocks by the sea, Nikos again told me that whatever happens between us depends on our being totally honest with one another. Even if I thought him ugly, I must tell him. No, I said, I didn't find him ugly.

———

Is it because I'm in Europe that I am so aware of World War II, and, behind that war, World War I, called the Great War? Our landlady, a delicate and dignified woman of extreme courtesy, on brief visits tells us of her driving a lorry during the last war, and I am aware that the wars did not take place 'over there,' but here, here, around me.

———

While alone here in our home in Wyndham Place, I filled a little notebook with what I can only think of as obscenities, all as if released from having been kept back during my life in New York, released now here in London, gross obscenities. I showed the notebook to Nikos, whose only comment was that the writing itself was good – was, because I then blackened the pages with black ink so that the text can't be read. And so, I think, I have blackened out my life in New York.

My life in London –

———

About Greece –

Nikos has a curious Greek national sense of connection with Prince Philip, whose mother Princess Alice lives in Athens, a nun. After Greek independence from the Ottoman Empire, the only person willing to take on the role of king, as at that time the titular head of any European state had to be, was a young royal from Bohemia, Otho. Princess Alice is by marriage connected to the lineage, and so, Nikos says, is Prince Philip. There are stories about her having hid Jews, and of having set up soup kitchens and having served the food to starving people, during the Nazi occupation of Athens. Apparently, she lives in a modest flat, and whether or not she has contact with her son or her daughter-in-law the Queen, very few people would know.

So I learn about Greece –

Nikos tells me there is no Greek aristocracy, which distinguishes the country from generations of European aristocracy. There are no medieval castles or Renaissance villas, for all the while Europe was evolving from the Middle Ages into the Renaissance, Greece was occupied by the Ottoman Empire. No Greek aristocracy developed around Otho or any subsequent king. The Greek royal family, Nikos said, speak German to one another.

Nikos has taught me to write the name Greece in Greek letters, which letters stand above the country's history like a temple:

ΕΛΛΑΣ

——————

I haven't kept this diary in some weeks, during which I think I went through the most emotionally violent time of my life.

Nikos introduced me to acupuncture, which had been introduced to him by the painter Johnny Craxton, for Nikos' migraines; as he found it helped him, he thought the same would help me with what a doctor in New York had suggested was a duodenal ulcer, due, no doubt, to my failed life in New York, a failure that was entirely my own fault, for in New York I had behaved badly, very badly.

The acupuncturist, Indian, Singha, had his surgery in the sitting room of a semi-detached house in Hendon, and I was very skeptical the first time I went as I lay on a trolley and heard pop music from the kitchen, where I presumed his wife was. But I allowed Singha to insert fine needles between my toes and fingers, after which he left me and I had the vivid sense of falling within myself. The sessions over the weeks become confused. I remember his pressing his hands on my chest, over and over, more and more emphatically, until I was breathing in and out in spasms, and I suddenly shouted for my mother and sobbed. He covered me with a blanket and left me until I again felt as if I was falling.

On the bus back to Nikos, I sensed the darkness of my New York – say, my American darkness – open up beneath me dangerously. At home, a deep tiredness came over me after the meal Nikos prepared, as I wasn't able to move, and he helped me to bed, where I slept for over twenty-four hours. The darkness deepened. On the weekends, Nikos and I would go for a walk in Hyde Park, where it seemed to me my very body was straining to go in many different directions at once, each direction to one of the many young men in the park who attracted me, and if I hadn't been with Nikos I would have tried to go in all the directions – as I had tried to do in New York. The fact is, I had come to Europe to be promiscuous, even more promiscuous than I had been in New York, as if in my fantasy Europe offered more sexual promiscuity than America, even New York, because in Europe I would be totally free and not think of being faithful to a relationship. Nikos would say, 'Breathe in, now breathe out,' which I would do, and then – what I longed for – back home for our afternoon nap, where the greatest reassurance beyond sex was falling asleep with Nikos.

The most shocking reaction to the acupuncture didn't occur at Singha's surgery, but back home, where, again, Nikos prepared a meal after which I became immobile, he more or less carrying me to our bed where I fell and suddenly twitched violently, then more and more violently, and I began to make hissing sounds through my bared teeth and then, with clenched fist, to make stabbing gestures. Worried, Nikos rang Singha, who told him to let me be, I would be all right; and I knew I would be, as I was able to look down at myself from a distance and tell myself that I could stop the fit if I wanted to, but, here, safe with Nikos, I could let the fit take its course. It lasted the night, Nikos sitting on the side of the bed. In the morning, I found that the palms of both hands were bleeding from my fingernails. I was in bed for three days, Nikos, before work and after, having to help me to the toilet.

When, back with Singha, I recounted what had happened to me, he appeared not at all surprised, and I thought, well, perhaps it was nothing to be surprised about, but when I left him, walking along Hendon Way, the sunlight slanting through the unpainted pickets of a tall fence, I all at once knew that there was nothing to worry about, that everything would be all right, and a lightness of spirit came to me.

Strange, it is as though I didn't go through all the above, as though it happened to someone else I hardly know.

But how can I not think but that Nikos has cured me of an illness I arrived in London with?

———

Nikos told me he had, before he met me, invited a French boy to stay with him in his flat, Alain, and because Alain, coming to London from Paris, was counting on staying Nikos couldn't tell him no. Nikos showed me Alain's letters, in which he wrote, 'I am quite the little homosexual.' Nikos said, 'He isn't. He's joking. He wrote this, flirting, just because he wants to stay in my flat.' Now Alain is staying in the flat with Nikos and me, and he sleeps on the sofa in the sitting room while Nikos and I sleep in the bedroom. He is seventeen.

———

Our first drinks party together, the wine and the spirits Nikos bought cheaply from the Greek Embassy for entertaining. Because I was drunk, the only person I recall enough to distinguish him was a very tall, broad, bald-headed man, whose skull appears to be close to the skin, John Lehmann, who is a poet and who was a publisher and who worked with Virginia and Leonard Woolf at the Hogarth Press. No doubt I distinguish him because he seemed to distinguish me from the others, and, before leaving, asked me to 'swiggle' (I think that's what he said) my name and telephone number on a piece of paper. When he saw the number is the same as that of Nikos, he smiled and said, 'You live together,' and I, 'We do,' and he left.

After the drinks party, Nikos and Johnny Craxton and Alain and I went out to a restaurant, and I found I was as bored as Alain because of the talk between Nikos and Craxton about people in London we didn't know. Nikos and Craxton, smoking cigars at the end of the meal, appeared to be settled in for hours, especially when they talked to each other in Greek, and I did feel, somewhat, that I was the boyfriend, as in the periphery as Alain, both of us silent.

Johnny mentioned Lucian Freud, and I, always curious (and perhaps more than curious, possessive of a world I don't know), asked if he knew Lucian Freud, and he said, simply, that he and Lucian Freud once had studios in the same house, and I had the sense he didn't want to say more. But now I make a connection between Johnny Craxton and Lucian Freud, and I wonder what other connections are to be made. Connections criss-cross, invisibly, through the air of London.

It would be disingenuous of me to write that I am not aware of all the connections, all, I imagine, finally connecting into a London world.

Johnny has a house in Chania, Crete, and paints scenes of the Greek countryside of goats eating figs from gnarled trees and young men playing backgammon at coffee-house tables.

———

Stephen Spender is back in London. Nikos wanted to see him on his own before he introduces him to me. They had lunch together in a restaurant, then came to the flat, where I was waiting with Alain. Nikos came in with Spender, who seemed to pay more attention to Alain than to me. I remarked that Spender is very tall, with very large hands and feet. He made a date with Alain for tea before he left. Nikos went with him to the entry passage to the street door, from where I heard Spender say, 'He's very nice.' I supposed he was talking about me, but maybe he was talking about Alain.

Nikos asked me if I liked him, and I said yes. 'I'm glad,' Nikos said, 'I was anxious that you and he wouldn't like one another, or that Stephen would be upset by your living with me.'

Nikos took Alain and me to dinner that evening, and back at the flat Alain again slept on the sofa while Nikos and I slept together in the bedroom.

I wonder what Alain makes of us sleeping together, and, he must hear, making love together. He simply smiles a large, clear, young smile.

What worlds within worlds am I living in?

———

I didn't come directly from New York to London, but from New York went to Boston, wanting to get away from New York, but I left Boston soon after to come to London for the same reason that I had left New York: not sexual promiscuity, but sexual unfaithfulness, the two different, for sexual promiscuity is in itself irrelevant to relationships, and sexual unfaithfulness is the cause of great pain in relationships. Well, perhaps the two overlap more than not.

Helen, my faithful friend beyond sex, is visiting from Boston. We went to Hampstead Heath. After a terrible automobile accident, she limps along with a cane (in England, a stick). We walked up and down muddy paths through over-grown, wet woods, and I got lost. We wandered for over an hour, until I realized I must find the way back toward Hampstead Underground Station, as I was to have lunch with Nikos and Spender, and the time was getting late. I thought the way must be in this direction, and Helen followed me. We came out into an open space where I was able to see, in the blue, hazy distance, hills and more woods. I said, no, we must go in that direction, and we entered the woods again. Almost two hours passed. We came on no one to ask directions from. I got into a panic. I didn't want to miss Spender, and I realized just how much I wanted to see him, as though so much depended on it, as though he would think I didn't want to see him if I didn't appear and he, then, would not want to see me again. And Nikos would be worried, as he always is if I'm late. I became impatient with Helen, my old, dear friend, but the more impatient I became I suppressed the impatience with courteousness, even if this meant missing Spender. I finally found our way out, Helen more relieved than I.

When I got back to Wyndham Place, Spender was leaving, and, out of breath, I apologized. He smiled, and it occurred to me that I shouldn't have panicked, that we'd see one another again.

He seems to leave his white hair uncombed.

———

Helen and I went with the artist Patrick Procktor to Regent's Park to lie on the grass, where Patrick did a sketch of me. With a high tone that may or may not have been ironical, he said something like, 'I'm so glad Nikos now has you as his friend.' After we left him, Helen asked me, 'What did he mean by friend? Is that an English expression for something?' I, embarrassed, said, 'I haven't been in England long enough to know.' I have a life in England I wouldn't admit having in America.

Patrick as an artist seems to me to be between two totally differ-ent worlds – one of languorous and druggy young men lounging on sofas and the other of Chinese Revolutionary Guards demon-strating for the Cultural Revolution of Mao – and I can't see any meeting of the two, for I doubt that Chinese Revolutionary Guards lounge about on sofas amid flowers and smoking hashish and reading the Little Red Book in quite the same revolutionary spirit as the young people Patrick depicts in aquatints, though I suppose there is a revolution occurring in both worlds. Is Patrick being ironical, as he is about everything?

He is a friend of Nikos from before Nikos and I met, and, as with so many of Nikos' friends from before, I have no idea how they came to be friends, and I am, I admit, jealous of his relationships that had to have excluded me before I met Nikos, an impossible jealousy. So, I don't want to know what Nikos' relationships were, not even, or especially not, with Stephen Spender. I want to think Patrick's friend-ship with Nikos began with my friendship with Nikos, want to think that all of Nikos' past friendships in London have begun with my meeting him. Even Nikos' love for Stephen.

———

Stephen Spender telephoned. I answered. He said how happy he was that Nikos should have such a nice friend. Stuttering a little, I thanked him a little formally, though I tried not to be formal. I can't yet call him Stephen. I said I thought it was unfair that I should know so much about him from his books and he so little about me, and perhaps he could get to know me without any books. He said he would like that. After, I wondered if I had sounded presumptuous.

———

Öçi came for drinks, and immediately he and Nikos connected by way of the names of people they know, or know of, in Greece, or names of Greeks they know, or know of, who live in London. Öçi wore a shirt made of white, diaphanous, finely pleated material, cinched in at his waist by a heavy belt made of big blue beads. I noted how large his nose is, with large pores. Nikos wore a brown cardigan, his white shirt open at the collar. His features are refined.

———

Patrick, dressed in tight purple velvet trousers, a loose shirt and a silk scarf about his neck, is very tall and lanky. The different parts of his body – head, arms, long torso, pelvis, legs – appear tenuously connected, so when he moves his body moves in different, swaying directions, as if he were slowly dancing, a cigarette poised in three fingers, the little finger held out.

He lives in a walkup in Manchester Street, Marylebone, decorated with Oriental-like cushions and rugs, a multi-coloured glass lamp hanging down in the midst.

David Hockney is painting a portrait of Patrick in his, Patrick's, flat, which I went round with Stephen Spender to see. Stephen and I often meet as if we had all the free time in the world, though Stephen will then say he feels guilty and should be at home writing; as long as I'm with him, I feel I am learning something about London. The large Hockney painting was in Patrick's sitting room. When I said how beautifully painted the basket is, Patrick, with a laugh close to a snort, asked, 'Which basket, darling?' and I noted the bulge in the crotch of his tight trousers.

He proposed doing a watercolour of Stephen and me, on his sofa. 'Get closer, darlings,' he said, and Stephen put an arm about me and I leaned against him. The portrait of Stephen is very good, precise, and Stephen's red socks and shiny black shoes are deftly painted; I, however, have a flat, grey face and a vacuous smile and most of my body is left blank. Patrick gave the picture to me.

Stephen asked me not to let his wife Natasha know about the picture.

I said, 'How could I let her know? I've never met her.'

He looked puzzled, as if this had not occurred to him.

He said, 'It's a bore, Natasha not wanting to meet you and Nikos.'

Ah, Nikos and me, Nikos and me, known as a couple more than we would be known singly.

Are we known as a couple whom Stephen dotes on? And how is this known by Natasha? If Stephen doesn't tell her, who does?

Stephen asked Nikos and me to lunch to meet Christopher Isherwood at Chez Victor, a restaurant writers have been going to for a long while. Isherwood, with his hair cut very short at the neck so his thin nape is almost bare but kept in long bangs over his forehead, looks like an aged little boy. He and Stephen giggled a lot, often at jokes Isherwood made about Stephen, the jokes all about Stephen's boyfriends in Berlin and how one cost Stephen an expensive suit, another an expensive meal. But whereas Isherwood seemed to make fun of Stephen, which Stephen enjoyed, or appeared to enjoy, Stephen didn't make fun of Isherwood.

Isherwood didn't pay much attention to Nikos and me, though perhaps he did by thinking his making fun of Stephen would entertain us.

When he left, to go on to someone he let us know was very grand, a movie star, Stephen said that Isherwood has never been interested in his friends.

———

A lazy Sunday lunch with Patrick. He said he had seen Alain, who has returned to Paris, and Alain had told him that Stephen made a pass at him when they were together for tea.

Patrick put Alain in a painting, among many young men all standing about as in a large room.

He did pencil drawings, one of me lying on the floor and reading the Sunday newspaper.

One of Nikos and me lying on the floor together.

Stephen is angry that Patrick has been telling people that he made a pass at Alain. His large face appeared to become larger the redder it got. He said, 'I didn't.'

Nikos, too, got angry. He said, 'Of course you didn't.'

I wonder why Nikos sided so quickly with Stephen against Alain.

———

Stephen will sometimes tell an anecdote about, say, Virginia Woolf – her telling him that a writer must not publish before the age of thirty – which I had read in his World within World, and I imagine him a mediator between myself and Virginia Woolf, whose advice Stephen no doubt thinks I should take.

———

When, I wonder, will I be able to write about an English character?

What I have understood about the English I meet is their suspicion of generalizations, of abstractions, so easy for an American. The American generalization about the English being reserved I've never in fact encountered. On a bus, I sat next to an elderly lady who told me, in a very matter-of-fact way, that she had just had a hysterectomy and this was the first time since her operation that she was out. 'I'm well now,' she said, 'well and well out of it.' I said, 'Yes, I must say, you're well out of it,' and she looked at me as if pleasantly surprised by my agreeing with her and smiled.

———

Stephen often asks me if I keep a diary, and I said, yes, I do, because I feel he wants me to. Today we were wandering together through the dark, narrow stacks of the London Library, where the floors are like cast-iron grills you can see through to the floors below, he looking for a magazine he needed but which we couldn't find. Stephen said, 'You can put this in your diary.' He couldn't find the magazine, and said it didn't matter. Leaving the library, we met Henry Reed, whom Stephen introduced me to, then Ruth Fainlight, whom Stephen also introduced me to. Henry Reed, Stephen told me, is a poet whose most famous poem is 'Naming of Parts', based on instructions given to soldiers about their rifles in World War II. About Ruth Fainlight, he said she is a poet and has a brother who is a poet, Harry Fainlight. Ruth Fainlight is married to the novelist Alan Sillitoe, whose novel The Loneliness of the Long-Distance Runner I had read. And so I begin to put things together, without really knowing, now, more than the names of writers. Then we walked to Cork Street, and we looked in all the galleries at what was showing. Stephen becomes especially animated when he meets someone he knows in a gallery, and, with a long, sideways undulation of his big body, he holds out a hand to me for me to come and be introduced.

Once, we were walking along Piccadilly and Stephen, spotting someone on the other side, ran across through the traffic to speak with him, an old man with bright white hair, wearing a bright blue jacket. Stephen waved to me to come, and he introduced me to Henry Moore.

———

I had this dream – that Nikos and I were sleeping together, as we in fact were, and that I was woken by someone out in Wyndham Place, calling for help. I also heard in the dream our landlady knocking on the door of the flat and saying, 'Mr. Stangos, Mr. Stangos,' to wake him, as I, too, tried to wake him by shaking him by the shoulder. But he wouldn't wake, and all the while the voice was calling for help from the street. Then I was woken by Nikos saying, 'Yes, what is it?' and as soon as I woke I realized that the voice in my dream was me calling for help from the street, which Nikos had heard.

———

The King's Road –

Along the King's Road on Saturday afternoon, Nikos and I went from shop to shop where clothes hang on racks from high up to low down, clothes that I consider costumes and Nikos as 'inventive' (a word he likes to use, as he does 'innovative' and 'original'). He was excited by a sailor's trousers, with the buttoned panel in front rather than flies, dyed bright yellow – bright yellow and now liberated from all military discipline.

He held the waist of the trousers up to his waist so they hung down, and he laughed.

I was jealous of his excitement, which seemed to me promiscuous.

I said, 'Come on, what would you do with a pair of yellow sailor's trousers?'

He put the trousers back on a pile of old clothes that smelled as though they had been worn and he turned away.

And then I grandiloquently said I would buy him the bright yellow sailor's trousers.

'No, no,' he said.

'I want you to have them,' I said.

There, here, my proof to him that I can be more expansively liberal than he is, here I am buying him a pair of bright yellow sailor's trousers that once fit, with sensual tightness, the thighs of a fantasy sailor. How much more liberal can I be?

But since then Nikos has never worn the dyed yellow sailor's trousers. I have.

———

I should keep a diary, Stephen has told me, for the sake of my writing, which writing I have, with Nikos' insistence, been devoting myself to. Stephen said I should use my diary to write with clarity and definition. He recommended that I simply describe.

As an example, he gave me a copy of Joe Ackerley's We Think the World of You, in which Ackerley had tipped in handwritten passages that he had had to censor from the book, about a love affair between an older man and a working-class boy, whose parents say about the man, 'We think the world of you,' but don't approve of his relationship with their son. The writing is very clear.

But there is so much to describe –

Describe Patrick's flat/studio, where Nikos and I were invited to tea before the big picture of demonstrating Chinese Revolutionary Guards he is working on. We had English tea, the cucumber sandwiches cut very thin.

He told us this story: he and Ossie Clark went to Harrods to buy scarves at the counter where ladies' scarves were sold and where, prancing, they tried on different ones about their necks and looked at themselves in the mirror, and when Patrick asked the sales lady which one she thought suited him best, she said, 'The green one, it's more masculine.' Patrick laughs, in bursts, through his nose.

Then David Hockney's flat/studio in Powis Terrace to look at the etchings of naked boys he was doing to accompany poems by Cavafy translated by Nikos and Stephen, the etchings spread out on the floor with male physique magazines from California.

David gave to Nikos some etchings that he rejected from the book to be published. One etching is of a naked boy packing a suitcase and beside him another naked boy either taking off or putting on underpants. Another is of two naked boys standing side by side and looking at themselves in a mirror. Another is of what David imagines to have been Cavafy's young, plump Egyptian Ptolemy with necklace and bracelet and painted fingernails.

Describe Mark Lancaster's loft, where he lives and paints. Mark is suave. He goes to New York often, and has, near the Angel, a loft, like the lofts in New York converted from urban industrial buildings. He has a miniature Empire State Building. Taken as he is by American popular culture, he is doing some paintings inspired by the orange and blue of the highway restaurants Howard Johnson, but abstracted into geometrical shapes; as are his works based on the film Zapruder, an amateur film taken by a spectator of the assassination of President Kennedy, again abstracted into pale rectangles of green. There is an ineffability to his work, the abstract shapes appearing to float off the canvas. As if in passing, he mentions that he was in a film made by Andy Warhol called Couch, in which he makes love with another guy. He wants to go live in New York, and with him I wonder if it was a mistake to have left that city, if in New York the air itself is so charged with creativity just being there makes one creative, creative in the use of the colours of Howard Johnson highway restaurants.

Mark said this about a difference between New York and London – in New York if you praise a picture you've painted as great it is believed to be great and if you self-deprecate and say it's nothing really it's believed to be nothing, but in London if you say a picture you've painted is great, or even good, you're considered pretentious and your picture not great or even good, but if you self-deprecate and say it's nothing really your painting has to be, if not great, good.

Stephen Buckley comes for drinks with his friend Bryan Ferry, both of them at art school in Newcastle. Richard Hamilton is their teacher, as he was Mark's. Hamilton is the British Pop artist, some of his works based on stills from advertisements or films which he cuts out and arranges in collages, or which he uses as the understructure for paintings, and I prefer the paintings for the wonder of the use of the beauty of the paint, missing as I do in Pop Art just that, the wonder of the use of the medium paint – as in the painting Stephen Buckley gave to Nikos and me, a finely fissured green wedge through which fissures a layer of yellow appears, the wedge upright against thickly painted brown.

He said, 'I tried to paint the ugliest painting of the twentieth century.'

Nikos and I are starting to put together a collection of pictures given to us by the artists.

Such as by Keith Milow, who gave us a work which consists of a magazine picture of a building cut up into squares and arranged on a grid, and on each square a little patch of metallic powder held in place by a clear plastic sheet, the whole in a Perspex frame.

He said he worries about his work being too elegant.

––––––

It comes to me: Nikos and I live together as lovers, as everyone knows, and we seem to be accepted because it's known that we are lovers.

In fact, we are, according to the law, criminals in our making love with each other, but it is as if the laws don't apply.

It is as if all the conventions of sex and clothes and art and music and drink and drugs don't apply here in London.

––––––

Mark came to dinner with Keith. They are having an affair that seems to be going badly, Keith saying to Mark, 'I know you don't fantasize about me when we have sex.'

How do we know so many artists?

I think it has to do with Stephen Spender's dedication to all artists, whom he introduces to us.

———

I should write that there is an essential difference between Saturday in the King's Road, which is a funfair, and Sunday on the King's Road, which is totally shut down.

In Marylebone, where we live, the very air on Sunday appears to go still and silent. There is a chemist's shop at Marble Arch that is open, but only for prescribed medications; a large grate shuts off the rest of the shop, and through the grate one sees rows of shampoo, deodorants, shaving cream, and even bags of sweets, all inaccessible. It is possible to buy lozenges for a sore throat at the counter.

Marylebone could be a provincial city within a metropolitan city. At our local greengrocer, I asked for green peppers and was told, oh, I'd have to go to Soho for that. I don't dare ask for garlic.

———

We went to Johnny Craxton's studio, the ground floor of a terrace house, the floors covered with sheets of plywood and the plywood covered with paint. Nikos told him to pay no attention to the bad reviews he was getting for a gallery exhibition of his work, too, the critics have written, picturesque. Johnny stuck out his lips so his moustache bristled.

Johnny told this story: he was spending the weekend at a country house, where the ladies left the men at the table for brandy and cigars, and where one of the men asked around, when was the last time any one of them had kissed a boy? The usual answer, at school, but Johnny, looking at his watch, said about an hour ago.

When I was alone with Nikos, he said that Greece, in the person of the Greek painter Ghika, has been a bad influence on Johnny.

Ghika is derivative of Picasso, and Johnny is derivative of Ghika. But then, Nikos said, almost all European art of Johnny's generation is derivative of Picasso.

There are the older artists whose work is derivative of Picasso and there are the younger artists whose work is derivative of Marcel Duchamp.

Nikos says that only the American Abstract Expressionists were capable of originality.

———

I saw in Oxford Street a man wearing a pinstripe suit, tight in the waist, and wearing a bowler hat and carrying a tightly furled umbrella, and I thought: but he must be in costume!

———

Patrick is one of the most intelligent people I've ever met, and also one of the people who most denies his intelligence. Listening to him talk high camp, the camp raised so high most likely by hashish, it's impossible to see him as the serious person who learned Russian in the Army, who translated hitherto untranslated Russian poets, who was among a group who walked from London to Moscow where they were allowed to demonstrate in Red Square against the atomic bomb, after which they were invited to tea with Mrs. Khrushchev. When he tells the story of the march – how the group would be picked up by a bus at night and brought to the nearest town, either back from where they'd come or forward to where they were headed, then brought back in the morning to where they had been picked up – it sounds as though no one, or at least not he, took the march seriously. As he tells the story, he plays languorously with the scarf about his neck.

His mother is often at his place, an elegant woman who, I think, runs a hotel in Brighton, and I cannot imagine what their relationship is or what she thinks of his friends, which, however, she seems to accept in an accepting English way. Is that English: not to question, but accept, the acceptance a vague cloud of unknowing that appears to float about some people's heads, their eyes unfocused?

The vague cloud of unknowing. No one seems to know, quite, what the boundaries of London are, as if London were itself within a vague cloud of unknowing. I have seen a map which left the boundaries of London open, but the metropolis centered on Hyde Park Corner, in a large black dot. When you arrive from beyond London into London, you do not arrive in any station that is identified as London, but Victoria Station, Paddington Station, Liverpool Street Station. There is no 'downtown' London.

I once thought that the English were the most adroit at defining, but almost every question I ask appears met with that vague cloud of unknowing – of, say, bemusement, as if it had never occurred to the person asked that such a question need be asked. My reaction is to think: well, really, there is no need.

———

Patrick did a watercolour of Nikos and me in bed, Nikos half under the covers, I naked, bum up, on top of the covers, which Stephen commissioned from Patrick. It cost Stephen £40. Looking at it, he said he had a drawer in his desk that he kept locked and he would put it there for safe keeping.

'I have to outlive Natasha,' he said.

He never mentioned this watercolour again, and I never asked, and I wonder if he, thinking better of keeping it from Natasha, tore it up and threw it away.

———

Stephen urged me to read Joe Ackerley for clarity. Yes, but I feel Ackerley's writing lacks tension, and in my own writing I want a low level of tension which I hope to get by bringing a slight degree of self-consciousness to the sentences, perhaps the self-consciousness of a light lyricism, enough to highlight them so that they suggest a little more than what they are literally, and therefore the low level of tension between the literal and the – what? – more than literal, whatever that more than literal could be. Stephen, noting this about my writing, said he was reminded of the self-conscious writing of Julien Green, the

American writer who wrote in French, and I took this as a warning from him, but a warning I thought English, and in my writing I'm not English, but, oh, a Franco-American, whatever that means.

What it means, I suppose, is that, though French has become submerged beneath English, English nevertheless floats on that primary language, and I do write conscious that I am writing in English, and, conscious as I am, I become self-conscious, but try to use the self-consciousness to be creative in the writing, to be more than literal, to sustain the tension between the literal and that light lyricism.

———

One of David Hockney's assistants is called Mo, who does stand-up cut-outs of animals and trees and flowers in vases from plywood. Nikos has known him since before he met me, and they have a warm relationship that I am left out of. Do I mind? I mind that Mo is one of David's friends within what I think of as a magical circle and from within that circle he looks out at Nikos with fondness and not at me.

But, then, Mo was a friend of Nikos before Nikos met me, one of a number of friends of Nikos who used to meet in Nikos' flat and smoke dope and recite poems and draw pictures. Nikos told me, recounting with excitement the event from before I met him, of getting high with friends and going off with them all to the Albert Hall for a famous poetry reading, Wholly Communion. Perhaps I am, as he tells me I am, envious of that circle of friends, and, envious, instead of joining in stand apart – stand apart from it mostly by my taking a stand against dope. Dope is a great unifier of friends, and I won't be unified with Nikos' friends from before he met me. Whatever friendships Nikos had from the past that were unified by dope, he has given up, no doubt reluctantly, because I won't be unified. I have made Nikos lose friends.

David Hockney says about Mo that if he had a factory producing hundred-pound notes he'd lose money on it.

———

I am beginning to see the English as distinct from the Scots and the Welsh or even the people from Yorkshire, and certainly from the Northern Irish, and leave it – again – as a vague cloud of unknowing as to what Great Britain is. I wonder if any Brit would be able to tell me. I guess the United Kingdom has entirely to do with the Queen.

———

To be in London because I am in love – amazing!

———

David Hockney's world –

He bought a gold lamé jacket and a gold lamé shopping bag to carry his shopping from the local supermarket, and with his hair bleached and his large round black spectacles, he has become an icon of the times, with photographers flashing photographs of him on his way back from the supermarket.

He said, in his matter-of-fact Yorkshire accent, 'I know a bit of show business is important.'

Seeing the exquisitely drawn portraits David has done of Stephen Spender, W. H. Auden, Christopher Isherwood, Isaiah Berlin, Cecil Beaton, I of course wish I too were drawn by David to rise to the level of the celebrated.

And when I stand before his portrait of his friends Celia Birtwell and Ossie Clark, with their large white cat, I feel they are in a magical world that David has merely depicted them in, but which they do in fact live in. So it is a surprise to find myself, with Nikos, in the very room in which Celia and Ossie were situated to be painted and to find it as magical as it appears in the painting. David does create a magical world.

And how he believes that there is no reason why anyone else should not love life.

Interesting about David is, though he has the reputation of being something of a pop star, his tastes in literature and in music and in art are far from what the world would expect those of a pop star to be: Proust, Wagner, and I heard him say that the greatest work of art is the Fra Angelico frescos of the Annunciations in the monks' cells in San Marco in Florence.

———

In Carnaby Street, looking in shop windows at blown-up cut-outs of almost naked sexy young men among fancy clothes, I'm at first pleasantly surprised at the eroticism displayed so frankly, and then I think, But why hasn't such eroticism always been on frank display? as if any opposition to such a display of sex suddenly becomes so obsolete I can't understand why it ever was in force.

Nikos said that the Soviet ambassador approves of Carnaby Street because it is essentially inspired by the young proletariat.

———

It comes to me almost as a recollection from a long time ago because I can't recall who the girl was I was with, nor where the lawn was that we were lounging on, nor why she suggested that we drop acid. She said, 'It has to be in the country, in the midst of nature.' I said, 'Yes,' outwardly agreeing with everything in general, as Nikos tells me I do, as a way of inwardly not agreeing to anything in particular. I was alone with her. I wonder now if the appeal of the agreement with her was that it excluded Nikos, for I would never ever take drugs of any kind with him, and I wouldn't, I know, not because I would separate myself off from him but because he would separate himself off from me, and this would enrage me, as it does when, rarely, he does smoke dope. Dope may be familiar to him as a Greek, for whom the hashish dens in the port of Piraeus are a part of Greek subculture, more than as a Londoner for whom the subculture of hashish is a fashion. He has no right – I give him no right – to enter so exclusively into himself that I do not exist for him. (And yet, friends are impressed at how we, at drinks parties, each go off to speak to different people, an indication of the respect we have for the independence we have for each other; an independence we do respect even when alone together, Nikos in his study and I in mine.) Am I being introspective, which I studiously do not want to do in this? I think I'm not so much introspecting into myself as introspecting into Nikos' self, in which I imagine him wishing, at least from time to time, for total independence from me. I will not try to introspect into my noncommittal agreement to drop acid, apart from Nikos, with the girl on the lawn.

When I returned home, Nikos, preparing supper, asked me, annoyed, 'Where have you been? I was worried,' and this reassured me totally in him, a reassurance that it excluded any introspection.

I want to be free of introspection.

————

Stephen asked me to lunch with him at his club, the Garrick. I had never before been in a gentleman's club. He told me to wear a tie. I always wear a tie. In the dining room of the club, Stephen said, pointing with two fingers at a table across from us, 'There's Benjamin Britten.' Against the light from a window, I saw a man with dense curly grey hair talking with someone at his table. Stephen kept looking toward him, but Britten never looked our way. As we were leaving the club, Stephen said, having, it seemed, thought a lot about it, 'I don't think he's ever liked me.'

Later, Stephen told me he had been reprimanded by the club because I, as his guest, had stood on a rug guests are not allowed to stand on.

————

'Your life is interesting to you and to me,' Nikos said, 'but don't presume that it is interesting to anyone else.'

————

I'm told that Nikos and I live in a world beyond which we can't see the outside objections to two men in love. No doubt, but I can't imagine any reason for objecting to it. Do we ever think that the

police may suddenly break into our flat and arrest us for the criminal activity of making love?

And the London world we live in is made up of many, many
such criminals as we are.

We never think of the sexes of people we entertain in our flat.

———

Patrick came to dinner. I never know if he is being ironical or
not, in such a grand way that he raises his chin and smiles and
looks down at me from his high height with half-shut eyes, his
lids fluttering, holding out the scarf from about his neck and
letting it drop so it seems to float around him, and drawling,
'Darling.'

During the meal, he said something from his height that
made me think that before Nikos met me he and Patrick had an
affair, or something like an affair. I laughed, again not sure if
Patrick was joking or not, but then I became very upset. I
thought Patrick, skinny and lanky, was not attractive, and I was
offended that Nikos would have found him attractive. After
Patrick left, Nikos sensed I was upset, and when we were in bed
together he asked me why. I couldn't tell him I was offended in
my sexual pride by his having had sex with someone I thought
sexually unattractive – but I said enough, finally, for him to tell
me I understand nothing about sexual attraction, which is
attraction, not, as he seems to think I think, towards a whole
generalization of people, but towards a particular person, love
making a conversation – the most intimate possible – between
two people.

———

When I saw on Nikos' desk an address book, I picked it up to
look through it. We are totally open to each other, so that I not
only don't mind Nikos opening my post, I want him to open my
post. I found that Nikos came to London with addresses and
telephone numbers given to him by the Greek Surrealist poet

Nanos Valaoritis, who had lived in London and made friends among the English poets. I saw, among other names, that of Stephen Spender.

Again, I have never asked him about his first meeting with Stephen, have never asked him about his relationship with Stephen. I have simply assumed that it was a loving relationship that has developed into a loving relationship between Stephen and Nikos and me as a couple. But there is a deeper reason why I don't want to know: that Stephen is so much older than Nikos, the sex between them sex I myself would draw away from with a shudder. And Stephen is so big! I am young, and in my youth my sexual attraction is to those as young as I am. Nikos is young, and, oh yes, he is attracted to me, as I am to him, but he allows that older men are attracted to younger, and that the younger have no reason to shudder at this attraction. Does this have to do with Nikos being Greek, and I, in my not even thinking of sex with an older man, an American of – what? – puritan principles, in the sense that puritan principles are self-righteous, self-regarding, even self-loathing if they are not self-righteous and self-regarding? In no way as promiscuous as I was in New York, Nikos has revealed to me his past sexual activities in Athens, which seem to have involved more loving emotion than sexual urgency (no pornographic impulses in him); Nikos is to me free of puritan principles, but the freedom makes him very vulnerable to tender emotions. These tender emotions I have to say I had never experienced before I met Nikos, who, in the enthrallment of love, cannot be but tender.

I recall a conversation Nikos once had with another Greek: it gives so much pleasure to an older man to have the pleasure of a younger, and it requires so little effort on the part of the younger.

And this: in a just-opened so-novel sex shop in Soho with the art historian Robert Rosenblum and his wife the artist Jane Kaplowitz, Nikos picked up an enormous dildo and laughed, and Bob and Jane laughed, because, after all, the urges of sex are not to be taken seriously, and do not command sexual pride. I take sex too seriously, and my sexual pride – that is, that I should only be known to love someone, such as Nikos, whom the world would admire me and even be jealous of me for – makes me a prude about sex, and embarrassed in a way Nikos isn't, so, in the sex shop, I had to force myself to laugh, and wished Nikos wouldn't joke about the grotesque dildo, though I could see, when he looked at me, that he was joking, with the slight mischievousness that makes his eyes shine, because he knew his joking embarrassed me.

When we were alone, he said, 'You didn't like my doing that.' And I, 'What do you think I am, a prude? Of course I didn't mind.'

He said, 'You're funny about sex.'

'You're funnier,' I said.

Bob Rosenblum has given female names to all his male friends: Nikos' name is Phaedra and mine is Faith.

————

Trying to learn Greek, which becomes more and more difficult as I try, I think how strange it is that I should be so close to someone whose native language I don't know. When I hear him speaking over the telephone to a Greek friend, I recognize words but not enough to know what this important conversation is about – especially the word 'catastrophi!' – important because it is in a language I don't understand. Do I think that he tells others in Greek what he wouldn't tell me? No, I don't, I'm not jealous of what he keeps to himself in his language. Or am I?

I'm very interested in reading his poems – written some in English, which he gives to me to read and which always impress me for the way he can make an idea appear to be as sensitive as the touch of a fingertip, and some in Greek, which he doesn't give me because I can't read them but which, I know, he wouldn't mind my reading – though, finding a poem in Greek exposed on his desk when he was out, I became determined to read it, to enter into his language, and I stopped on:

ΩΡΑΙΟΣ ΕΦΗΒΟΣ

which words I did not understand at first reading, but which suddenly revealed themselves as:

BEAUTIFUL BOY

and, yes, for a moment I was jealous of whoever that beautiful boy was, hidden away in Nikos' poem in Greek, even if that beautiful boy existed only in the poem. I was suddenly jealous of Nikos for being Greek, for being able to claim a sensibility, a sensitivity, that allowed and still allows boys to be beautiful, that allowed and still allows the sensible, the sensitive appreciation of beauty.

There is so much to write about this: Nikos as Greek.

He smiles at my speaking whatever Greek I know, and tells me that I get the genders – of which there are three in Greek, masculine, feminine, neuter – all mixed up.

I call Nikos Αγάπη μου, my Love.

———

I think back at my fantasies of Greece before I met Nikos, fantasies that go as far back as myself as a pubescent boy looking through the Encyclopaedia Britannica that my father, always aspiring for a higher education than his eighth-grade parochial school education, had bought from a door-to-door salesman, an encyclopedia that offered me a world view, which world view I found more arresting in the photographs than in the text, a world view that suddenly focused on photographs of ancient Greek statues when I turned the page and they appeared, statues of naked gods. (Stephen told me that as a boy his first sexual arousal came with studying, under a magnifying glass, Greek postage stamps with statues of nude gods.) I had never seen any depiction of nudity, and though I was sexually aroused, I was aroused by Greek nudity, which was the nudity of gods, which was idealized nudity, which made arousal god-like, idealized. And so, whenever I encountered, in whatever form, some reference to Greece – always ancient Greece – the reference was to the Greece of Greek gods, was an idealized Greece. Reading the orations of Pericles (one of the few books we had in our house, kept on glass-fronted shelves above a drop-leaf desk) I felt rise in me the idealizing devotion to the great patriot, the hero, the god-like. Studying photographs of Greece in a large picture book, I was, yes, aroused by the vision of asphodel in a stony field illuminated by the essential light of Greece.

And so the fantasies of an idealized Greece in all the Western world, with varying attempts to realize the idealization.

———

Leaving for New York, Mark asked us to care for his cat, a Burmese named Jasmine, which Nikos loves more than he loves me.

Johnny Craxton did a drawing of Jasmine:

The cat fixes us more than ever in our lives together: a pet to take care of.

After Mark left, I, feeling that there was more than friendship between him and Nikos, asked him if he and Mark had been lovers, and he asked, 'Would you be hurt if I said yes? He loved me.' And that Mark had loved Nikos made me think: yes, of course he did.

————

At times, usually at a meal, when Stephen and Nikos and I are together, I listen to them talk, say, about Russia and America. I note how Stephen, who so likes to speculate about international affairs and will make references to what someone told him when he was in Washington, will try to be deliberate in his speculation, and how Nikos will seem to be impatient with Stephen's deliberations and will suddenly make a statement that totally undoes those deliberations, an impertinent statement such as, 'You believe what you heard in Washington? Why not Moscow?' and Stephen will frown and blink and seem to wonder if Nikos may not be right.

Nikos once said to me, 'I should be elected President of the United States,' and when I told him he couldn't as it is in the American Constitution that all presidents must be born within the United States, he said, 'The Constitution should be changed,' and then laughed that beguiling laugh that makes me laugh.

————

Mario Dubsky, who paints large abstractions with heavy brush-strokes, gave a party for a houseful of friends on Guy Fawkes night, and in his garden set aflame odd pieces of furniture, including a bedstead, the roaring fire terrifying. Many people gathered round, illuminated by the flames they stared into, people I can now consider friends, all of us as if in flames.

I noted the painter Maggi Hambling, her necklace of brass bullets glistening in the flames, she staring out with narrowed eyes.

Also there, the artist and set and costume designer Yolanda Sonnabend, with long black hair that she keeps shaking back, and wearing large bracelets that move up and down her slender arms as she gestures. She is a close friend of Maggi, as is Antoinette Godkin, who works for an art dealer, whose beauty appears accented by a bright beauty spot on a cheek. The three seem to be the goddesses

of some esoteric rite that is exclusively female, and one does not
ask what goes on in the rite.

And, yes, I have to include Helen McEachrane, very beautiful and
also mysterious, as I'm not sure where she is from or what she does,
but, wherever she is from and whatever she does, she moves with
style, always dressed as if in veils that move about her as she moves.

———

It sometimes happens that when I am speaking to Stephen over the
telephone, he will suddenly ask, 'Natasha, Natasha?' and I will hear
the click of a telephone receiver put down, Natasha having listened
over another telephone. That Natasha, whom I have not met,
should be a presence looming in my friendship with Stephen is
very strange to me, and makes me wonder if Nikos and I loom in
any way in her relationship with Stephen.

When I told him this, he laughed. He said that he had been talking
over the telephone with his brother Humphrey, Humphrey in a telephone box from where he exclaimed that Stephen should see the
beauty of a young man passing outside, and Stephen heard the tell-
tale click of the receiver of the other telephone and knew that Natasha
had been listening. Why Stephen laughed I don't know, though
perhaps I do, in a way: to keep Natasha alerted to his sexuality without
admitting it to her, to make her wonder. This seems to please him.

———

Now I find that Öçi is having an affair with Mario, with whom
Keith had an affair. Do I, in a way, feel left out of these criss-
crossing sexual affairs, which I only hear about incidentally, by
living with Nikos, with whom I have more than an affair? Perhaps,
at moments, I do, but only at moments, when, at a gallery opening,
I talk to someone in the crowd whom I think sexy. But I know
from New York about affairs, and it is always a relief to go home
with Nikos and go to bed with him.

———

What is the desire – the felt need – to have lived Nikos' life with him, to have always been there with him? Is it possessiveness that makes me want to have been with him when he was eight and his father died on the day the Nazis left Athens; when, to his total bemusement, a man next to him in a cinema undid his flies and masturbated him, his first sexual experience; when he was a student at Athens College and secretly mimeographed Communist propaganda; when he was in America and for a summer worked in a meat-packing factory; when he scrubbed floors in the army; when he was rejected by a lover on holiday with him on the island of Poros? So many events, so many, and I want to have been there, just to have been there. Is this love? Is it love to want to be with him when he dies, and close his eyes?

———

When Stephen, at dinner in our flat, said he had to go to the South of France, though he didn't want to, to get trees planted in the garden of his and his wife Natasha's house there, Nikos said, 'Why don't you ask David to come with you?' This seemed to puzzle Stephen for a moment, but after that moment his face became animated and he said, his head thrust forward and his eyes wide, 'That's a brilliant idea.'

Paris

In Victoria Station, as soon as we sat in our seats on the train, Stephen jumped up and went across the aisle to speak to two men who were already seated. They were Francis Bacon and his friend George Dyer, also going to Paris. Bacon will have an opening at the Galerie Maeght, and said Stephen and I must come, which meant Stephen would have to postpone our going to the South of France to plant the trees in his and Natasha's garden, but Stephen appeared very excited, blinking his eyes a lot, and said we'd love to come to the opening. And as it turned out we were all staying at the same hotel in Paris, the Quai Voltaire, where I am now, looking out at the Seine, green-grey, as I write at a little French table sitting on a little French chair, the kind of table and chair I imagine Stephen, who is so big, would break just by writing a letter here.

Stephen asked me, at the hotel reception, if I wanted my own room, and I said no, I'd be happy to share a room with him.

I put my clothes away neatly, and he throws his all over the room.

I've spent the day alone, and will spend the evening alone, as Stephen had to go to Geneva, he didn't explain why. Francis Bacon had asked me to have dinner with him and his friends, but as it turned out plans had before that been made for him which he couldn't break. I can't see where all the horror comes from in him:

he is physically so soft, and always so polite, with strands of hair combed carefully over his forehead.

Alone this afternoon, I took a long walk. When, six or seven years ago, I lived in Paris as a student, the city was all soot black and water-streaked, and many walls were pockmarked with bullet-holes from the war. But now that it has been cleaned up it is all pink, and in the electric street lights it seems to sparkle here and there, which may simply be reflections in newly cleaned windows that are not closed by shutters. I walked around the parts of Paris that are familiar to me, and I kept wishing I could show my Paris to Nikos. My Paris? It is very strange: streets and shops and cafés here once had all kind of associations, and now I don't sense them, and I know it's because I can't associate them with him, except to wish he were here. I wore the cap Nikos gave me because he said it'd be cold in Paris.

I went to see a church that I love, Saint Severin, so old all its pillars and walls lean a little in different directions, and there I lit a candle, a big one, for Nikos. It is a Greek Orthodox church. Then I went up the Boulevard Saint Michel and down the rue des Ecoles where I lived right across from the Sorbonne, an American student imagining he could be, simply by being there, Parisian. I ate at a small Breton restaurant I used to like very much on (Stephen would say 'in') rue M. Le Prince, which has dark wood wainscoting and serves cider and crêpes. I ate potage, then veal and spinach, and drank a whole brown pitcher of cider. And I hurried to a cinema to see Ten Days that Shook the World, which I thought was the best film I have ever seen. The first scene shows an immense statue of the tsar, and suddenly hundreds of people appear with ropes to pull it down, so an arm falls off, a leg, and then suddenly all the ropes disappear, and all the people also, and the statue continues to fall apart. Then I walked back to the hotel.

I am tired, as I didn't sleep well on the train, though we had berths in a carriage that was disconnected from the rest of the train at Dover and put on the ferry and reconnected to another train at Calais.

What shall I do this evening? I hate going to a restaurant by myself. Why isn't Nikos here? Why did he insist I come without him, with Stephen? Paris is so unfriendly. The rudest city in the world is the most beautiful. On my walk, asking for directions, or in the restaurant for lunch –

Which makes me think: I once said 'lunch' to Stephen, and he corrected me by saying 'luncheon,' and I presumed that in England lunch is a verb, 'to lunch,' like 'to dine,' and 'luncheon' is a noun like 'dinner.'

– everyone was so rude, and I almost exploded with anger, as Nikos hates me to do, so, thinking of him, I remained composed.

I love him and think of him all the time. It's five o'clock here, four there. He's in his office at the Embassy, having to deal with Greek over-complications, which he can't stand. I wish he could get another job. What did he do at lunch time (which is an American way of not saying 'luncheon')? What will he do for dinner? I hope he's not frightened to stay alone in the apartment. I want to be with him and hold him and kiss him and love him –

I think the candle I lit for Nikos in Saint Severin must still be burning.

———

Stephen has come back. He came with a lot of Swiss francs, and asked me where he should hide them in the room, but I didn't say, and didn't watch where he did hide them. He's having a bath, and then we go to the Francis Bacon exhibition.

Now hours later –

About to go to sleep. Stephen already asleep in the other bed.

At Francis' exhibition, George, very drunk, took me in hand, and, all in Cockney, told me which paintings were of him, and did I recognize him? I didn't, really, but he said he saw himself in them, in the way Francis painted him. One was of him as a mutilated lump of flesh sitting on a toilet.

Stephen introduced me to many people, including Sonia Orwell, the widow of George Orwell, and the novelist Mary McCarthy and Mary McCarthy's husband and Philippe de Rothschild, and told them all, giggling, that he and I are going to the South of France to plant trees together in the garden of his and Natasha's house. He was very amused that someone named Plante would be planting trees with him.

I suddenly wondered if Natasha, whom, after all, I have never met, knew that I was going to her house with Stephen to plant trees in her garden. She gave him instructions for the planting, with a drawing, which he showed me. Where a row of cypresses are to be planted are a row of dots.

We are on a train, heading south for Avignon. It is raining, and everything is grey, dun, pale green outside – and very flat.

When I woke in our hotel room I found that Stephen had left for an early appointment. I met him at the Grand Palais. We went into the Hommage à Picasso exhibition, which was not yet put up completely, so we walked about cables and crates scattered on the floors. We saw drawings that Picasso did when he was thirteen, and from there to now masses and masses of drawings, paintings, etchings, sculpture, pottery, tiles, as if he never for a moment stopped, and, at eighty-five, has not stopped. He must be the most impatient man in the world to create, create, create as much as, or more than, anyone has ever created, and I wondered if the way he works has a lot to do with impatience. Stephen said the exhibition made him twenty years younger.

No artists we know, especially Hockney, could be painting what they paint without Picasso. Certainly Francis could not paint the way he does without Picasso having first distorted the figure, though, as David H. says, Picasso never mutilates the figure the way Francis does. Stephen said the Picasso exhibition made Francis' exhibition look pale. I said that he couldn't compare, that it was unfair to any artist since Picasso to compare that artist to him. Stephen nodded, the way he nods, blinking also, when you say something he evidently agrees with but that seems at the same time to bemuse him.

We met John Russell, the art critic, in the exhibition, and he was also enthusiastic, but I sensed in his enthusiasm the isolation, almost the loneliness, of the critic.

Stephen and I walked back to the hotel, and on the way he insisted on buying a camera to take pictures. In the hotel lobby were gathered Sonia Orwell, Mary McCarthy and her husband whose name I can't remember, the Baron de Rothschild, Francis, and John Russell. George was too drunk to come. We all went to lunch in a restaurant in Les Halles. I was wearing Nikos' cap, which, as we were taking off our coats, Sonia grabbed from my head to put on hers, laughing. She said she must buy one, and I wondered if she was implying I should give this one to her, but I didn't say anything. Nikos did tell me to be careful of her, and I was. When we all sat at the table, the cap was passed around from person to person to put it on and joke.

David in Nikos' cap

I sat next to Mary McCarthy, who was cold at first, then warmed up, I think, when, after having asked her if she thought of writing about Rome and she answered no, I asked her if she had read Eleanor

Clark's book on Rome, a great gaffe, because I suddenly realized that Eleanor Clark was married to Edmund Wilson, who of course was once married to Mary McCarthy. But, though I may have read about these relationships, I forget what I've read when I meet the person in fact, as if the person I'm meeting in fact can't really have had anything to do with the person I've read about. She didn't say she had read Eleanor Clark's book, but she laughed. When she raised her wine glass, her small finger, slightly crooked, extended in a feminine way, I was struck by how masculine her hand was.

She asked me where I'd been to college, and when I said Boston College, she said, 'You were educated by the Jesuits.' 'Yes,' I said. She said, 'I was educated by the Sisters of the Sacred Heart,' and added, as if I might not know and she wanted to make it clear that my being educated by Jesuits in no way put me at an advantage, 'the female equivalent of the Jesuits.' 'They are, yes,' I said.

Having been listening to us, Sonia, across the table, said, 'Mr. Plante, I was brought up a Catholic too.'

Philippe de Rothschild, bald and stout, was very animated. As if he were playing tricks, he parodied certain philosophers, and Mary McCarthy was the only one to become engaged in the talk. She said, 'You're an idealist,' and this made Philippe de Rothschild stop.

He asked Francis if he would design a label for a special de Rothschild wine, and Francis, with a shrugging laugh, said yes, of course.

As if, suddenly, no one knew what to talk about, Sonia brought up Stephen taking me to the South of France to plant trees, and there was some joking around the table about Mr. Plante planting trees, with advice from various people on how to plant them. Stephen seemed to like this joking.

John Russell, attentive to everyone and smiling a bright if tight smile of pleasure, again appeared to be isolated, if not lonely, in the midst of the party.

Philippe de Rothschild, who said he must go, left, but came back to tell us he had paid the bill, which, he said with great surprise, was remarkably cheap.

Before the rest of us broke up, Stephen asked Francis if he and

George would like to come stay with us in the South of France, and Francis, with that shrugging laugh he has, said yes. He won't come, I thought. I also thought: my God, I hope he doesn't come, because if he does how are Stephen and I going to find the time to plant the trees? Stephen has already told me he has great fears that Natasha will arrive next spring to find three withered trees leaning toward one another on the horizon, all he and I were able to do. He also said he was counting on me to get all the trees in the ground so that Natasha will in fact find everything she asked for done. I think Stephen imagines I'm filled with common sense and stick-to-it-iveness, more than he is, and what he is counting on is that we get the trees planted so that Natasha, if she knows about us being together, will not complain that he brought me with him just to have a good time. So I'm determined that we do get those trees planted, and I am trying to emphasize my common sense and stick-to-it-iveness. But how will we be able if we are spending our time with Francis and George, if they come?

As Francis was leaving, Mary McCarthy asked him if he would come with her to visit the studio of a friend of hers who painted owls, and Francis said of course, of course he would, there was nothing he'd like more than to see a studio filled with paintings of owls. Francis left with John Russell and Mary McCarthy's husband.

After he left, Mary McCarthy said, 'I'm interested in those owls because they look just like Edmund,' and she smiled her hard smile, all her teeth showing as in a stark rectangle.

She, Sonia, Stephen and I went to the rue de Rivoli for coffee. Sonia, maybe a little drunk, talked a lot in a high voice, to no one and to everyone, often in French. She spoke so quickly, I couldn't understand most of what she said. Mary McCarthy left. Stephen said he wanted to see Ten Days that Shook the World, which I had talked about. Sonia asked if she could come with us.

I suddenly had this feeling: that Sonia was interested in – more than interested, excited by – my friendship with Stephen.

Sonia loved the movie, and so did Stephen, who recalled having seen it in Berlin when he lived there in the thirties.

Stephen and I returned to the hotel, where we found Francis and George and others drinking in the bar. Annoying everyone, I think, Stephen insisted on taking photographs, but, as must happen with every mechanical device Stephen has ever in his life attempted to use, he couldn't get the flash to work, and then, as I'm sure always happens to Stephen, it suddenly did work.

Francis said, with a laugh, that he would never, ever design a label for Philippe de Rothschild's bottles.

I left them to go up to our room to rest. After a while, Stephen too came to rest.

At eight-thirty, a car came for us to take us to dinner at the de Rothschilds' house. The car drove through a strange quarter of Paris, among factories and what looked like warehouses, and stopped in a dismal little street. Stephen and I got out, went through an iron-grill door, then through another door, then another, as if there were deep secrecy at stake, and finally into a magnificent pavilion with an illuminated garden beyond showing through French windows.

I kept putting my hands under my arms to dry them in preparation to shake hands, as my palms were sweating.

Philippe de Rothschild told me he had just a short while before moved into this house, and when I said, 'Bonne chance,' he grabbed me by the shoulders and kicked my shins and laughed. 'I'm sorry,' I said, and said, 'Merde.' 'That's better,' he said. I had the sense from him of his being totally friendly with me because I was his guest, but that, the moment I ceased to be his guest, he wouldn't think for a moment that there was any reason to see me again.

He introduced me to his wife, the Baroness Pauline de Rothschild, tall, with a very aristocratic nose, an American who was not identifiable as an American. She was just courteous toward me.

She said she loved the new style of clothes for young people, and had been struck by a photograph she had seen in a newspaper of a group of young men wearing these clothes. She asked a footman to get it from her bedroom. He did, and she showed it to me: three or four very beautiful young men, all, as evident from the caption identifying them, from aristocratic French families. A deep sense of exclusion from their world came over me, but then I wondered if she showed me the photograph to put me at ease for the clothes I was wearing, the brown-and-white-striped Carnaby Street suit Nikos bought for me, which was inappropriate for the dinner party.

The other guests were Louis Aragon and his wife Elsa Triolet, and a Russian couple who had come recently from Moscow. Stephen explained to me later who they were: Elsa Triolet's sister Lili Brik, once the mistress of the early Soviet poet Vladimir Mayakovsky, and her husband, Osip Brik, who was one of the founders of Russian Formalism. Elsa Triolet was small and thin, her hair short and loose, and Lili Brik small and plump, wearing a stark black dress, her hair in a large, smooth chignon held by a net. We were asked into the dining room, where Pauline de Rothschild assigned me to sit at the top of the table on a grand gilt and velvet chair. Stephen was seated at the opposite end of the table. I said I was embarrassed to be given such a position, and after we were all seated Philippe de Rothschild made a face at Pauline de Rothschild, who apologized and asked me if I wouldn't mind changing. I stood. She asked the husband of Lili Brik, sitting on one of the more modest chairs along the side of the table, if he wouldn't mind changing, and he too stood. I thought she meant that he and I should change places, but footmen came and one took my grand chair away while the other took his chair away and, while we stood away, exchanged them, and I sat back where I had been but on a modest chair and he sat where he had been on the grand chair.

The de Rothschilds were trying to arrange to rent a mansion in Russia for the summer. To do this seemed to them as matter-of-fact as Lili Brick and her husband coming from Moscow to visit in Paris.

There was talk about references to the Rothschilds in literature, and I said I remembered that in Dostoyevsky's A Raw Youth the main character says his great ambition is to become as rich as a Rothschild.

In the drawing room after dinner, talk about Ezra Pound, whom Aragon said he detests. Stephen told me later Aragon detests almost everyone. He was very rude to Stephen when Stephen said, yes, Pound is horrible for being Fascist and anti-Semitic, but there is something tragic enough about him that all the horrible things he did take on the dimension of tragedy, and Stephen was drawn to the tragedy of Pound. He said the last time he had seen Pound he had found him in a grave depression, not interested in his poetry, thinking his whole life had been a waste. Aragon jingled his keys impatiently, looked at me and made a face of French intolerance.

I told Aragon how much I admired Le Paysan de Paris and asked if he minded talking about the Surrealist movement. Not at all, he said. He hated Breton. He said the movement had its value, yes, but it was never meant to wipe away the past in favor of something revolutionary. He himself had always read Hugo even when the Surrealists were disowning him. He said, rather bitterly, that the movement was dead, and he saw no point in trying to revive it, as he thought people now in the sixties were trying to do, with drugs and hallucinations.

Then, suddenly, the room was filled with rapid, crackling, flashing talk. I had come thinking I would be intimidated and unable to say anything, and I was intimidated, even frightened, but just because of this I made myself participate. And as I found I was communicating, I became excited and maybe spoke too much.

At the end of the evening, Aragon read a long poem he had written for Mayakovsky, and read it very dramatically. I was very moved, and told him so and for a moment I felt we had a contact.

He asked Stephen about me, 'Est ce qu'il a déjà publié un livre?'

'Pas encore,' Stephen answered, 'mais il en publiera.'

Aragon turned away.

Stephen and I stayed a little while with Philippe and Pauline de

Rothschild after the others left, and I felt a charm from them that, if I had counted on it, would have made me think we had become close friends.

In the car back to the hotel, I told Stephen that my fear of French cultural superiority might have something to do with my being a provincial Franco-American who grew up speaking a crude, seventeenth-century French I was aware was not, as an aunt used to refer to it, the real French French of France. But, Stephen said, he has always been frightened by French superiority, and speaking especially with André Malraux, minister of cultural affairs in France, always frightened him. Yet, he said he didn't think the French so intelligent; they're simply calculating, coldly logical, and definitive. I was sure he was thinking of Aragon.

I said, 'The relationship between the de Rothschilds and Russia must be very close for them to think of renting a mansion there.'

Stephen frowned and shook his head with disapproval. He said, 'Imagine, the de Rothschilds renting a mansion in the Soviet Union.'

The train is passing through rolling countryside, with ploughed fields.

———

We are still on the train. We left Paris at 9:15 a.m. and will arrive at Avignon at 4:30 p.m. The countryside gets more and more dramatic.

Stephen is reading, and while he's been reading I've been thinking about him and what he is doing for Nikos and me: he has opened a whole world to us. He and I were talking about Nikos, as he says we always do, and he said, 'I wish that when I was your age I had had what you have now with Nikos.' I said, 'But, Stephen, you are giving us both what you didn't have at our age.' I feel he has given Nikos and me a world in which our relationship can expand and expand, so that in discovering the world he has opened to us we are discovering one another.

But it had shocked me a little after I talked to Nikos by telephone from our Paris hotel room to feel a small flash of jealousy from Stephen, jealousy maybe not because he loves Nikos and I have him or Nikos loves me and he has me, but jealousy because we have each other. He laughs that I want to talk about Nikos so much, that I'm always writing letters to Nikos, but maybe I am exaggerating our relationship to keep him at a distance from me while I'm with him. Maybe I want to keep reminding him: I'm Nikos', and I can't be anyone else's.

The country is all round, stark hills. We'll hire a car in Avignon and drive to Stephen's house, outside Maussane. I am anxious to start digging.

When Stephen asked me if I'm writing a letter to Nikos, I said yes, and he asked if he could add to it. I gave him a blank page from the block of paper I'm writing on.

Dearest Nikos,

We are in the train on the way to Avignon, and David has been writing a letter to you. He will have told you all the news fit to print like the New York Times. David is still all in one piece and very helpful. Maybe he got a bit spoiled in Paris but that was only two days, and the digging will doubtless correct any bad results from Paris. The only qualification of this is that Francis Bacon may decide to join us. But we'd have to dig anyway. We are going to christen all the trees. Nikos will be an almond tree (or would you prefer fig?). Perhaps an oleander would be best of all. We think of you all the time and never talk of anyone or anything else. All my love always, dearest Nikos, Stephen

Mausanne

There is no electricity in the house, so Stephen and I use oil
lamps.

I got up at dawn today and went out to dig. I dug two holes
before breakfast. It's cold, and a strong wind is blowing. The
air is brilliantly pure and, just as Van Gogh described the
country to his brother in his letters, seems to magnify the
colors. After breakfast, I dug thirteen holes. Workmen arrived
to put up a fence, and I felt, oh, so authoritative telling them
what to do.

Now I'm resting. Stephen and I share his large upstairs room,
with a bed at either end. He has lent me Van Gogh's letters, so I can
see Provence as Van Gogh saw it. Stephen has gone to Arles to see
a lawyer, I think, on business that annoys him to have to do. As it
annoys him to have to get through to Malraux in Paris to ask him
to help get electricity to the house, which he said Natasha insisted
he do.

Last night at dinner, Stephen and I again spoke about Nikos,
and again he told me how fortunate I am. I have become close
to him. I told him I'm sure I've become a different person since
I met Nikos, more sure of myself, confident of things develop-
ing naturally without my having to force them. Stephen agreed
that he was sure I had changed. My separation from Nikos has
made me realize this very much, and it is Stephen who has

given me the perspective to see Nikos and me together and how being with Nikos has changed me. What he says about us is always so right.

We talked about the stories I gave him. He said he liked them, but there are certain things I must be careful about. I must not write carelessly (which I do now and then), and I must read each story over and over, twenty and thirty times, until I have a definite sense of each one. He said he sensed a lot was in the stories, but what's in them is never fully expressed. Then he said, 'Be sane.' I was struck, and not sure I understood. He told me not to worry about making my stories imaginative as there's enough imagination in me that will come out. He said, 'Don't try to be mad, you're mad enough.' He told me not to be hysterical, because the hysteria always seems unmotivated and therefore boring. And then he said I must listen for my own voice. He asked me, 'Do you know what I mean?' 'Oh yes,' I said, 'but I wonder if my voice is locked in and I am locked in with it, and I do nothing but listen to it but can't make it heard.' 'That may be your greatest danger,' he said.

I know what we can get Stephen for Christmas: a briefcase.

———

I brought all three of Nikos' letters, all arrived at the same time, to Avignon and read them sitting in the square. Stephen had dropped me off for a couple of hours while he went to arrange for the delivery of the trees for which I have dug the holes. I think Nikos is lonely and depressed, and I want to go back to him. I want to tell him: you don't write rubbish in your letters, and you especially don't write anything I shouldn't, as you say, concern myself with. Your wanting to do something with your life concerns me greatly, as I assume what I do with my life concerns you. You are right to tell me you feel that I want you to remain in the position of a clerk in the Greek Embassy for my security, and you are not perverse in suspecting this in me. You will always have to fight against my wanting you to be the one with the solid job, the regular income, the one in whom I find security. You must demand security from me.

While I was in Avignon, I went to the Popes' Palace, with huge, draughty halls, great flights of stairs, narrow and high corridors, all in stone, grey, whitish, clay-color, and crumbling everywhere. After wandering around in the cold, I found the papal chapel warm with sunlight flooding through the windows. The chapel is huge and absolutely stark, and echoes in such a way that when you let out a faint shout it is like striking an immense tuning fork.

Back in the house, Stephen gave me a letter Nikos sent to him:

November 18, 1966

My dearest Stephen,

Thank you so much for taking David with you to France. I am sure that it will be very good for him for his health, and good for him to meet interesting people and to be with you in the country which I imagine being so beautiful. I wish I could have come with you but I do not resent not being able to come. On the contrary, I think that I am with you through David. You are both marvellously good to me always. Sometimes I doubt that I deserve it. I hope with all my heart that everything will go well in France and that you will love David as much as I do. I am sure that you will create a beautiful love-garden that will, perhaps, remain in history as the most beautiful love-garden in the south of France, made by the last great English romantic, the last New England idealist, both inspired by the last Greek before Greece sinks like the Atlantis.

I will be thinking of you both and imagining you planting, talking, reading, writing and being happy.

All my love,

Nikos

Reading this letter, I thought, but the garden is Natasha's!

Αγάπη μου,

We are on the train, in a compartment, Stephen, Francis, George and I, all headed back to Paris.

Though I can hardly understand what George says, I know he likes me as much as I like him, so I smile at whatever he says, and that's understanding enough between us. We will see them both in London. Francis has already suggested that we all go to a Greek restaurant together. You see, I've talked about you to them too!

They arrived Saturday afternoon, and that evening we had dinner together in the restaurant of their hotel and talked about the Picasso exhibition. Francis said he can't admire the man enough, but when I said, 'I see your work, the studies for heads, come right out of Picasso,' he looked at me with one fixed eye while the other eye seemed to drift off to the side and I felt he was, with a slight frown, thinking of how to take what I said, then he simply smiled and said nothing. I thought, though, that I should be careful of what I say to him, especially about his own work.

Francis said he had gone with Mary McCarthy to see the paintings of owls, which were dreadful, so dreadful he couldn't believe she had any appreciation of art, any at all. He laughed.

We all talked about different people, such as Sonia, but also many people in London I don't know who appear to make up a world.

George told us about his world — about being in borstal and later in prison. Everyone listened to him attentively, especially Francis, as if he had never heard George talk about his time incarcerated, and the talk appeared to excite him.

When Stephen and I got back to his house and his big room, he said to me, his hand on my head, 'I hope you won't be spoiled by all the people you're meeting.'

Feeling suddenly self-conscious, I said, 'I hope not.'

He put his hand on my head and turned it a little from side to

side to look at my face carefully, then he laughed and said, 'You look like a young French priest that older women fall in love with,' and I was relieved he was joking.

I changed into my pajamas and got into my bed at my end of the room and Stephen said to me, 'Sleep well, David.' I thought, I do love him, and how can I let him know I love him without making love with him? I fell asleep before he got into his bed.

Sunday morning, he, Francis and George and I went, Stephen driving, to Montmajour, where we took photographs.

Then we went on to Arles, where we stopped for a long time in the Roman amphitheater, Stephen and Francis talking about Shakespeare, especially Macbeth, about which Francis had strong if simple views as a tragedy, and Stephen, I noticed, agreed with everything Francis said, even, as if with excited enthusiasm, affirmed what Francis said. When Francis, as if a little impatient with Stephen's agreeing with him, said, 'But what do I know?' Stephen frowned and shut up. We took more photographs in the amphitheater.

We went to Tarascon, where we ate a bad meal. Stephen seemed embarrassed by the meal, as if he were responsible for it, but Francis and George seemed not to care, with a lightness that made me think they didn't care much about anything. Stephen whispered to me that we were lucky that Francis and George were in very good moods.

There appeared to be a lightness to Francis' very body, the way he moved in sudden, quick ways, as if he were weightless and attached to the ground by a string, and only a string, and the string jerked him into walking and sometimes gesturing, his arms held out, laughing his abrupt laugh. George, who never laughed or smiled much, always appeared very fixed to the ground.

In the evening, we had dinner in the restaurant of Francis' and George's hotel with the prefect of Maussane and his wife, whom André Malraux, an acquaintance of Stephen from a long way back, had telephoned from Paris to tell him that electricity must be brought to the Spender house. And the painters Rodrigo and Anne Moynihan, who live part of the year in the South of France, also came to the dinner.

George, who sat next to me, told me, or I think he told me, how much he loves Francis. He put his arm over my shoulder to tell me this again and again.

Alone with Stephen in the house, I felt as he walked about in the light of the oil lamps that his loneliness was as big as he is. I said goodnight and went to bed before he did.

The next morning, Monday, I dug a little until the men from whom Stephen had ordered the trees arrived and said that they would have dug the holes, and, seeing the holes I'd dug, obviously thought they'd have to improve on them.

Stephen and I picked up Francis and George at their hotel and went to Aix, where we had a great lunch, saw a little Rembrandt self-portrait Francis admired for the way the face so obviously emerges from paint.

On the way back from Aix, we passed an accident at a crossroads where a big truck load of pigs had smashed into a tree, and the roads were littered with dead, bloody pigs. Francis, his eyes wide and head turning in all directions, got very animated by the sight as we drove past.

He said, 'It's so beautiful.'

At Maussane we again had dinner in the hotel restaurant.

Before we left Avignon this morning, we took lots and lots of photographs in an automatic booth in the train station. Francis said he uses them to paint from, especially if they're blurred or contorted in some way, so we all tried to make ourselves as blurred and contorted as possible. Francis took a bunch, Stephen did, and I have some. The best ones are of Stephen when he is not blurred or contorted. He looks marvelous, monumental, with a beauty only very few older people come into, I think.

In our compartment, which for hours we had to ourselves, the talk was very intimate, about guilt and love and sex and homosexuality.

Francis said a lesbian can pretend to be heterosexual just by lying there, but a homosexual man can't pretend to be heterosexual with a woman.

We've passed out of the sunlight of Provence into a grey fog. Stephen, Francis, George are sleeping. A Frenchman has come into our compartment, and, seeing me write this letter, has just said, 'Les lettres d'amour ne sont jamais terminées.' I wonder how he knew.

Αγάπη σου
Stephen wants to add to this letter.

Dearest Nikos,

When I first met you I couldn't have imagined that anything so wonderful would happen as you and David finding one another – still less that if it did I could be so with you both. I am very glad this has happened.

Always with my love,
Stephen
David doesn't do anything but write letters to you.

Paris

We are back in the Quai Voltaire, though we have decided to leave tonight rather than tomorrow. Mary McCarthy had invited us when we were last in Paris to dinner this evening, but when Stephen telephoned her to confirm she said something had come up and she couldn't have us. It occurred to me that she is a friend of Natasha and maybe, thinking about it, decided she shouldn't invite Stephen and me to her home. God knows what everyone thinks of my relationship with Stephen, even though he makes a point of telling everyone it is not sexual.

Last night, after we got back to Paris, Stephen, Francis, George and I had dinner in a restaurant, and for the first time I saw Francis in terms of his pictures. He got drunk, drunker and drunker, and kept repeating over and over that people are horrible, life is horrible, that everyone is scum. George, also drunk, didn't appear to be hearing. Stephen and I listened, and were defenseless. When Francis started to denounce Christianity, citing Macbeth as the most profoundly atheistic work ever, Stephen said he thought he was Christian at least in believing we must all help one another.

Francis, his lower lip stuck out and his smooth jowls bulging, fixed on him, and then he said, 'Practically, do you help others?'

'No,' Stephen said, 'I don't, and I certainly wouldn't give everything I have away to the poor, but still I believe I should.'

Francis stared at Stephen for a longer time, his lower lip stuck out more, as if, frowning deeply, he were considering deeply. He said, in a harsh voice, 'Rubbish.'

I thought, Well, of course he's right, but then I suddenly became upset, partly, I think, because he was attacking Stephen, and there was nothing I could do to stop him. I could have sided with Stephen, I guess, but I didn't, because I knew that Francis was right.

When Stephen and I got back to our hotel room, I all at once began to weep.

Stephen asked, 'Is it because of what Francis said?'

I said I didn't know.

Stephen said I should consider that Francis' paintings are just a part of life – as the war in Vietnam and all viciousness were parts of life – but that there are other parts to life, parts that Francis himself is aware of and enjoys, such as landscapes and intelligence and friendship. Hadn't I seen this side of Francis in Provence? Stephen said, 'You saw the best of Francis when he and George were with us in Provence.'

This morning, the four of us met again to go once more to the Picasso exhibition to see what we hadn't been able to see the first time, but maybe we had seen too much that first time (also Picasso, Picasso, Picasso is everywhere in Paris) because we came out feeling less than enthusiastic. Or could this have been because of Francis, who, after he started out by saying everything was marvelous, stopped saying it, but began to frown, his lower lip stuck out? Stephen has bought Nikos the catalogue as a gift.

We all had lunch with Mary McCarthy in a restaurant. Francis said he thought the paintings of the owls were marvelous. She smiled her hard smile.

Stephen and I went to look at some art galleries, then came back to the hotel to rest, and decided we would leave tonight.

So I will wake Nikos up in the morning and get into bed with him.

London

Nikos' cousin Maria is staying with us for a while before she moves into a flat in Mortlake with two other girls, all of them going to a mysterious 'school' Maria talks about cryptically. She is a dark young woman with large dark eyes made all the larger by large dark circles around them. Because she is so secretive about her school, Nikos and I wonder if it is the school of Scientology or Economic Science, which, along with schools of Indian meditation, are advertised on posters in the Underground stations. Nikos has no tolerance for such places, but he is very tolerant of Maria, who is herself so tolerant, as if some deep sadness in her has made her so deeply tolerant. Her laughter is very sad.

Like Nikos, she won't go back to live in Greece, but has decided to make England her home. In Athens, she said, she was talked badly about because she wore a skirt and blouse to a wedding. She wants to paint, to write poetry, to wear what she wants.

She says, 'I want my life to mean something.'

I am with her often, and we talk.

She is teaching me Greek.

———

Francis, with George, invited us and Stephen to dinner at the White Tower, which he chose because Nikos is Greek. I wanted so much for Nikos to like Francis and George. I am never sure that he will like the people I do. He tells me I like everybody, and expect everybody to like me. Francis was very lively, passing out pound notes to anyone who served us, even if it was just to refill our glasses with wine, and sometimes held out pound notes to people passing as if they were serving us. George smiled a contented smile, as if pleased that Francis was with people with whom he was being so spontaneously lively.

Francis said, when Stephen asked him, that he doesn't see Lucian Freud any more.

George said, 'Lucian borrowed too much money from Francis that he gambled and lost and never paid back. I told Francis, "Enough, Francis, enough of that."'

Francis laughed.

There was talk about Henry Moore, and Francis, laughing, said that Moore's drawings were knitting, just knitting. Nikos, who, I knew, could have easily disagreed with Francis in a way neither Stephen or I would dare to, said, 'That's it, they're just knitting.' After, Nikos and I walked home. He didn't say anything. I asked, 'Didn't you like Francis?' He said, 'I'm thinking.' We walked on. He said, 'He doesn't take anything for granted, anything at all. He's totally original. I think he is amazing.'

Keswick, Cumberland

I don't like being away from Nikos. I really am anxious all the while. I had thought it would be nice to get away with Maria, who said we should simply take the next train from Euston Station that was leaving after we got there, which seemed an exciting idea. But I think of Nikos all the time and want to be with him. There were moments on the train when I felt I wanted to turn right back to him. I used to enjoy travelling, but I don't now, perhaps because I feel being with Nikos is as far as I could ever hope to travel. Perhaps there's a horror in all this that I feel: we're so entangled with each other, and though the entanglement is freedom for me, I can't begin to imagine how horrible it would be if Nikos felt limited by it. I think, sometimes, I do limit Nikos, and he resents it. But I know that he frees me, in the largest sense, and I can only hope I do the same for him, in some sense.

The next train leaving Euston was to the Lake District. It took about six and a half hours, with two changes. The trip was pleasant, but towards the end when it got dark and we were told that most hotels would be closed, we had a moment of panic. But we found a hotel easily, in the center of Keswick, where I am now in bed in my room. We took a walk, but it was too dark to see anything. We talked. Nikos would not be very tolerant of our philosophical discussions about life and death, but I am enough like Maria that we get a lot from them, and sometimes she does say remarkable things.

I wish I could get the train ride in: at first leaving London, buildings grey, then green and dun-colored fields with placid cows, then it clouded over and drizzled, and as darkness came so did fog, and I felt rather sleepy so dozed a little and woke to find we were in the midst of very high, bald hills, the darkness a kind of blue-black light that made everything gleam, and then it got too dark to see anything, and going through a valley, where the train stations were illuminated by one weak lantern hung on a branch or the picket of a fence, I had the feeling that the train had left the earth and was rattling through the dark sky, and that all the very distant, very pale lights were stars in that sky. I then felt a horrible anxious-making desolation come over me. I really don't have any other stability but Nikos.

It's early, around 9:00, but we both wanted to sleep. Because of the cold damp, the bed has an electric blanket.

Bowness-on-Windermere

After breakfast, we came by bus to Friar's Crag on Derwent Water, where we are now. We're sitting, completely by ourselves, on a rock thrust out into the lake. There are dark islands, and behind them vague mountains covered in mist. In the foreground are pine branches. It is very, very quiet, the quiet that Maria calls 'silence that goes beyond silence.' But I've started to notice matchsticks and bits of paper and rubbish on the ground around us. I think we'll go.

Later. We're in Bowness-on-Windermere, in a lovely hotel right on Lake Windermere. There's a large party on downstairs, and I can hear voices and music from my room.

As we're here off-season, the rates are very reasonable, and we are indulging ourselves in ordering tea from room service and having tea together in Maria's room by the electric fire.

She says, 'It's a funny thing, this earth we walk on,' or 'It's a funny thing, hurrying and worrying about life,' or 'It's a funny thing, life,' and while she smiles, her large, dark eyes, surrounded by dark rings, are very sad.

———

Maria said she woke this morning feeling better than she has in months.

In the lounge after dinner yesterday, she told me just a little about her 'school' – or rather suggested something about it by asking me if I had ever stood up among people I didn't know and told them honestly everything I have ever done in all my life, however bad? I said no. She said, 'It's the hardest thing to do.'

London

B ack home with Nikos, who I know is the centre of my life.
He is the centre, and about him are the now many friends
we refer our lives together out to, all these friends aspects of life in
London, where we are extended into a world.

Yet, do we – no, do I, for Nikos is not interested – know
anything about what is meant to be the class system of Britain?
Here, I belong to no class, or imagine that I don't. Nor does
Nikos belong.

———

I guess the real invention in keeping a diary is the way it is written,
so allow myself to think back, inventively, at the time Nikos and I
were in Venice, our first trip abroad together after we met, on our
way to Yugoslavia. We were there for the festival of the Redentore,
and, sitting on the steps of the Salute, we watched the fireworks in
the warm, clear night, starting with a shocking bang that made the
night itself seem to shake, and then, over and over, great balls of
red, silver, gold rose into the sky and, one after another, exploded
into red, silver, gold suns that held themselves still for a moment
then, from flashing cores, were shattered into bright sparks that fell,
slowly and silently, down, down, down, and disappeared into the
darkness that appeared to be as deep as it was high. We were
witnessing the beginning and the end of the universe.

———

Stephen asked me if I would write a letter to Natasha to reassure her that she would have approved of my having gone to the South of France with Stephen, which Stephen told me she had known nothing about (and I more than suspected that Mary McCarthy, who had invited Stephen and me to dinner, cancelled after having spoken to Natasha over the telephone, Mary McCarthy referring to me and surprising Natasha that Stephen was not alone, upsetting her very much).

I wrote her this letter, hoping to humour her, hoping to impress on her that I am, oh, charmingly innocent. But I haven't sent the letter, and think I'd better not. That I started the letter addressing her as Dearest Natasha shows that I was writing to a fantasy person I've not met, and am rather frightened of meeting.

Dearest Natasha,

When Stephen said he had to go to the South of France to plant trees, I thought he'd been invited by some state cultural institution, perhaps within the realm of André Malraux as Minister of Culture, to participate in a ceremony of tree planting. He said this as if looking into the far distance at a scene of himself throwing earth into the hole around the base of a tree held by an official, and he frowned. He said, 'I'm going alone.' Nikos said, 'Why don't you have David go with you?' Stephen smiled and said he'd like that, and I had the image of myself standing behind him, feeling awkward and at the same time proud to be there, as he gave a little speech after the tree was planted.

It was only when we were on our way to Saint Rémy that I realized he was meant to plant trees – or what he called trees – in your garden. He said something like, 'My God, I forgot Natasha's plans for what we should plant where.' I was relieved that what I'd imagined a public ceremony would be private – because planting a tree must be, I felt, something of a ceremony of some kind, even if private. When we arrived at the house, Stephen, looking through folded papers that he took from all his pockets so there was a stack of them, with unused postage stamps, spectacles, pound and franc and even lire notes, and old, cancelled airplane tickets among them, he found the plans, but as clear as they were, we, not quite gardeners, prepared more for the ceremony of planting rather than the practicalities, and couldn't quite match up the sketch of the garden it would be with the garden as it was. We stood in the wind, your careful plans flapping. The light was very clear on the foothills of the Alpilles along the horizon.

Monsieur M., the French gardener, came and helped us. He wore a sagging blue overall and thick black shoes, and he listened to Stephen as if torn between his duty to do what Stephen told him what you wanted him to do and the need to tell Stephen what to do. He took the plan and turned it to the right way up, and indicated where the holes for the bushes, not trees, were to be planted in a row to form a protected walk that was to be covered in gravel. Now, the walk was uneven and weedy. Monsieur M. said he would deliver the plants.

They arrived – twigs with earth-filled pouches about the roots – and the next morning, a cold November morning, Stephen and I went out after breakfast to dig holes for them. I still felt I was about to perform a ceremony, and I thought that, as ceremonies are meant to be effortless, digging holes would be effortless. The ground was frozen, and I had to use a pick-axe to break it up, and then each time I shoved the spade into the loosened earth it struck a stone. Stephen would shovel out the earth, then I would, each in turn, and when the hole was about a foot deep Stephen would say, 'I think that's deep enough, don't you?' He or I would go for a twig, undo the pouch, and one of us would hold the plant, its roots sticking out, upright in the hole while the other replaced the earth and stones, and we'd both, each on a side, stomp. The freezing air was electric, and that electricity seemed to be the source of the constant, bright white, almost blinding light. That morning, we dug three holes and stomped three plants into them.

> *Monsieur M. appeared, and, examining our work, looked, again, anxious. He obviously wanted to tell us we weren't doing the work quite as it should have been done, but he was too respectful of our efforts to. His dark eyes were filmed with tears, though the tears were probably caused by the cold wind that made the twigs stomped into the earth sway.*
>
> *Monsieur M. said that the earth was too frozen in fact for digging properly, and that we must not derange ourselves with trying to plant now. He would deal with that when the weather was better. Stephen and I went to lunch at a restaurant in Arles, one of those restaurants with dark wood wainscoting and where the steaming soup tureen was put on the table with an old, dented ladle. The wine was in a carafe.*
>
> *I think we had some sense of celebrating our accomplishment, even though, as Stephen has told me, we planted the wrong coloured flowering bushes in the wrong place.*

I haven't sent this to Natasha because, she not having met me, she most likely would think I am patronizing her, trying to make her feel that she must find Stephen's and my planting plants in her garden funny, and as funny excusable. But I like the details in the description.

———

Öçi tells me that I have such interesting friends, which surprises me, as I always assumed his friends, for simply being his friends, were more interesting than any I could have.

He asks me about America, in particular about New York, where he wants to go, and where I do not want to return to.

It reassures me that Nikos reads my diary, which he says he likes to read to find out what we've been doing in this record of our lives together. I do not hold back from writing whatever I want, which allowance he not so much gives me as never questions.

This comes to me as something of a surprise: that there is no fantasy in my relationship with Nikos, in our love for each other.

––––

Walking along Piccadilly, Maria and I saw on the newspapers being sold at little newspaper stands the headlines about the military coup in Greece by some colonels. She laughed both sadly and nervously.

Because I have no experience of an American national political catastrophe, I cannot imagine the effect of one, and I am unable to make the connection between Nikos and Maria, whom I know, and the catastrophe of a dictatorship in Greece, about which I know only by what I am told by Nikos. I'm unable to make a connection between him and modern Greek history, he having lived that history and I not. It is a history of many catastrophes, and therefore Nikos' so-often-used word 'catastrophe' for missing a bus, or breaking a glass, or forgetting where his spectacles were last put down. How can I know what it means to a Greek to have the country dictated to by petty colonels, and especially what it means to Nikos, working at the Greek Embassy, and, too, what it means to us together?

––––

Some men, including Sonia Orwell's ex-husband Michael Pitt-Rivers, were arrested and imprisoned for homosexual activity; so many people objected to the unfairness of these convictions that the Wolfenden Committee was set up to study the law that gave rise to them, and its report recommended decriminalizing homosexual relations among consenting adults. Years after, years since the report was published, a bill has been passed in Parliament, and Nikos and I are no longer criminals. We never felt we were.

––––

The military dictatorship in Greece made it politically and morally impossible for Nikos to continue to work at the Embassy, so he quit.

He had no money, but I had $3000 savings. We moved to a top-floor flat in Battersea, in Overstrand Mansions on Prince of Wales Drive, London S.W.11, overlooking the large, dense green trees of Battersea Park. The flat, with slanted ceilings because we are under the roof, has three small rooms off a corridor, which we painted all white.

Johnny Craxton gave us some furniture, some beautiful chairs and an antique chest of drawers, and the rest we bought at a huge second-hand furniture warehouse in Peckham Rye.

As Nikos says, we are creating our lives together.

My desk cost two pounds ten shillings. I've begun to write reports for different publishers, to translate technical books from French, and to write fiction.

Many of Nikos' friends from Athens have come to London in exile, and we often have them staying with us.

Through Stephen, Nikos had a few interviews with publishers. Charles Monteith at Faber & Faber told him that he should start out by getting a job in a bookshop. Nikos said, 'I didn't do all that graduate work in philosophy at Harvard in order to become a sales clerk in a bookshop.' Patrick introduced him to Anthony Blond, who was publishing guidebooks about the night life of capital cities called London Spy or Paris Spy or New York Spy and asked Nikos to do Athens Spy, but Nikos said he was not interested in the night life of Athens, where, in any case, he would not go. John Lehmann invited Nikos to lunch but had no advice.

Nikos said, 'Well, they must think I'm asking for a lot – not being English, my first language being Greek, and having no experience in publishing.'

I looked for a job teaching English to the children of families at the American army base at Ruislip, but many other young Americans wanting to live in London without work permits were also trying to get jobs there.

Then Nikos, at a drinks party, met an editor at Penguin Books, Tony Richardson, who was leaving Penguin and said there was a job going there, and why didn't Nikos apply? He went for an interview with Allen Lane, the founder of Penguin Books. The position left vacant by Tony Richardson was to be editor for poetry, art and architecture, cinema, theatre, and town planning, and Nikos got the job. He started working as an editor at Penguin Books.

He recounted to me a long walk he had with Tony Richardson, who, very ill, perhaps fatally, had to take long walks for whatever medication he was on to circulate throughout his body. He told Nikos that the only appreciation he has in art, music, literature is for the greats: Michelangelo, Rembrandt, Haydn, Mozart, Beethoven, Dickens, Dostoyevsky, Tolstoy. Recounting this to me, Nikos, as he does when he is very moved, raised his arms and lowered them, and said nothing. Tony Richardson died soon after Nikos took over his position at Penguin Books.

Nikos was granted resident status by the Home Office.

With Stephen guaranteeing me, I have also become a resident.

We see a lot of Stephen, who, when he first came to our Battersea flat for dinner, said it was just the kind of place he'd always wanted to live in.

All this is just summary, as I write only occasionally in my diary.

———

I have been reading Victor Shklovsky, who, with his friend Osip Brik, was one of the founders of Russian Formalism, and who wrote:

Sometimes books are not written; they emerge, they happen.

And suddenly, thinking of having met Osip Brik and his historical involvement with Russian Formalism, there comes to me the small shock of having met Lili Brik whose photograph by Rodchenko was used in perhaps the most famous Soviet poster, that of a woman wearing a bandana, an open hand to the side of her mouth, shouting out the good news of Communism!

And because of the way I like connecting people I've met with people they have met, as if these greater connections expand my world into that greater world, a strained sense of possessiveness comes to me with the thought that when I shook hands with the Briks I shook hands with the Russians they often had to their flat in the 1920s, including Boris Pasternak, Maxim Gorky, Vladimir Mayakovsky, Sergei M. Eisenstein, Kazimir Malevich, Alexander Rodchenko, Varvara Stepanova, Yuri Tynyanov, Vsevolod Meyerhold, and who knows how many others?

And it comes to me, belatedly because it did not come to me at the time, to wonder what Osip and Lili Brik thought of my relationship with Stephen Spender, Stephen and I perhaps to them a strange couple who, especially for Soviets, could only have come from a world so foreign to them that they must have wondered at it.

A cultural difference between Nikos and me, which difference makes him always more attractive to me. As a provincial American who grew up in a small, isolated, French-speaking parish in Yankee New England, I held and still do hold celebrated writers in some awe, and that awe is certainly a dimension in my friendship with Stephen Spender, for often I step back from our friendship and see him as a celebrated poet who is a friend. Nikos, a Greek born and brought up in a cosmopolitan family in which some of his relatives are themselves celebrated writers (among others, his aunt Tato, a novelist) and who know celebrated writers, seems to take for granted the celebrated writers in London as if he were simply transferring his familiarity with Athenian writers to familiarity with writers here. He sees Stephen as a friend who writes poetry.

And as for my awe of publishers, I once saw a commissioning editor in a publishing house as having the power to determine my life. And now Nikos is such a publisher. But, as he explains, in Athens it is no very great distinction to publish a novel or a collection of poems, as there are many publishing houses which, in the old way of publishing houses, have their own bookshops, and more often than not the writer will pay for the publishing of his or her work. Publishing a novel or collection of poems may add something to one's life, though, really, one's life is determined somewhere else, mostly by one's family, for whom publishing a novel or a collection of poems is simply a part of the family culture. Nikos is so unassuming in his position as a publisher, I sometimes wonder if he is at all aware of his power, as if to be a publisher in London were to him to have no more determining power than a publisher would have in Athens. When I visit him in the Penguin offices, I am very impressed by how matter-of-factly he appears to take to dictating to his secretary, to talking business on the telephone, to having his own personal cup for coffee on his desk.

No doubt aspiring British editors are resentful that Nikos, not British, should have such a powerful position as editor.

Nikos as poetry editor with Borges.

In Nikos' presence, though I can't recall where and to whom, I said that I don't understand how anyone can say, 'I like him' or 'I dislike her,' nor do I understand how anyone can say about a country, 'I like Italy' or 'I dislike France,' people and countries too large and complex in character to have any opinions about them. Some time later, again I can't recall where or to whom, I heard Nikos say he didn't understand how anyone can say about another, 'I like him' or 'I dislike her,' or about a country, 'I like Italy' or 'I dislike France,' and I suddenly felt in our relationship a transference that would have him repeat what I had told him as though the thought had come from him. In what other many, many ways does this transference occur, from me to him, and, more importantly to me, him to me? I find myself saying to another, 'We went to France for a weekend,' and it is with great pleasure that I hear him say to the other, 'We went to an exhibition of Courbet at the Grand Palais.'

At a dinner party, a guest said she had been to Paris for the Courbet exhibition and came away not liking Courbet. Nikos sat up straight and said, 'You can't say that, you can't say you don't like Courbet.' The guest, a woman, said, 'But I have the right to my opinion,' and placed a hand about her throat. Nikos said, 'No, you don't, you don't have the right to an opinion about Courbet.'

————

Nikos was among many people at a meeting in the Friends' Meeting House in Marylebone Road to speak against the dictatorship in Greece. The house was packed. He started by saying that when he was in school, at Athens College, he was threatened with expulsion for reading poems by the Greek Communist poet Ritsos and playing a Soviet oratorio by Shostakovich at an event organized by a cultural society which he was president of. He said 'ah' a lot while he spoke.

He told me that while at Athens College he had in fact been a member of the Communist Party, which was outlawed by the government. He would risk getting up during the night from his bed in the dormitory of the boarding school and go down to an office for which he, then president of the student council, had keys and where he would mimeograph propaganda, then, with the sheets hidden on him, would on a free evening go to cinemas in Athens and throw the sheets from balconies into the audience. It was dangerous to do, but he was never caught.

Nikos knows of the horrors of Communism in Soviet Russia. I would never ask him to justify his belief in Communism, the meaning of which is deep in his Greek history, but which meaning is in my American history anathema.

————

Stephen telephoned from Paris. He is staying in a hotel on the rue des Ecoles. He said that last night around three o'clock students overturned cars and set them on fire just outside his hotel window and bombs were thrown. He has been out on the streets himself, on the side of the students. One asked him if he was Herbert Marcuse, and he was very pleased, but had to say no. Demonstrations of students and workers go on day and night: speeches, marches, riots.

———

An uncle of Nikos, Stavros Stangos, has left Greece to live in London. He is, Nikos tells me, a well-known journalist, Leftist. He came with his wife for a meal and talked of how he used to go into the poor areas of Athens to recruit people into the Communist Party, dangerous. He talked of the defeat of the Communist Party during the Civil War, which he fought in, and which Nikos, younger, remembers. I feel that what the Greeks I have met most have to bear is the defeat of their social ideology.

Greek friends of Nikos, also having managed to get out, visit, and some stay with us for a few days until they are able to settle. Nikos and they talk in Greek, the only word comprehensible to me being 'catastrophe'.

The great Greek actress Aspasia Papathanasiou has come to London, and Nikos visits her. She is an ardent Communist. She gave a reading of Yannis Ritsos' 'Epitaphios' at a poetry reading in the Festival Hall, a lament on the death of a young Communist soldier during the Civil War, and in her declamation was the tragic voice of Greece.

W. H. Auden read on this occasion. He kept looking at his watch when other poets read. Later, he said he disapproved of Papathanasiou's recitation: one does not weep when reciting a poem.

It is strange to meet people who are exiled, people who talk of prison and torture. Though I hear about 'catastrophe' in the personal terms of people I meet through Nikos, I can't see anyone truly suffering the 'catastrophe,' certainly can't see anyone in prison and tortured, as if suffering is far beyond this or that single person but is some vastly impersonal suffering. I wonder if this has to do with the impression I retain of World War II – only an impression, because I was a little boy – of suffering on such a scale that it is difficult to reduce the suffering to someone I could possibly know, or even meet.

How my mind makes tangential connections as I write, tangents always occurring to me to draw me away from now to then, until now and then become so connected I don't make a distinction between the two. So a dinner party occurs to me, given by Nikos and me, at which Frank and Anita Kermode came with the Italian writer Luigi Meneghello and his wife Katia, on whose forearm I noted a blue, tattooed number from when she was a prisoner in Auschwitz.

Nikos told me that, after years of youthful taking for granted the Parthenon on the Acropolis, one day he looked up at the temple on the rock and the meaning came to him overwhelmingly. I can only guess what that historical meaning was – is – to him, a Greek.

———

A Romanian friend, Roxanne, whose aristocratic family in Romania lost everything to Communism, and who has shown us letters from her mother that have obviously been censored with faint pencil marks underlining sentences before they were allowed to be sent, admonished Nikos that he should be grateful that Greece has been kept free of Communism. Nikos closed his eyes and lowered his head.

How can I not feel in him the defeat of his ideology?

Nikos asked Roxanne if her family were Greek Phanariots from Constantinople sent to Romania by the Sultan to govern the country.

Yes, she said, four hundred years ago.

———

On the crowded 137 bus from Marble Arch, alone, I stood next to a young man and as the bus moved we were jostled against each other, and each time we were jostled against each other we looked at each other in the eyes. That sense came over me as of there being no two other people in the world but the two of us, we at a centre and nothing around the centre. He must have felt the same, because when I got off the bus at Prince of Wales Drive he did too, and we walked together along the drive, hardly talking, but he came with me up to the flat and we made love. I did not learn his name.

When Nikos came home I told him, and he exclaimed, 'Not in our bed!'

———

I saw Öçi alone. He said, 'I am not an envious person, but I admit to you that I'm envious of your relationship with Nikos.'

———

James Joll, historian of anarchism, and John Golding, historian of art and also a painter, live in Prince of Wales Drive. (Francis Bacon lived here once, and the woman he often paints, Henrietta Moraes, still does, the windows of her flat all year long decorated with Christmas lights.) Nikos and I were invited by John and James for a drinks party.

At the drinks party were Richard and Mary Day Wollheim. Richard is a philosopher of aesthetics, Mary Day a ceramicist of elegant pots. Richard talked of people he knows, always with a look on his face of the improbability of knowing such people, half frowning and half smiling, and making ambiguous gestures with his fingers. There was the story of the couple who, when travelling by ship from New York to Southampton, took a stateroom apart from their own for their parrot. The man will say to his wife that he cannot sit at the opera surrounded by others, so she, with the money, will buy a block of tickets, and an hour before the performance he will say he is too tired to go.

Richard and Mary Day were with Sylvia Guirey, who was once a lady friend of Richard, and is now a friend of both Richard and Mary Day.

She is in some way a descendant of Hugo von Hofmannsthal, the poet and librettist for Richard Strauss, and is more immediately connected to the American Astors. Inspired by Richard, she left her past life to lead a more imaginative, creative life in the present. She is a painter.

Because married to a Circassian prince, she is a princess. Mary Day said, 'Anyone from Circassia with a pair of boots is a prince.' Her husband the prince lives in Ireland.

From John Golding's book, Cubism, the first line: 'Cubism was perhaps the most important and certainly the most complete and radical artistic revolution since the Renaissance.'

Nikos has commissioned John Golding to write a short essay on Cubism for an anthology he is editing, Concepts of Modern Art.

———

Not I, but Nikos was invited by Stephen to the Neal Street Restaurant, a new restaurant that is meant to attract interesting people, with W. H. Auden and Cyril Connolly and Pauline de Rothschild. Nikos wore a brown overcoat and Connolly said to him, 'Brave of you to wear brown in town,' which Nikos didn't understand was not done in London, but which amused him (I would have thought, Oh, I should have known, and clearly I don't know). He said Connolly ordered a partridge, which bled when he cut into it, so he sent it back, and when the bird came back burnt black, Nikos saw Connolly staring at it with tears running down his cheeks. Stephen laughed. Pauline de Rothschild ate only one pear. W. H. Auden was silent.

———

When Nikos is with Greeks, the sexual leanings of someone not known will be questioned, and one of them, leaning his head a little to the side, will say, as if the expression has to be in French, 'Il est un peu comme ça.'

———

The Greek novelist Costas Tachtsis is staying with us. Nikos suggested to Penguin Books that the novel by Costas, The Third

Wedding, be translated into English and published, as a way of Penguin making a positive statement about Greek culture during a time when culture in Greece means nothing more than propaganda. Was Costas happy with the translation and the publication? Is Costas ever happy about anything? I arrived back home a little late to find Costas, sitting at the top of the steps to the landing outside our front door, keening, 'Ach, ach, ach!' Alarmed, I asked, 'What's wrong?' and he, throwing his arms up and raising his chin, cried out, 'My book! My book! They've destroyed my book!' He disapproved of the translation.

Praising the book, Nikos is amused by the transposition of the raving Greek female characters from raving Greek male friends.

Costas travels with a special trunk of women's clothes, not fashionable frocks, but dowdy tweed skirts and cardigans and heavy stockings, which he dresses into to – as he says – faire le trottoir along Queensway in Bayswater. He plucks his beard so he doesn't have a stubble. The men he picks up, he insists, never know that he is a man, but a woman who excuses herself from not having frontal sex because she is having her period, but is happy with backside sex. Costas earns his money, not from his books, but as a transvestite prostitute.

Johnny Craxton invited the three of us to a drinks party in the large house he lives in, Kidderpore Avenue, where, it seems, many people live and where large drinks parties are given. (Johnny's father, Harold, is famous as a coach to pianists. I once heard him say that when he was a young musician in a group of musicians, they would, when invited to play at an event at a country house, be told by the chief butler to use the servants' back entrance.) Stephen Spender was at the drinks party, and while he and I stood apart without understanding, Costas raved, as one of his female characters raves, all in Greek, which Nikos and Johnny understood and listened to without expression. Later, Nikos told me that Costas was raving about Stephen – how, in the crudest way possible in Greek, he had fucked Stephen, who, now, didn't recognize him. Knowing Costas, Nikos said, he dismissed Costas' raving against

Stephen as resentment that Stephen didn't recognize him as Greece's greatest living novelist.

I have helped Costas refine the English in his own translation of a short story, and was struck by the image of a man's large red cock as if the large red cock of a blank wall.

As for everything connecting, how can I not put in here this? Edna O'Brien invited Nikos and me to dinner with the Australian novelist Patrick White and his Greek partner Manoly Lascaris. I asked him, being Greek, if he knew of a Greek writer named Costas Tachtsis? and he, scowling, said, Yes, he once knew Tachtsis, who for a while lived in Australia. Did he? I asked. All Lascaris said was, Yes, he did, and I knew not to ask more.

———

As poetry editor, Nikos has many poets wanting his attention, poets who send him or arrange to meet him to give him the kinds of publications that originated in America, the mimeographed typed text stapled together. One is The New British Poetry. Nikos and I are archivists, and I suppose we do think that whatever is of interest now will be of even more interest in the future, including the names of the New British Poets: Allen Barry, Don Bodie, Alan Brownjohn, Jim Burns, Dave Cunliffe, Paul Evans, Roy Fisher, S. A. Gooch, Harry Guest, Lee Harwood, L. M. Herrickson, Douglas Hill, Pete Hoida, Anselm Hollo, Michael Horovitz, Alan Jackson, Peter Jay, David Kerrison, Adrian Mitchell, Tina Morris, Neil Oram, Ignu Ramus, Jeremy Robson, Michael Shayer, Steve Sneyd, Chris Torrance, Gael Turnbull, Ian Vine, Michael Wilkin, W. E. Wyatt.

Some of these poets Nikos has published: Alan Brownjohn, Harry Guest, Anselm Hollo, Michael Horovitz, Adrian Mitchell, and a poet he especially admires, Lee Harwood, whose love poetry has great tenderness, and who earns his money, Nikos said, as a bus conductor collecting fares in Brighton.

———

Asked to contribute a one-line poem to an anthology, Roy Rogers, Nikos asked me to help, and I suggested:

(   )

which Nikos submitted.

———

A group of American poets came to London to give a reading and invited Nikos, who asked me to go along with him, in a small hall, which I remember as black with a spotlight on the narrow stage. The poets were Aram Saroyan, Patti Smith, and Andrew Wylie.

GOLD

Andrew Wylie

They all appeared to form a cult, a New York esoteric club. Patti Smith had long black hair and Andrew Wylie wore a beret and dark spectacles, and Aram Saroyan appeared even weirder than they for wearing rather college-like button-down collar and chinos. They gave Nikos collections of poems in small booklets, published by Telegraph Books, one of the booklets photographs of scars instead of poems put together by Brigid Polk, one of the Andy Warhol people.

A poem by Gerard Malanga, one of the Warhol people:

> My dreams come true
> Even the bad ones

A poem by Aram Saroyan:

> HAPPY!!!
> INSTANT!

A poem by Andrew Wylie:

> I fuck
> your
> ass
>
> you suck
> my cock

To his amusement, the writer on art, Marco Livingstone, told me that when Nikos visited him in Oxford to discuss a book, Nikos, noting on a shelf a long playing recording of Patti Smith singing, said he hadn't been aware that she is a singer as well as a poet. Though he couldn't see how he could publish her poems – which, come to think of it, read as if the lyrics of songs – Nikos was impressed by how original she was in herself, and he liked her.

Mark Lancaster gave to Nikos a recording of songs by Janis Joplin, and after he played one song he put the recording aside, but he kept up his interest in Janis Joplin in herself as a renegade.

Nikos likes renegades.

As for their music – as driven as it is, Nikos says there is hardly any invention in it, and invention is what Nikos is acutely attentive to in any art; their music relies on an obvious beat and does little to develop the beat, does little, if anything, to invent on the beat.

That is, when he is attentive to the music. When recorded rock music is played at a party, he likes the background beat; and though he is not at all a good dancer – at best, he sways back and forth – he likes to see me dance, which I do to the driven beat, and he stands back and smiles, and I like to think I am dancing to make him smile.

About Bach, and especially Glenn Gould playing Bach, Nikos will from time to time cry out, 'It's so inventive!' and suddenly Bach *becomes* his music, and I think of Bach, who lived within the conventions of his time, as one of the most original people who ever lived.

———

Nikos has learned that a close friend of his in Athens has been arrested, George Kavounidis.

From time to time Nikos has mentioned this George Kavounidis, who was a diplomat in some South-east Asian country from where he brought back to Athens two miniature gazelles in his diplomatic luggage, one of which died of suffocation and the other Nikos described sliding about the shiny parquet floors of Kavounidis' flat. My sense from what Nikos has said of Kavounidis is that it was through him that Nikos was able to enter into the world of diplomats and then within that world on to London, and my greater sense is that Kavounidis had an entourage of young men whom he helped, for whatever personal satisfaction. What interested me is the notion of diplomats once forming, in Greece, not only a world of people engaged in politics, but of people noted for their culture. So, the poet George Seferis used his diplomatic postings to further his career outside Greece, and so, too, Nikos, posted in London, used his post in the Press Office of the Greek Embassy to establish himself in London. About George Kavounidis – who, from what Nikos says, was a social figure in Athens – I imagined him to be in a nineteenth-century, or even traditionally older, Athenian social world in which diplomats were invited to formal occasions, and Nikos, a sortable young man as Sonia would say, was invited by Kavounidis to come with him. Nikos will say he hated such occasions in Athens, but I am struck by the formal attire he brought to London from Athens: his – as he calls it – 'smoking' (what I call tuxedo), cummerbund, shiny black pumps with little tassels, an overcoat with a velvet collar, a white silk scarf, in case his posting in London required him to attend a formal event, for if Nikos does enter into such a social event he behaves accordingly. That Kavounidis' entourage of young men was homosexual was known and, as if this was a tradition among diplomats and their entourages in that social world, accepted.

That now is past history, the colonels as dictators, Nikos said, totally uncultured, crude, stupid.

New galleries keep opening. Garage is a venue for exhibitions of art and of readings of poetry founded by Tony Stokes. Everyone is in love with Tony, including Nikos. Tony flirts with Nikos, and Nikos flirts back. Tony organized at Garage an exhibition of the works of Jennifer Bartlett and Joel Shapiro.

Tony is married to Teresa Gleadowe, who works for the Arts Council. She sometimes cares for our cats when we are away, Jasmine and, now, Mustafa. The cats are known to be very neurotic, especially the female Jasmine, who, jealous of other females, hisses at women, so Teresa had to lock her in the bathroom.

I think more of Nikos' social life in Athens, as when he told me that, to be relieved of military duty by his commanding officer on New Year's Eve, he gave him a gift of a pair of expensive leather gloves and so was free to go to an all-night party with gambling, and I wondered if such a relief by an officer of a soldier for a pair of expensive gloves was indicative of a world that has had its precedents in many many years of past military social history. I imagine that Athens, being provincial and yet, because provincial, alert to what cultured Athenians imagined to be happening in the capital cities, preserved social ways that no longer existed in Berlin, Paris, London.

———

At Garage, Nikos organized a reading by Kenward Elmslie, whose poems Nikos published, and I remember the beautiful, resonant lines:

Madonna, Madonna

read in a dry voice.

Is there in his poetry a movement away from any explicit or even implied meaning, to a lively, slap-happy activity of the mind?

> The sluggish choreography of shadows bumping,
> burping and bloating, hunching and gnarling,
> has the marijuana tempo of sex sometimes.

Kenward wears on a thin chain about his neck a locket with a black and white photograph of Joe Brainard, Kenward told me when I asked, touching the little round cut-out photograph.

Joe Brainard does drawings based on ordinary objects, a lot on comic strips, such as on the comic heroine Nancy.

IF NANCY WAS A BOY.

Joe Brainard has written a book, I Remember, which consists of one-line recollections that bring back to me so many similar recollections:

> I remember my mother's sticking toothpicks into cakes to see if they were done or not.
> I remember Dole pineapple rings on a bed of lettuce with cottage cheese on top and sometimes a cherry on top of that.
> I remember continuing my return address on envelopes to include 'The Earth' and 'The Universe.'

———

The poet Harold Norse is in London, having come from living for some time in Athens, where there is what he calls a 'scene' despite the colonels. Nikos has published him in the series Penguin Modern Poets, along with Charles Bukowski (whose poems are brutal, filled with booze and whores and death, and who sends Nikos long, long, typed letters that read as if spilling over the edges of the pages with beer) and Philip Lamantia (the American Surrealist poet admired by André Breton who writes such wonderful lines as 'The mermaids have come to the desert'), poets Harold recommended to Nikos.

No doubt Harold brings with him a world, the, say, Beat world of America, inhabited by Allen Ginsberg and Gregory Corso and William Burroughs, but I'm not sure I'm so very interested in that world to hear about it from someone who himself inhabits it. No, I'm wrong – I do find the world fascinating, but the truth is I am so jealous of it the only way I can deal with it is to tell myself I am not interested. But I also have to admit that in the person of Harold, whom I don't in himself find very interesting, the 'scene' does contract from fantasy into the ego of a man Nikos and I find more and more difficult to indulge, as he seems to want more than we can give.

Yet, Harold's poems are so much about egolessness, expounding on mantras and karma and nirvana and the cosmos and the Hub of the Fiery Force.

I like this couplet he wrote: 'Comme c'est beau / de chier dans l'eau.'

He told us this story: having met W. H. Auden at some literary event in New York, Auden invited Harold to Saint Mark's Place, but somehow Chester Kallman thought the invitation was meant for him and he appeared first at the door of Auden, who, opening the door, said, 'Wrong blond,' for, improbable as it seems, Harold was blond, as I suppose Kallman was. Harold told this story with such animated resentment at having been outdone by Kallman, and with such insistence at getting the facts right, that I have forgotten why Kallman rang Auden's bell instead of Harold. Auden must have taken to Kallman enough because Kallman stayed on.

———

The police rang Nikos to say someone named David Gascoyne, who claimed to be a poet, had asked Nikos to be called, as David Gascoyne had been arrested for trying to get to the Queen in Buckingham Palace to inform her that her life was in danger from someone wanting to kill her. Nikos went to the police station in support of Gascoyne. Nikos believes Gascoyne to be a major poet, a true Surrealist, as the English cannot be, and a Surrealist, inspired by the French, who transformed himself into a poet of some of the most movingly vulnerable spiritual poems in modern English, which, too, put him apart from the other living English poets. From Farewell Chorus:

> 'The silence after the viaticum.' So silent is the ray
> Of naked radiance that lights our actual scene,
> Leading the gaze into those nameless and unknown
> Extremes of our existence where fear's armour falls away
> And lamentation and defeat and pain
> Are all transfigured by acceptance; where men see
> The tragic splendor of their final destiny.

This poem is dated New Year, 1940.

I also think that David Gascoyne has written the most heart-wrenching poems about World War II, as in these simple lines:

> Go to sleep. Put out
> That light! The War is over now. It's late.
> Why don't those people go to bed?

And this makes me wonder what the generation of David Gascoyne, which of course includes Stephen Spender, for whom World War II is a lived experience, can make of England now, in which it seems that that war, or any war, is so distant in time that Joan Littlewood's Oh, What a Lovely War! comes as shock from a past that the present needs to be reminded of. Perhaps David Gascoyne, in his madness, still lives the horrors of the war.

Does Stephen? Stephen seems to live more in the present, to be amused by the style of the present, as when he showed us a new greatcoat he had had tailored especially for him by the fashionable Mr. Fish, a long, wide greatcoat with wide lapels, mauve. He laughed with pleasure when he showed it off to us.

Which reminds me – reminds me, too, of so much I don't put into this diary, as though I think of so much as insignificant, whereas it may all be wonderfully significant if this diary is ever read, as it were, historically – that Nikos bought me a greatcoat (as Stephen calls an overcoat) designed by Ossie Clark, a pink and grey tweed, which I wear with the awareness that I am wearing an Ossie Clark greatcoat that others would recognize as by Ossie Clark, making me, oh, in style!

———

How I enjoy Stephen's levity, the somewhat guilty pleasure he takes in a fancy greatcoat, in fancy restaurants, in friends, in giggling at stories he tells about himself and others – guilty because I sense in him that he feels he doesn't really deserve such pleasures but that they are generous gifts to him from a world he is bemused by – and how I am always aware of a weight in him that that levity has to sustain.

I read his poems about grief, and especially the grief of his war poems, and often enough have the sense in him of that grief when, at the news of yet another wartime horror in Vietnam, he will press his lips together and stare out and shake his head a little, and I think of his writing about:

> That wreath of incommunicable grief
> Which is all mystery or nothing.

———

It seems to me that so much history is in the 'insignificant' particulars, and that in a hundred years' time these very details will say more about the past than generalizations.

———

How did Nikos learn about contemporary British poetry? How did he know of F. T. Prince, whom he published, and whose The Tears of a Muse in America I read as a hymn to America. I think that if Henry James had been a poet he would have written such a poem:

> here resolutions bristle,
> For the cause seems to shine out at me from the moment
> I grant him all the mind I can; when I in short
> Impute to him an intemperate spirit . . .
> . . . It comes to me afresh,
> There glimmers out of it upon me that I want
> Nothing of it to come at once. It glimmers,
> It glimmers from the question, of how, how shall it fall
> The moment of the simple sight?

———

Thinking of 'insignificant' details – they come to me, one after another, and I'm not able to place them, but when each appears it brings with it, as if momentarily filling out the darkness, a whole world evoked by the detail. So this: hanging from a long, twisted flex over the high headboard of a bed, a light switch which is turned on or off by pressing a button. A tray on an unmade bed with a small coffee pot on it and cups with the dregs of coffee and plates with the crumbs of rolls and the unfolded wrapping of butter and little empty jars of jam. Two towels hanging over the rim of an old, claw-footed bathtub, the floor small black and white tiles.

When I described to Julia Hodgkin the light switch at the end of a flex, she said, 'You've brought back my entire childhood,' and I was amazed that a detail that meant something to me was so meaningful to her.

———

Harry Fainlight, whose poems Nikos has been urging him to be published, came over. Though Nikos has great patience for him, thinking him a more than worthy poet, I find him too mentally shat-tered, I suppose by drugs, to make any sense of what he says. (Too, I'm frightened of drugs – hallucinogenics – for the disarray they would cause in what I feel my already disarrayed mind.) Harry gives Nikos poems to be published, then takes them away, and Nikos doesn't press him. He had come to give Nikos his poems but he left with them.

We do have a chapbook collection, Sussicran, Narcissus spelt backwards, published by Turret Press under Ted Lucie-Smith, and these lines from a poem about lying in bed with a stranger after sex struck me:

> Thrown by the pattern of holes in the top
> Of an old-fashioned paraffin stove, a magic
> Cathedral window glows on the ceiling.

Nikos and I had a paraffin stove when we first moved into Over-strand Mansions, as we couldn't afford central heating.

———

What the derivation is I don't know, but the word 'gay' has come to mean being sexually attracted to one's own sex. Frank Kermode's colleague at University College London, Keith Walker, said he thought a lot about what people who are attracted to the opposite sex should be called, and came up with 'glums.'

Stephen is teaching at the University, but feels he is doing so badly he wants to go into the loos and write on the walls SPENDER MUST GO!

———

Often, looking at Nikos sitting across the room from me, he read-ing, it comes to me, as with a little flash, to wonder what was it like to have a German officer billeted in his family house? What was it like to see a German soldier shoot a little boy for stealing a potato? What was it like to hear a man with a wheelbarrow call-ing out, each morning, for those who died of starvation because of the German occupation? What was it like to live in a country where torturers wiped their bloody hands on a schoolroom wall? And to live through the German occupation only to have civil war replace the occupation and having to hide under the dining-room table when the nearby airport was bombed? And to be taken out to Communist rallies by the maid, who, when no one in the family could kill a dearly bought chicken, said, 'Kill a chicken? I kill men every night'? In him, in his history, I am aware of World War II.

The dead, starved to death by the Nazi occupation, being taken to a mass grave outside of Athens.

———

Kenward Elmslie publishes a literary magazine, Z, another Z added with each magazine, and in ZZZZ is a draft of Nikos' 'Pure Reason'.

———

Stephen, Keith Milow, Nikos and I spent an afternoon together. Keith took photographs:

Stephen says Keith looks like a mischievous fawn.

Always in a suit and tie, his rigidly parted hair combed flat against his small, round skull with a lot of water, his slightly Asian eyes bulging behind his pink-rimmed spectacles as if to look in all directions at once (his paternal grandmother was in part Malaccan), John Pope-Hennessy's body appears too constricted to contain a soul. Too intellectually brilliant for any shadows in him, the impression he gives is of a man totally self-confident in his intelligence and knowledge and worldliness, all of which precludes any need for more than what he already has himself, and least of all any need for belief in God.

Asked at an airport check-in if he had packed his own bags, he answered, in his high pitch, 'Of course not!'

Though he always wears a tie, the collars of his shirts appear always to be wrinkled.

From time to time we meet for lunch (I imagine he would say, 'luncheon') in an Italian restaurant in Soho called Bianchi's, where on a shelf are novels written by people who frequent the restaurant, among them the novels of Iris Murdoch.

Christmas time, on my way to have lunch with him, I stopped in a shop and bought a little carved rhinoceros, Indian, for tuppence, which I gave to him. He studied it carefully, said, in his high-pitched voice that was close to being a squeal, 'Very nice,' and put it into a side pocket.

We talked about a series of books published by Penguin Books, called Style and Civilization. Nikos is the editor. Pope-Hennessy (can I possibly call him John?) said, 'I don't like the word "style."' I didn't know what he meant, and I never do dare ask him what he means – not because I think he would be offended by my asking (it is hardly possible to offend him), but because I feel that if I asked him what he means he would have had every right to ask me what I mean, and for me to try to get into such a conversation with John about style would expose my cultural limitations and pretensions. I like John, I like being with him a lot, and not only because in my deference to him I would learn so much from him, but because he seems to respect my ignorance. With him, it is better to ask, 'Who was Giovanni di Paolo?' than to suggest any insights into the artist's work.

We talked about mutual friends. He was amused to hear funny stories about these friends, none art historians, anecdotes that made him laugh a high, abrupt laugh that brought his voice up to a level I had thought impossible for a human.

If he doesn't like someone, he will say, looking down, his heavily lidded eyes half closed, 'I don't like him,' and then look up and away as if the person, who seemed to have been standing before him in judgment, suddenly ceases to exist. He particularly dislikes most art historians.

———

On a Sunday afternoon, Nikos and I will amuse ourselves by lying on the floor next to each other and painting in watercolour.

One afternoon, we amused ourselves with this:

TITLES TO ALTOGETHER DIFFERENT NOVELS

It is a truth universally acknowledged, that a single man in possession of a good fortune, must be gay.

Halfway down a by-street of one of our New England towns stands a rusty wooden house with a flat roof and a small chimney in the middle.

Call me Jezebel.

During the whole of a lively, bright and laughter-filled day in the spring of the year, I had been passing with a riotous group of joking friends, on horseback, through a colourful tract of country, and at length we found ourselves, as the sun shone at its fullest, in view of the slap-happy House of Usher.

Under certain circumstances there are few hours in life more agreeable than the afternoon hour of everyone dancing naked on the lawn.

All drinking families resemble one another, but each teetotal family is unhappy in its own way.

Longtemps je me suis couché très tard.

Once upon a time and a very bad time it was there was a lorry coming down the road and this lorry was coming down along the road and hit a nicens little boy named baby tuckoo and killed him.

Mrs Dalloway said she would buy the whip herself.

Robert Cohn was once a drag queen in a bar in New Haven.

One may as well not begin.

———

John Ashbery, in London to give a reading in his flat but somehow resonant voice, came to supper with his past lover from Paris, the poet Pierre Martory. Nikos is the first publisher to publish Ashbery's poetry in Great Britain.

John said he is working on a book to be a Henry James novel without characters or setting or plot, and this interested me, thinking everything Jamesian in the book must be all in the writing.

I never know if John is being wry or not, as when he said his mother rang him to tell him she was at an airport, and when he told her, no, she was in a home, she answered, yes, of course she knew that, she was in a home at the airport. He said he would never be explicit about sex in his poetry because his mother might be shocked, and did worry about having included in a poem something about a sexual act wiped up in a tissue and flushed down the toilet. I laugh, but he doesn't laugh, and stares at me with a slight frown.

He gave us some long-playing records of a group of comedians, called the Firesign Theatre, which he said reaches an even funnier level with a bit of smoke. After John and Pierre left, Nikos and I listened to the Firesign Theatre, but I guess with smoke they would have elicited little more than chuckles. Perhaps I do wonder if I am missing a lot missing smoke.

I once said to Stephen, 'I don't understand the poetry of John Ashbery,' and he, as he sometimes does as if to avoid making a comment, stepped sideways as if to go away, but he said, 'Neither do I.'

———

Stephen gave us a set of Horizon magazine, reprinted and bound in volumes – rather, he gave the set to Nikos, with a dedication thanking Nikos for allowing him to 'seduce' me by taking me to France. I look through the contents pages of the issues of Horizon and think, with the wonder of it all, so many of the people listed we've met.

There's Julia Strachey, whom we've visited in her walk-up flat in Percy Street, a small flat with slanting floors and slanting ceilings and, dominating, a large bronze bust by Stephen Tomlin. In her droll, laconic way, she complained of the rats pulling off her bedclothes, disturbing her sleep. There is a telephone service, DIAL A CHICKEN, but she prefers DIAL LIVER.

And there is Lawrence Gowing, who stutters so his saliva runs down his chin, which he wipes with his tie, a man of wonderful enthusiasms. When he became professor at the Slade, he, as an art work, had his female students outline his body as he lay naked on a sheet of plywood, spreadeagled, and, he said stuttering, 'Some-some-some-sometimes they get-get-get-get my penis pointed and some-some-some-sometimes blunt.' He and Julia Strachey were once married.

The interconnections among all the people we've met defeat me. I've read Julia Strachey's Cheerful Weather for the Wedding, laughing. Her wonderfully extravagant metaphors and similes: 'Dolly's white face, with its thick and heavily curled-back lips, above her black speckled wool frock, glimmered palely in front of the ferns, like a phosphorescent orchid blooming alone there in the twilit swamp.' It was published by the Hogarth Press by Leonard and Virginia Woolf; and then The Man on the Pier, with a jacket design by Barbara Elizabeth Hepworth, published by John Lehmann.

———

Öçi has left for New York, where he intends to make his life.

———

Nikos is very rational, so when he engages in what I think of as the irrational, I baulk – as when he has a flu and he sets up on the bedside table a glass of water, a needle, a little heap of cloves and a candle in a candlestick that he lights to perform the ritual of: inserting a clove on the needle and holding it in the candle flame and reciting, 'If David gave you the evil eye, may his eyes pop out' (he having told me that only someone with blue eyes can give the evil eye, and not intentionally but unintentionally through someone else intending evil, so it would not be my fault if the evil eye were cast on him through me), and if the clove simply sizzles I have not given him the evil eye, that burnt clove then dropped into the glass of water, and then another clove on the needle is held in the flame with the

names of everyone he can think of with blue eyes; but if the clove
pops when my name is pronounced, I have given him the evil eye,
and the spell is broken, after which the burnt clove-flavoured water
is drunk. He laughs when I say no, no, I will not assist him, but then
when, his face illuminated by the candle, I see him perform the
ritual, a sense comes to me of a cultural loneliness in him that may
go back for centuries and still isolates him in a belief that has nothing
to do with the world he lives in, and I wonder how much from his
ancestry does isolate him within some form of cultural loneliness
that separates him from the world he lives in.

The ritual is called Moschokarfia, and it is unique to Greeks
from Asia Minor.

Does he actually believe in the ritual? I once asked him if he
believes in God, and he answered, 'That is a question I never ask
myself.'

He also told me that there is a special prayer, recognized by the
Greek Orthodox Church, for breaking the spell of the evil eye.

———

John Ashbery has sent us a copy of the kind of publication that
proliferates, mimeographed typewritten pages stapled together, this
with a large black and white photograph of John on the cover,
barefoot and walking near a seaside beach with bathers, the text
called 'The New Spirit'.

> I thought that if I could put it all down, that would be one
> way. And next the thought
>   came to me that to leave all out, would be another, and
> truer way.

Reading, I found that, though I didn't understand what the text
was about, I became more and more engaged in the writing, and I
was reminded of what John said when he came to supper, that he
was trying to write a Jamesian text that left out everything James

would have included, character, setting, plot, for the way the Jamesian prose in itself enchants. Even in reading a James novel it happens that I don't know what is going on but I am sustained by the wonderfully elaborate and always inventive prose.

I'm reminded of what Gertrude Stein wrote about Henry James in What is English Literature:

> In the meantime Henry James went on. He too needed the whole paragraph because he too was just there, but, and that is the thing to notice, his whole paragraph was detached what it said from what it did, what it was from what it held, and over it all something floated not floated away but floated, floated up there. You can see how that was not true of Swinburne and Browning and Meredith but that it was true of Henry James. And so it makes it that Henry James just went on doing what American literature has always done, the form was always the form of the contemporary English one, but the disembodied way of disconnecting something from anything and anything from something was the American way. This brought about something that made neither words exist for themselves, nor sentences, nor choosing, it created the need of paragraphing, and the whole paragraph having been being made the whole paragraph had rising from it off of it its meaning.

What rises from and floats above John's poetry, it seems to me, is some sense of meaning without my knowing what the meaning is, but the sense engages me enough to make me wonder, that wonder in itself enough to keep me reading.

My impulse is to get everything in.

Lucca

We are staying with John Fleming and Hugh Honour in their house, the Villa Marchio, in the hills outside Lucca. As they are advisory editors for Penguin art books, including the series Style and Civilization, Nikos has come to discuss work with them, and I have come along.

We were given separate bedrooms, but decided, as we were alone in a wing of the house, to sleep together in his bed. We were woken this morning by the housekeeper, Gilda, carrying in a tray with breakfast, which we didn't expect, and when she saw us both in the same bed she exclaimed, 'Ai!' and immediately withdrew. We found the tray on a table on the landing.

When I told John what had happened, he said, 'Don't worry about it.'

It is beautiful here.

The villa is eighteenth century, with mottled pink walls and green-shuttered windows and a double stone staircase up to the double doors into the main hall and wings on either side, built by local builders who perhaps didn't work from an architect's plan but their own idea of what a villa should be, and though the symmetry of the house is off it is balanced by two huge palm trees growing on either side of the double staircase. There are great terracotta pots with lemon trees leading to a loggia that overlooks a lotus pool, and the surrounding garden appears stuffed with flowers, vines, flowering trees, cypresses, all pressed together by the garden walls, in a corner of which is a chapel. There is a cantina, a long, dark-beamed hall filled with enormous tuns, demijohns, great green bottles, and very worn, wooden wine presses. John and Hugh have their own wine, olive oil, fruit, vegetables, cheese, eggs, poultry, nuts, berries. The land outside the wide gate to the garden slopes down to outbuildings and houses where peasants live and, beyond the buildings, to terraces planted partly with vines and partly with olive trees, then down steeply to dense, cool, very green woods and a small stream. All the valley is terraced with vines and olive trees, and here and there are pink stucco houses and blue-black cypress trees. Poppies are still blossoming, and yellow daisies, and lots and lots of tiny lavender flowers. John and Hugh have filled the villa itself with what they have no doubt been collecting for years: small bronzes, medallions on small round tables, huge parchment-covered books, paintings, chairs that look like large silver open shells, one shell the seat the other the back, not to be sat on, and in the sitting room there is a fresh bouquet of flowers picked by Hugh.

We were sitting under the loggia when Gilda appeared and said, sternly, 'È pronto,' meaning lunch was ready, and she served it in the dining room with a stern face. Nikos kept telling her how delicious the food was, and she did smile a little.

John and Hugh told us stories about Percy Lubbock, for whom they had been readers in his late years in Lerici when he was blind, and who, they said, would tell them stories about Henry James, one particular story about a painting that had been given to James. 'What was I to do?' Hugh said mimicking Percy Lubbock who had mimicked Henry James. 'It was of a nudity!'

This afternoon, John and Hugh took Nikos and me into Lucca to see the town, and when we came back for tea under the loggia John brought me a beautiful first edition of Italian Hours so I could read what Henry James wrote about Lucca, and reading it while he and Hugh talked to Nikos about art historians I realized what the villa had inspired in me: what I imagined a nineteenth-century

Jamesian appreciation of such a villa from all my reading of James. I know my appreciation is a fantasy, but I am possessive about the details of what I see here: the roses, the fireflies in the bushes, the smell of drying hay.

———

Hugh has a very distinct way of pronouncing various words – not 'wisteria' with the accent on the 'ster,' but 'wis-te-ri-a,' with the accent on the final 'a,' and as for place names, not 'Calay' for 'Calais' but 'Caliss,' and not 'Marsay' for 'Marseilles' but 'Marcelles,' and as for the city of Milan, he pronounces it, he said, as it scans in Shakespeare: 'Mill-an,' with an accent on the 'Mill.' And so arcane English pronunciations are preserved by an Englishman living in Italy, and who thinks of Britain, as he has said, as a small island off-shore from Continental Europe.

We slept separately last night, but this morning the breakfast tray was on the table on the landing, and we realized Gilda is allowing us to sleep however we choose.

And thinking of Jamesian fantasies –

John and Hugh took Nikos and me to meet Harold Acton in his villa just outside of and overlooking Florence, La Pietra. A cameriere in a white jacket showed us into a large, dim drawing room with sunlight showing through the closed shutters in slits onto the rich furniture and Oriental rugs. Acton, in a three-piece suit, was waiting for us, and offered us drinks, which the cameriere poured out. There was a smell of old wood smoke and parched roses. The gilt frames of the paintings glinted here and there, but the pictures themselves were shadowed. Acton seemed to be the very embodiment of the most extravagant fantasy any American could ever have of the cultured European. He was all Oriental politeness and good humor as, with a springing step, he showed us around the gardens, and at lunch in a restaurant in the country he continued to entertain, with lightly told but intimate stories about artists and writers, historians, antiquarians, about aristocrats and ambassadors and friends of de Gaulle.

He said that the damage caused by the flood in Florence is still being suffered by the working class and the peasants outside in the countryside. Shopkeepers were given money to repair their shops, money which came mostly from outside, as the Florentine upper classes did very little to help, so the shops are now bright and shiny for the tourists. But lots and lots of the money collected for the flood relief which first went to Rome remained in Rome and never got to Florence.

Back at the Villa Marchio, John and I sat together under the loggia and I listened to him talk about Acton, who, John said, has a music-hall comedian's sense of timing, making hand gestures and rolling his eyes at the most effective moments, while he also keeps a respectable exterior. He might, for example, tell an anecdote about how uncomfortable life at the Sitwells' was, as when his mother, on a visit, asked for a lavatory, and was taken down a long passage into Lady Ida's bedroom, where she was given – here Acton would pause, then say the rest quickly, with the last word as if sung out on a high note – a chamber pot!

Nikos was not impressed by Harold Acton, whom he thinks of as trying to live a fantasy he imagines is not a fantasy. Acton, in any case, does not have the socialist credentials that would make Nikos respect him. I found him fascinating, to, I think, Nikos' amusement.

———

I woke up from a very deep sleep, a sleep that, it seemed to me when I was fully awake, was composed of layers upon layers of impressions that have piled up over the few days we've been here, starting with leaving grey, dismal London, the plane ride to Pisa (the plane at moments seemed to stop, motionless, and float in the air), the arrival at the small airport, John and Hugh meeting us, the Italian advertising, the particular smell of an Italian farmacia we stopped in on the way to the villa, the Villa Marchio here, and especially Harold Acton's villa La Pietra and its gardens, the blurred sense of cypress alleys, complicated box hedges, wisteria-covered arbors, statues tangled in the rich vegetation, fountains at the end of sudden vistas. I woke from all this after Nikos had left me, woke to the high, large, lumpy bed I was in with a headboard of wrought iron, to the stained whitewashed walls and ceiling, the huge wardrobe, the flies droning in the hot, still air, the painted plaster Madonna's head above the bed, the open window framing palm fronds, the old tile floor, and everything appeared suddenly familiar.

Last night, as Nikos and I were making love, a firefly came in through the open window, and the dark room silently pulsed with the palest green light.

———

After our visit to La Pietra, John handed me Harold Acton's two autobiographical volumes, Memoirs of an Aesthete and More Memoirs of an Aesthete, and, yes, he became a fantasy figure to me, someone not only from another world but another century. My fantasy is of a world and a century of the salon, his villa itself a major salon, in which he could, just by pulling on a thread, pull together a whole tangle of interconnected aristocrats, politicians, artists and, too, homosexuals. If I were a minor Marcel Proust, what I could have made of it all!

He lived his youth, not only in terms of a villa with some sixty rooms with a grand staircase and huge tapestries and immense statues and fountains in the garden and thirty-five servants, but a style of life that allowed him to take it for granted that when he traveled he would stay in the best hotels, dine in the best restaurants, go to the best tailors. He could take it for granted that it was possible to meet anyone he wanted. When he was a boy, Serge Diaghilev and Léon Bakst, who were themselves fantasy figures to Acton, visited La Pietra. Of the older generation, he knew Bernard Berenson, Edith Wharton, Max Beerbohm, Oscar Wilde's old friend Reggie Turner, D. H. Lawrence, Norman Douglas, the Sitwells, Gertrude Stein, and of his generation pretty much everyone, Evelyn Waugh, Nancy Mitford, Diana Mosley, George Orwell, Cecil Beaton, Cyril Connolly, Henry Green, Anthony Powell, Graham Greene. He could devote his life to the purely aesthetic pleasures, such as the ballet and poetry and rococo art, and he could decide, with no worry about how he would support himself, to be a writer.

Of course I see him as a fantasy figure. He has inherited fantasy, without his having to supply one silver spoon to it, from his parents. Does Acton ever think he is living a fantasy? There have to be moments when he thought he did – as when, at Eton, he and his close friend Brian Howard, even more aesthetic than he, hired a room at the back of Dyson's, a jeweller in the town, where they played records of Russian ballet music and danced together the parts they had seen Massine and Nijinsky, Karsavina and Tchernicheva dance at performances of the Ballets Russes. Or when, later at Oxford University, he went 'tittupping' along the High Street with a gray bowler and a tightly rolled umbrella, wearing, under a long, tubular, black velvet coat, silver, mauve or pink trousers that were so wide at the knees and ankles they looked like a pleated skirt, a style he invented which was copied by many others and was finally known to the outside world as Oxford bags.

Nikos stops me from even trying to act on fantasy.

———

We went into Florence, just Nikos and I, with a guidebook. Repairs to damage caused by the flood are going on everywhere, and a lot of places are closed. And yet it is remarkable how quickly and efficiently the rebuilding was done. Along the Arno, for instance, there are photographs outside a coffee bar that show the almost irreparable damage, but the bar is now bright and new. So Harold Acton was right. You can still see the high-water marks on the buildings.

As for what we saw in Florence – I used to think that art historians might have knowledge about works of art that I didn't have, but I assumed, in my uneducated way, that if I didn't have their knowledge I had a sensitivity to art that they didn't have. I couldn't have been more wrong. In these past days, hearing John and Hugh talk about art with the greatest of outward knowledge, I realize their inward sensitivity to the art is as great. What was most wonderful in what we saw were the frescos in San Marco by Fra Angelico, but for me to try to comment on them, or to try to comment on anything else we saw, would be to presume on knowledge and sensitivity I don't have. So I'll keep my appreciation to myself, as, I realize, I already keep any appreciation of books and music that presumes on commenting on them to myself. No comments, none, on Fra Angelico or Masaccio or Ghirlandaio or Donatello or Michelangelo or Cellini or Brunelleschi or –

I tell myself: forget what you think or even feel, and simply describe.

For example, the little devil's head soldered to the barred window in Savonarola's cell, perhaps to warn him of the dangers of looking out.

I look out of the little window above the table on the landing where I'm writing and see: a rising landscape of dark and light, green and yellow, and on the top of a hill a hamlet of stone houses with red tile roofs.

———

At dinner, then after with coffee in the sitting room, John and Hugh often recount stories about people they've known, or about people known by people they've known, and it is as if great bubbles rise from their mouths and expand and expand with the actions, words, interrelationships of such people as Berenson and his entourage, Percy and Sybil Lubbock, George Santayana, Howard Sturgis, Logan Pearsall Smith, E. M. Forster –

About Sybil Lubbock: Percy, her third husband, had built for her a villa in the most beautiful place possible, on a promontory in Lerici overlooking the Ligurian Sea, and brought her to see it for the first time on a moonlit night, she, however, simply saying she was very tired and must go to bed. The Italian navy was practicing maneuvers off the coast, shooting cannon, which noise annoyed Sybil, so she rang the admiralty and had it stopped. Coming down to breakfast, she said she hadn't slept all night, reading Pico della Mirandola.

Hugh, who is the real raconteur, said that Percy Lubbock once told them he had told E. M. Forster, 'Morgan, one day they'll all see just how thin your books are,' to which Forster replied, 'I dare say they will.'

Lubbock's stepdaughter, Iris Origo, came to him, more or less on his death bed, to tell him he had no more money, to which he replied, 'Oh dear, I thought it would last at least another fortnight.'

I realize that here I am within a world of English expatriates (though John is Scots) who retain an Englishness that has gone in England, retained mostly in anecdotes about people once known but now dead, people who once did represent a world within the greater world of what was once the British Empire.

———

John and Hugh brought us to Pietra Santa to meet the wife of an art historian friend of theirs, the art historian Robert Goldwater, his wife Louise Bourgeois, who is a sculptor. We met her where she has her workshop – rather, a kind of open stall along a line of other stalls – and she showed us a sculpture that had just been finished, not by her but by one of the workmen, of what looked like a bunch of marble male erections stuck together, and while we all studied the sculpture I noted she seemed to study us with a wry smile. She brought us to another stall where the maquettes by Henry Moore are enlarged into monumental sculptures, and the man presiding, a large man called Agostinelli with a folded newspaper cap set firmly on his head, picked up a maquette and then showed us the monumental replica he was carving in marble. He said the final work is done in the light of a candle, which interested Hugh very much, as he said that Canova – Hugh's book on whom is his lifetime's work – did the same when refining the surface of his sculptures. Then we all went to the main piazza for coffee, and, I don't know why, I wondered about the little figure of a Hawaiian girl in a hula skirt on the side of the little cups, perhaps because the figures appeared so culturally incongruous to having coffee with Madame Bourgeois in Pietra Santa. Robert Goldwater is a scholar on African sculptures and the director of the Museum of Primitive Art in New York, and the talk about him among Louise Bourgeois and John and Hugh seemed to open up another incongruous world about us about Africa. Nikos and I, within these worlds revolving around us in a café in Pietra Santa, were silent.

———

I asked John F. if he had asked Percy Lubbock what accent Henry James had, and John answered, yes, as a matter of fact he had, and Lubbock told him that James didn't have an American accent, but neither did he have a British accent.

My fantasy of being a Jamesian character in Europe is over, and it didn't take much, I see, to put an end to it – just being in a place I might have once imagined where a Jamesian character would have flourished. I realize I in fact have so little to do with being an American Jamesian character I could have only ever had a fantasy of what it was like to be one, because I, from a small, French-Québécois-speaking parish in Yankee New England, am American in a way no character in James is.

Yet, I sense some affinity with James as an American, if to be an American is, as James wrote, to be possessed and to possess one's possession. Ezra Pound wrote about James that he knew the world is spherical, and his possession was to possess that spherical world, to possess it in his books and then let it go in his books. I tell myself: the letting it go is necessary for the world to be, on its own, round and whole.

———

What I most like here is the little chapel in the corner of the walled-in garden. I go in by way of the entrance at the back which opens up from the garden. It is small, damp, crumbling, with a few very dusty vestiges of its sanctity: grey and wet altar cloths, broken candlesticks, a crucifix with broken arms hanging loose from the nails in the hands, holy water fonts stuck in the wall and filled with rags, squares on the walls where pictures had hung. There are even two pews, with a very dusty wine bottle occupying one, having been there long enough for cobwebs to attach it to the seat. The stations of the cross – small, colored pictures in black frames – are still in place. I go in and I sit by the wine bottle and I close my eyes. Though I tell myself I am a total non-believer, with my eyes closed I know it is the religion I was born and brought up in that most deeply, most helplessly, makes me what I am, and this Henry James certainly knew nothing about.

While sitting there, a peasant woman came in from the front entrance opening from the dirt road to place a small bouquet of roses before a little shrine to the Blessed Virgin Mother.

John said the chapel is still consecrated.

San Andrea di Rovereto di Chiavari

We have come to stay in a little house on the Ligurian coast for our summer holiday. The rent is five shillings a day. The house has two rooms downstairs and two up, and is in the midst of an olive grove. The steps up to the house from the street are crowded on one side with pots and old tins of flowering plants. Hydrangeas are in bloom.

The view from the house, high on the side of the coast, is a steep descent, thick with olive trees, down to a blue-green sea. On the

right we can see all the way to the tip of Portofino and on the left to Sestri Levanti. At night fishing boats are like large lapping stars.

Nikos loves it here for its simplicity.

This occurs to me – I listen to him talk about politics, and I realize that before I met him I had none. I suppose I still have none, and have assumed his.

A few mornings ago I got up very early, went outside and sat on a step. A young woman, all round curves, passed me going down the stairs, having come from the olive grove behind, carrying a large, sloshing bucket of milk. She left a trail of splashed milk all the way down to the street.

After going down to the sea today by way of a narrow path through the lush vegetation, we took a nap. The room is all white, with a red tile floor, and very simple. We were covered with a stiff, almost canvas-like sheet that you get in cheap hotels in Europe, and the white afternoon light, so penetrating I imagined all the outside world was dissolved in it, burned about the edges of the closed shutter, and one long thin crack of light fell into the dim, hot, fly-buzzing room and across the sheet.

We are happy.

Trying to find short cuts to the sea, Nikos and I follow steep paths through olive groves, vineyards, and through woods. Just off one path we found a cement bunker from the war, like a huge, square eye closed to a slit and staring through the foliage out over the Tigullian Gulf. We found the entrance and went in. It smelled of shit. I, frightened, said we shouldn't go in, but Nikos lit a newspaper he found on the ground and we went in, crouched. There were a series of cemented caves along each side. As we went deeper into the bunker we heard voices behind us, and quickly turned back to get out and met a group of boys with a flashlight coming in. When they saw us, they, more frightened than we were, scattered.

My sexual fantasies almost cease to exist while I am with Nikos. Certainly sex doesn't obsess me as much as it did before I met him. But, then, so much in me has changed since I met him.

———

We met Stephen at the train station in Chiavari. He was wearing a shirt with the cuffs unbuttoned and dangling, and he looked very hot in the Italian heat, but we got him into a taxi and into the cool hills of San Andrea. He has come to join us for a few days. He is staying in a small hotel in the village, where he works during the day while Nikos and I go down to the beach. Every day we take the train to Chiavari, Nikos and I to shop for our meals – fish, vegetables, fruit, cheese – Stephen to buy the English newspapers, and we have meals, cooked by Nikos, in our small house. We are all three happy.

Stephen was filled with his experiences in Paris where he was during the student demonstrations. He let us read the first draft of chapters for a book, and he read out some of the students' slogans he had copied from walls in the Latin Quarter:

Prenez vos désirs pour des réalités.

Toute vue des choses qui n'est pas étrange est fausse.

Plus je fais l'amour plus je fais la révolution, plus je fais la révolution plus je fais l'amour.

———

Stephen and I took a walk before he left, just the two of us. We found ourselves lost on the paths through the tangled woods, then came across a disused railway track and we followed that to a small house, maybe a signaling station for the railway, the windows of which were burnt-out holes and the roof falling in. We went inside. The floor was covered with bits of plaster fallen from the walls, stones and branches and garbage, and where the walls weren't soot black from fires there were large pornographic drawings in charcoal. We went upstairs, where in one room all the walls were painted with murals, one of a woman in a green dress sitting in a chair, on either side of her a large red rooster, and near her and looking at her a smiling young man with horns and a garland of flowers about his head.

Stephen asked that his visit to us be kept a secret.

London

More and more, I wonder how it happened that Nikos and I are living together, the wonder, as wonder will do, making it all strange.

———

In homage to his beliefs, I suggested to Nikos that we go visit the tomb of Karl Marx in the Highgate Cemetery. He brought along a red rose which he placed at the foot of the huge granite plinth with the incised motto WORKERS OF ALL LANDS UNITE, the massive bronze bust above. Nikos was silent, and I sensed in him his inability to articulate why a vision that should have brought equality and justice and peace to the world went so wrong, and it seemed to me an impertinence to say to him that the vision all went wrong because of human failings, a cliché. I am always aware, against my American simplifications, of Nikos' own Greek awareness of complexities too great to react to with anything more than a pained look in his eyes, and silence.

———

A friend of Nikos, Ersi Hadgimihali, is in London from Athens, opposed to the dictatorship, but secretly.

She came to supper. A sophisticated, elderly woman, she recounted, in English, stories about escaping Nazi-occupied

Greece to go by boat to Egypt, there where the Greek royal family were in exile. Before leaving for Egypt for the long night-time crossing, Ersi had bought a watch, for which her husband commended her as keeping time was important for the crossing; but he kept complaining that he should have the watch, really it was more important for him to have a watch than for her, and she, fed up, took the watch from her wrist and threw it overboard into the sea. She writes poetry and paints very primitive paintings in bright colours. She comes from a famous family, an aunt of hers commemorated by a bust on a plinth in a square in Athens, or so Nikos told me.

Nikos seems to know a cultured class of people in Athens.

He told me that Greeks with a surname beginning with Hadgi are descended from ancestors who were baptized in the Jordan, which made me wonder what connection there could possibly be in the use of the word among Muslims who once in a lifetime go on a pilgrimage called, I think, the Haj.

To see everything, every single event, every single word, every single thing, every single person in terms of history –

––––––

I waited for Nikos near the Greek Embassy in Brook Street, just behind the American Embassy in Grosvenor Square, as we had planned to meet there before joining the demonstration against the dictatorship in Greece. The only other people there on the pavement were an old woman in severe black mourning and a young man. Clearly, they wondered, as did I, where the demonstration was, and in my bad Greek I said I was waiting. The old woman asked me, in Greek, if I'm Anglos, and I answered, 'Oxi, eimai Americanos,' which made her draw back from me and spit at me, a great gob of her spit landing on one of my shoes. Never before had anyone spat on me, and that I was spat upon for being an American roused a rage in me. I wanted to tell the old woman that I was an exceptional American, not, as the Americans of the Embassy, supporting the dictatorship, but out to demonstrate against it. She, with the young man, his shoulders hunched over, left, and I, in my rage, thought of leaving also.

I walked out to Park Lane and saw the demonstration advancing, and waited until I saw Nikos in the midst, he talking animatedly with John Berger, whom he admires for his political vision, and whose book on the success and failure of Picasso Nikos had published at Penguin. I joined them, and in my continuing rage told Nikos about the insult and that I was not going to demonstrate, but would go home. He calmly said that the old woman was probably a Communist who had suffered terribly under the American Truman Doctrine which outlawed membership in the Communist Party as a capital crime. So, I was seen as representative of the Truman Doctrine. Nikos introduced me to John Berger, and we marched on.

We passed the Greek Embassy, where Nikos had once worked and where people he had known still worked. The curtains were drawn, as if the building was abandoned, but as we passed under the windows, jeering, a hand appeared from between closed curtains to give the march the finger.

Along the way, I noted Ersi Hadgimihali appear on a side street, half hidden by the corner of a building, the collar of her coat held up to hide her face.

The march ended in Trafalgar Square. There was a huge crowd, Melina Mercouri on a platform in the midst wearing her red blouse with, it appeared, nothing underneath, so that whenever she raised her arms high to shout out against the dictators the nipples of her breasts pressed through the cloth, and the crowd roared.

———

I hear Greeks, having got out of Greece, talk about their recollections of the German Occupation of Athens and then the Civil War, hear them describe how during the occupation people in the streets cried, 'Pinow, pinow, pinow' ('I'm hungry, I'm hungry, I'm hungry') and died there in the streets, so others walked over their bodies; hear them describe how, during the Civil War, unspeakable atrocities were committed on both sides; hear how, now, when a group of friends go to the house of a friend for a name-day celebration and find he does not appear they know he has been arrested and interrogated and most likely tortured by having the soles of his feet beaten so no scars are left – and I react with horror, but they look at me as if I haven't in fact understood, as of course I haven't because I haven't lived through what they have. I asked Nikos' cousin Stavros, who is severe, if my expressing horror was sentimental, and I was told, severely, yes, it was.

I think of these people as having lived through brutal history, and to say to them how horrible it was makes them react, if not with a severe stare, with counter-stories of joyful times at the worst of times among families and friends, so that when there were curfews they would hold dances all night long, in which couples would meet and fall in love and eventually marry.

I asked a friend of Nikos why there is no Greek mafia, and he said because no two Greeks can agree enough to form a mafia.

Another Greek said, 'But there is a mafia – it is called Greek Government Ministers.'

––––––

What does Greece mean to Nikos? The country means more to him than any other, and I know that whatever he says that rejects his country is in proportion to the meaning it has for him. And I have learned this: if I say something disparaging about Greece, repeating something he has said, he will stop me with, 'What do you know about Greece?'

What does Nikos being Greek mean to me?

Do I look in him for some Greekness that antedates my knowing him, some past fantasy of Greece inspired, say, by reading Plato's Symposium, so that I fantasize his participating in that fantasy? The fantasy is there, but, in my close relationship with him, I am able to look over his shoulder at the symposium of ancient Greek literature with more of a direct view into it than ever before. Past Nikos, I see beyond Aristotle, beyond Plato, into the Pre-Socratics, who have become more and more interesting to me, as if I were seeing into them the very origins of my own thoughts and feelings, as, in essential ways, I am, and the essential way is to believe that the origin of the concept of the ONE is as central to me as it was to those ancient philosophers.

How essential to me this:

All things come out of the one, and the one out of all things.

Heraclitus

As for what Nikos reveals of Greece – within his history of living through the German Occupation and the Civil War, I think of his more personal history on the island of Poros, where he was abandoned by a lover, and where he sat on rocks by the sea, the wind-wafted scent of blossoming lemon trees from the mainland his consolation. In him, I sense the consolations of Greece are made so very poignant against the losses.

———

A sponsor for anti-dictatorship action in London invited Nikos to an event in someone's flat in North London to raise money, and I went along. Melina Mercouri was there, in the midst, dressed in a blouse and slacks and sitting cross-legged on the floor, her hair a mass of long dangling blonde curls. All I remember of the evening was being introduced to her and she looking up at me with large eyes and her wide smile and saying, in a low, slow, seductive voice, 'I love Americans.'

———

At a drinks party given by John Lehmann, I met his sister Rosamond, who, large and with bright white hair, appeared to me to be a moon goddess. When I said I'd just come back to London from Lucca, she asked, as if there could be no other place to stay there, had I stayed with John Fleming and Hugh Honour? Yes, I had. 'Then you must be very privileged,' she said, 'because I've never been invited.'

John's sister Beatrix was also there, but every time I found myself, moving among the guests, facing her, she turned away, and I wondered if she took me for a boyfriend of John whom she disapproved of, not, perhaps, because I was her brother's boyfriend, but because she assumed I was his boyfriend only for the privilege of meeting her, the actress Beatrix Lehmann, at a drinks party where she would be present.

As if to educate me about Stephen, John said to me, 'Our Stephen is very good at intuiting, and all his best writing comes from his intuition, but he's hopeless when he tries to reason a situation or problem out logically.'

I want to get this in: John once said that on a visit to Greece he had had a boy with a perfect ancient Greek profile, and I was reminded of what Nikos once said about Northern Europeans fantasizing about Greek boys.

And I'm reminded of this line from Stephen's poem 'The Funeral':

The decline of a culture
Mourned by scholars who dream of the ghosts of Greek boys.

———

Nikos does have one Greek friend, whom he seems more to tolerate than like – Rea Seferiadi, by marriage a (I think) sister-in-law of the poet George Seferis, shortened from Seferiadis. Nikos is not a great admirer of Seferiadis' poetry and derides him for deriding Cavafy's poetry as a pedestal without a statue. Also, Nikos thinks it morally weak of Seferis to have made, after a long period of silence, a weak statement against the dictatorship – calling it an 'anomaly' – to save his face among those opposed, especially non-Greeks outside of Greece who oppose (Greeks are more attentive to opinion from outside of Greece than from within, and wait for a writer to be praised by non-Greeks before they themselves praise him); whereas the poet Ritsos has been sent to a concentration camp on an island for being, as a Communist sympathizer, opposed to the dictatorship. But to get back to Rea, who speaks with a very upper-class English accent, and who gives the impression of knowing just what is going on in the royal family, such as the Queen will abdicate to give over her position to her son Charles, said with such authority that I thought she must know, until Nikos told me not to believe anything she says. She is a compact woman who wears plain close-fitting dresses with a pearl necklace, her hair dyed black, her large eyes black. We were invited to her flat where, in her sitting room, she made pronouncements about world news with such authority that she might have been connected at least to the ambassadors of all the most powerful countries, from whom she gets the news. Pointing to a little painting by the French painter Hélion of lips, she said, 'Those are my lips,' and this made me imagine her connections to the whole of the French art world. Her husband, whose first name I can't recall, said nothing; he works in the City, but in what capacity I don't know. Nikos makes fun of Rea, and when I asked him why he is friendly with her and her husband, he said, 'They suffered the Catastrophe,' and I had a sense of how those dispossessed people do form almost a racial group, even to intermarrying.

Natasha away, Stephen invited Nikos and me to a dinner party, where, Stephen told us, the other guests to arrive were Julian Huxley and his wife. Clearly, Stephen was excited to make this introduction to someone we should have known about, but whose name for me only conjured up a vague sense of a British dynastic family of many distinguished members, Aldous Huxley only one of them. Nikos of course knew who Julian Huxley is, and was able to ask him about animal charities, to which Nikos gives a lot of money, harking back to when Huxley was a zoologist and his great concern the wellbeing of animals. I had no idea what to talk about with Julian Huxley. After the dinner party, when Nikos and I helped with the washing up, as we always do, Stephen seemed annoyed with me for not having responded, as Nikos had, to meeting Julian Huxley, and all I could think of to do was shrug, which made Stephen press his lips together and turn away, and I worried that he thought I was ungrateful for the privilege when I was simply embarrassed. Yes, I should have known who Julian Huxley is – should have known his history.

———

The leaves are falling from the trees in Battersea Park. The sunlight is bright, the sky absolutely clear. There is a smell through the open window over my desk of burning leaves.

I can do so much. I know it, I know it.

And yet, if I were to step back into myself, which I keep myself from doing to be more outward than inward, I would ask myself, How do you know you will? and I would step back out of myself and insist, I will.

———

Stephen invited me to lunch at the Lyons' Corner House in Piccadilly with Elizabeth Glenconner.

With amusement, Elizabeth remembered Nikos offering her a pink gin when she came to his flat for drinks, this before Nikos and I met; the amusement was that Nikos, a Greek, should offer her a drink that was once so fashionably English, and now so out of fashion.

Stephen and Elizabeth talked about many people I don't know and couldn't place in the English world, though I listened with attention to try to make connections among them all – among all the Tennants, of which there seem to be a very complicated number, starting with Elizabeth's husband Christopher Tennant, Lord Glenconner – but the connections are too complicated for me.

When I said this to Elizabeth, she smiled and said, with a slight drawl, 'It's all very simple, really.'

They talked about someone named Anne, but I thought it would be impolite to ask who Anne was, but Stephen informed me, 'You've met Anne, Anne Wollheim, Elizabeth's sister,' which did not seem simple to me, because I have met Anne, the former wife of the philosopher Richard Wollheim, he now married to Mary Day Wollheim. Here I am, trying to interconnect people I've met. Anne Wollheim has twins, Rupert and Bruno, by Richard Wollheim, and two daughters by a former husband, Philip Toynbee, Polly and Josephine Toynbee. Josephine has a child, Pip, by a Mexican lover, a boy of great charm, who especially loves the art historian Ben Nicolson whom he greets with, 'Ben!' at a dinner party at Anne's that Nikos and I are also invited to, where Pip runs to Ben for Ben, laughing his gurgling laugh, to take him in his arms. How sort all this out in a diary? And how sort out Elizabeth's family with her husband Christopher? Leave it for now, to be sorted out later, if there is a later.

I can't recall why, but Stephen said to Elizabeth that he is 'dead middle class,' which I took him to mean that Elizabeth wasn't, and I was impressed for I had not thought of Stephen as belonging to any class, had never before heard anyone define his or her class to another.

She asked Stephen about Natasha, and I felt that for her at least there exists a world in which everyone totally, if somewhat vaguely, accepts everyone else without question, perhaps even me. Her eyes seemed to be always slightly out of focus.

She went off to a Greek lesson, as she and her husband have built a house on Corfu and will move there.

This was said with no reference to the dictatorship. When I told Nikos this, he simply said he loves Elizabeth, and I felt in that, not an excuse, but some kind of acceptance that belies Nikos' principles, which are in fact much more complicated by his history lived in the particular than I know the abstract puritan principles of my history to be.

———

Stephen asked Nikos and me to the Garrick Club for lunch with Cyril Connolly and W. H. Auden. Cyril Connolly wants one of the kittens born from Nikos' cat Jasmine, but when Nikos said they cost twelve guineas each he became thoughtful and said that a cat in his garden would upset the birds and destroy the balance of nature. Nikos spoke at length to Auden, who was very spirited and obviously liked talking with Nikos. While we others listened – and I had the impression that whenever Auden spoke Stephen and even Connolly simply listened to him – he and Nikos talked about personal happiness. Nikos wasn't going to simply listen, but had a two-way conversation with Auden, who said, when Nikos asked him, that he thought he was happy.

Part of the conversation was about the next Professor of Poetry at Oxford; Stephen, Auden, Connolly all supported Roy Fuller. At one point, Cyril Connolly asked Auden:

'Is that person who kicks over a little stone in Letter from Iceland a real person?'

'Yes.'

'May I ask who?'

'Robert Medley.'

Connolly's review in the next Sunday Times included this information:

For sheer pleasure, the 'Letter to Lord Byron' from Letters from Iceland (1937) with its mixture of candid autobiography, journalism and genius is unbeatable – and witty as well. Who cannot thrill even now to his admission:

> One afternoon in March at half past three
> When walking in a ploughed field with a friend;
> Kicking a little stone he turned to me
> And said, 'Tell me, do you write poetry?'
> I never had, and said so, but I knew
> That very moment what I wished to do.

The friend was the painter Robert Medley.

There was speculation about the relationship between T. S. Eliot and Jean Verdenal, to whom Eliot dedicated Prufrock and Other Observations, and what the love was that Eliot had for him, Connolly quoting from the epigraph amor ch'a te mi scalda.

Coming out of the club, Auden took somebody's big black bowler hat from a hook and put it over his head. It dropped down over his eyes, and all one could see of his face was a great mass of broken wrinkles, and in the midst of the wrinkles a smile.

Connolly left us, and then Nikos to go to the publishing house, and I followed Stephen who followed Auden to the department store Simpson's in the Strand, where in the shoe department Auden bought a pair of carpet slippers, as, he said, his corns make wearing shoes too painful. The salesman at first was at best deferential, but then recognized Auden and was reverential. Auden wore the new slippers and left the old behind, and, again, Stephen followed him, and I followed Stephen down to the Piccadilly Underground Station.

Auden called the round station the Fairy Circle, and when I asked what that meant, he answered, as though a mother instructing a son in the facts of life, that this is where gentlemen pick up young men in need of financial help. He said, 'The arrangement is simple: you need sex and they need money,' and that, coming from him, sounded reasonable. Stephen said nothing. A man, recognizing Auden, went to him to ask if he would sign a book, and Auden said, 'But I don't sign books I didn't write.' I felt oh, that I belonged to a little inner circle of people among whom one is famous, and if anyone looked at me as belonging to the little circle he or she might wonder who I was to belong to it.

As we were about to part to go in different directions, W. H. Auden invited me to stay with him when I next go to New York, and this made me think, Well, he likes me enough to invite me to stay with him. When I told Nikos this, he said, 'You think it's because he likes you that he invited you to stay with him?' I thought, for a flashing moment, to be able to say I stayed with W. H. Auden in New York might, just might, be worth whatever reason he has for inviting me!

Later, as if to warn me, Stephen told me that Auden's house in Saint Mark's Place in New York is as messy as the way Auden packs a suitcase: he simply loads all the clothes he needs onto a table, places the suitcase on the floor at the end of the table and then shoves all the clothes off the end of the table into the suitcase then closes it.

And a little revulsion at the possibility of eating there came to me when Stephen said that Auden's lover Chester Kallman makes the chocolate pudding in the bathroom washbasin.

And I'm reminded by my using 'washbasin' of the time I said 'bathroom sink' in the presence of Sonia, who stopped me with 'washbasin.'

———

In a taxi, as if being in a taxi together allowed such an intimacy, Stephen told me that when he and Natasha were in Germany after the war, on a train, she proposed that they exchange their pounds on the black market, but Stephen said, no, at the official rate; Natasha insisted, and he insisted, her insistence driven to such an extreme that she threatened to throw herself off the train if he didn't agree with her.

He said to me, 'She is that willful.'

When I asked, 'Does she do that often?' he looked out the window of the taxi and didn't answer.

———

Thomas Hardy, in Life's Little Ironies, writes about London: 'There are worlds within worlds in the great city.'

———

I sent £5 to Frank Kermode as a contribution to the memorial slab to commemorate Henry James in Poets' Corner in Westminster Abbey, and I was invited to the service. Nikos was invited by Stephen. We met by the Great West Door, where we were presented white tickets. Robert and Caroline Lowell came behind us, but because they didn't have tickets they were told to wait. Everyone was treated brusquely, which I tried to take as a formality. Nikos and I were separated, he to sit on one side of the nave, I on the other, next to Tony Tanner. The Lowells, finally admitted, sat next to me, he in rumpled suit and perhaps the last of the truly Yankee writers, and Caroline kept biting her nails. Tony and I joked, identifying people passing to go to their seats: C. P. Snow, Anthony Powell, Victor Pritchett.

The psalms from which the James took the titles The Wings of the Dove and The Golden Bowl were read, then Ralph Richardson read a passage from Portrait of a Lady, after which Tony leaned towards me and said, 'Henry James isn't getting a memorial slab in Westminster Abbey for *that*.' The dean and various prelates in red soutanes or academics in black gowns processed down the aisle, followed by Leon Edel and Stephen and a professor from the Sorbonne, and James' great-great-nephew, Alexander, carrying a laurel wreath, all wearing red carnations on their lapels. They disappeared into Poets' Corner, so we had to imagine Henry James' great-great-nephew unveiling the slab and placing the wreath. Then we heard, amplified over loudspeakers, Stephen give a short address in which he said that James was aware of the class struggle, or at least of the bankruptcy of the middle and upper classes. The Professor from the Sorbonne claimed, in French, that James was a French writer. The procession filed back down the aisle, and I heard, 'Pray for the soul of Henry James,' and for the first time I was moved. Edel started with a eulogy on the name Henry James: both given names, both democratic, and yet both the names of kings. More prayers, the organ played, and I met Nikos and we presented pink tickets to get into the Jerusalem Room for sherry. Nikos asked me, 'Weren't you moved?' I said, 'A little, but not really.' 'You weren't? Henry James means so much to you. I was. I had tears in my eyes. I couldn't keep myself from weeping when I saw Henry James' great-great-nephew, such a beautiful young man, carrying the laurel wreath down the aisle. And all the old English writers, sitting in the stalls, watching him.' 'Yes,' I said, and felt ashamed that I hadn't been more moved.

Seeing Henry James' great-great-nephew standing alone – which is an English habit I have often noted when the guest of honour is often left alone as if it would be considered a presumption to engage with him or her – Nikos and I went to speak with him, Alexander James, Jr., who was twenty-six. His charcoal-grey suit from the 1950s was, he said, borrowed, as he didn't own one. With it, he wore a white shirt with a button-down collar and a thin dark tie. His long hair was parted in the middle and combed back over his ears, and he had what I thought of as the pure features of a Yankee – a strong forehead, nose, jaw and neck – and pale but intense eyes. A great-grandson of William James, he was studying, appropriately, to become a clinical psychologist. He loved to garden. He said, quietly, 'I'm not at all used to the kind of attention I'm getting here.' Nikos stared and stared at him.

Nikos and I left with Tony Tanner to have lunch. We talked a little about British writers today. I asked, 'Is there a British writer today who is great enough to be given, after his or her death, a memorial slab in Poets' Corner?' 'No,' Tony said, 'no, no.'

I once thought that Henry James had a secret, the secret of being an American, which was to be a Yankee American, which I am not. If my sense of Henry James having a secret went, everything would go. And it did go. The straining consciousness of James – straining in the very elaboration of the writing for the totally inclusive 'everything' – seems to me the possession of a man who always feared that 'everything' was a horrifying 'nothing'.

It was in rereading a commonplace book, from those years back when I strained for the realization of 'everything' and copied down passages from Henry James' autobiographical books – not his novels, for his autobiographical books brought him closer to me as a person – A Small Boy and Others, Notes of a Son and Brother, The Middle Years – and rereading the passages revived in me a sense of – what? – a sense, of course, of 'everything.'

'. . . the wonder of consciousness in everything . . .'

'. . . It was big to me, big to me with the breath of great vague connections . . .'

'. . . an air of possibilities that were none the less vivid for being quite indefinite . . .'

'. . . my vision loses itself withal in vaster connections . . .'
'. . . who should say now what a world one mightn't read into
   it? . . .'
'. . . the far-off hum of a thousand possibilities . . .'
'. . . in the beauty of the whole thing, again, I lose myself . . .'

Reading a long, long passage of Henry James, I from time to time
forget – I am, by the elaborations detached from – what the often
repeated word 'it' refers to, so 'it' becomes 'big, big with the breath
of vast vague connections,' and 'it' becomes 'everything,' 'everything'
sensed as if as a pulse in the very consciousness of the universe. All
his life, I imagine, Henry James expected 'it' to be revealed to him.

———

Auden invited Nikos and me to have lunch at Chez Victor. He
held the menu wide open before him and, reading it, said, 'The
tomato soup looks good,' and Nikos and I knew we should order
the tomato soup. Then he said, 'The cold chicken and salad
looks good,' and again Nikos and I knew we must order the cold
chicken and salad. The point of the lunch was for Auden to give
Nikos a sheaf of poems by Chester Kallman for Nikos to consider
publishing.

After our luncheon, Auden looked tired, but when I said something about a nap, he said, 'Mother wouldn't allow it.'

Later, Nikos said he was very moved by Auden asking him to
consider Kallman's poems, moved and embarrassed, because he
could not see that it was possible to publish them.

———

Stephen rang to say that Wystan has left. He was staying at the
Spenders', and Stephen is relieved that he has left; he drinks
immense quantities, smokes so the whole house stinks, never
washes, goes to bed at 9:30. Stephen said Lizzie always wants her
bedroom fumigated after Auden has used it.

Stephen said that once, when Auden was staying at Loudoun

Road, Natasha rang him up to say she would be late, and would he put the chicken in the oven? Auden did – he simply put it in the oven, didn't put it in a pan, didn't turn the heat on.

For the past weekend, Nikos has been in Manchester with Mark Lancaster and Richard Morphet, Assistant Keeper of the Modern Collection at the Tate Gallery; they were invited to judge the Northern Young Contemporaries Exhibition. So I slept alone, and slept very badly. The award went to Stephen Buckley.

Richard's enthusiasms for British art make me enthusiastic, so when he, in an excited voice, talks of an artist I've never heard of – such as the mystic Cecil Collins – I want to find out about the artist. He and his wife Sally invited us to lunch with the widow of Cecil Collins, who wore a mink hat, and talked of her life with Collins, when the kitchen was a gas ring on the landing.

Stephen has a painting by Collins, which, Stephen said, was painted to depict him, Stephen, as a holy fool, a painting especially meaningful to Stephen.

———

Mark Lancaster picked me up in his car, in a row in the back seat three sisters close together – Henrietta and Amaryllis and Fanny Garnett, all, I think, the daughters of Angelica Bell, the daughter of Vanessa Bell, the sister of Virginia Woolf, as Mark, who is inspired in his painting by Bloomsbury, had explained to me. He had also explained that Henrietta was married to Burgo Partridge, the son of Frances and Ralph Partridge, with whom – Ralph, that is – Lytton Strachey had been in love. And to complicate it all, Ralph Partridge, before Frances, had been in love with Dora Carrington, who, out of her impossible love for Lytton Strachey, killed herself. Burgo Partridge died just a few years ago. I may have got this all wrong. Mark took us all to a queer club, which, in the early afternoon, was empty except for us. Mark and I sat at a table and watched the three sisters, all in long dresses with embroidery across the bodices and even longer scarves, dance together, their clothes swinging.

Days later, Mark rang me to tell me that Amaryllis drowned herself in the Thames.

————

Stephen is finishing his book on the students, The Year of the Young Rebels. He said he is giving a lot of thought to the construction, which he thinks of as musical. 'Not that anyone will know.' We sometimes meet, after he picks up the neat chapters from his typist, at the National Gallery. He gave me two typed chapters. I found them, I'm afraid, rather dull. I said, 'I'm a little disappointed that you didn't put more of yourself in.'

'I didn't want to,' he said. 'I didn't want to make it refer to me.'

He rings up almost every morning. The conversation is something like this:

'How are you?'

'Very well. And you?'

'Oh, very well.'

'Are you working hard?'

'Yes, very hard. And you?'

'Very hard.'

'How's Lizzie?'

'How are the cats?'

He said that Natasha will be going to France for a week, which means he'll be completely free and won't have to think up excuses when he sees us. He'll come to dinner on Saturday, and we all plan on going up to Cambridge on Tuesday to see Mark, now artist in residence at King's, and, I hope, E. M. Forster.

————

Mark is fascinated by Bloomsbury and once introduced us to Angelica Garnett, who wears a colourful bandana tied tightly about her head, always appears distracted, as though by some shock. She asked us to supper. When I asked her about Amaryllis, she said she hasn't been a good mother. She seems to live within her own world, painting her charming, Bloomsbury paintings with cross-hatchings and playing her cello. She invited Nikos and me to stay at Charleston – where she more or less grew up not knowing that her father, a constant presence, was Duncan Grant – but she warned us that the roof leaked, and Nikos, as much as he likes Angelica, didn't fancy sleeping under a leaking roof. I imagine Charleston as filled with sunlight and flowers in vases and all the furniture painted in different colours, the walls painted too, always with cross-hatchings, and Vanessa Bell in one room painting, and Duncan Grant in another room painting, and Angelica, a little girl, talking with Virginia Woolf in the garden – about what?

I find I still fantasize about Bloomsbury, which fantasy I suspect will change during my life in London. But I am in the thrall of Mrs. Dalloway arranging a large bouquet of flowers in a vase; and Mrs. Ramsay reading and Lily Briscoe painting at an easel; and Percival listening to the sea waves with a shell to an ear. And characters from another writer appear. On a little pool made by rainwater, naked, splashing one another, are Mr. Beebe, George and Freddy. One of the trees is a wych-elm, and by it sits Helen Schlegel, writing a letter and hearing someone sneezing, 'a-tissue, a-tissue.' And somewhere beyond the trees, in an open space, a cricket match is being played.

It is as though I am nostalgic for a world that I in no way lived in except in the novels set in that world. Sentimental of me!

Nikos has no interest in Bloomsbury at all, and if he were to ask me what my fantasy is I wouldn't be able to say, wouldn't even be able to say what the word 'Bloomsbury' represents to me.

At the luncheon with Connolly and Auden, at one point everyone got involved in the discussion Nikos and Auden were having about happiness, and everyone, unable to say who was an example of a really happy person, agreed that Sonia Orwell was the unhappiest.

I saw her at an immense party (there must have been more than a thousand people) for an immense poet (Adrian Henri) at the Institute of Contemporary Arts. She grabbed me by the sleeve and we talked, wandering through the gallery, and only half looking at the Apollinaire exhibition, for about an hour. She is still beautiful, though rather dry and puffy around the eyes. Stephen says she used to be known as the most beautiful girl in London, the Venus of Euston Road, because she posed for the painters of the Euston Road School, which included Stephen for a short while. She laughs hysterically, is always running her fingers through her hair and pulling it, and she speaks so rapidly it's difficult to follow her.

(John Lehmann said, narrowing his steel-blue eyes, 'You know, old man, everyone says that her marriage to Orwell was a mariage blanc.')

Nikos told me of a dinner he had at Sonia's house before he met me – she, he, Johnny Craxton, her ex-husband Michael Pitt-Rivers from whom she had just got divorced, and Michael Pitt-Rivers' boyfriend. Nikos said it was the most unbearable dinner party he had ever been at. Sonia up till then had been rather seductively interested in Nikos, but after this dinner party she simply cut him whenever she saw him.

I recall a New Year's party at the Craxtons'. As Nikos and I entered, Sonia rushed out from another room, kissed me and fussed over me, speaking in very rapid French, but Nikos, standing right beside me, she refused to see. Johnny came and tried to get her to acknowledge Nikos, but she kept talking to me as if I were alone, and I stupidly did nothing but smile a fixed smile at her; she grabbed my sleeve and dragged me into the room where she had been, saying, still in French, that I must help her, that I, knowing about things French (which is hardly true), would understand. A young cousin of Johnny, previously married to a queer, had been talking all evening with a nice, very straight man who, though he showed signs of interest, didn't seem likely to go so far as to ask her for a date. I was to flirt with the cousin (Sonia confessed later she found the cousin 'rather tiresome'), so that the nice straight man would, through jealousy of me, ask her for a date. We all sat together. I didn't say a word. Sonia spoke without stopping. She said, 'They took away the drinking laws, everyone became an alcoholic; they took away the gambling laws, everyone became a gambler; now they're taking away the laws against homosexuality, and everyone is becoming queer.' Then she jumped up, grabbed me by the hand and pulled me out of the room, saying, 'Did you hear? Did you hear? He made a date with her!' I hadn't heard.

Last night at the ICA she and Nikos greeted one another perfunctorily and coldly. She invited me to dinner but not Nikos, and I said I couldn't go.

Stephen said she's well known for breaking up couples, especially homosexual couples.

At the party I spoke to, it seems, hundreds of people: David Hockney, Alan Ross, Patrick Procktor, Mark Lancaster, Ted Lucie-Smith, Stephen Buckley.

Alan Ross is the editor of the London Magazine, for which he asked Nikos to write a 'Letter to Athens'. Nikos wrote of his involvement, when he lived in Athens, with an avant-garde magazine, Pali, that tried to bring new inspiration into Greek letters, badly, Nikos said, needed.

I learn from Nikos the names of Greek writers I had not known, not only contemporary, but from the past, and outstanding poets they are: Andreas Kalvos, Dionysios Solomos, Kostis Palamas, Angelos Sikelianos. And though I had read the poetry of Constantine Cavafy, it is with Nikos that I feel I am in the world of Cavafy, for the evocation of sensuality, Nikos' delicate sensuality, and the evocation of history, Nikos' Greek history. I live with Nikos in a Greek world within the outer world of London.

ΑΓΑΠΗ ΜΟΥ.

Together, we translated an erotic novella by the poet Andreas Embirikos, Voyage of a Balloon, which Alan Ross has published. It is a Surrealist novel, as there is, Nikos said, a deep Surrealist unconscious in Greeks.

———

My cousin Bryan came to stay with us. He left the States in protest against American forces fighting in Vietnam. I found out for him the address of an organization for young Americans in London who are resisting being drafted into the war. He went and when he came back said the people he spoke to were limp and altogether pathetic. He returned to the States to join the military.

———

Do I ever think of becoming British?

I have, in a way, a claim to be a part of British history, for my father, born in Canada, in the French-speaking village of Saint Barthélemy in the Province of Quebec, was born a subject of King George V. At the age of two he was taken in the arms of his mother across the border by train between Canada and the United States – no Ellis Island initiation into a different world, no passports, but a relocation from one part of North America into another. His father was a carpenter. They settled in a French-speaking parish in Providence, Rhode Island, where my father grew up as within a palisaded fortress against the Yankee outside world, and he lived as a subject of King George V in that palisaded fortress until, at the age of twenty-one, he and his father became citizens of the United States. I doubt his mother – my illiterate grandmother, who never left the fortress – ever did become a citizen.

I recall visiting my grandmother – whom I called Mémère – and sitting with her in her kitchen with my father and younger brother, he and I standing still on either side of our father as he spoke to his mother in French, she hardly responding, and most of the time all of us silent, as if the silence was communication enough.

———

We were taken to dinner by the poet Ted Lucie-Smith at an Indian restaurant. Stephen had wanted to have dinner with us that evening, and we asked Ted if he could come along. Ted said he'd be honored to have Stephen. Adrian Henri was also there.

At dinner, Ted spoke endlessly about his poetry, and though the poet Adrian Henri tried to be funny and sometimes was, the talk always came back to Ted's poetry. He sat, fat and motionless, presiding at the top of the table, his bulging eyes fixed, his smooth face fixed, and only his mouth moving. I could sense Stephen closing in more and more. He left immediately after dinner, and Nikos and I, going out to the street to say good night to him, watched him walk away, a huge figure in a raincoat, listing a little as he walked as if he were not quite sure where he was going. He rang the next morning to say he had become depressed at dinner, where he had felt too much self-importance was given to being a poet.

He came to dinner at our flat last night. He had a basket of bottles of wine and was in very good spirits. Stephen Buckley came too. Stephen B. made Stephen S. giggle, Stephen B. lightly irreverent towards Stephen S., which Stephen S. apparently enjoys.

This is totally true of Stephen S.: that he is supportive of the young.

———

Stephen Buckley often comes from Newcastle to stay the night in our spare room. We have just a little more money than he, as a student, has, so we find it a little presumptuous of him to say at dinner with us, 'What, liver again?' He said to us, 'I don't at all think of you as a homosexual couple, but just as Nikos and David.' As beautiful as he is, he likes, I think, to be admired by homosexuals, but has his lady friends of potent, if difficult, character. He flirts with Stephen Spender, and always makes him giggle.

Nikos and I now have a representative collection of Stephen B.'s work: heavy, the layered colours rich and sometimes brutal, the canvas often cut up into strips and interwoven to deepen the primacy of the materials, pictures that, for all the references to other artists, exist in themselves so emphatically that these non-figurative pictures are not abstractions, but have a thick, dense presence that makes the room they hang in appear abstract. They have spirited humour and, too, irony, which are Stephen's spirited humour and irony. He will say about a work, 'Oh, just torn-up bits of canvas,' and sniff, and then smile in such a way that belies what he said. He never ever talks abstractly about art, but instead will go on about the London bus routes.

———

A book launch for Cyril Connolly's collection of reviews, The Evening Colonnade. I wondered who arranged for Nikos and me to be invited, though Nikos said he wouldn't come – Sonia, near the entrance, who was very friendly and told me she thought I would be amused to be there. Stephen was not there. I saw Cyril Connolly talking to an elderly, refined-looking man wearing a white Stetson hat and white bandana tied about his neck, and, excited, I went to Connolly to tell him some gossip that I had had from Stephen which I assumed would impress him for my being close enough to Stephen that he would confide in me: a big row in the Spender family. Connolly simply stared at me, as did the man in the white Stetson, who, when Connolly introduced me to him – Cecil Beaton – turned away with a frown of, who is this presumptuous young man? Well, I thought, I've made a fool of myself, and so there goes Cecil Beaton.

———

Stephen gave me a first edition of E. M. Forster's The Longest Journey, published almost a hundred years ago. Stephen thinks the novel Forster's best. Reading it, I did not think so, but in it I found a vision entirely that of Forster, and whenever I came across sentences and paragraphs and passages that seemed to me original to Forster I copied them out, rearranged them and created in fragments a whole that is distinct from the novel itself as a whole. What the passages reveal is a very British – even more, Northern European – idealization of classical Greece.

He looked at the face, which was frank, proud, and beautiful, if truth is beauty . . . Certain figures of the Greeks, to whom we continually return, suggested him a little. One expected nothing of him – no purity of phrase nor swift-edged thought. Yet the conviction grew that he had been back somewhere – back to some table of the gods, spread in a field where there was no noise, and that he belonged for ever to the guests with whom he had eaten.

Ansell said, with irritation, 'But what can you expect from a person who's eternally beautiful?'

Rickie thought, 'Do such things actually happen?' . . . Was Love a column of fire? Was he a torrent of song?

He said again that nothing beautiful was ever to be regretted.
'You're cracked on beauty,' she whispered – they were still inside the church. 'Do hurry up and write something.'
'Something beautiful?'
'I believe you can. Take care that you don't waste your life.'

He revisited Cambridge, and his name was a grey ghost over the door.

Ansell was at Sawston to assure himself of his friend's grave. With quiet eyes he had intended to view the sods, with unfaltering fingers to inscribe the epitaph. Love remained.

Let us love one another. Let our children, physical and spiritual, love one another. It is all that we can do. Perhaps the earth will neglect our love. Perhaps she will confirm it, and suffer some rallying point, spire, mound, for the new generation to cherish.

———

Everything David Hockney does seems an occasion for celebration, as his arrival in Victoria Station on the boat train from Southampton, where he'd arrived from New York by ship, with an American boyfriend, an art student he had met in America, Peter Schlesinger. I joined some of David's friends, including Ossie and Celia, to celebrate the arrival. David stepped off the train smiling a broad smile, and then Peter Schlesinger stepped off, as if in a daze, his blond-brown hair swinging over his forehead, walking away from us with a slow swagger to his hips and shoulders as if, curiously, he was alone. I suppose I might have gone off with them all, an animated entourage around David and Peter, but I held back, feeling that I didn't really belong among them, envious of them for a levity I wouldn't be able to sustain among them. It happens that, as much as I want to be light spirited, a sudden heaviness will come over me and lower me, and I will feel I am pretending to be light spirited, so it is better for me to withdraw.

———

We went to a poetry reading, among the poets Adrian Mitchell who seemed to sing out, as a refrain to a long poem, 'To Whom It May Concern (Tell Me Lies about Vietnam)'. There are many poetry readings in London.

I recall a poem by Spike Hawkins was read:

Pig, sit still in the strainer,
I must have my pig tea.

———

Stephen came to lunch, just the two of us. He brought a big bunch of asparagus, which he loves; I cooked it and we ate it with butter and lemon, the game pie and salad, and wine. We talked about the English class system and the American class system.

I said I didn't know if it is a matter of class, but certain English I've met seem to have the ability to loathe a person and be kind at the same time. He said that Annie Fleming, the wife of Ian Fleming and a grand hostess, would invite people to dinner whom she hated, and be very kind to them. I said I wondered if Natasha had this ability, and he responded, 'Oh no, not at all.'

He said she annoys him when she will say 'chimneypiece,' which is not of her class, instead of 'mantelpiece.'

About the American class system, he said it depended on where in America you are.

I said I know where I am there.

If to be English, or even to be British, is to be aware of where one is in a class system – a system that some people I've met say no longer exists, as does the editor Caro Hobhouse, for example, who, being a Hobhouse, should know – the system in no way exists among the people I know in London. Whatever the originating class of the people we meet at dinner parties, drinks parties, book launches, in the foyer of Covent Garden, at these occasions they appear to me so interconnected with one another that they form a class that I think of as London.

———

I met Stephen at Liverpool Street Station, and we trained up to Cambridge. On the way, he read and corrected proofs of his book about the young rebels. From the Cambridge train station, we took a taxi to King's and to Mark's rooms.

Mark had a little sherry party before lunch, and a few

undergraduates came, all with very long hair and all terrifyingly intelligent. They seemed to talk of nothing but pop music and violence. One student, with whom I sat on the floor, said he sometimes hoped the war in Vietnam would become another world war, because he believed that only violence could produce synthesis. I said I thought he was being very selfish. What an incredible level of intellectualization and inexperience they live on.

After lunch in a pub Stephen and I went to visit E. M. Forster.

When Stephen first suggested that Nikos and I meet Forster, Nikos had been against it, insisting we would be visiting a literary monument, not a person, and Nikos especially objected to my wanting to take flowers. Stephen tried to arrange a meeting with Forster through Joe Ackerley, and when Nikos saw all the wheels put into motion he said he'd come also. But then we got a letter from Forster – actually written by Joe Ackerley and signed by Forster – saying he was ill and would be going to Coventry (to his former friend's house, Stephen said, a policeman, now married), so we didn't go up to Cambridge. We had lunch with Joe Ackerley at Chez Victor. He appeared thin and wan, and as he was hard of hearing it was difficult to talk with him; in any case, he didn't seem very interested in us, even bored. He asked a waiter about a dog the restaurant used to keep as a mascot, and he was told by the waiter the dog had died. (Talking, finally, to Forster, I mentioned Joe Ackerley, and said how sad I thought it was that he should dedicate his posthumous book to his dog Tulip. Forster said, 'Oh, Joe used often to bore me with his dogs.') I sensed Ackerley had become, I thought, intentionally indifferent when Nikos and I said we wanted to meet Forster; I saw him viewing us as two crude opportunists, especially when Nikos said he had heard Forster had lots of Cavafy papers, which might have sounded as if Nikos wanted to see them. Joe said he didn't know about any Cavafy papers, and, leaving the restaurant with us, said that Forster was accessible and liked the company of young people, but he obviously left the going to us. He went to a Japanese film. Shortly after, he died. So we didn't go to King's College,

Cambridge to meet Forster, and, hearing that he had become senile, we decided we shouldn't go.

But then Mark, as artist in residence at King's, said he saw Forster daily, and he was very well and clear headed. Nikos couldn't come on the day Stephen was free to go, and, in any case, wouldn't have come, because he thought I wanted to meet Forster only to be able to say I met him.

How did he know that for years and years I have blazoned across my mind the admonition from Blaise Pascal, 'Curiosité n'est que vanité le plus souvent, on ne veut savoir que pour en parler, autrement on ne voyagerait pas sur la mer pour ne jamais en rien dire et pour le seul plaisir de voir, sans espérance d'en jamais communiquer,' making me feel guilty of the sin of pride for voyaging on the sea only later to write about it?

I told myself, no, I had a legitimate reason for meeting E. M. Forster: his famous epigraph to Howards End 'Only Connect' seemed to me more than a moral imperative, it seemed the very reason for my wanting to see him, to, however briefly, connect with him. So, as if justification were needed, I was justifying meeting him by referring to one of his most famous epigrams.

I knew that Stephen had read E. M. Forster's unpublished novel about male lovers, which I'd heard about, as literary gossip, in New York, as if knowledge about it were knowledge about some secret homosexual world only a few people were allowed into. On the train, I asked Stephen, 'What is the novel like?' imagining I now would be allowed into that closed world, as closed as the Cambridge Apostles I'd read about. Stephen frowned and said the novel, Maurice, didn't quite come off, and he wondered if it should ever be published. This was the first criticism I had ever heard about E. M. Forster, whom Stephen called Morgan, and I took it to be the criticism, not of outside gossip, but of inside knowledge.

Stephen knocked on Forster's door and a delicate voice said come in. He, short and bent, was in his shirtsleeves. 'I've just seen the doctor,' he said, 'I've just seen the doctor.' 'Are you well?' Stephen asked. 'Oh, indeed, indeed.' Stephen introduced us, and when I shook his hand I imagined shaking hands, as if all their handshakes remained like hundreds of invisible hands about his, with Virginia Woolf, with Maynard Keynes, with Lytton Strachey, with all of Bloomsbury – and, extending even more out into the world, with Constantine Cavafy in Alexandria. He went into his bedroom to put on his jacket and on the way out shut the door of his bathroom, where I saw a long, claw-footed Victorian tub that listed. We sat before his fireplace, above which were oil paintings and, I gathered, family photographs. The furniture was all Victorian, rather old-maidenish, with knitted arm covers on the chairs. High bookcases, with big yellow and brown books, lined the walls one after another like large rectangular librarians standing at attention. I think the wallpaper was of yellow flowers. One of the oil paintings, all in vivid yellow, red, green, was of King's chapel done by an undergraduate, another a mountain scene by Roger Fry, and on a wall between the bedroom and the bathroom was a reproduction of Picasso's young man leading a horse. Forster had had painted the bottom panes of the windows so he wouldn't have to see the ugly modern building, the Keynes Building, across the way.

He paused for long periods between sentences, and seemed always to repeat what he said twice.

But when we talked about the military dictatorship in Greece – I saying I had hoped to go to Greece with my partner, Nikos, who was Greek, but as he couldn't go neither could I – he said, 'Yes, I understand. But one recalls instances in Greece that were beautiful even though the country, even then, was imbedded in muck. Somehow one's dearest memories are of events that, if one saw them in a greater context, were always imbedded in muck.'

Stephen joked about Mount Athos, the Greek peninsula of all-male monasteries where, supposedly, not even hens are allowed. Forster said he'd once been on a boat that was on an excursion to Mount Athos. 'The men got off,' he said quietly, 'but I stayed on board with the ladies.'

After a silence, we talked about Mark's paintings, which Forster said he viewed with compassion, but not much understanding.

After twenty minutes, Stephen said he had to get back to London, so we left. Mark drove us to the station, and on the way Stephen said, 'There was a lot of Forster in that remark about one's dearest memories always being imbedded in muck.' 'Oh?' I asked. 'His insistence on the muddle and confusion enclosing personal moments of vision,' Stephen said. At the station, he said there was no reason why I should go back to London with him, and Mark said I could stay with him in his rooms. I thought: Nikos won't mind. We left Stephen off and I returned to King's with Mark.

I rang Nikos, who didn't mind, but told me to spend the night.

Mark signed me in for dinner at High Table (how strange, I thought, that Forster's name should be matter-of-factly written in among the others), and we went back to Mark's rooms, where more undergraduates came in and talked about pop music, about which Mark appears to know everything. He played records.

Before dinner, he took me into the combination room for sherry. On the red walls were portraits of Bloomsbury people, such as Rupert Brooke, which I had seen in reproductions in books about Bloomsbury. The fellows appeared in their gowns hanging half off their shoulders. It was amusing to see Forster come in wearing his gown, smiling generally at everyone but not talking to anyone, and moving about quickly as he got his glass of sherry and went to the back of the room and sat in an armchair by himself. Mark introduced me to the provost, who asked me to follow him into dinner, where I sat at his left. The provost asked me what I do, and when I said I'm a novelist he said, 'Do you know we have Morgan Forster sitting at our table?' 'Oh, indeed, indeed,' I said. I saw Forster, toward the end of the table, eating with quick movements and looking up and only smiling at anyone who spoke to him. His moustache was short and stiff.

In the hall, the undergraduates, with trays, were sitting down to or getting up from their meals. The provost told me that the undergraduates had decided that they no longer wanted formal meals with the fellows, but to eat off trays. Therefore, the High Table had been moved from the far end of hall to the end near the combination room, so the fellows would no longer process through the students to the far end. And, again because of student protest, High Table was no longer on a platform, but, like all the tables the undergraduates ate at, was set on the stone floor.

After dinner, Mark said we should go back into the combination room. Forster was sitting alone, drinking coffee. Mark asked if we could sit with him, and he said, Oh, it'd be his pleasure, it'd be his pleasure. We talked about student demonstrations, about the war in Vietnam, more about the dictatorship in Greece.

And then, as if I must take advantage of this moment for some knowledge that no one would know but I because I would be the first person E. M. Forster told, I said, 'You met Cavafy,' but he only answered, 'Yes, I did, I did.'

I had to be content with the thought: though he would not remember me, I would remember him, and I had connected.

Mark asked him if he wanted to come to a Guy Fawkes party. At first he said yes, but then, as the energy visibly drained from him, he said he thought he'd perhaps better go to bed.

I left him thinking how utterly unmysterious he is. It seemed to me that he must be aware that he is the greatest living writer, and that there had to be a mystery in his being that, but he seemed not to be at all aware, and not once referred to his books. He's a few weeks away from being ninety.

The Guy Fawkes party was given in a small Victorian row house by two male friends. There were about fifty people, of all ages and, evidently, sexes. They, as mixed as they were, moved about among one another with great ease and cheerfulness. At one point the lights were extinguished, one of the hosts put on a record of the Fire Music from The Ring, drew back two curtains, opened French doors onto a balcony overlooking a back garden, and announced, 'Ladies and gentlemen, the fireworks!' From the garden, Catherine Wheels, Roman candles, flares, high-rising rockets, all in great gushes and geysers, kept people on the balcony and upstairs windows for about an hour.

Then a fire was lit in the garden, and people upstairs threw books down into the flames. Someone said, 'But you're burning Patrick White. You can't burn Patrick White.' After, there was a buffet of curry.

I fell a little bit in love with an undergraduate who kept refilling my plate.

At around one-thirty in the morning, Mark and I went back to King's and watched a bit of the American elections live on television, then went to bed, he upstairs in his bedroom, I on a sofa in the downstairs sitting room. I did think: if Nikos had once had sex with Mark, why shouldn't I? I jerked off into a handkerchief, which, in the morning, I stuffed into a pocket of my trousers. Not thinking it showed any evidence of what I'd used it for, I took it out in Mark's presence to blow my nose, and he, no doubt seeing that the handkerchief was stiff in a way it shouldn't have been, smiled, but said nothing. I've never mentioned to him his affair, however brief, with Nikos.

———

Stephen often asks me about this diary, as if he wants to be reassured I am keeping it. I feel I don't put everything in that I should or, perhaps, that he would want me to. After I came home from an afternoon with him, during which he had said something about Auden or Isherwood, I thought I ought to record his comments in my diary, but, thinking further of it, I decided it was wrong of me to record the comments, as, Stephen apart, their relevance was not to Auden or Isherwood, but to me as the diarist. For so many years before I came to London, I kept my diary recording relationships within my family and close friends, people who were relevant and important to me. But Auden, Isherwood, Forster, however often I might meet them, are not my friends, and everything I record about them can only be of an almost irrelevant literary interest – the very interest Nikos so derides and tries to break in me. But, even so, given that I am a writer, how can I not write about them? And now I regret not having recorded what Stephen told me, which I've forgotten.

As for Stephen in himself, I sometimes wonder if he wants me to write in my diary events in his life that he himself would not write in his – as his telling me, with glee in the telling, that years ago he was in Switzerland and had sex with a young man in a bush, after which he gave the young man a huge Swiss note, but the young man thought this too much, so he gave Stephen change. Stephen was bright red with laughter.

———

Some time after Nikos and I began to live together, he showed me a poem he had written before we met, called 'To a Friend Who Regretted Leaving Three Days Later,' a title that suggested more to me than I wanted to know, dedicated to someone named Toer Van Schayk.

He is, Nikos said, a Dutch ballet dancer and choreographer.

Some time later, Toer Van Schayk, in London, rang wanting to see Nikos. Nikos told me to come along, my jealousy softened by my curiosity, and we met Toer Van Schayk in a simple cafeteria. I had come thinking that if he had found Nikos attractive, he would find me attractive also. I found him attractive, a slim, elegant man, whose demeanour was self-contained and modest. He could speak Greek, which he had learned living as a local on the island of Paros, where he would enter the ancient Parian marble quarry for marble and carry out lumps to carve them into heads he would then leave about the countryside. He and Nikos spoke Greek while I listened, and the more they spoke the more stiff I became, my arms crossed, until Nikos and Toer sensed my disapproval and spoke in English, though Toer still concentrated on Nikos. He evidently did not find me attractive. My jealousy became stark, and I leaned towards them and stuck out my chin to interrupt them and said to Nikos I had to go, and if he wanted to stay that was up to him. This surprised Nikos. He knew from the past that he could, in my presence, turn his attention to someone else without intending me to feel he was being inattentive to me, he knowing that I would of course understand that he was meeting someone he hadn't seen in a long while who meant something special to him, and in the past I had understood and had deferred, especially when a Greek refugee comes to our flat for supper. But now, not looking at Toer but at Nikos, I stood, and Nikos stood, and turning away I didn't say goodbye to Toer Van Schayk.

Nikos was silent on the way home, and, at home, asked me, 'Why were you so unkind to Toer? He is a pure person, and I loved and love him.'

———

Stephen came to dinner a few nights ago with Patrick and Patrick's new, beautiful friend Gervase. Stephen spoke about his friendship with Christopher Isherwood when they were in their early twenties, when they didn't know anyone famous. He said, 'I'm sure I did more sincere work then, when I was twenty-three, when I didn't know anyone famous, than the work I did after I began to meet famous people.' We discussed successful people – that is, people who could confidently enjoy the fact that they are successes, such as E. M. Forster, Henry Moore, Francis Bacon. Patrick and Nikos said no one should allow himself to think he's a success. Stephen said, 'Well, I know I'm not a success.'

After dinner, Patrick made a reefer and passed it around. I didn't take any, nor did Gervase, who sat quietly still all evening, but Stephen and Nikos did, Nikos staring me straight in the eyes as he took deep puffs, and I went into a funk. I don't know why the very subject of hashish causes all kinds of jealousies, anxieties, depressions in me, but it does. Nikos says it is because I want to be in control, and hashish puts him beyond my control.

———

I mentioned to John Lehmann that I was looking for a job, as I'd run out of money. He asked me if I wanted to be his secretary a couple of mornings a week, sorting out papers, typing, answering business letters, and I said yes. He invited me to lunch in his flat to talk about what I would do. I went reluctantly. At lunch, he asked, slitting his eyes and leaning over the table toward me, 'Tell me, old boy, just what is your relationship with Stephen?'

When I next saw Stephen, I told him I saw John, but not why, and I said, 'He really is unpleasant, isn't he?' I said this because I knew Stephen wanted to hear me say it.

Nikos, at lunch alone with Stephen, told him that I was going to work for John, and Stephen rang me up. He said, 'Nikos told me you're going to work for John.'

I said, 'I don't really want to. What do you think?'

'Well,' Stephen said, 'I suppose it'd be silly if you turned him down.'

We talked about it for a long while, and I decided: 'I won't work for him.'

Stephen said, 'Well, perhaps I'm being unjust, but I would prefer it if you didn't. When I heard you were going to, I thought: I won't see David any longer. It's the first bad thought I've had about you.'

'I don't want you to have any bad thoughts about me,' I answered.

When, a couple of weeks later, Nikos and I saw John Lehmann again, he asked, 'When are you going to start working for me?' 'Oh,' I said, 'I don't think I'll have to now.' He said, 'I didn't think you would.'

John has the vulgar habit, on greeting Nikos and me, of kissing us on the mouth and jutting his tongue between our lips. Nikos, in front of him, wipes his mouth, but I am too intimidated by John to do anything but smile a weak smile.

———

Stephen, I think, creates guilt, both in others and in himself. We were going to the Italian Cultural Institute on Belgrave Square, as he had to copy down some Italian translations of English poems for a lecture he was to give in Rome. On the way, we passed Magoushe Gorky's house, and Stephen said, 'We mustn't let Magoushe see us. She'll tell Natasha we're together.' Magoushe is the mother-in-law-to-be of Stephen's son Matthew. After we left the Italian Institute, going back to his car, Stephen said, 'Let's go to Magoushe's and have tea.'

'But, Stephen, you didn't want her to see us together,' I said.

'Oh, it doesn't matter,' he answered. 'It's a great bore, Natasha's disapproval of you and Nikos.'

We went and had tea, and were welcomed. Magoushe and Maro, with whom Matthew has been living for years, were writing out invitations to the wedding. There was a lot of talk about who was Hon. and who not, and what titles people had. In came three women, a mother and two daughters, with the names Chloe, Clare, Chlochlo, though I was not able to sort out who was called what, all Peploes, who appeared to me to be mythological creatures. Leaving them all, Stephen paused in the street and said, 'I hope Magoushe doesn't tell Natasha we went to tea.'

———

With a single tulip, I visited David Hockney, who was surrounded by what I took to be dealers who so closed in on him all I could do was hand him the tulip and say hello. I wandered about among other visitors and noted in the middle of a room a double bed, unmade, and by the bed on the floor a large jar, the cover off, of Vaseline.

———

To my surprise, Stephen suggested we make a television script of Henry James' story 'The Author of Beltraffio,' in which a wife allows their son to die, so outraged she is by her husband having published a novel that she finds morally corrupt. That Stephen chose this story can only make me wonder what the significance of it is to him as a writer, and to him and Natasha as husband and wife. To what degree does Stephen feel that he has had to censor himself in his writing, not wanting to upset Natasha in revenge against what he would like to write? And to what degree does Stephen feel he, married to Natasha, should have the freedom to write what he wants? And write about what? Sex? I can write about sex because of the freedom the world more and more allows. Stephen is still in another, a residual world in which to write about sex is not allowed, and that other, residual world censors him, that other, residual world in which he places Natasha as a guard against the moral corruption of unlawful sex. I think: Stephen may feel that to write about sex is to break free from that other world, is to break free from Natasha as the guardian of that world. But isn't there, within their relationship as husband and wife, something more binding that holds them together, and isn't that something the source of some of Stephen's best and most moving poems, the love poems about Natasha? I am gathering together an image of Natasha that, from Stephen's telling me about her, is complex, as are his feelings towards her. It would be too easy to simplify Natasha as a willful woman who will get her way, or to simplify Stephen's relationship with her as subservient to her will, which he resents but cannot escape. Of course, I do wonder why he wants to do the adaptation of 'The Author of Beltraffio' with me. Anyway, what I cannot understand is that sex should have been, in a world not so very far removed from the world in which Nikos and I love each other, considered morally corrupting.

———

I like to think that Nikos and I together belong to three nations – both of us British, both of us Greeks, both of us Americans. What the cross-overs from country into country could mean I can only wonder.

———

I met Stephen at the Tate, where we went quickly through the de Kooning exhibition, with those large women with large staring eyes and large teeth and short legs sticking out from under voluminously painted skirts, who made Stephen giggle; then we got into a taxi as he had to go pick up plane tickets for Israel (he and Natasha are going for two weeks) and then in the same taxi went on to his publisher, Weidenfeld & Nicolson, where he was to correct the proofs of his book about the students. He wanted me to come in the taxi with him as he said that would be the only time he had to be with me.

I didn't mention that John Lehmann was coming to dinner, as I know he doesn't like Nikos or me to see John. But Stephen rang up while John was here. He rang, just before he had to get ready to leave for Israel the next morning, to give me a sentence for a blurb I'm writing for the Edward Upward novel In the Thirties. I was sure Stephen could hear John's voice and laughter, perhaps made loud because John knew Stephen was on the phone. After I wrote down the sentence, I said, 'John Lehmann is here.' I sensed Stephen's disappointment. He said, 'Well, I hope you don't prepare him as magnificent a meal as you prepare for me when I come.' 'Not nearly as magnificent,' I said, and he laughed, but I felt vaguely guilty.

I don't at all understand Stephen's relationship with John Lehmann. I sense Stephen has more resentment toward John than John toward him, if John has any resentment toward Stephen. In fact, I think John is rather large about Stephen, and though he'll say such things as 'Oh Stephen, thy name is naïveté,' there doesn't seem to be any bitterness in it. Stephen's comments about John, however, are often bitter. He thinks John mean-spirited. Stephen once gave me the plot for a story: two well-known literary figures, who look somewhat alike, are often taken for one another at parties, and act the parts of one another, while in fact they despise each other. But, as big as they both are, Stephen doesn't look at all like John. John looks sinister, his skull large and very near the surface, his eyes narrow and staring with fixed concentration, and Stephen looks the very opposite of sinister, always blinking as if innocently bemused.

John brought a bottle of Osbert Sitwell's wine when he came to dinner last night: Vini Chianti Montegufoni, proprietà Sir Barone Osbert Sitwell.

He said that if one asks for a lavatory in the castle, one is shown the way by a servant along many passageways to a room with a chamber pot – a story I have heard from someone else, but can't recall from whom.

———

We could hardly understand Stephen when he rang for the background noise of music and talk at the wedding reception of his son Matthew and now his daughter-in-law Maro. Stephen, sentimental about how Nikos and I love each other, sounded drunk, and Nikos and I were embarrassed for him.

———

Because Nikos couldn't come, I tried to excuse myself from going to lunch at John Lehmann's house in the country, Lake Cottage, near the town of Three Bridges, and over the telephone said I was waiting for an important call that I had to stay in London for, but he insisted: he had prepared lunch for me. The lunch consisted of a slice of meat pie with the endless egg in it, frozen peas, and a puddle of instant potatoes. John showed me a collection of photographs of young men taken just before the war, mostly in and about Vienna: blond, thin, fresh, smiling, all lovers. One was wearing the uniform of a Nazi air force man. John said, 'These aren't all of them, duckie; there were lots more.' Perhaps I'm making him sound crude. He wasn't, or if he was the crudeness is held within a tremendous, even ponderous structure of English graciousness.

He let me look through his library, all smelling of damp, of the books he published, of an extraordinary high quality. Everyone says he is a much better editor than poet.

In the entrance hall of the cottage is a large round table decorated by Denton Welch, whose delicate novels I have admired with the admiration of someone who thinks, falsely, that the admiration is unique to oneself, though in fact the admiration is of a cult. But his presence suddenly appeared unique to me, long after his death, in the solid table painted in bright red and green and yellow.

———

The more I get to know Greeks, the more I think they are people who do not make moral judgments, but who, living the facts of history, have a very deep, unspoken, instinctive moral sense which they live by historically, and which is very accommodating of human failings. It comes to me more and more forcefully that Greece is not a country of puritan principles, unlike America, but a country deeply layered with the facts of its history that belie making judgments raised up on unaccommodating high principles.

A Greek friend of Nikos, who, as Nikos did, worked in the Greek Embassy in London but left and is now stranded because he can't return to Athens, is staying with us for a few days. He laughed saying that all Greeks are guilty, all, of complicity in deals, which are kept secret. 'Greece,' he said, 'is run on don't tell, don't tell, keep it a secret, because if you tell you bring on the evil eye.' What surprises me is that Greeks will admit this with a laugh, and then make a gesture of disgust and turn away as if from all of Greece.

But if ever I, enas xenos, a stranger, ever repeat what a Greek – even Nikos – has said to me about Greece, the look I will get – and, in the case of Nikos, the reprimand that I'm not Greek and don't know about Greece – shuts me up.

For all of that, I have fallen in love with a country I don't know.

––––––

Stephen came to supper, then the next day rang to say that when he arrived back to Loudoun Road, where he lives, he found a taxi, its door open, waiting, and, inside, Natasha, with Sonia attending, packing to leave because she knew he had been with us. Sonia left and he calmed Natasha.

Perhaps I concentrate too closely on Stephen and Natasha in this diary, leaving other people we see outside, but it is as if I see them more and more as within a narrative that keeps me attentive because Nikos and I are in it.

We could of course tell Stephen that we think it best for Natasha and his relationship with her that we don't see him, but we won't do that.

Maro Gorky, as if to find out who Nikos and I are, came to visit, and informed me, as with delight, that Nikos is a C.I.A. agent. I thought: well, at least they – she, Matthew, Magoushe, and, too, the Peploes, Clare and Chloe and Chlochlo, all that world – are all talking about Nikos.

Nikos told me that, before he met me, the Italian writer Niccolò Tucci had stayed with him, having had to escape from the Peploes because of their pet snake. I imagine them, mother and two daughters, with names all beginning with C, in an apartment that could be anywhere in the world, in which they, in long loose frocks and barefoot, and speaking many languages, wander from room to room, with no other reason for being who they are but that they have a pet snake, which is all I know about them.

Tucci came to a meal, an elegant, multi-cultured man who seems to use three or four languages in every sentence. He has just published a novel, called Before my Time.

I was born before my time. When my time came, the place was occupied by someone else; all the good things of life for which I was now fit had suddenly become unfit. It was always too early or too late.

When Anne Graham-Bell, who is a presence in the literary world of London and who wants to bring accord to all the world, arranged for Nikos to have lunch with her and the mistress of Allen Lane at Bianchi's restaurant, Nikos thought Tucci would charm them both and asked Anne to include him, and he did charm them both, so all Nikos needed to do was sit back. Later, Anne said to Nikos that she hoped that Tucci was discreet enough not to let on that he had had lunch with the mistress of Allen Lane, and Nikos assured her that Tucci had often had lunches and teas and drinks and dinner with the mistresses of powerful men, and knew about discretion.

San Andrea di Rovereto di Chiavari

We are again in San Andrea. Anne Graham Bell is staying with us.

She encourages me to write. Her devotion to literature is great, and will have her pestering agents and publishers to give the writers she is most devoted to the attention she believes they deserve. There is a story that a publisher, knowing that Anne could not be stopped by his secretary from entering his office, hid away on the balcony. She writes articles warning reviewers that they must read the books they are reviewing through to the end, shocked as she is that reviewers don't read books through to the end. The shock is registered in her round staring eyes and her mouth a little agape in her long face. She will suddenly become serious about the way the standards are being lost, that look of shock leaving her bemused at how this could happen.

And of course I enjoy the connections she will refer to lightly, married to Graham Bell who was one of the group of painters called the Euston Road School, among them Lawrence Gowing and William Coldstream and Rodrigo Moynihan and Adrian Stokes and, for a while, Stephen Spender; and, after Graham Bell was killed in an airplane crash, Anne married Gerald Reitlinger. She said about Virginia Woolf that she always appeared to be dressed in dusty curtains. Anne likes to joke that by marriage she is also related to Alexander Graham-Bell, the inventor of the telephone. She laughs a laugh of astonishment at all this happening to her, she, as she likes to say, a provincial girl from South Africa.

All together, we take the bus to Chiavari to shop. In the market, she was very keen to buy a punnet of wild strawberries, for she must have wild strawberries, however much they cost.

More than amused by her, Nikos and I love her for her enthusiasms.

She was with us when Stephen came to visit us, he staying in a hotel. It embarrassed Nikos and me that Stephen paid little attention to her. We all had lunch in a restaurant in San Fruttuoso overlooking the Ligurian Sea.

The photographs perhaps say more than I could.

Stephen and Anne have gone.

Today it is raining, so we've stayed in, reading and writing letters. The little whitewashed house on the high steep slope of the Ligurian coast is enveloped in cloud, pouring down over the mountain ridge above us; there is a smell of mint everywhere.

Stephen went from us to Paris to meet Natasha. His trip to Italy is a secret from her. He said, 'She's suffered so much from my friends in the past, I don't want her to suffer any more.' Another time, he said, 'Natasha despises weak people. I'm weak. I don't understand why she doesn't despise me.'

While he was here, he and I took a long walk up the mountain. Stephen was filled with anecdotes. About John Lehmann: 'Rosamond and Beatrix and John were waiting together as their mother was dying. After some time, John took out his watch and asked, "How long will this take? I have many things to do."' About Auden: 'Wystan said he would write a poem for my birthday. I thought, How nice, a poem for my birthday. Then he said, "I didn't have time to write a poem, so I sent a letter to the Guardian." But the letter didn't appear, and Wystan told me they must have lost it.' Talking about poetry, he said, a very revealing thing about Auden's poetry is that it completely lacks mystery. The same applies to Isherwood's prose. He thought that mystery is what his own poetry is essentially about.

The day after Stephen and Anne left seemed vacant. I said to Nikos, 'It is so mysterious when people leave: I can't really imagine

Stephen now on the same train on which we saw him off, settling into his compartment and reading his newspapers. Separation is incomprehensible.'

'I hate it,' Nikos said.

———

We go to the beach every morning and stay until the afternoon. At lunch time, the beach becomes almost deserted, and it is hot and absolutely still. The few people remaining lie motionless on the pebbles, and waves of heat rising about them distort them.

I am never bored with Nikos. Last night, we sang songs to one another that we made up. Mine was in French:

> Sur la table,
> dans un rayon de soleil,
> se trouvent
>
> un verre d'eau
> et une pomme rouge.

His was in Italian, a tango:

> Prosciutto e melone,
> un po' di provalone . . .
> Zabaglione.

I thought, the other day, walking down the path to the beach with him: if ever I am unhappy in the future, I will have these days, these three years, with Nikos to look back to as proof that I can be happy. I'll never be able to say that I wasn't happy. I think of the change in my life from before I met him to being with him essential.

London

Back in London, where everything seems to be working for me. The short stories in Penguin Modern Stories One, with Jean Rhys, will be out soon, and two novels have been accepted by Macdonald. Of course I am pleased, and I tell everyone. But I find myself becoming depressed, and I don't know why.

Nikos says to me, 'Don't disappoint me.'

———

Nikos likes to say we are both refugees.

My father was born in Canada, in the province of Quebec, and when he was two years old was taken by his parents across the border between the United States and Canada to Providence, Rhode Island, forced out of their home because they had been reduced to poverty by the English, who dispossessed them of their inheritance, for the French were the original settlers. So, in a sense, my father's mother and father took refuge in the United States by settling anew in a Quebec French parish in Yankee New England, where the work allowed the refugees was in factories owned by the Yankees. I was born and brought up in that parish, and in all my youth I felt that we Québécois-Americans, we Franco-Americans, were a race apart.

Nikos has said he never felt he belonged in Greece, and I have never felt I belonged in the United States. To be, as I am, a

Franco-American, meaning a French-Québécois-American, is to be no one in America, because we have no identity there, none. Nikos' identity, even to his singular accent from beyond mainland Greece, was at best marginalized as a refugee.

We grew up, in our different worlds, fantasizing about a world outside which we could belong to, and that world is, if not England, and even more if not Britain, London.

I must put in that Nikos and I met the old writer Raymond Mortimer at the writer Raleigh Trevelyan's flat (and of course I'm aware of the name Trevelyan as having a long British history), and all I can recall of Raymond Mortimer is his saying he had met 'a charming blackamoor,' this said with a knowing smile, he obviously knowing that he was affecting the offensive 'blackamoor' as justified by the history of the world from centuries past.

———

Whenever Nikos and I are out in a crowded street and an old person carrying a suitcase appears, Nikos says, 'I can't bear it,' and I see tears rise into his eyes.

———

John Pope-Hennessy had a brother, an historian, known most notably for his book on the slave trade between Africa and the Americas, in which the more horrifying aspects are detailed. I visited James Pope-Hennessy in his flat above a pub in Ladbroke Grove, he thin and pale and gracious, the other guests a languid young man who never rose from the armchair under which cushion he seemed to have been born and which he did not have the strength to rise from, and a vigorous furnace stoker from the Battersea Power Station. Everyone was very friendly.

James, a masochist, was found tied up and murdered by an overly inspired sadist. John described going to the morgue to identify the corpse of his brother, his face with a dissolute, almost evil expression.

Still, John had a Roman Catholic Mass said for him. The Mass revealed to me for the first time that John himself was a Catholic, but I did not know if practicing. When I told Sonia Orwell that John Pope-Hennessy was a Catholic, she shouted, 'How can he be?' as if his being a Catholic were an outrage.

John went to Florence where an exhibition of great medieval silver chasses helped him to recover from the death of his brother.

————

Stephen invited Nikos and me to have lunch with Auden at the Garrick. Auden looks older than what I remembered, and more slovenly.

I notice, whenever I'm with Stephen and Auden, Stephen becomes very quiet and reserved, as if in recognition of Auden's superiority; he never disagrees with him, and when, a few days after our lunch at the Garrick, Auden came to dinner and Nikos argued with him about the Vietnam War (Auden is for withdrawal, but is sure this will cause chaos in South Vietnam) Stephen seemed to slip into a position that was almost reactionary in his seeming, a bit embarrassed, to support Auden.

He and Auden were coming to dinner on an evening when John Lehmann had invited Nikos and me to drinks. There didn't appear to be any reason why we shouldn't go to John's and hurry back to give Stephen and Auden dinner. An hour or two before we were to go to John's, he rang up:

'Look, old boy, Auden is coming for drinks also, but has to leave early because he and Stephen have been invited to dinner. So why don't you and Nikos come early, fifteen minutes or so, to meet him.'

I paused. 'But, John, he's having dinner with us.'

'Is he? Isn't that amusing? Stephen didn't mention a word of that.'

'Well, I wonder why.'

'You know Stephen.'

Nikos and I did go early. There were John, Robert Medley, Auden and Stephen. Auden said little. Later, in the taxi, he complained that when one's invited for drinks, there should be proper drinks, and not just champagne. Stephen had sent us a cheque to buy a big bottle of vodka for him, and when he got to our flat he made himself a huge Manhattan, took off his slippers, sat, came to the dinner table in his stocking feet, and talked the whole evening – that is, until 10:00, when, way past his bed time, he told Stephen they had to go. We'd asked John Golding and James Joll also.

Because Nikos and I are foreigners and don't really know the accords of who likes whom or the discords of who dislikes whom, and, too, because we don't think in terms of liking or disliking (or as foreigners don't have the social confidence to be able to), we're happy when, on having different people to supper, we find that among them one of them is very fond of another and both are happy to be brought together unexpectedly, or we're disconcerted when one of them very much dislikes another, and the consequences of that have led to some disastrous supper parties, as when someone was so insulting to another the only accord I could think of to bring everyone together was for everyone to sing 'Jerusalem,' after which, at 9:30, everyone left. We've been told, because our ignorance must be generally known, by a friend not to be invited with another friend, and so we learn about accords and discords, without quite knowing why so-and-so doesn't want to be invited with so-and-so.

It does surprise me when I am enthusiastic about meeting someone – and Nikos, too, who will say about someone recently met, 'She's wonderful!' – I find someone else I am also enthusiastic about knowing will say, 'I don't like her,' or even, 'How can you be friends with her?' leaving me to wonder which of the friends I should be more friendly with, and leaving Nikos to laugh a light laugh.

James and John had not met Auden, so Nikos and I thought they would be pleased.

Stephen had said, the best for Auden would be grilled chops and root vegetables, no salad, no pudding, but cheese for after. Wanting to do something special, I prepared what I found in a cookbook to be called something like Hamine Eggs, eggs boiled in onion skins for an hour or so, with mayonnaise for first, which Auden so liked he asked for the recipe and said he would tell Chester to make them.

James Joll said that he recently told the critic George Steiner that he would never speak to him again after Steiner wrote in an article what James thought unjust, but, as it was a rainy night, he offered Steiner a ride to his house, where he left him off with a final goodbye.

Auden seemed not to hear. ——————

Auden appeared not to be interested in anyone, and I tried to rouse his interest by asking James if he had to do a lot of research as he was writing Europe since 1870. He said, 'No, I've done the research,' so the history of that period was now of an interconnected world revolving in his head, a world that to me occurs in disconnected flashes that have no chronology, none, that I can put together.

Auden did look at James for a moment, as though his attention held for a moment in which he wondered who James is, but he quickly lost interest.

Throughout the evening at supper with Stephen and Auden, John and James, it seems, said very little, but then who can say much when Auden says everything?

John Golding did say he thought that though Picasso has illustrated books he has never read a book in his life.

Stephen says Auden, in conversation, is like a great big bus with a very determined route, and either you get on and listen without talking, or you jump off. There's very little communication with him. And yet, he was very open to having anyone board him as a bus, was very relaxed, said how nice he thought our flat is, how good the food, and he was, in the way a great big red bus can be, very amiable.

I wonder if Stephen has ever admitted in print, or even in conversation, that his friend W. H. Auden is a very great poet.

Thinking about history –

History for me is always a surprise as to what happened to the past in relation to what is happening now, though I am acutely aware that what is happening now is in direct relation to what happened in long past battles, though I cannot remember dates, who fought whom, and why the battle determined the fate of the world I live in. I defer to historians for keeping the history of the world together.

But in his introduction, James does write: 'Episodes which seemed immensely important at the time sink into insignificance in the wider view. This is especially true of the history in the last twenty-five years. Since the end of World War I it is hard to decide what is important and what is ephemeral in our history. Down to the end of World War II we at least know, when writing history, what was going to happen. For the more recent past we do not know the outcome of historical events in which we are still personally involved.'

————

What to make of this, which I take to be entirely English only, I suppose, because it took place in England, or, more specifically, in London? Nikos and I were invited by Robert Medley to a drinks party, and there he, left aged by the recent death of a lover with whom he lived and whom he cared for over many years, introduced us to a slim young man with bleached-blond hair, and we imagined him to be Robert's young lover, given the way Robert laid a loose arm about the young man's shoulders. There were many black people there, and the music was reggae, and the young bleached-blond man danced with a young black woman, and the way they danced, and the way they held each other even when they were not dancing, made me wonder what possible relationship Robert could have with the young man.

Maggi Hambling, whom we see from time to time, was there, standing apart, smoking a rolled-up cigarette, with narrowed eyes looking upon all the proceedings.

She said she often goes to a bar in Battersea Park Road, just behind where we live, and suggested we go with her one evening, and Nikos, who likes her a lot, said yes, yes, and so I said, yes, yes.

———

Stephen is away, teaching at the University of Connecticut.

John Lehmann is at the University of Texas.

At a party for the writer Jessica Mitford, I spoke to Sonia, who looked older and had put on a stone if not more, and who seemed a little cool perhaps because I hadn't seen her in a while because of her treatment of Nikos.

Sonia said, looking past me, 'There is Natasha,' and I turned and saw a tall, striking-looking woman with a broad, blonde Russian face talking to a man. I suddenly became very uncertain of myself, and squeamish. I wondered if I should go and introduce myself to her, because, after all, she would know who I was from my having gone to the South of France to help Stephen plant trees in the garden of their house, and I decided, yes, I must. The man she was talking to had hair like white plucked chicken feathers and very yellow teeth, the painter Julian Trevelyan. When I introduced myself to Natasha Spender, she appeared not to have heard of me. She talked on with Julian Trevelyan, and I just stood by, smiling stupidly, and commenting on what she said, 'How nice,' as if I were in fact participating in the talk.

The fact was that I knew about everything she mentioned: Stephen in America, the birth of Matthew and Maro's daughter Saskia, Lizzie, that the house in Loudon Road needs rewiring, that the garden of the house in the South of France is coming on, that Stephen was going to get the English Chair at University College – though, as this hasn't yet been revealed, Natasha hinted at it by saying, 'We're hoping this will be my husband's last extended trip abroad. It's time he put on his carpet slippers and settled.' She spoke with great articulation, her lips forming the words almost exaggeratedly. But I couldn't let on that I knew about Stephen getting the Chair. As friendly as I am with Stephen, with whom I talk very intimately, he as much about Natasha as I about Nikos, I am a total stranger to Natasha. I couldn't possibly say, 'Stephen rang up from Connecticut last week to say hello.'

I couldn't see myself as I listened to Natasha speak, my awareness of myself a kind of blur out at a distance from myself, that distant blur suddenly referring back to me only for a second when I raised a hand to touch my nose and realized that it was in fact my hand, but, standing before Natasha and listening to her, I thought that she saw that my hands, my face, my body were all mine, and that she must be judging me for the way she saw me. What did she see?

(I suppose the attraction of looking at photographs – or, more, of film – from a party after the event is to see oneself as others saw one, and perhaps to think: really, that's me?)

Natasha seemed not to be seeing me at all, and I turned away from her after a while and let her go on speaking to Julian Trevelyan and spoke to someone else.

Later, I talked to Sonia, who said she had wondered if Natasha and I would meet and speak to each other.

'Oh, we did,' I said.

'Yes, I saw you. You seemed to be chatting away intimately.'

'No, not at all. She talked with Julian Trevelyan, and all I said from time to time was, "How lovely."'

'Oh?'

'It's too stupid. And all for nothing. My relationship with Stephen is so innocent.'

'No,' she said, 'it isn't. It isn't innocent. Nothing involving feelings is innocent.'

'Perhaps you're right.'

I sent Sonia my novel, The Ghost of Henry James, and she sent me a sweet letter thanking me for it.

————

We went to the bar, Sporters, in Battersea Park Road with Maggi H., she dressed in khaki. There was an all-women band playing extravagantly, the drummer wearing a jacket covered in blue sequins that flashed as she swung her arms.

Maggi told us that once when she was in the bar, in came a group of men in drag as women, and some of them chatted her up and asked her if she'd like to go to a T.V. party, and Maggi, wondering what kind of party there could possibly be of men in drag watching the television, but, curious, said she'd love to go. She was taken in a lorry, the driver having to hike up his/her dress to drive, to Clapham Common, where more and more men in drag collected. Maggi asked, 'Where's the television?' and at her question the room became silent and she suddenly knew that T.V. did not mean watching television, and that the men in drag suddenly knew she was a woman, and that if she didn't get out of there as quickly as she could she'd be raped.

In the bar, Nikos appeared excited to be in an extravagant world of working-class people who, within their world, allowed themselves freedoms that were theirs entirely, a world I felt he genuinely admired, but one he could never ever be a part of.

———

To celebrate the publication of my novel, The Ghost of Henry James, Nikos invited some friends to the only truly Greek restaurant in London, in a mews off Queensway, where I drank and drank and drank and smashed the glasses on the floor. Back home, I was sick in the toilet bowl, Nikos standing above me, and between bouts of vomiting I said, 'I'm so happy, I'm so happy,' and Nikos laughed and put his hands on my shoulders.

———

Back from America, Stephen recounted how, when asked if he knew of any good new literary magazines in the States, he was amused to answer, 'Yes, Fuck You.' He laughed his high laugh, his shoulders shaking. He gave us some copies, rough paper, roughly printed, stapled, rough drawings in the Egyptian erotic style, the editorial page called EJACULATIONS FROM THE EDITOR, with exhortations IMMEDIATE GRATIFICATION, FREEDOM FOR HALLUCINOGENS, GROPE FOR PEACE,

DISOBEY!, GOD THROUGH CANNABIS, KEEP HUMP-
ING, MUSHROOMS, RESISTANCE AGAINST GOON
SQUADS, and entries by Allen Ginsberg, Frank O'Hara, Peter
Orlovsky, LeRoi Jones, Robert Duncan, William Burroughs,
Robert Creeley, Charles Olson, Gary Snyder, Gregory Corso, John
Wieners, Norman Mailer. One issue has a long poem by W. H.
Auden, 'A Platonic Blow', which, with many rhymes internal and
external admired by Nikos, such as:

> It was a spring day, a day, a day for a lay when the air
> Smelled like a locker-room, a day to blow or get blown,

describes a blow job that is not Platonic. Stephen said Auden does
not deny he wrote the poem, but is annoyed that it was stolen from
his desk.

Stephen asked for the issue with the Auden poem back.

Though Nikos Georgiadis and my Nikos are Greeks, I note the
difference between them when we visit Georgiadis in his flat/
studio, where, with the theatricality of a set designer, he puts on
display evidence of the different cultures within Greek history
noted by, say, Herodotus and his travels throughout the then
known world: large picture books on Palmyra, the ruins of
Carthage, Thracian gold; swaths of embroidered cloth with East-
ern patterns; ancient clay vases and glass vials and alabaster cups;
and, surmounting all, the cover of an Egyptian mummy with
large staring eyes. My Nikos would consider all this as merely
picturesque, and I remark that the only Greek artifact we have in
our home is a komboloi of large blue beads given to Nikos by
someone from Greece.

We went with Nikos Georgiadis to an art film at the Curzon
Street cinema. After, in the men's room, I, turning away from the
urinal, saw Rudolf Nureyev peeing in the next urinal. Outside, I
joined both the Nikoses on the pavement, and when I mentioned

that I had just peed next to Rudolf Nureyev, Georgiadis, instead of leaving us, talked about the film until Nureyev came out and, seeing Georgiadis, joined us. Georgiadis had designed the set for the Prokofiev Romeo and Juliet in which Nureyev and Margot Fonteyn starred. He didn't introduce Nikos and me to Nureyev, and we all went our separate ways. Nikos said that Georgiadis had intentionally waited for Nureyev to come out and speak to him as a way of letting us know he knows Nureyev, and, too, that Georgiadis was letting us know that his friendship with Nureyev was exclusive of us. The next day Georgiadis rang to apologize – Nureyev had rung him to complain that he, Georgiadis, hadn't introduced us.

I thought, just as well, really, just as well, I sensing that Rudolf Nureyev could be a threat to Nikos and me.

———

Sonia's house in South Kensington has polished parquet floors and bright rugs and small, round tables with long and delicately curved legs and, always, vases of flowers on the tables, and books. There are, around the sitting room, shelves and shelves of books, for Sonia is a great reader. The fire in the fireplace might be lit. The air in her house appears filled with reflected light from polished surfaces, from crystal, from mirrors even on grim, gray days. There are drinks in the sitting room, then dinner in her basement dining room where the table is set with a starched white cloth and starched white napkins and gleaming china and glasses and silver, at the center a small bunch of pretty flowers. She wants everything to be pretty. The meals she prepares are mostly French, as are the wines she has opened and put on the buffet to breathe. A Francophile, she says the French enjoyed life more than the English, and, at the end of a meal, instead of asking everyone to go upstairs to the sitting room for coffee, she keeps her friends around the table for the coffee and more wine and talk, as she says is done in France.

She is always exhausted, as her dinner parties require of her a great effort, a duty even, and after having made the effort, performed the duty, as if to confirm that the things of this life matter because there is no other life, she hardly eats what she has prepared, but sits a little removed from the table and drinks and smokes as her friends eat, and as the evening deepens she takes a more and more commanding view of her friends, all of whom she devotes herself to. And it usually happens, when everyone is sitting about the table long past coffee but with smudged glasses of wine, that there occurs in Sonia's devotion, which is like a great cloud that envelopes everyone, a sudden shock of thunder and lightning. She attacks a friend for something he – always, as far as I knew, he – said.

At a dinner party, she suddenly attacked a friend, in the context of a conversation about the Nazi concentration camps, for the friend expressing horror at them. There was, she would insist, no expression of the horror of the camps that was equal to what they had been. She recounted having been to, I think, Belsen with her friend Marguerite Duras and her rage when Duras expressed horror, Sonia answering Duras' horror with, 'What did you imagine it would have been like? What?' To Sonia, the extermination camps were so indicative of the fact of human baseness, she took them as a given: of course people would exterminate other people, for whatever reason, of course. She even became angry at her Jewish friends for any bewilderment they might have had about why the camps: they, above all, should know why, which is the baseness of humanity. When Sonia read the unpublished memoir of a former inmate of a detention, not an extermination, camp which he was trying to get published, she said, 'He was in a very minor concentration camp.' Friends took this as a parody of Sonia's snobbism – and she is, she herself admits, an intellectual snob, perhaps instilled in her by the Sacred Heart nuns, also intellectual snobs: if you read about the French philosopher Jacques Lacan in the review section of newspapers, you soon met him at Sonia's house – but her denouncing the former inmate of what Sonia called a minor camp for presuming to use his experiences there to promote the publication of his memoirs, which Sonia found badly written, showed the depth of her basic conviction that everyone really is vain, that vanity really is everything. Beyond stating the starkest facts, you cannot not express any feelings about horror that are not expressions of basic vanity, and the more emotional the expressed feelings the more filled with vanity.

I admire her, I admire her even when, drunk, her denunciation becomes relentless. 'How could you say that? How could you? How?' You draw back into silence, and the other guests try to change the subject, but Sonia keeps after you: 'How could you have said that?'

I never mind Sonia denouncing me at one of her dinner parties, not only because I know she will telephone the next morning to apologize and to invite me again, but because I believe that she has the right to, believe that in her rejecting a faith that tried to destroy her in the name of trying to save her she has earned the right to denounce hypocrisies, has learned that all expressions of feeling are in an essential way hypocritical. It reassures me for my hypocritical, because false, expressions of emotion to be denounced by Sonia.

Nikos is aware of these false expressions of feeling from me, but is gentler than Sonia in making me aware of them.

Francis Bacon gave Sonia a painting of a head, done in savage brushstrokes, which hangs in a gold frame to the side of Sonia's sitting-room fireplace. He is often at her dinner parties. When I, drunk, asked him, as I often asked him, if he had ever had any religious feelings, he, also drunk, said, as he always said to my question, 'Never, never, never, never, never, never, never.' But Bacon was a cynic, and Sonia not. Sonia came over to Francis and me and asked what we were talking about. Francis said to her, 'David asked me if I've ever had any religious feelings.' Sonia frowned one of her severe frowns at me and said, 'You couldn't have.' I said, trying to justify myself, which was always a mistake with Sonia, 'I just wanted to know if Francis ever in the past believed in God.' 'Don't be stupid. Of course he didn't,' Sonia, angry at me for my presumption, answered.

I had already set myself up to be denounced by Sonia that evening, so when I said, drinking more wine at the table and more drunk than before, that I wondered if, even for an irreligious writer, it was possible to write a really deep book that wasn't religious, she denounced me for not being a deep writer – she repeated, 'You can't be a deep writer if you say that. No one who says what you've said can be a deep writer' – because, she said, religion in a novel, in any work of art, made the work obvious, made the work banal and pretentious. 'I know you're right,' I said, 'I know,' and I had that curious, slightly thrilling sense of having said what I'd said just to get Sonia to react as she did. Maybe I risked bringing up religion with Sonia so she would reproach me for bringing it up. I was drawn to Sonia partly because she reassured me in my being lapsed, and I sometimes made provocative statements about religion that I knew she'd condemn me for, because her reaction, which I could count on, reassured me all the more about my being lapsed, and, more, the very attention she gave me by condemning me reassured me. I almost felt rejected by her when she desisted.

She said, 'Hrumph,' and, as if to make up for turning her attention away from me, asked me to open more bottles of wine, which were on the buffet. I did, with pleasure. Wine was essential. Food was essential. Dinner parties were essential. And in fact this evening, maybe because of Francis whom she was intimidated by, she didn't attack anyone else after she had attacked me, and certainly not Francis, and the party was altogether as pretty as the flowers at the center of the table.

She invited me to tea, maybe to reassure me after having attacked me at her dinner party. I found that when I was alone with her she would get onto a subject – almost always a friend – and talk and talk about that friend as if the talk itself would sort that person, who badly needed to be sorted, out. Most often when I tried to add to the sorting out, she would say, 'You don't understand.' This afternoon, a grim winter afternoon with her sitting room warm with a fire and bright with all the lamps lit, the person was the writer Rosamond Lehmann, whom I told Sonia I had met. I described Rosamond Lehmann, tall and big-boned with a very white face and long, white hair, as looking like a moon goddess, which I'd thought original of me, but which made Sonia frown severely at me as if for trying to be colourfully original. I should have known by that frown not to continue to talk about Rosamond Lehmann, whom Sonia evidently disapproved of, but whom she nevertheless felt compelled to sort out. I said I wondered if what explained Rosamond Lehmann, whom I didn't know at all well, was her belief in the ghost of her dead daughter appearing to her, which she'd written about in her book The Swan in the Evening. Sonia frowned even more severely.

'You read that book?'

'Yes, I did,' I answered.

'How could you have? You don't believe in ghosts, a stupid, childish, self-indulgent belief, so why should you indulge someone else's belief in ghosts? I don't understand.'

'I wanted to find about what she had to say.'

'About a ghost appearing to her?'

'Yes.'

'That interests you?'

'Well, yes, it interests me, in a way.'

'How could it? How could you be interested in anything so stupid, childish, self-indulgent?'

'I guess it is stupid, childish, self-indulgent.'

Sonia lit a cigarette and shook her hair back and stared at me with narrowed, blood-shot, angry eyes and said in a low, hard voice, 'It is.'

While she talked, the smoke of her many cigarettes making the air dull, I had one of those moments of wanting to die. I told myself I must not indulge myself in it any more than Sonia would indulge me in it. But I wasn't able to concentrate on what Sonia said. I wanted to be as hard on myself for the longings that occurred to me as I thought Sonia would have been had she known about them, longings the very fact of their occurring she would have considered only as evidence of my weakness, of my inability to finally and forever deny them. And she would have considered any expression of my longing to be in a world where I would no longer have to endure the agony of the longings as nothing more than an expression of my vanity, because, again and yet again, there was no other world.

As soon as I was out in the street, I saw through the windows, over which she hadn't drawn the curtains, the lights in the sitting room go off abruptly.

———

Among the British writers whose work I read, Rosalind Belben has the most distinctive style, the writing in itself in tension with the literal, a tension that causes in the literal the sense of something much more vibrant in the literal than the literal. There are other British writers whose styles try for the more than the literal, writers whose work the writer Giles Gordon has brought together in an anthology called Beyond the Words: Anthony Burgess, Alan Burns, Elspeth Davie, Eva Figes, B. S. Johnson, Gabriel Josipovici, Robert Nye, Ann Quin, Maggie Ross, and Giles himself. And he asked me to be among them.

———

A description:

Nikos and I in Rome, where he had never been, the city, in my recollection, all flesh pinks and tans, great phalluses chalked on the walls, and the sound of water running. The presence, in museums, in public squares, in niches, of marble and of bronze, of statues glorying in their nakedness, in their sexuality, even the statues of emperors fitted with armour that, formed in the musculature of naked chests, appeared to expose their bodies beneath. The languorous nudi of Michelangelo's Sistine chapel, surrounded by phallic acorns, seeming to bulge out from the painted fresco, and the floating angels in the paintings of Caravaggio seeming ready to fall into one's arms. We stopped along the Tiber to look across at the Castel Sant'Angelo, and Nikos, pressed against a wall, said, 'I have an erection.'

———

Sonia, alone, to supper, which we ate in the kitchen. There were
two bottles of wine on the table. She studied them for a while, then
asked if we would mind if she paid to have a third bottle. 'Three
bottles of wine are reassuring.' We didn't accept money from her,
but I went out for a third bottle of what is called plonk.

———

I returned home from an evening at a dinner party Nikos had
declined going to, saying he needed a quiet evening at home, but
he was not at home. He came shortly after to say that Nikos Georgiadis had rung him and invited him to a party with Nureyev and
Margot Fonteyn, both of whom Nikos had talked to animatedly.
When Nikos told me, I became jealous of him, and he laughed.

———

The newspapers have been filled with the story that cannabis was
found by the police in Francis' flat. Francis, who declares he doesn't
smoke because of the asthma that he's suffered from all his life and
that kept him out of the military during World War II, has accused
George of planting the cannabis and alerting the police. There's
been a court case, in which the police had to admit that information about the presence of the drug came from George. Francis was
acquitted.

This afternoon, I was on a bus crossing Chelsea Bridge in the
rain, and I saw, from an upper-deck window, George, out in the
rain, walking along the pedestrian way of the bridge. The Thames
was dark gray beyond him. His hands were in the pockets of his
raincoat, but his head was bare and water was running off his hair.

———

Auden came to dinner with Stephen of course. We also invited
Johnny Craxton and his new friend, a bricklayer who was very
warm and personable, and whom I thought Wystan liked, but
when I asked Stephen later if he had Stephen said he hadn't,
because 'he wasn't a looker, wasn't bright, didn't have anything

to make Wystan interested.' 'That's monstrous,' I said. Stephen answered, 'I think Wystan is becoming more and more of a monster.'

When he arrived, he was obviously in a sullen mood – so far to come, all the stairs up to our flat – but we gave him lots to drink (actually, Nikos made a mistake in mixing the Manhattans, putting three parts vermouth to one part vodka instead of the opposite, but Wystan didn't seem to notice this), made him the absolute center of attention, to the point where I felt we were ignoring Stephen, Johnny and the bricklayer, and gave him a very good meal, all of which revived him, and he began to tell jokes, laugh, give his calculated opinions on anything that was mentioned: cigarette lighters, cars, South Africa, recruiting students into the military on university campuses, which he approves of because that ensures educated people in the military.

He told Nikos that Greece, in all its history, was best under the Turks, because it was at its most efficient under the Turks. But Nikos told him that was ridiculous, and he smiled at Nikos for a moment as if amazed that someone was telling him he was ridiculous, then as if with the appreciation of someone telling him just that.

When Auden said that he thought Cavafy's erotic poems – not his historical poems – camp, Nikos said they have to be read in Greek, which Auden can't read.

Auden said something disparaging about Samuel Beckett getting the Nobel Prize for Literature. Nikos said, 'Who else is there?' Auden shook his head so all the sagging wrinkles shook and said, 'There's me.'

What upset me most about what he said was, in giving a sermon on hell (he said he is very fond of giving sermons, and confessed, in a game he proposed in which everyone was to say what he had most wanted to be if he hadn't been what he was now, that he had wanted to be a bishop), that each man creates the hell he deserves, so that if a drug addict can't break his addiction it's his own fault and he should use a little extra will power to get himself out of his situation.

I am making him out to be more simple-minded about this than he was, but the startling fact about him was that he did insist that everyone was always responsible for his actions. I said, 'But sometimes one simply doesn't have the will power to be responsible.' He didn't listen. To make the point, he told us of a servant he had once had, a young Spaniard, who stole some money from him, and, Wystan said, 'Of course I fired him.' I got angry, thinking, and you didn't for a moment consider that he might have needed the money, or that you had been paying him so little he had to steal?

When, at about 9:15, he said he was rather tired, he got up to leave.

It surprised me that, after Nikos had opposed him on so much, he seemed to single out Nikos for special thanks, even affectionate thanks.

As for myself, I thought, well, really, there's no reason to see him again.

I mentioned my anger at Auden to Stephen over the telephone the next day, and he said he knew exactly what I meant, and that it was highly unlikely that the servant, whom Stephen had known, had stolen the money, as Wystan often imagines things are stolen from him when in fact he has lost them.

Stephen said, 'Wystan's only interested in himself, in no one else. He doesn't listen when anyone speaks to him, and he isn't interested in any case.'

Still, Auden is a very great poet, any number of examples of his poems testament to his greatness. How moved I am every time I read 'In Praise of Limestone' for the intelligent lyricism of the flowing lines, as if the very lyrical intelligence of the poem is what makes it so very moving – and mysterious!

———

After a recital at Festival Hall of Bach by Rosalyn Tureck – a pianist Nikos admires, though he said that she did often hit the wrong note (he is much more educated in music than I am as he had wanted to be a pianist but was discouraged by his mother who even refused him piano lessons, for she had it in mind that he should be a medical doctor) – Nikos and I were invited by Rodrigo and Anne Moynihan to their large house for a post-recital party. We knew almost no one, so, unlike us, we stood together and looked about at others. I noted a little old man, with long white hair round his bald pate, and, seeing me look at him with interest, Rodrigo brought me over to meet him, Sir Francis Rose, to whom I said, to let him know that I knew, 'You were a friend of Gertrude Stein,' and he, smiling a tender smile, said, 'Yes, yes, I was,' and he seemed to wait for me to ask him questions about Gertrude Stein.

She was someone whom I used to, as a student, fantasize about, reading with wonder The Autobiography of Alice B. Toklas, writing a paper in college on Tender Buttons (not then knowing that tender buttons referred to the female anatomy and trying to make sense of a portrait of a Red Stamp as 'lilies are lily white if they exhaust noise and distance and even dust'), and, more, to playing, to the distraction of my roommate, Gertrude Stein reciting in a recording, 'Portrait of Picasso: Shutters shut and open so do queens,' as if she were opening up not just a way of writing but a way of life – the fantasy certainly an impulse to my first going to Paris and searching out 27 rue de Fleurus to stand outside and wonder at all of her world coming to visit.

But, suddenly, I had nothing to ask Sir Francis Rose about Gertrude Stein or her world, and that world vanished here in London, and I realized it was an American fantasy world, of little interest to the English, and not at all to the French.

As for the lack of interest among the English in William Faulkner, this puzzled me until it came to me that his novels are not within the narrative of English history, in which history the sale of slaves may have been a source of colonial income, but a history not wounded in the land by mass slavery, the deep and lasting wound in the land of my country.

———

Had lunch ('luncheon'?) with Stephen before he left for the South of France with Natasha. He told me to meet him at Chez Victor, where another guest – a Polish poet – was to join us. I arrived before Stephen, and taking off my coat asked for Stephen's table, and the headwaiter, big, blocking my view, turned and pointed to the table behind him where Natasha was sitting with a man I presumed was the Polish poet. We looked at one another, I, I'm sure, as expressionless as she was; then I quickly went to her, said how nice to see her, and, to my surprise as she had the last time we met ignored me, she introduced me to the Polish poet. There was another woman at the table, and when Natasha stood the other woman stood, and they both went to another table and left me sitting with the Pole.

He said that Natasha told him that she had arranged with her friend to have lunch at Chez Victor without knowing that Stephen had also arranged to have lunch there. I got up and went to Natasha and said how sorry I was we weren't all having lunch together, and suggested that Stephen had invited me because I had wanted to see Richard Wollheim, whom Stephen had invited. She smiled, and, trembling, I left her.

Stephen appeared with Richard outside, saw me through the window, which he knocked on to say hello before he came in. Natasha was in a little alcove and couldn't see him. When Stephen did come in, taking off his coat as he advanced to the table, I said, 'Natasha's here.' 'Where?' I pointed. He went to speak with her, then came back, red. All during lunch with Richard and the Polish poet, we kept looking at one another, he smiling and blushing. We finished lunch before Natasha and her friend, and, leaving, I said goodbye to her. Outside, the Polish poet left us, and Richard said something that let Stephen and me know he understood the situation.

At home, I told Nikos, and he said, 'Well, does it surprise you that Richard, that everyone, knows about Stephen and us? Thank God I wasn't there.'

Stephen, ringing that evening, said that Natasha hadn't mentioned a thing about it when she got home.

Natasha has become a big presence in Nikos' and my life, though we don't in fact see her. We dream about her, sometimes have nightmares about her. We both think she has been treated unfairly by Stephen. I think, of course: if we were really on her side we'd stop seeing Stephen, but that is impossible.

———

I have heard the curator of exhibitions and writer on art David Sylvester say that there is not a drop of English blood in him, he a Jew who dresses like a large rabbi in black with a large-brimmed black fedora, which made me wonder what it is to be English. I asked him what he considers himself, and he answered: British. The differences among the Welsh, the Scots, the Northern Irish, even, I feel, Yorkshire people as distinct from the English becomes more and more marked, and not only in my awareness but in what is called devolution. Devolution from what? From England? But what is England? I may become British one day, but I'll never be English, though I wonder who does know what it is to be English? I would say, once again, the name connotes a vagueness as vague as the boundaries of London, with, perhaps, Hyde Park Corner as the centre of the outlying vagueness. Perhaps, in my own vagueness, I can now call myself a Londoner.

———

From James Joll's The Origins of the First World War:

Men are not motivated by a clear view of their own interests; their minds are filled with the cloudy residues of discarded beliefs; their motives are not always clear even to themselves.

I remember the end of World War II, Victory Over Japan. I was five years old. However unaware I was of the world, I, by being historically a part of the world, grew up in a world more outside me than inside me, a world that, after World War II, belies personal history for world history. As ridiculous as this may seem, given how personal my history appears, I think that really I am much more in world history than I am in my own.

It seems to me that my life occurs, in ways far beyond my interests, my motives, outside in the world, however the world outside is filled with residues of discarded beliefs, and far from any clear motives.

And Nikos is much more in world history than I am.

And think of Stephen – Stephen during the Spanish Civil War, Stephen as a Communist, Stephen during World War II, Stephen in Germany after the war, when, in Berlin, he picked up fragments from the top of Hitler's desk, for which he paid a few cigarettes to an old woman selling the fragments. Back in London, he propped the fragments on a mantelpiece until one day, studying them, he was shocked by their presence, and threw them into the rubbish.

———

We went to a party at Mark's, who had just moved into a big bright white flat near Belsize Park. We knew Stephen and Natasha were going to be there. Stephen met us at the door, smiling mischievously. Nikos asked, 'Is Natasha really here?' 'Yes,' Stephen said, 'she's in the sitting room.' Neither Nikos nor I went in for a while, then finally did. Natasha was speaking with Ted Lucie-Smith. I went up to Natasha, said hello, said hello to Ted, and went for a drink. Nikos went straight for a drink.

I was at one end of the room talking with John Russell and Nikos was at the other talking to Stephen Buckley and his new lady friend. Natasha was in the middle, on a sofa, from which she suddenly got up and went straight to Nikos and started to talk to him. Stephen B. withdrew.

Nikos told me later that they talked for about an hour, all about Nikos' upcoming operation to have a rectal polyp removed – an operation that, given the presumed nature of our sexual relationship, makes me wonder if people are somewhat amused by it, though it is hardly up to me to tell them sex is for us rather in the intercrural ancient Greek way. Natasha, Nikos said, was very concerned, advised him to have a blindfold so he would be able to sleep with the lights on, to take lots of cologne, and said that if there was anything she could do for him to let her know. Nikos said he was sweating, and the talk was very stilted, but she wouldn't stop.

Everyone was aware that they were talking. Mark came over to me and said, 'I listened in. They're talking about hospitals. It sounds rather awkward.'

Finally, Stephen went over and broke them up to go home. As he and Natasha were leaving, he turned to Nikos and said, 'We'll see you tomorrow at Richard Wollheim's.' Nikos told me that Natasha's face fell, surprised by yet another of Stephen's 'conspiracies' behind her back.

Richard and Day, having invited Nikos and me and Stephen and Natasha to dinner, wondered if they might have done the wrong thing, and Richard rang Nikos to ask him if he or I would be offended that they'd also invited Natasha. 'It's Natasha who might be offended,' Nikos said. So Richard rang up Stephen, who insisted that we should all go but that he wouldn't tell Natasha, who'd simply find Nikos and me there. But for some reason he decided to let Natasha know at Mark's party.

The next evening at Richard and Day Wollheim's, in their large studio in Pembroke Gardens, there were Stephen and Natasha. I went to Natasha immediately and began to speak to her, but she seemed to me stiff and not willing to talk. Stephen came over to us and said she had been in bed all day. Richard came over to introduce someone to Stephen and Natasha, and I left to get a glass of wine. I thought, Well, Natasha is offended.

When I turned back into the studio room, I saw her talking with Nikos, both of them with hands gesturing with great animation, their voices bright and engaged in whatever they were talking about. (Nikos said later it was all about Encounter magazine, whose chief editor, Melvin Lasky, held back from Stephen and Frank Kermode the fact that the magazine was financed by the C.I.A.-funded Congress for Cultural Freedom, a fact that, when revealed, made Stephen and Frank resign, Natasha enraged by the duplicity that Lasky forced on the unknowing Stephen and Frank.) She talked on and on.

Stephen went up to them finally and said to Nikos that he wanted to introduce him to someone else. Natasha said, 'But we're talking!' Stephen went away, then, blinking rapidly, came back a short while later and again tried to get Nikos away. Natasha got angry. Stephen left, only to go back soon after, blinking more rapidly, and almost pulled Nikos away from Natasha. I saw Nikos give Natasha a look of helplessness and shrug his shoulders. But later in the evening they were together again, Natasha now advising Nikos once again about his time in the hospital.

As she and Stephen were leaving, she came to me and said, 'You will let us know how Nikos is in hospital.'

I can't help but wonder what she wondered about in Nikos having rectal polyps.

Stephen seemed anxious to leave. They did leave, but a moment later he came back, his huge overcoat flapping, his face red, his white hair flying about, as though he had been running, only to blow very demonstrative kisses to Nikos and me, who stood and smiled back with silly smiles.

The revelation is quite simply that Stephen seems more responsible for the separation between Natasha and us than Natasha herself.

Nikos went into hospital on Monday, was operated on on Tuesday, and came home on Thursday. I went to see him twice a day, was only happy when I was on my way to see him or at the hospital bed beside him, and I hated to leave him. I minded his being there, I think, more than he did. All my hatred of hospitals came out: I resented the nurses touching him, the doctors examining him, the operation itself.

He became friendly with a Russian sailor in the ward who had had an accident on a Russian trawler off the coast of England, and had had a leg amputated, but who was very lively. He loved the care he was given in England.

While he was in hospital his cousin Maria had a total breakdown, and was in a locked ward at Friern Barnet. She finally

believed she was possessed by the devil, and had to be taken away
by the police in a straitjacket. When I wasn't visiting Nikos, I was
visiting her.

———

Trained in philosophy, Nikos will explain to me, say, Kant's cate-
gorical imperative, and for a second I understand, but then the
second of understanding goes, and I am left, not with understanding, but a 'sense' of the concept, which 'sense' I am not able to
articulate, but which appears to be a little, radiating globe in my
mind.

I think I don't have ideas, am incapable of ideas, but can only
have a 'sense' of meaning, the 'sense,' however, filled with more
meaning than I could ever state. I have a 'sense' of meaning without
knowing what the meaning is.

What is odd is that this 'sense' of meaning seems to come not
from within me, but from out in the round world, for that is where
the greatest meanings are.

———

Richard Wollheim had us invited to a drinks party given by a friend
of his, a large queenie man dressed in a loose white caftan, his flat
as if transported from Morocco, or what a European imagines a
Moroccan interior to be –

(I realize that Nikos doesn't try to transport Greece into our flat
with Greek artifacts, but, as if to identify the flat as Greek more
than American or English by referring to what to me is the richer
world of Greece, which I, living with Nikos, make a show of
belonging to, I will buy in a Greek shop a spice, machlepi, which,
however, is never used, or a little coffee-making pot – briki – or
backgammon – tavoli (Nikos prefers Scrabble, he always winning)
– these little attempts to bring Greece into our flat amusing to
Nikos)

– the lighting in the Moroccan-like flat was somber so the people
appeared to move about slowly as if the air was thick, and, in the

midst, a tall, wide armoire on top of which was a human skull. We were welcomed with a grand indifference by the man, as if we were there to prove ourselves before he would pay particular attention to us, and soon after Nikos suggested we leave; together, we thanked the man, who said, 'Go, go, go,' and we were being dismissed before we had the chance to say we were leaving, so we left feeling belittled, but relieved. The man, we understood, has a shop for antiques in Chelsea.

Stephen Buckley came to have lunch with the artist Jennifer Bartlett. She once had a show in Tony Stokes' gallery, Garage.

I think I amused her by reading out from Gertrude Stein's Lucy Church Amiably:

After all there are very many knives that have wooden handles.

It has been said that clouds can meet but it has not been said whether the clouds were of the same size and thickness . . .

It is always a mistake for the sun to come through the window from within to the outside.

She has an easy manner, an easy sensual manner, as if her body were one with her easy thinking and feeling, and yet, oh, there is beneath the easiness an absolute devotion to her art. She will never self-deprecate, but will say about her own work, 'It's great, isn't it,' not as a question but as an indisputable affirmation that it is great. She has a light, ironical laugh that seems to belie her seriousness, but her seriousness is absolute.

She is a friend of the artists Jan Hashey and Michael Craig-Martin from when they were all students at the Yale Art School.

After seeing the documentary by Alain Resnais, Night and Fog, about the death camps, Nikos and I were silent, and went home to a meal in silence, and after our meal Nikos said, simply, 'Let's go to bed.'

In bed, I sensed his thinking about what has no words, thinking about what is happening in the world for which there are no words. I wonder what any self-awareness in personal introspection, in therapy or analysis, can do personally to accommodate the suffering of the world; and, given such depersonalizing awareness, what any analyses of nations, of governments, of politics, of history itself, can do to make somewhat comprehensible the sufferings of the world, and, with some comprehension, accommodate the sufferings of the world.

Again, some days later, home from the publishing house, Nikos said, 'It isn't that I commission books, especially of poetry, in defiance of the horrors, because the horrors are too great to defy, but because I believe poetry is a moral and spiritual recourse for the defeated, as, I suppose, we all are.'

———

A friend came from New York to visit.

Hearing me speak – my pronunciation of certain words now deliberately British, as aluminum, vitamin, tomato – he said, severely, 'You're American, speak like an American.'

For a moment, I saw myself from his point of view as an American pretending to be British, and, more, from his point of view saw my entire life in London as pretentious, an accusation that for the moment shook me. I felt pulled back to New York, where I had felt imposed on me the condemning self-consciousness that in New York made me think that everything I did was phony. Then I thought, this is where I live, here in London.

It is because of Nikos that I began to use English expressions. Nikos is not American, and he does not have the American suspicion that Americans who speak in foreign ways must be phony (such an American expression that: phony), which suspicion Americans visiting from America have about Americans living here, perhaps because Americans have retained from

American independence a way of speaking that sets them off from the English, and, moreover, sets them off from any Americans at the time of independence who, with pretentious foppish superiority, continued to use the King's English. I know now that my self-consciousness was American enough that to shift prepositions from 'a quarter of three' to 'a quarter to three,' or from 'living on a street' to 'living in a street,' or to pronounce 'alou- mi-num' as 'al-you-minium,' or to call 'a flashlight' 'an electric torch,' was to risk being a phony. Not only is Nikos not American, his accent is not American, so he is free of any American telling him to speak like an American. He is free to choose to speak another language in any way he likes. With him I'm freed of so much of the American self-consciousness imposed on me by America that for too long has condemned me as phony. I use the English expressions he uses.

He has a delicate and precise way of speaking.

———

Sunday, and Nikos has gone to visit his cousin Maria at Friern Barnet. He has been away about two hours. I've been writing, but suddenly a feeling comes over me that he has been away for an intolerable period. I want him to be here. I feel unreserved love for him. I want to write this in here because I realize as I've never realized before how much I love him.

———

During the Nazi occupation of Athens, an aunt and uncle of Nikos hid a Jewish family in their apartment, but when the occupation ended the Jewish family refused to leave, so Nikos, visiting his aunt and uncle, would see figures passing behind semi-transparent sliding doors, the Jewish family so settled in that the aunt and uncle left the flat to them and moved elsewhere. Telling this, Nikos laughs, and my historical awareness now includes something that I would not have imagined because I was not there to have experienced the occupation and the aftermath.

And Nikos does say that he was happiest in his extended family, including the maid, when all lived together in one apartment during the Nazi occupation. He remembers bean soup, mock coffee infused from carob pods, overcoats made from blankets.

As if he were still a pubescent boy, Nikos has wet dreams while asleep; they wake me up but he goes on sleeping, but if he wakes he will say, sleepily, that he was dreaming of someone from his boarding school in Athens.

I thought of Nikos' interest in Giambattista Vico's investigation into the history of language as our richest history when I heard him discuss with his cousin, from Athens visiting London, the use of the word 'moro' in Greek – the cousin insisting it comes from the Italian 'amore,' and Nikos that the word is Turkish. This linguistic Turkish residue acknowledged by Nikos surprised me, as he always refers to Constantinople, not Istanbul, as the capital city his mother comes from.

Also, he says his knowledge of the purist language Katharevousa, which was meant to purify the Demotic Greek language of all Turkish expressions after Greek independence from Turkey, is in fact shaky, so that he had to ask his cousin to write a letter in Katharevousa for the historian Steven Runciman to send, I think, to the Patriarch in Constantinople in thanksgiving for some accolade. I rather doubt Steven, who claims to be a polyglot, knows even Demotic Greek, for when Nikos speaks to him in Greek he simply opens his hands as in a gesture of acceptance, and smiles.

But there is a big difference between speaking a language and reading it. Steven recalled his approaching the formidable historian of the ancient world, J. B. Bury, when he walked each afternoon along the bank of the Cam in Cambridge (his wife kept students away from him), and Steven revealed to him that he was interested in Byzantium, to which Bury reacted by asking Steven if he could read Russian, and, given that he could, he would be able to read Bulgarian, and should go to the library to look up a certain Bulgarian historian. Steven can read Russian, Bulgarian, Romanian, Greek, and no doubt the more esoteric languages.

About Nikos' cousin visiting from Athens – I would have thought that, under the dictatorship, Greece would be a closed country, no one allowed in and no one allowed out, but in fact there is a lot of toing and froing. Those who leave and don't return are those opposed, and I imagine those who are there and opposed hide their opposition, though Nikos tells me that many opposed are arrested and tortured. He learns about this by visiting Greeks in exile, among them the actress Aspasia Papathanaseou, in long night sessions in flats I can't picture, except as dim and filled with smoke. But he in no way disparages those people in Greece who keep their mouths shut and get on with their lives as of course has happened over and over in Greece for centuries.

I recall the wonderfully witty writer Edith Templeton saying about life in Communist Czechoslovakia, 'You keep your mouth shut and you can have a very good life,' including special retreats for writers and extra square meters of living space for their flats.

———

Because he knew I was interested and he wasn't, Nikos suggested that I go visit the Bloomsbury painter Duncan Grant to pick up the uncollected poetry by Paul Roche, close friend of Grant and often his model, to give to Nikos for him to consider the poetry for publication by Penguin. ('No chance,' Nikos said.) Duncan Grant, lively and sweet tempered, reminded me in his openness and matter-of-factness of his contemporary Forster. His little basement flat in Park Square West was stuffed, in an almost Oriental way, with ceramics and bits of mosaics and embroidered pillows and, of course, pictures both propped up on furniture and hanging all over the walls. As he was showing me the pictures, only a few by him, others by Vanessa Bell and minor French artists, another guest arrived, also American, and also called David. We all sat, and Paul

Roche gave me and this other David tea in two-handled cups.

I didn't like this other David. He must have known Duncan
Grant well, as he called him by his first name, and, lounging back
among embroidered pillows, asked Duncan Grant – no, didn't ask
him, but, with what I felt an ostentatious over-familiarity, entered
into Duncan Grant's life with the presumption of knowing everything about it all by saying something like, 'Duncan, you really
were mischievous, you know, you and Virginia and Virginia's
brother Adrian.' As presumptuous as I thought this, Duncan Grant
responded gleefully. 'You mean,' he said, 'the Dreadnought hoax.'
His lashless pink eyes blinking, he told a story, with long pauses, of
a hoax that Virginia Woolf (then Stephen), her brother Adrian and
others played on the British Navy: disguised as Abyssinian Princes
they were welcomed aboard one of HM's ships, treated with great
deference and unsuspecting interest, even when their beards began
to come off in the wind. I didn't know this story, which I would
have known only by having read about it, but didn't know it had
been accounted for in any book, so I imagined I was hearing something that could only be known uniquely from Duncan Grant, and
this of course gave me a sense of privilege. But the reaction of the
other David, with overly demonstrative laughter and interjections
of 'Duncan, you devil you,' which Duncan Grant appeared to love,
made me feel embarrassed for my sense of privilege. There was no
way I could compete with this other David for the attention of
Duncan Grant, and I didn't want to compete; and if I was aware of
being envious of him for his flamboyant intimacy with Grant
(which Paul Roche, perhaps seeing how much Duncan Grant
enjoyed it, deferred to), I was more aware of myself as being all too
similar to this other David and liking myself even less than I liked
him. He took over, offered to heat up water for more tea, kept
asking Grant to tell stories, all the while reminding Duncan Grant
what a fantastic life he's led. I left.

On the tube on my way home, I thought: there is enough
Bloomsbury left for someone to feel a part of it in its residue. After
all, Ben Nicolson is a friend, and his Christmas dinners in a Greek

restaurant in Soho, with Julia Strachey and various other Bloomsbury descendants, might have been like an occasion of fifty or sixty years ago. And Angelica Garnett is a friend. There are many people I've met who are doorways through which I could step into the company of so many more people to meet whom I have heard or even read about – such as Mary Hutchinson, born in 1889, whom I did meet with Stephen at Chez Victor, and who couldn't have more credentials for belonging to Bloomsbury, her cousin Lytton Strachey, her lover Clive Bell when he was married to Vanessa Bell, the mother of Angelica whose father was not Clive Bell but Duncan Grant, all of which Stephen told me before I met Mary Hutchinson at lunch, and, also, that Mary Hutchinson was the character in T. S. Eliot's play The Cocktail Party who keeps forgetting her umbrella – but I tell myself to stop at the doorway, because I wouldn't go in to know these people for themselves but for me to say, having entered through the open doorway and come out, oh you have to know whom I've met! I understand so clearly now what Nikos accused me of in wanting to meet E. M. Forster: I saw him as a monument I had wanted to visit to be able, after, to tell people – oh, friends in America – I have, amazingly!, met E. M. Forster. But how can I not step through the doorway opened to me and not come out and try to account for those whom I met inside, the account I of course hope to be read by someone who wasn't there at the right time at the right place at the open doorway?

———

When Nikos tells me I am deep down a negative person, he senses something in me that I too sense is true, but any investigation of why would be endless. Still, yes, it is true that I feel the world is one of moral and spiritual darkness, and stories of the horrors of Greece, and, too, the world wars, confirm for me that moral and spiritual darkness in the darkness of world history. It is as if the outer world darkness relieves me of any inner darkness, and, instead, of indulging in personal darkness, I am indulging in the darkness of the world – for the darkness of the world is not my fault, is not darkness I have to blame myself for, but is the fault of history, and history is to be blamed.

Then Nikos tells me a funny story about how, during the German Occupation, his family kept a turkey on the balcony, but the turkey one day flapped its ineffectual wings and instead of flying fell down to the street, where a man, amazed that a turkey should fall from the sky at his feet, ran off with it. And of course I laugh, and now think that, really, I must free myself of wanting to hear the dark stories, as the bright stories do belie the dark, even in history.

I visited Henrietta Garnett in hospital. She told me about her attempted suicide, speaking in a low voice but enunciating every word very carefully with large, beautiful lips. Her large, wide eyes in her thin face were shining. She laughed, a slight laugh that was hardly more than a breath, from time to time. She had wanted to throw herself off from the whispering gallery in Saint Paul's Cathedral, but arrived too late, the gallery now shut. She then drove around London looking for a place high enough for her to jump from, and decided, finally, on a room high up in a hotel that she thought would do. She jumped from the window, but didn't kill herself; and though she couldn't move, she was aware of people walking past her, imagining, she thought, she was drunk. Hearing Henrietta moan, someone stopped.

Robert Medley came to dinner. I mentioned how sweet I thought Forster was. He said, 'Don't be fooled, my dear. He liked to give the impression that he was sweet and gentle, but he had claws tucked away in his soft paws and could and did use them. He could be a real bitch.'

Robert also said something about having been given some very early poems by Auden which always went to pieces in his pocket. I said, 'I didn't know you were an old friend of Auden.' 'You didn't? My dear, we were more than friends.' And then I recalled the reference to Robert in Letter from Iceland. But I also recalled that when I saw Wystan and Robert together at John Lehmann's, Wystan hadn't said a word to him. I mentioned this to Robert, who said, 'But Wystan's a monster. Of course he wouldn't speak to me now.'

———

Nikos has heard from his mother in Athens that Maria has died of cancer.

I went to her flat in Mortlake to sort out her belongings, but her two flatmates had already claimed most of them, one saying that Maria had promised her her record player, the other her easel and paints for painting, and both claimed her clothes. I didn't argue. When I asked about the school Maria had been to, which Nikos and I are sure was the School of Economic Science as advertised in Underground stations, they wouldn't say anything except, 'Maria had to learn to deal with her problems herself.'

———

A 'sense' of meaning – this 'sense' is in my awareness of everything, cups and plates, tables and chairs, doors and rooms, houses, trees, clouds, sky, and, oh, people and their connections one to the other, everything, somehow, connecting beyond my ability to make connections. Is the 'sense' of meaning in this: that everything, in ways beyond me, does connect?

———

A dream about my parents. They had moved to a very damp and humid country, where they lived in a huge shed built on stilts. I went to visit them. There was a bamboo screen over the entrance to the shed, wavering in a breeze, and behind the screen I could make out two people sitting motionless side by side. I knew that the two people were my mother and father and that they had committed suicide. Frightened, I raised the curtain and went into the room. On their laps were newspapers and magazines they had been reading while waiting for the poison to take effect. Their faces were hideously distended and green, already rotting. All about was great stillness and silence. Then, suddenly, my father raised his arms laboriously toward me and opened his eyes, and my mother, with great difficulty, said, 'Help us,' and I woke up.

———

We look forward to a quiet but full winter – no dinner parties, at most relaxing Sunday-afternoon teas, writing during the day, in the evenings playing Scrabble. I feel well, and everything is promised.

It seems to me that I have lived for so many years – for as far back in my life as I can remember – for the day when I would be on my own, when I would travel, when I would write. Nothing really existed in the present – not even friendship – but in terms of that very dark future. Now, for the first time, but not with complete certainty, I am living in that future, and it is not dark, but bright. I know I could never be happier with anyone else but Nikos (given our differences, our uncertainties, our anxieties), I love London, and I feel, with a fullness that is so rare I doubt it at the same time, I feel in control; the world is whole and globed.

———

It occurred to me that Nikos and I never think about 'bad sex' or 'boring sex' or whatever that we hear other couples talk about, heterosexual and homosexual. We never talk about our relationship in terms of sex, and yet I'm sure that our relationship would change if we did not make love.

———

We spent a Saturday with a young friend of Nikos, Henry, tall and good looking. They had met at a drinks party given by the Moyni-hans, and Nikos sees him from time to time for lunch. Henry grew up in Canada, on a ranch, and used to ride his horse over the Cana-dian countryside. He is, Nikos said, pure, as a horse is pure. He is heterosexual. The three of us walked through Hyde Park, and I noticed that Nikos was lively because Henry was with him. We went to a tea shop, where Nikos sat next to Henry on a banquette behind the small table, and Nikos sometimes reached an arm to place it along the back of the banquette, almost on Henry's shoulders. After Henry left, I told Nikos that it was evident his spirits were raised because of Henry. 'Really?' he asked. I answered, 'Come on, you know his being with you pleases you very much, enlivens you, and that's as it should be, because he's young and beautiful, and, honestly, I'm moved that you should be so responsive, and I think, yes, Nikos is alive to youth and beauty.' Nikos laughed.

More about Henry James. For so long, reading his novels in America, I imagined that his London was the true London, the London he not only accounted for in his novels but the London he dined out in, almost every evening of the year. I imagined he knew the lords and ladies, the dukes and duchesses, and, if princes and princesses, foreign ones (Italian) living in London. Certainly the London I am getting to know is not the London he knew, and his London, for so long, appeared to me the London that hovered above mine, and, up there, was inaccessible to me.

But the more I live in London the more I look at the London of Henry James as a fantasy – his fantasy! His novels are fairytales!

Andrew Lord makes ceramics, which are not to be used but are works of art, such as large, misshapen jugs with extravagant curlicue handles. I went with him to see a collection of Chinese porcelain. We were alone in a room, looking at delicate vases in an illuminated glass case, and I had such a sudden sense of Andrew's body next to me I turned and put my arms around him. He laughed, a light, shy laugh, and his body seemed, abruptly, to elude me and I dropped my arms. We continued to study the porcelain. Other people I have spoken to about Andrew are also drawn to his physical presence, solid, and at the same time elusive. He wears jeans and tee-shirts, and his hair is crew cut. As powerfully present as he is, Andrew is elusive because his center seems somewhere outside himself, and he is himself drawn to it. That center, which obsesses him, is his work in ceramics. When I am with Andrew in his studio, I imagine he has no other life but there. I are not sure where he reads and listens to music and eats and sleeps and makes love.

I was late getting home, and Nikos was obviously upset when I told him whom I'd seen. 'You can do what you want,' he said. I said, 'No, I can't, and don't want to. I don't want to hurt you, so if my seeing Andrew upsets you, I won't see him.' 'No, you must see him,' he insisted; 'it doesn't hurt me, it simply proves to me what I've always known.' 'What is that?' I asked. 'That you aren't and never were attracted to me.'

I suddenly realized this about him: that he is always looking for proof of what he thinks is the truth that I don't love him, that we are too different (he being Greek and I American) to understand each other, etc.

I said, 'You know, when you asked Stephen to take me to the South of France with him shortly after you and I met – I've often wondered why you did that. Didn't it occur to you that he might want to make love with me?'

'I was sure of it.'

'Then why did you send us off together?'

'To prove that I was right.'

'About what?'

'That you would love him more than me – or, at least, that you and he have more in common than I have with either of you.'

'But your experiment didn't work. I didn't make love with him. I've never felt I have more in common with Stephen than with you.'

'That's not true. You do – you do with all your English friends as well. It is purely a cultural thing. I don't, as a Greek, belong here, and you as an American do. I know, in fact, that when we're in company you're often embarrassed by me.'

'Embarrassed?'

'Yes.'

'Sometimes, yes, when you become needlessly difficult and argumentative, as the other night at the Stokes' when you told that woman she had no right to say she didn't like Courbet.'

'If you really loved me, you'd never be embarrassed by me. You'd agree with me that no one has a right to say he or she doesn't like Courbet. You should agree with me, because I tell the truth.'

I feel that Nikos and I are now within the globe of London, and within that globe are connected to friends within the globe.

Melvyn Bragg's novels about his native Cumbria are as rich as the earth he so earthily describes, such as a farmer's heavy boots of leather encased in heavy boots of mud. He is usually a reticent person, but I feel he feels close to me, and talks freely. He told me about his first wife's suicide. The last time I saw him, he said, 'I want to write about a love affair. I want it to start as a happy, a magnificent love affair, and I want it to end a happy, a magnificent love affair.'

His wife, Cate Haste, writes about how women have changed – in part have been changed and have changed themselves – since World War I, the book a testament to how World War I and World War II form a continuing consciousness for Europe.

I saw Edna O'Brien, the novelist, at a party Sonia gave for her fellow novelist Vidia Naipaul. Edna asked me to sit with her on the same small armchair. 'You won't leave me, will you?' she asked. 'No,' I said. She was wearing a fringe of jet beads across her forehead. 'I think,' she said, 'I'm going to cry – because people are so cruel to one another, so dishonest, so inhuman.' She did cry, great soft tears that dripped down her cheeks and collected under her nose.

I once asked Ben Nicolson if there is anyone he can think of in London who has a salon, and after a long pause, his fingers to his chin, he said, 'No,' then after another long pause, he said, 'Yes, Sonia Orwell.'

———

As our circle of friends grows, Nikos and I are invited for weekends – to the house, formerly an old mill, of Howard and Julia Hodgkin, in a Wiltshire valley with a stream running through the valley and grazing sheep. From our room, in bed, we hear the sound of the voices of Howard and Julia in bed in their room talking, which go on, we think, past our falling asleep. In the morning, Howard brings us large, golden cups of tea while we are still in bed. The walls of the rooms are painted a pale green, what appears to be a Hodgkin colour.

All together, we take walks in the countryside, often up to a hill where there was once a Roman villa, the tesserae of a mosaic still to be found on the ground.

Some weekends, we are invited by Joe and Jos Tilson, in Wiltshire, where a number of British artists have moved to – including Hodgkin, Peter Blake, Dick Smith – Joe and Jos in a huge old rectory with grooves in the stone floor from the tea trolley passing from the kitchen into the sitting room. Joe is making ladders – not that one can use, but inspired by – and on each rung he burns words: YEW, MOTHER, WINTER, NIGHT, SWORD, SEED. Jos spins yarn from natural wool at a spinning wheel and knits beautiful rough jumpers, scarves, caps. Joe is very generous and gives us copies of his prints.

On a weekend at the Tilsons' with Frank and Julia Auerbach – rare, as Frank hardly leaves his studio – Frank did some etchings on a press that Joe had set up, one of Julia and one of Joe. He had not done etchings in years. He gave Nikos and me etchings, one of Julia and one of Joe.

With money from an advance on a book, for £500 I bought, on Nikos' urging, an etching by Lucian Freud of his mother.

And Johnny Craxton gave us a painting of a Greek young man smoking a cigarette.

We are building up our collection.

Barry Flanagan, artist, will from time to time ring the bell and come up, though I'm never sure what our conversation is about. I asked him what he was doing, and he replied, 'Dentures,' paused and nodded as if to confirm what he had said, 'yes, dentures,' and I wondered if he was making dentures. 'How is that?' I asked, and he answered, 'It's like a double helix on either side of the Stone of Scone, and that's no crucifixion,' and, not ever understanding Barry, I took him literally. He gave us little pieces of stiffened burlap with what might be thin white plaster dripped on the burlap.

Jan Hashey and Michael Craig-Martin, who live in Greenwich, organized a picnic on the Greenwich Common. Friends invited were asked to bring picnic food, which, on the blanket, did not appear to have the congruity of a picnic. Jan and Michael's daughter Jessica, ten or so, was very impressed when David Hockney arrived with a crate of oranges. David wore a pale green suit and a red knitted tie. Barry and Sue Flanagan were there, he wearing his three-piece tweed suit and sandals without socks; when I asked him how he was, he said, 'It's all coming in through the toes,' which Sue, smiling, clearly understood, and if their young daughters Samantha and Tara didn't, they seemed to accept as a matter of fact that a father is not necessarily understood. Mark Lancaster arrived, apparently having come, as always, from an exclusive club he had access to, Stephen Buckley with him.

Thinking about works of art: Jan – who, Michael said, was at Yale when he and Jennifer Bartlett and Richard Serra were there, and who was the best of them all – does drawings of domestic objects, such as a brown bowl, on two overlapping sheets of paper, a sheet of carbon paper between, so the top drawing is in full colour and the one under is a ghost of the bowl so the bowl becomes mysterious, and yet remains the depiction of a simple bowl, implying to me a lively irony that may be an irony that Jan herself enjoys – say, in ending a meal at her and Michael's with simple frozen orange pops, which pops suggest all kinds of ironies about being original in the face of not being able to afford anything more elaborate than pops, and, too, about the pop culture we seem to live in, a culture Jan is vividly aware of. Jan certainly has style, and will appear wearing an Ossie Clark snakeskin bomber jacket or a Vidal Sassoon haircut, always appearing to be stylish within the wider awareness that style is in so many ways culture, and this makes me see Jan as more acutely aware of the culture I suppose I too live in but am in no way as aware of as she is. She makes me wish that I had more style, and that I could be as stylish as she is in serving frozen orange pops at the end of a carefully thought-out meal. And I must mention that the meal is served within, but not on, a Barry Flanagan tablecloth: a sheet of burlap from which all the rectangles at the place settings are cut out and folded back to expose the table top with the plates and glasses and knives and forks, all of which place settings would be covered if the cut-out flaps were folded down, and so the meal becomes something of a Barry Flanagan art work.

One afternoon, Michael came round to our flat to show us his latest work: little 'stories,' as he called them, written on file cards, one sentence to a card, and each story has to do with a different way in which he saw himself and how he thought others saw him.

———

How odd it is to see in public places works by artists one knows, or simply has met, such as the mosaics designed by Eduardo Paolozzi in the Tottenham Court tube station –

And, to see, in an exhibition, a portrait by Lucian Freud of Kitty Godley, staring out with wide eyes and apparently strangling a cat she is unaware of – Kitty, the daughter of the sculptor Jacob Epstein, married to Wynne Godley, economist, who asked me if I thought it a good idea to buy an old, semi-ruined house in Italy, which Nikos and I did and then sold to great profit, almost as though we were speculators in property, so I said yes; but Wynne and Kitty seem to lose more and more money, moving from lesser and lesser houses, until they live in a workman's cottage in the high street of a provincial town, and we have lost contact with them. I look at the portrait of Kitty with the wonder of knowing her and yet, in the portrait, of not knowing her at all, as if in the portrait Kitty has the most esoteric relationship with the Kitty we know.

———

Dinner at Anne Wollheim's, Nikos and me and Ben Nicolson.

Ben said that Virginia Woolf would make fun of him whenever he was invited, by Royal Command, to Buckingham Palace: 'Poor Ben, having to go to the Palace.' He laughed his long nasal laugh.

He told us this: as a boy he visited his grandmother who told him that his mother, Vita Sackville-West, was a raging lesbian and as for his father, Harold Nicolson, he was never out of bed with Raymond Mortimer, which information he thought about on his bicycle back to Knole, where he asked his mother if she was in fact a raging lesbian and as for his father was he never out of bed with Raymond Mortimer, to which they answered, simply, yes. Telling the story, Ben laughed a kind of deep gurgling laugh.

Anne has a constant look of bemusement and will almost always make a comment about what she has said, 'Well, I'm not sure,' and run her tongue over her lips.

She will suddenly, unexpectedly, reveal past friendships, such as Henry Green, whom she knew as Henry Yorke.

She rang me to ask if I had rosary beads, as her former husband Philip Toynbee, living in a commune with his second wife Sally, had converted, or hoped to convert, to Catholicism, and he wanted rosary beads to say his prayers on. I do have a number of rosaries, placed without my knowing in my suitcase by my mother every time I visit and found on my return, and I offered her one, to be passed on to Philip Toynbee. She invited Nikos and me to dinner and I gave her the rosary. I didn't know that Anne was brought up a Catholic, but when I expressed some hint of common interest, she laughed a light laugh and sniffed and said, 'No, no.'

After a supper party at Anne's, I spoke with Alexi Russell, a former wife of John Russell, she leaning against a door jamb as if for support and I in front of her. In a low, rather sad voice, she said, 'If you and Nikos live long enough together, you'll find that what you now think of as detracting from love – age spots, wrinkles, all of that – will make you love each other more.'

What came to me, forcefully, is this: that Nikos and I are in London loved as a loving couple.

Anne had just bought an antique rug which Nikos got down on his hands and knees to examine. He said, 'Anne, there's a defect in your rug.' She said, 'Go home, Nikos, go home.'

———

Ben Nicolson delights in telling stories, his delight making him seem to gurgle as he speaks. Here is one: J. P. Morgan had a very big nose, grotesquely big. A society lady invited him to dinner, and thought she would put her attractive daughter next to him to entertain him, but she warned her daughter not to stare at Mr. Morgan's nose and in no way refer to noses. All during the meal, the lady was apprehensive about her daughter offending Mr. Morgan by referring to noses, all too possible because she was warned not to. But all went well, the lady congratulating her daughter. In the drawing room after, the lady, serving coffee, asked, 'Mr. Morgan, how much sugar do you take in your nose?' Ben laughed, his laughter even more of a gurgle.

He said about his daughter Vanessa, 'I will accept everything about her, but if I find she is uncivil I will come down on her –' and here he slapped one palm against another hard – 'like a ton of bricks.' His wife, Luisa Vertova Nicolson, lives in Florence. What their relationship is I can only think of as incomprehensibly British.

He seems to be in love with a young beautiful man with dense black curly hair called Simon, whose interest in art history Ben encourages.

Ben's great expertise is Caravaggio and his followers the Caravaggisti.

I tell myself not to make comments, but simply describe, but how can I keep myself from noting that Ben is one of the most loveable men I have ever known?

———

Among the people we meet at Anne Wollheim's dinner parties are the art historian Francis Haskell and his Russian wife Larissa. He had been to Moscow and there visited Guy Burgess, who had escaped, or was allowed to escape, to Moscow after it was discovered he'd been a spy for the Russians. Francis said that Guy Burgess stood in the middle of his sitting room and looked up at the chandelier which he knew was bugged so everything he said would be heard, and he shouted, 'I hate Russia.'

As Francis and Larissa stay with John Fleming and Hugh Honour, Nikos and I were able to make a connection through them, even share in what it is like to stay in the Villa Marchio.

———

Sylvia Guirey does paintings of many many dots on canvas. She gave me one, of many black dots, based, she told me, on an idea I gave her, so she has dedicated the work as from me.

Nikos and I often go to her for her meals, cooked on a cooker with large iron burners in large copper pots and pans.

She gave to Nikos a delightful spoof cookbook that she wrote, called La Cuisinière Provençale, based on a recipe for cooking sausages:

She put in thyme, a bay leaf, pepper and celery salt.

Couvez et laissez cuire . . .

She found the corkscrew and opened a bottle of white wine.

　She poured some into the pan, stirring as it hissed all around
　the sausages and smelled bright and brown.

She poured herself a glass of wine.

The man came in.

She poured him one too.

He said he would read his newspaper. He read the financial page.

She put the wine back in the refrigerator. She read the recipe
　again.

Sylvia has a Philip Guston abstract painting.

She likes to shop in a shop at the World's End with a large clock in the window the hands of which go backwards very quickly. The shop seems to specialize in black leather skirts and black very high stiletto-heeled shoes.

Minor, I suppose, but perhaps not, to note that when I used the word 'drapes,' Sylvia, as if she heard in that word all my American background, corrected me with 'curtains,' which I assumed to be what Americans of her background say.

———

Francis King to supper with the writer Olivia Manning.

In London, I see people in the context of their lives more than for the few hours we are together; so I see Olivia Manning within the context of her Balkan Trilogy, which I take to be autobiographical and, as autobiography, history, for in those three novels she recorded not only the displacement of the British in Romania, in Greece, in Egypt, in Palestine because of World War II, but the disassembling of the British Empire. She appears, in herself, to be displaced, dissatisfied, as though something were missing that would make her whole and that something whole, perhaps once imagined to be possible, is now known never to have been possible.

Olivia is thin, almost gaunt, and she whines, as though inside her are taut fine wires through which she speaks.

'What should I read?' she asked with a whine. 'I've read everything I want to read. I have nothing left to read.'

Perhaps, she thought, she would write a book about cats; everyone loves cats.

Francis sustained a sad smile.

I remark, in the Trilogy, someone saying about another, 'He rides the choo-choo.'

———

At Anne Wollheim's we met Ben Nicolson's wife Luisa Vertova Nicolson, whom Anne seemed uncertain about, as if Luisa might suddenly say something outrageous. She did go on about Harold Acton and how Harold will not recognize the fact that he has a half-sister in Florence, though all of Florence knows that Harold's father had a mistress with whom he had a daughter.

I like the 'all of Florence,' which seems to me a nineteenth-century term that really only applied to the English and American community there, with perhaps some Florentine aristocrats married into the community. I doubt that there was as much contact between that 'all of Florence' and the 'all of Florence' of the old Florentine families which Henry James fantasized about. There is no contact at all in the novels of E. M. Forster, his middle-class English very much a foreign community enclosed within itself in Florence, any contact with primitive sexual Italians as shocking as it is tempting, Forster's fantasy.

The fantasy of other countries!

I once read Henry James' comment: for an American all things foreign are sacred.

Luisa said that Harold's mother would not have anything to do with Florence, not after the way she was treated by the Fascists at the beginning of the war – imprisoned with prostitutes as an enemy alien – and in no way would the Uffizi get the Michelozzo painting of the Holy Family the museum wants. What Harold will do with La Pietra she didn't know, but she did know that Oxford University had turned down the offer to inherit it.

———

Nikos has translated poems by Yannis Ritsos to be published as a volume in the Penguin series of Modern European Poets. Ritsos, the winner of the Lenin Peace Prize for Literature and renowned in Russia, has been sent by the Greek dictators into internal exile, in a concentration camp on an island, where he continues to write, his poems now referring directly to ancient Greece. These poems move Nikos most:

. . . the symposia of our philosophers have all vanished . . .

Our paper and our books are burned, / the honour of our country lost.

. . . a cloud at sunset, deep, violet, moving, behind the barbed wire . . .

. . . maybe a new Kimon will arrive one day, secretly led / by the same eagle, and he'll dig and find our iron spear point, / rusty, and that too almost disintegrated, and he might go / to Athens and carry it in procession of mourning or triumph / with music and with wreaths.

Perhaps in response to the dictatorship in Greece, Nikos tells me about ancient Greek history as if he himself is renewing it, as when he told me that the leader of the Athenea, the yearly festival of Athens, was a young man especially chosen for his beauty, who for a year was not allowed to touch metal, and in a pure white robe led the procession up the massively cobbled way and up into the Acropolis and into the Parthenon.

How could I not see Nikos as the leader of the procession?

And how could this not bring tears to my eyes?

Strangely, this comes to me: that the only 'impure' part of Nikos' life I can think of, which he was forced into, was his time in the military when he had to wear a uniform and was made to shoot a rifle and use a bayonet.

Michael Craig-Martin has had an exhibition that consisted entirely of an ordinary glass of water on a high glass shelf, the glass itself the idea one would have of an ordinary glass. The glass of water on the glass shelf is high up on a blood-red wall, the whole length of Waddington Gallery. But, as an accompanying card informed, printed in red on white pasteboard, the glass of water is no longer a glass of water but an oak tree.

Michael was brought up a Catholic, which he has, as I have, rejected, but what else but his religion informs the miracle of the transubstantiation of the glass of water into an oak tree?

But, more than our shared Catholic pasts, I have my own view of Michael's work – which he seems to respect but not to be convinced by – in our both having been taught by Jesuits. I went to Jesuit Boston College and was taught Scholastic epistemology, which discipline has remained with me as my essential sense in my own apprehension of the world. I like to think that Michael was just long enough at the Jesuit university of Fordham to have been inspired by some idea of Scholastic epistemology, and to be intrigued by the mental process by which a specific object such as a glass of water is held in a state of momentary suspension before it is judged as this or that glass of water, so that in that state of suspension, of apprehension, the water glass becomes an oak tree.

———

We've become regular guests at the Queen Anne house of Adrian and Ann Stokes in Hampstead, with sherry first in the sitting room hung with a large nude by William Coldstream, and considered by Adrian a major work. Dinner downstairs in the basement, by the Aga, the table laid with Ann's pottery, with large ceramic animals as centrepieces.

Adrian especially warm towards Nikos, whom he embraces whenever we arrive, Nikos appearing to revive in Adrian a youthful erotic attraction to someone as attractive as Nikos.

As for worlds revolving around Adrian – think of Ezra Pound, think of Osbert Sitwell, think of all the Saint Ives artists including Barbara Hepworth and Ben Nicholson and Naum Gabo and . . .

And Adrian knew D. H. Lawrence, whom he visited when Lawrence lived in Italy, in the Villa Mirenda – not only knew Lawrence, but delivered Lady Chatterley's Lover to Lawrence's Italian publisher Orioli, no doubt reading that novel on the train!

Nikos is very impressed that Adrian was analyzed by Melanie Klein, and thinks that the great disappointment in Adrian's life is that analysis could not cure his daughter Ariadne of schizophrenia.

———

R. B. Kitaj is painting an almost life-size portrait of Nikos.

R.B. and his wife Sandra come to meals, or we go to them. At their large round dining table there are always interesting people to meet, as if R.B. (Nikos calls him Ron, but he prefers R.B. or, simply, Kitaj) sees his friends as references to the richness of culture as he sees the figures in his paintings as referring, too, to the richness of culture.

His library, with high shelves of books, forms part of his studio, there where a punching bag hangs, and I easily imagine Kitaj punching the bag when he gets frustrated at a painting not going well.

He can have a mad look.

There are so many references in his paintings. In the branches of a tree hung what looked like red ribbon, and I asked him what it referred to. He said, off-handedly, 'I just wanted a bit of red there,' which impressed me, for I sometimes think that Kitaj will sacrifice composition to the references.

At the large round table in the basement kitchen, Nikos and I have met the very old American painter Raphael Soyers and his wife. R.B. is keen on artists of the 1940s Fourteenth Street School of painters that included Reginald Marsh, Isabel Bishop, Kenneth Hayes Miller, all figurative artists, as R.B. is trying to promote figures in paintings as opposed to abstraction.

Other people we've met at their dinners:

The painter Avigdor Arikha and his wife Anne.

The film maker Kenneth Anger, whose Inauguration of the Pleasure Dome I'd seen years before. As good looking as he was, I was frightened of him because I'd heard he was under a satanic bond to kill someone.

The poet Robert Duncan, whose portrait Kitaj has drawn and who clearly has exhausted both Kitaj and Sandra by his relentlessly inventive talk, as he exhausted Nikos and me when he came to supper, theorizing about, say, Gertrude Stein in terms of the inner tensions in her work, his mind, it seems, filled with inner tensions that flash out in different directions while one tries to make the connections among all the flashes. His lover Jess Collins sat back.

Robert gave us some of his books of poems, with photomontages by Jess. So we are building up a collection of signed books given to us.

Also at Kitaj and Sandra's, we met a coroner, who said that there was nothing more beautiful than the naked chest of a dead young man.

When you meet someone at Kitaj and Sandra's, you feel the person must be rather esoteric to be of interest to them, and, in meeting this esoteric person, you hope you are rather esoteric too.

Kitaj, an American, wants to belong to what he calls the London School of Painters, wants, I think, to become as much a part of the art world of London as Whistler and Sargent were.

He is close to David Hockney, with whom he appeared on the front cover of the New Review, both of them naked, arms across shoulders.

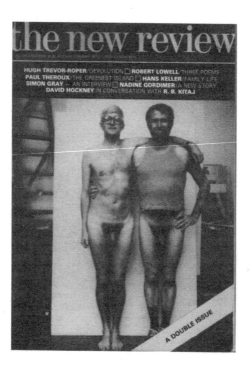

Sandra asked to paint my portrait – in the nude, if I didn't mind.
I didn't mind. Then she suggested I come again and pose with
another male model, very sexy, both of us nude. 'And you never
know what will happen.'

She and R.B. go to Amsterdam to the live sex shows and afterwards clap.

Kitaj likes to go to the airport and take the next flight out to
wherever, the last time to Athens, where he went to a whorehouse
and waited until a large woman came out and, raising her arms
high, shouted, 'America!' He tells this story before Sandra, who
laughs, I think a strained laugh.

Their understanding is: never with friends.

Sandra is very beautiful, with a wide white smile.

———

I have no idea what it is in me that responds so with the love of
details, so that, on a walk in the Wiltshire countryside, Nikos and I
spending a weekend with Joe and Jos Tilson, I, after the visit and
back in London, can remember almost nothing of the conversation,
but remember details of the countryside, and in accounting for as
many details as I can remember I feel that the visit is now fixed on a
walk through an arboretum with the sunlight level through the tall,
thin, straight poplar trees, the branches high up so the trunks are
bare, the sunlight and shadows appearing to multiply the tree trunks,
so I am in an imaginary wood; and, too, I am imagining the bracken
on either side of the path, bent, bright green, thinly serrated fronds;
as I am imagining the mushrooms in open spaces among the bracken,
imagining a brown beer bottle, an old shoe, a tin, the details all
together demanding that I make something more of them than what
they are, this something more my love of them.

And at the same time I am accounting for the details as I imagine
them – because, of course, they are no longer what they were – a
sense of such tediousness comes over me in the effort of the
accounting that I think, oh, let them all go, it would be a relief to
let them all go, let my possessive love of them go. And I think of

writing without any details, writing in some way that frees me of this possessiveness. Or not writing at all.

Nikos admonishes me: 'Enjoy the event in itself, don't try to possess it, because you falsify it by elaborating on it.'

And I try, I try, I do try not to try to account for all the details of a dinner party on a dining-room table – the large round pan of paella with black mussels and shrimps and red peppers imbedded in the saffron-yellow rice; try not to retain the details of a view from the window of a country pub – hollyhocks in the garden of the public house, seen through a many-paned window, bicycles leaning against a garden shed; try not to possess the details of a parade of cavalry passing – they in tight, dark blue uniforms with yellow braid and a red stripe down the side of the trousers, and dark blue casques with cockades of white plumes, riding horses in parade with silver cannon on large black wheels. I try not to, as much as I honestly do find it a bore to look and then record, but I fail.

———

I've been making pottery at Ann Stokes' two afternoons a week, listening, as if in sympathy with the Greeks, to Greek bouzouki music. (Nikos is indifferent to bouzouki, as he is indifferent to anything he deems folklore. He is keen on Ann's pottery, of which he has bought stacks of plates, cups and saucers, bowls at her annual pottery sale, and she has given us vessels copied from ancient Greek types. When Ann made, in ceramics, a Free Greece medallion, and gave it to Nikos, he was very touched.) Adrian paints up at the top of the house in his studio, and comes down at tea time and we all have tea. I made a version of a Minoan storage jug, about three feet high.

Natasha saw it during one of Ann's pottery sales and wanted to buy it for the garden of their house in the South of France, to go at the end of a cypress avenue. I gave it to her. We were talking very easily with one another and tensed up, both of us, only when Stephen came to find out what we were talking about.

———

Sometimes I wonder who, really, are our close friends? and answer myself, the people I write about in my diary, and these include our friend Stephenie Bergman.

Stef lived for a while in Soho, her lover a man whose business was making pornographic films. When he died, Stef did what he had requested be done with his ashes: strew them in the gutters of Soho.

Stef is a ceramicist, and works in the pottery of Ann Stokes. We have some of her pots, collected by many people.

After one of her supper parties, she wheeled in from another room a large ceramic lorry loaded with oranges.

Her great friend is Roxy Beaujolais.

After an event in London we'd attended together, they, Stef driving, said they'd take me home. We crossed Battersea Bridge, in the middle a stand where hot dogs and drinks are sold and always surrounded by bikers in black leather jackets and their big black motorcycles. Stef said to Roxy or Roxy to Stef, 'Let's get rid of David and come back here for some fun.'

Roxy is a publican, and is the best-connected person I know in London, from politicians to City gents to artists.

She likes to wear her dress with the top slung low to expose her beautiful shoulders.

Nikos makes no generalizations about poets, but sees each in his or her self, and as an editor he remains open to whatever world they may come from. So, he has published in one volume of Penguin Modern Poets John Heath-Stubbs and F. T. Prince and Stephen Spender, and in another Geoffrey Grigson and Edwin Muir and Adrian Stokes.

He is especially moved by Adrian's poem 'Schizophrenic Girl', about his daughter Ariadne, his beautiful unbending daughter, who keeps at bay the horror of her nothingness.

At the Stokes' house, she would sometimes come into the room where I was alone working on a pot, and she would simply stand against a wall and stare. Once she undressed and stood naked, and I went on working until Ann came in and took her out. Another time she dropped a torn bit of paper on the floor near me and left and I picked up the paper and read, in upper-case letters, MUDDLE HEADED. She has been accepted into a home run by nuns, where she will spend her life.

———

I'm sometimes surprised by the independent intellectual life Nikos has. His main interest is in aesthetics, which was his graduate concentration at Harvard University. Hearing him talk to Adrian Stokes or Richard Wollheim about aesthetics, it occurs to me that they are all within a sphere of interest that is theirs, and into which I can't enter. I am always very pleased that Nikos should be within that sphere, partly because I admire his superior knowledge and intelligence, and also because, as we are a couple, his superior knowledge and intelligence reflect back on me as if I were someone who would be equal to him in conversation with Adrian and Richard, while, on the other side of the sitting room, I am talking to Ann or Day about pottery. But I do hear enough of their conversation to recognize that the main topic with Adrian and Richard has to do with the psychoanalytic interpretation of aesthetics, a subject, I feel, that is very much within the circle of philosophers and psychoanalysts referred to in their conversations, such as Donald Winnicott and, most meaningfully, Melanie Klein.

Adrian had analysis with Melanie Klein.

I know of Nikos' interest, but I was surprised when, one evening on his return from work, he asked me what I thought of his starting Kleinian analysis.

I didn't know what that meant.

It was the most rigorous form of analysis, starting as far back as the good or bad breast.

This seemed to me to have nothing to do with our relationship, so I said I thought if he wanted to go into that analysis, he should. I imagined it had to do with some deep – the deepest – appreciation of the aesthetic. Nikos has collected a significant library about aesthetics, and I imagined his wanting to go under analysis was a more profound investigation into the state of mind when we think of something as beautiful. He inspired me with the acute sense of beauty – in his poetry, and also, when we were together on, say, an Underground train and he would whisper about a woman standing at the other end, 'How beautiful she is!' someone whose looks I would have not noted at all – and I believed I would, on his enhancement of his sense of the beautiful by analysis, find my sense also enhanced.

Through Richard, he was able to have a meeting with Hanna Segal, the custodian of the analytical approach of Melanie Klein. When he came back from the meeting, he told me that she had asked him basic questions – what kind of homosexual was he? promiscuous, in that he went cottaging (a term neither he nor I had heard of, but that means having sex in public loos, as Hanna Segal had had to explain to Nikos), or monogamous? He told her about us, and she said that if he were to enter into analysis he might find that his relationship with me would change fundamentally, and that he should discuss this possibility with me.

What did I think?

As he asked me this not long ago, I have to ask myself: what do

I think? I'm not sure I think anything. Is it because I feel so secure in our relationship that I don't feel any threat in his talking about our relationship with someone who sees it as if apart from us? I see our relationship from within, and to me the view is steady.

I told him to start analysis.

———

Bruce Chatwin needs to give the impression that he knows everything, needs to be able to tell you, when you stop with him at an antique-shop window off Bond Street, what factory the tea pot came from, and its date. And I'm envious of him because he does seem to know everything – my envy, again, of those who are able to make connections that I'm not able to make.

He invited me to lunch in his new flat in Belgravia. I praised it to him, but thought to myself: it is really very, very tiny. The only object he had hanging on his severe walls was a highly lacquered yin-and-yang disk from a Japanese temple. On a table he had a small collection of objects: a fragment from Persopolis, an Eskimo toggle, a pre-Colombian bit of polished black stone.

As Howard Hodgkin, one of Bruce's closest friends, says, 'Bruce is both mad and a snob about objects.'

The bathroom is very small. I said I love big bathrooms, with large baths, where I do a lot of writing in my head. 'Baths!' Bruce exclaimed. 'Oh, no, no baths! I hate bathing!' He shook his head. 'No, no.'

He placed the food we were to have on the small table – duck breasts and wild rice and a bottle of good wine – and, talking, not about baths which didn't interest him, but about writing, which did interest him, he sat and served himself first, then, still talking, touched the serving dishes with his fingertips to indicate that I should go ahead and serve myself. I was still standing.

In a high voice, speaking as if at a pitch against universal ignorance, Bruce said, 'The fact is that no one has ever understood what Hemingway was trying to do in In our Time. I ask you, has anyone ever asked why he called the vignettes that appear between the stories chapters? The book has to be seen not as a collection but as a whole, and it is, I'm convinced, a Cubist work of fiction.'

I sat and served myself and said that was fascinating.

Bruce ate quickly and went on talking, his voice rising higher and higher in excited pitch. His talk about Hemingway was fascinating.

He asked me if I'd like fresh fig, with a tone that I felt suggested he'd prefer me to say no, thank you. I said yes.

After lunch, he prepared for me a large, brown nut, a silver rim about the opening, filled with maté tea to be sipped through a silver straw with a little silver strainer at the bottom so the powdered tea wouldn't be sucked up, and then he occupied himself, it seemed to me with business: a letter he signed and folded and put into an envelope addressed, I saw because he did hold it so I could see it, to William Shawn of the New Yorker. He showed me a photograph of himself at his most stunningly beautiful, in sandals and a straw hat, and said, 'A photograph of the author.' He showed me an Italian edition of one of his books, of which he read a paragraph. It only occurred to me later that Bruce had left the letter, the photograph, the book about to impress.

When I was leaving, he gave me a copy of In our Time. He gave me a number of books, among them a collection of Ivan Bunin's short stories, and The Chinese Written Character as a Medium for Poetry by Ernest Fenollosa and edited by Ezra Pound. And when he, excited, recommended a book, I went out and found it: Xavier de Maistre's Voyage autour de ma chambre.

His excitements inspire me, but, as usual, I'm not entirely convinced by them, because they seem to me impersonal, not personal, and somewhat affected.

So, for example, Bruce will ring, and I'll ask, banally, 'How are you?', wanting to enter into some personal conversation with him, but he won't answer, and instead say, 'I think I've discovered where the socialist red flag comes from.' He thinks he's traced the flag to the bloody aprons of Argentinean butchers in an abattoir. I suggested he talk to James Joll about this, and he did, and James later told me that Bruce may have a point.

Whenever I hear that Bruce has had sex with some man, I

wonder why I do not find him sexually attractive, as beautiful as he is. He appears to me too bright to have any sexuality, too impersonally bright, as if he doesn't have a deep emotional life, or any great capacity to love. The falseness I feel about him may be the falseness of too much articulated brightness, which belies what to me is a deeper, more inarticulate sexuality. I imagine Bruce talking and talking and talking while making love, as if to make love making all articulation.

Still, I am envious of him for his ability to talk. Nikos does not at all understand this envy.

————

Nikos is disappointed that Hanna Segal will not take him on for analysis, but has recommended a Miss Richards, who has her office in a basement flat in Bayswater. Their first session, Nikos recounted a dream, and Miss Richards, he told me, said, 'You've brought me a gift.' Whatever Nikos thought, I thought this a presumption on the part of Miss Richards. Nikos tells me all his dreams.

————

Nikos is keen that I go on writing my diary, and I wonder if he thinks that I am preserving something that he wants me to preserve. As we have no secrets from each other – in fact, he reads all my post, as I read his – he will from time to time pick up the notebook in which I am currently writing and read. He says my diary makes him aware of what we are doing in a way he hadn't been aware before. And he glosses corrections in the margins.

————

The flat has been filled all day with a succession of redolent smells: the Christmas tree which I brought in this morning, bunches of hyacinths and anemones and irises Nikos brought in, then the smells of cooking cranberries and fresh bread (Nikos makes bread every week) and mincemeat pies, and finally the smell of pine bath salts which spreads out on the heat and steam from the bathroom.

All the smells combine in the awareness that this is my home.

Boxing Day

So many people over the past weekend –

Christmas Eve, Nikos and I went to church briefly, to the Brompton Oratory to light candles, then came back to the flat to have champagne and mince pies and open gifts.

Christmas Day, Richard and Mary Day Wollheim came, Adrian and Ann Stokes, Richard and Sally Morphet, Mark Lancaster, Barry and Sue Flanagan and their daughters Samantha and Tara, and Sylvia Guirey and her sons and daughter. Samantha played her viola. How did we all fit into our small flat?

Then in the evening Nikos and I went to Edna O'Brien's. Sonia and Francis Bacon were there. Francis left early. Sonia stayed and got very drunk, so I thought I should take her home. Nikos was annoyed, and I told him to stay at the party, but he said he'd come with me. (Later, he said I'm a victim of women like Sonia who have made and are responsible for their own hideous lives.) In the taxi, she babbled, in a strident, accusing voice, about how violently unhappy Francis was, George dead only six weeks.

'You don't understand – none of you understands – what desperation is. You won't help. You don't know how to help. I could kill, kill, kill, kill you all for your lack of sensitivity. Francis is suffering. Do any of you care? Do any of you ring him up? Fuck all if you do.'

Nikos got very angry, but contained his anger.

The next time I saw Francis, I said how sorry I was about the death of George, and laughing a little from the side of his mouth Francis shrugged one shoulder.

———

Nikos gave me a printing press as a gift, and the first item I set and printed out, on rough brown paper, was an invitation to be sent out:

NIKOS STANGOS

READING

FROM A WORK IN PROGRESS: PURE REASON

YANNIS RITSOS: A TRANSLATION

THE POETRY SOCIETY

21 EARLS COURT SQ.

While he read from 'Pure Reason' in his light but precise voice, I had a sense of someone near and far, someone I know and don't know, someone who loves me and someone for whom love is out there where love is a universal.

It is in being most abstract in his poems that he is most concrete, as if ideas for him have colour, shape, weight, can be seen and even smelled and touched; at the same time, they are ideas, and do not have colour, shape, weight, cannot be seen or smelled or touched. These antinomies – to use a word that Nikos likes to use himself – of the abstract and the concrete, the present and the absent, the defined and the indefinable, the invisible and the visible, create the ambiguity of both seeing and not seeing, smelling and not smell-ing, touching and not touching, knowing and not knowing, all at the same time.

John Golding, who came to the reading, said about Nikos' poetry that it is 'intellectually and emotionally plangent.'

———

When Steven Runciman taught at Trinity, Cambridge, his first student was Guy Burgess. In his early days, Burgess, though a bit grubby, was bright and had charm. As he got older, the charm got murkier, and after he became a Communist he never washed. 'Everyone knew he was a Communist. All the young men were Communists. They didn't sing too much about it, until the Spanish Civil War, but then people like Guy didn't go off to fight in Spain. In any case, Russia wasn't the enemy then. Russia was subversive, but Germany was the enemy. I rather mocked Guy's Communism, and, as I hated societies, mocked the Apostles, who were a supposedly secret society at the University of Cambridge devoted to high-level talk. When they got into official positions, it was thought they'd converted. I asked Guy, after he got a position with the B.B.C., "What are you doing there? Surely your Communist principles . . ." Guy said, "It is all rather different now.'" It was Burgess who, through machinations, got Steven his first job, in 1940, in the Ministry of Information. The Ministry needed someone to take over the section on Bulgaria, and Burgess knew that Steven read Bulgarian. Shortly afterwards, in the early summer of 1940, Steven was sent to be press attaché in Sofia. He stayed in Bulgaria until the Germans invaded, in 1941. From there to Egypt, Cairo, to organize news broadcasts in the various Balkan languages, Serbo-Croatian and Romanian, as well as Bulgarian. Then to Jerusalem, where he was a film censor for Palestine, which suited him well because there were hardly any films, so he studied religions. 'Religion is a necessary part of the human condition, even if it is a wild anti-religion. I love the study of religion.' At the time there was a détente between the Jews and the Arabs, and Steven used to invite professors of the Hebrew University to meet with Arab intellectuals, for some of the professors of the Hebrew University were deeply interested in Arabic studies. One Orientalist, Leo Mayer, was so highly respected by the Arabs that several learned Hebrew to attend his lectures. It was while he was in Jerusalem that the idea of writing the history of the Crusades came to him. 'Unfortunately – or fortunately – for me, the President of Turkey, driving around the streets of Istanbul one day, saw a building he didn't recognize, and asked what it was. Eventually, someone said he thought it was Byzantine, but no one was able to say more. He said angrily, "Do you mean to say that no one in this city knows anything about Byzantium? After all, it is a period in the history of our country." Turning to the Minister of Education, he said, "Find me a Byzantine professor at once!" The Minister of Education went to see an old friend of mine, the historian of the classical world Michael Grant, then head of the British Council in Turkey, who said they'd better get me. I received a letter from the Foreign

Office instructing me to leave my present job in Jerusalem to go to Istanbul to be a professor. I lectured in English, but the seminars and examinations were in Turkish. If you house-keep in a country, you learn the language.'

Everyone in Istanbul was praying that Anthony Eden, the British Foreign Secretary, would not succeed in bringing Turkey into the war. When the Turks did enter, on the side of the Allies, it was quite clear how the war was going to end. 'Everyone's always suspected me, I find, of being a secret agent when I was in Turkey. Not a bit of it. I was a straightforward Turkish professor. The Turkish secret service was very good at spying. At one time, when I had hepatitis and was recovering at a resort, I talked often with a charming Turk of the secret police who was there and wanted to learn English. He had been in charge of looking after foreigners in Istanbul, and the things he told me about the private lives of my English friends were absolutely amazing – things I hadn't realized. One had to be very careful. When the Italians caved in, they gave all their secret papers to the British, and in their list of British spies I was put at the top. Molto intelligente, molto pericoloso. One of my best tributes, and entirely false.' The Turks were liberal about allowing foreigners to travel as long as they kept away from the military zones, so Steven was able to do most of the Crusader journey. During his holidays, he went to Syria. Because of the appalling climate in Istanbul, he had sciatica for months on end. When the British Council asked him if he would go to Athens to direct its organization, he said he would go for two years, since Athens had a marvellous climate for rheumatism.

———

A Sunday evening, we went to the Spenders' in Loudoun Road for drinks. We were meant to give the impression, which Stephen had asked us to give, that we had never been in the house, which, however, we had been in when Natasha was away. Stephen appeared to be bigger than ever and spilled the wine as he poured it out, and he seemed very bored. Matthew and Maro and their little daughter Saskia, who only understands Italian, were there. Also Johnny Craxton. Natasha dashed about here and there, trying to be kind to Nikos and me as well as to the other guests, telling Stephen to refill glasses, asking Matthew and Maro to show us some of their paintings. She asked Nikos and me to stay on for sandwiches after everyone else had left, and we went down to the kitchen with her to help slice the turkey, butter the bread, get out plates. Nikos all the while, with pressing insistence, was saying how much he liked the house and asking about the paintings in the sitting room upstairs as if he hadn't seen them before. Maro came down and with a kind of cackle said from the side of her mouth, 'What's this little intimate scene all about?' Natasha, Nikos and I laughed, but a terrible boredom descended on me suddenly, and I knew I couldn't any longer sustain any niceness, appreciation, talk, so I became silent and wanted to leave.

But Natasha wanted to talk to me about Sonia. She said that Sonia is helpless and hopeless, and Natasha wondered if it was part of her own neurosis to find herself more and more involved with people the more helpless and hopeless they become.

We were all invited to David Hockney's flat in Powis Terrace for a late party. Stephen said he wouldn't come. Natasha drove Nikos and me, and Johnny followed on his motorbike.

I felt old compared to everyone else at David's – all young people bumping about – but Natasha didn't seem to be aware that she was in any way different. While Nikos, who likes young people, bumped among them, Natasha and I stood apart and talked more about Sonia.

Natasha said, 'Sonia has always been drawn to men who were in one way or another inaccessible – either inaccessibly married, or inaccessibly dying, or inaccessibly queer.'

I left Natasha to get a drink, then didn't return to her, but spoke with Johnny, then to Mark Lancaster and to Keith Milow. I wandered around the flat and found Natasha sitting on the floor in the bedroom watching television. A young man was sitting on the bed, and I sat next to him. He seemed to be a young man only because he didn't have any breasts, though his plump face was hairless and he had shaved his eyebrows and penciled on two long black lines and he wore mascara on his lashes. He told me that his friends are the Queen, the Queen Mother, who likes gin and tonic, and Pablo Picasso.

He said, 'One of my closest friends is Sir Francis Rose. You know who he is, don't you? The intimate friend of Cecil Beaton, Gertrude Stein, and Hitler.'

Natasha didn't seem to pay any attention to him, but continued to watch television. After he left, she looked round at me and asked, 'Who was she?'

I said, 'It was a he.'

Having kept them all, an inveterate archivist, I have been going through masses of papers from as far back as my adolescence – such adolescent essays called IMPROMTUOUS (sic) THOUGHTS ON NOTHING – to insert them into the pages of a bulging note-book of my diary, as if to incorporate the long ago past into the present. My feeling is that I am taking my past before Nikos into my present time with Nikos, but he told me that I am jealous of his going into his past in his present with Miss Richards so I am bring-ing my past into my present.

But, wondering if Nikos talks to Miss Richards about our rela-tionship, I was told by a friend who knows about Kleinian analysis that, as he is only months into his sessions, he has hardly approached the fact of being born.

On a bus home from a dinner party, Nikos said to me, 'You talked too much this evening.'

'Did I?'

'You talked to try to get people there to like you. You want everyone to like you. They think you are trying to impress them.'

'What about me am I trying to impress them with?'

'You talked to be nice, too American-nice, saying over and over, "That's so interesting, that's fascinating, that's wonderful," so no one believed you.'

'Do I do that with you?'

'I make sure you don't.'

'You don't indulge me.'

'No, I don't indulge you in that way.'

'So, I don't try to make you like me, but you do like me.'

He pressed his shoulder against mine and said, 'With some reservations.'

'Thanks.'

'Why is it that Americans so want to be liked?' he asked.

'Am I so American?'

'Aren't you?'

Steven Runciman came to supper, as always with six eggs from his hens wrapped in newspaper.

Steven does not keep secret his grand life as an historian. He holds honorary degrees from the four oldest English universities, Oxford, Cambridge, Durham, London, and from the two oldest Scottish universities, Saint Andrews and Glasgow, and in America his chief honour is to belong to the American Philosophical Society founded by Benjamin Franklin, and in Turkey he was President of the British Institute of Archeology in Ankara, and in Greece Foreign Fellow at the Academy of Athens, and he is an honorary member of the Academy of Palermo and a Corresponding Member of the Royal Academy of History in Madrid. He likes to say that when he is at a gala dinner, at, say, an embassy, he will, just by looking at the other guests, know where he will be seated. And he likes to refer to his 'royal' cousins on the Continent, whom he sometimes visits.

And, too, he will say he and George Orwell, then known as Eric Blair, were at Eton together, taught by Aldous Huxley.

He is not an Englishman – or, rather, Scot – who keeps to himself the people he knows and has known, but, with a display of amused wonder, his chin raised and with a vague smile, will recount how he played piano duets with the last Emperor of China, Henry Pu Yi.

Steven talking:

After he got his degree, in 1924, he stayed up in Cambridge to study with the older historian Bury, who never took on students but took on Steven because Steven was interested in Byzantium, which no proper historian at the time was interested in, assuming, as influenced by Gibbon, the one thousand years were years of Roman decadence. He came down with flu, which led to pleurisy, and he was quite ill for a time. Doctors in those times used to say, 'The boy should go on a long sea voyage.' He told his parents he would go on such a voyage if he could go to China, so he went to China. He arrived in the middle of a civil war. Though he hoped to go straight to Peking, he had a high fever, and by the time he was well again the civil war had broken off connections. This meant he was stuck in Tianjin where Feng Yuxiang, the Christian warlord, was besieging the troops of Zhang Zuolin, the Manchu warlord.

(I have to break off here to insist that as Steven talks, he remembers the names of all the historical figures, and I stop him to ask him to spell the names, which he does as if annoyed.)

He was staying with the consul-general, a cousin, at the British Consulate. Tianjin was not an exciting town, just a port town without antiquities. The Chinese Emperor, Henry Pu Yi, aged about twenty, was living there in the Japanese garrison. One day, his Australian tutor came to see the consul-general about some matter, and when the tutor met Steven he asked him if he played the piano.

'A little,' Steven replied.

'Oh, just a little is needed,' the tutor said. 'The Emperor's started having piano lessons and likes simple duets in which he plays the top part with both hands together while someone goes thump-thump on the bass.'

Would Steven come?

He went twice to the imperial residence and thump-thumped on the bass while the Emperor played nursery rhymes with both hands in unison, and when they stopped they had excellent tea and then talked a bit. He was an etiolated young man, not good-looking, with a tremendous air of aristocracy. He spoke quite good English, and told Steven that since he had the greatest admiration

for the Tudors he called himself Henry. He didn't like his chief
wife, whom he called Mary, after Bloody Mary, but his chief
concubine was charming, and she was Elizabeth. Steven was not
allowed to meet the imperial ladies.

The Emperor remained a puppet of the Japanese for years, as the
Emperor of Manchukuo, until Mao conquered Manchuria. The
Emperor didn't mind. If the Japanese wanted him to be an emperor
he would be an emperor; if Mao wanted him to be a market
gardener, he would be a market gardener. Mao liked him, and got
him to write his autobiography – or, rather, sign one written for
him. The last that Steven heard of him was from Queen Maria José
of Italy, the daughter of the Red Queen – Queen Elisabeth of the
Belgians, who always visited Communist states before anyone else
did. In the early sixties, Queen Maria José went to China with her
mother, and Mao provided as their dragoman the ex-Emperor – a
charming gesture of Mao. 'She told me about it when she got back,
and I said I wished I'd known beforehand, because I'd liked to have
known how the Emperor's piano playing was getting on, though I
fear it would have been discarded. He died soon after.'

Nikos told him about his beginning with analysis, and Steven,
the last person to have any understanding of the value of undergo-
ing analysis, looked at me first as with an attempt to understand
what I thought, which was, really, nothing, then he said to Nikos,
'I would suggest a long sea voyage.'

———

When I stare at – stare into – this photograph of Nikos as a boy long,
long before I met him, a sense of incomprehension comes to me that we
did meet, in the same way that when a coincidence occurs there also
occurs a strange sense that the coincidence has a meaning, but a meaning
just beyond one's comprehension of it. I can name the contingencies
that came together in our meeting – simply, that I was given his telephone number by a mutual friend in Boston and told to ring him when
I arrived in London – but the contingencies don't add up to understanding that elusive meaning of our meeting, a meaning rather beyond the

contingencies. That we did meet strikes me all the more strange, the meaning of our meeting all the more elusive, because I cannot, staring and staring into his photograph, connect with that boy, so remote from me in his different world that there is no way I could have met him; and, not having been able to connect with him then, my connecting with him now seems so strange, the meaning of our connecting so incomprehensible as to be – to use a word he uses – mysterious.

I stare more deeply into the photograph, and wish I could have known him as he was then, and, too, to have loved him then, and in my love have saved him from what he now appears to me to be in his delicate beauty: vulnerable, lonely, unhappy.

And then this happens: mysteriously connected, I see into the photograph of Nikos as a boy Nikos now, and project the loneliness, the vulnerability, the unhappiness of Nikos as a boy onto Nikos now, and I love him with the impulse to save him from the vulnerability, the loneliness, the unhappiness I see in him now.

He calls out to me, as he very often calls out to me, 'Where is the book I was reading?' and I go to try to find what he can't find and is irritated at not finding, suspecting that the cleaning lady misplaced it, or I did.

———

Roxy and Stef, who are something of a collective conscience to me, tell me I drop names.

———

In warning me that I may be basing my life too much on Stephen's, is Sonia warning me against the possible allegation that Stephen is so social his poetry is incidental to his social self? And Natasha, she claims, is as social.

How could I tell her that Stephen and Natasha impress me for their enthusiasm for going to and giving parties? Sonia would ridicule both Stephen and Natasha and me by my recounting Stephen once telling me that he and Natasha were in a quandary, as they had invited Philippe and Pauline de Rothschild to dinner but worried about what wine to serve, so Stephen rang the Wine Society to explain the problem and ask for advice. Stephen so enjoys social life, and so does Natasha. I wonder if one of the reasons why Stephen and Natasha do bond is in their attraction to going to and giving parties. Perhaps I am open to the allegation of wanting a lively social life, that I, unlike Nikos but like Stephen, so enjoy going to and giving parties.

Why will someone such as Steven Runciman be found amusing for his social life and Stephen not? Is it because they are from different classes? I came to London with the American idea that British society is structured by class, and that the classes range from the working-class navvies who work digging in the streets up to the Queen, and now I find that all this, too, becomes a cloud of unknowing. Is Steven, from a Scottish ship-owning family, upper class? I once heard Stephen Spender tell Elizabeth Glenconner that he is middle class. Perhaps it would be best not to think of classes, but of social worlds, so that Runciman belongs to a social world and Spender to another, and the navvies belong to a social world and the Queen belongs to a social world, and though the worlds overlap, they sort of float about in the cloud that is Britain.

Steven, in his world, amuses himself and amuses others, not

simply because he so enjoys it, but because of the high-pitched wit and irony in his voice which suggests that such enjoyment must not be taken seriously, must amuse; and Stephen is from a world without such irony, so his social life does not amuse. If there is irony in Stephen, it is mostly in self-deprecation; Steven's irony has a high degree of self-regard in it. Or so I sense. If I were Proust, I would develop this, especially from the point of view of Nikos and me, for though we are friends with both Stephen and Steven, they are hardly friends with each other, but seem to belong in different worlds within the world of Great Britain.

Steven has, he has said, 'endless anecdotes,' and will ask, 'Would you like to hear the story of my dancing with a lady who danced with the Prince Consort, Albert?'

Yes, we would.

'She was the daughter of the Duke of Montrose. Her mother was, I think, the Mistress of the Robes at the time that she came out, at the age of seventeen, and so a ball was given for her at Windsor, and, as it was for her, the Prince Consort danced with her. I met her when I was in my late twenties and she was in her eighties. I remember I sat next to her at lunch, and then I met her a little while later at a party where there was dancing. I very seldom dance – except in Scottish reels, at which I am quite good – but I couldn't resist when she suggested we might take a few steps together. She knew perfectly well why I was doing it, and after about three or four minutes – she really was past it, and I never really got to it – she said, "Well, now you can say you danced with someone who danced with the Prince Consort."'

He made a face as of mocking himself, drawing down the corners of his lips in the opposite of a smile, and he looked away.

———

Christopher Isherwood is staying at a friend's in South Kensington. He asked me to visit. I brought along a copy of The Ghost of Henry James and held it out to him when he opened the door, and he, seeing it, exclaimed, 'I've already read it! I love it!' and he showed me into the sitting room and pointed to a copy propped on the mantel of the fireplace.

As enthusiastic as he was, I felt something put on in the enthusiasm, as if he was trying to impress me for more than his enthusiasm about the novel, but with his own ability to enthuse exuberantly. I felt this, too, in the way he would from time to time exclaim, 'Gee!' the exclamation seemingly unrelated to whatever he was exclaiming 'gee!' about. I thanked him but kept my thanks somewhat reserved, because Nikos has told me often that I can sound affected by overstating my appreciation of another's appreciation of me, which affectation he calls the American need to be liked by everyone. Has Christopher himself become American in that way, for I so felt he wanted me to like him? I recall Stephen telling me that Auden said of Isherwood that he was 'falsch,' using the German, so perhaps Christopher has always given the impression of overstating both approval and disapproval in an over-exuberant way.

We went to a restaurant where we sat at a small square table with a votive candle between us, his gaunt but young face lit by the candle as he leaned towards me to speak. Again, I felt there was an overstatement in his telling me how happy he was that his lover, Don Bachardy, was now having sex with someone in London, Don Bachardy in bed with someone else as Christopher and I sat across from one another at the restaurant table.

He asked me if Nikos and I have an open relationship. I said, no, no, not really. Though Nikos has said that I can do whatever I want, he has also said I must not go to him after as if he were a father confessor and ask for his forgiveness. And, really, why should I have ever wanted to make love with anyone else when I have him?

Christopher smiled a rather compressed smile.

He did not ask more about Nikos, nor did he mention Stephen.

What did I feel, on my way home, about having spent the evening with someone who had been to me one of those mythological figures in a mythological world of cabaret? I felt that that world was 'falsch,' appropriately defined so in German because of

Christopher's Berlin stories, and that any attempt to hold it with nostalgia against the horrors of history – oh, to be in Weimar Berlin and indulge with wonderful freedom in sex while the Nazi troops are parading the streets! – is a very great affectation.

More and more, mythologies I once fantasized participating in fall apart when I am in contact with the people whom I once imagined mythological.

I told this to Stephen when I next saw him, and he stared at me, as if it hadn't occurred to him that I could begin to be critical of a world that I, standing outside, had no right to criticize.

Stephen once told me that his first sexual experience was with Wystan Auden when they were undergraduates at Oxford, any mythological vision of which has to be mitigated by Auden, in his rooms made dim by the curtains drawn all day, saying to Stephen, 'Now, dear, don't make a fuss,' and Stephen, always complying with a giggle to the matter-of-factness of Auden, not making a fuss.

———

After supper, sitting with Nikos on the sofa and together listening to music – Artur Schnabel playing a Beethoven sonata, the music as always chosen by Nikos, to whom I defer – I looked at him, his head lowered and his eyes closed to concentrate, and I wondered what his inner world is. Again and yet again, I imagine that inner world more historical, and as evolved from his history more cultural, than psychological. Today, he had a session with his analyst, and though he didn't talk about the session, and I did not ask him about it, I realize more than before that I'm not interested. I do not believe psychoanalysis can reveal in him what would be revealed by his history, by his culture, history and culture in one; and I think of Nikos' character, the character of his inner world, as formed by what I like to think the aristocracy of his being a Greek, of being able to claim a lineage, century upon century, through ancient Greece, through Hellenism, through Roman conquest, through Byzantium, even through the fall of Constantinople and the Ottoman occupation, through Revolution, and, as he lived it all, through Nazi occupation and through Civil War, through his education in Europe and America, through a Greece struggling to assert the ideals that Greece stands for, the surviving lineage evident, as I envisage him, in his delicate features, in the way his head is lowered and his eyes are closed as he concentrates on the music.

———

Because of the success of The Ghost of Henry James, I was asked by a producer at the BBC. if I'd be interested in doing a filmed tour of the house in Rye where he wrote his great novels.

The occupants of Lamb House are the novelist Rumer Godden and her husband. Part of the agreement in renting the house is that they would show visitors about, a duty I felt they found imposed on them a little when it came to a young American who couldn't know as much about Henry James as they did, and for whom it would have been more appropriate to give a televised tour. I did say I had read Godden's novel The River and liked it very much indeed. She gave me tea in the sitting room and informed me, as if to make her own presence more felt by me, that all the furniture in the room was hers. I recall chintz-covered armchairs and misty white curtains over the windows through which the trees outside were diffused into bright green blurs.

I had no sense of the presence of Henry James – none at all – and wondered what I had expected. In fact, according to Godden, there was very little in the house that had belonged to James, and all of what remained was in one room, just off the entry hall, which James called the telephone room as the telephone receiver was kept there. This was, if the truth be told, the only room normally open to visitors, at certain hours. I asked if I could see into it. Rumer Godden said, 'You won't see much,' and she and her husband let me go on my own.

The door to the telephone room was open. Inside, I looked at what had been recovered since the nineteen-forties, when most of James' possessions were sold at auction: his desk, some photographs, a walking stick, a cigar cutter, some books from his library. There was no telephone. Feeling low, and feeling, too, all the pretensions of my expectation, whatever my expectation had been, I left the room and closed the door. My hand on the door handle, it occurred to me that James had held the same handle and closed the same door, and a shiver passed up my arm.

When I returned to the sitting room, the tea things had been cleared, and Rumer Godden was gone. Her husband stood there, and I knew I must go. But, perhaps to make up for something, the husband, whose name I hadn't heard, told me there were still books from Henry James' library – old, uncut French novels – which I might find in secondhand bookshops in Rye, if I cared to look. He also said that James' knife boy – a boy who sharpened and cleaned the knives before stainless steel was invented and did other chores and errands – Burgess Noakes was still alive, and if I went to a certain pub I'd be bound to see him, a small, crumpled man, who would talk to me about James in exchange for a pint. Godden's husband warned me, however, that if I did speak to Noakes I'd find he remembered little about Henry James, and was not interested except for his pint.

I thought I wouldn't go to the pub, but I happened to pass it on my way down the hill on which Rye is built, and, drawn as I was to make whatever connections were available to me, I went in. The inside was musty and hardly lit with sunlight through the small windows, and there I saw a small crumpled man standing at the bar, wearing a hearing aid and blinking. I thought he must be Burgess Noakes, and I wanted to shake his hand, but he appeared too isolated to approach. I left.

Yes, gone, the ghost of Henry James.

———

While I'm making pottery with Ann, Adrian works in his study, but at tea time she asks me up to his desk and we have tea from Ann's cups.

I always bring Adrian little gifts, mostly postcards. One was of a Mughul miniature, which he liked. Another was of a Surrealist painting, and this he did not like, though his way of indicating he doesn't like something isn't to say so, but to laugh a little. Later, he told me he didn't like the Surrealists, but as an aside. My little gifts – besides postcards, a volume of three Greek poets, fancy cakes from a pastry shop in Hampstead – are offered partly with the wonder of how he will react to them.

I have no idea what Adrian's likes and dislikes are, and I realize that this both intimidates me and excites me. All I know for sure is that he has a vision, and vision excites me.

Once, having been first to Stephen Buckley's studio, I went to Church Row with a little work of Stephen's under my arm which I showed to Adrian: he looked at it for a long time on his desk, and I, standing by, wondered what he was thinking. When he said, 'Yes, I like it,' I was very pleased.

I'm always aware that his appreciation of something is, in a way, reflective, that it has to do with deciding something about the object. His appreciation is, I feel, based on the object's standing up or not to Adrian's awareness of it. I don't think: Adrian is coming to terms with the object. I think: the object is coming to terms with Adrian.

———

One afternoon, Henrietta Garnett came to visit me. She was wearing a huge ring, made, she said, from a fourteenth-century Portuguese sailor's silver buckle and an aquamarine which Ottoline Morrell (Henrietta called her 'Ot') had given to her grandmother, who had given it to her mother, who, Henrietta said, 'found it in a drawer among dirty socks, put it in an envelope which she didn't seal, misspelled my married name and got my address all wrong, and sent it off to me, and it arrived. And that is Bloomsbury.' Henrietta took the ring off and threw it across the room for me to catch.

———

Sonia invited Nikos and me for a birthday party for Francis. I sat next to Francis, and across the table was David Sylvester. I asked Francis if he ever worried about the meaning of art. 'No,' he said, and laughed.

'I just paint. I paint out of instinct. That's all.' 'Then you're very lucky others like your work,' David said. 'That's it,' Francis said. 'I'm very lucky. People, for some reason, buy my work. If they didn't, I suppose I'd have to make my living in another way.' I said, 'I'm sure people buy – or, if they can't buy, are drawn to – your work because you do paint out of instinct.' 'Perhaps it's just fashionable for people to be drawn now,' Francis said, and I said, 'No, that's not true, and you know it's not true.' He said, 'You're right. I do know. Of course I know. When I stop to wonder why I paint, I paint out of instinct.'

David looked very thoughtful. He sat away from the table, his large body a little slumped forward, his hands on his knees. Slightly wall-eyed, he stared at the table as he thought, and he finally asked Francis, very slowly, 'How does luck come into your work?'

Francis answered, 'If anything works for me in my paintings, I feel it is nothing I've made myself but something luck has given to me.'

David asked, 'Is there any way of preparing for the luck before you start working?'

'It comes by chance,' Francis said. 'It wouldn't come by will power. But it's impossible to talk about this.'

This excited me, and I immediately asked, 'Because it's a mystery?'

Francis jerked round to me, his eyes wide. He said flatly, 'I don't think one can explain it.'

I knew that I was trying to push Francis into saying something that I wanted him to say but which I also knew he disdained, as he disdained all forms of the mysterious.

Nikos warned me. 'Do you know what you're asking of Francis?'

I took the risk and asked Francis, 'Do you ever think that if one knew enough one might be able to explain the mystery of chance? And if one could explain would the mystery go and the work be destroyed?'

Francis pursed his lips. He could sometimes appear to be paro-dying the expression of deep thought. He asked me, 'Are you asking me if I ever think I could destroy my work by knowing too much about what makes it?'

'More than that. I wonder, have you ever wanted to explain what makes a painting work even though you knew the explanation would destroy it? I mean, do you ever worry that your work is too explicit in its meaning, not latent enough?'

Francis said, 'I can't wonder about that, because I know I would never be able to explain.' He laughed.

───────

I take in the names – Hobhouse, Trevelyan, Huxley, Strachey – as almost words for a certain British history, and for a while I think of myself, in my name David Plante, as without history, until it comes to me to recall the Christian names of my parents – my mother Albina, my father Anaclet – or of aunts and uncles – Aldea, Cyriac, Homer, even Napoléon – or the names of nuns who taught us in my parochial school – Mère Saint Félix de Valoix – and my history takes on a deep historical depth, as far back at least to French neo-classicism if not further back, that French history transposed in name only to French Canada, but then lost in my French parish in New England when transposed from French Canada, so, really, I am disconnected from the French history in which such names had meaning, a history totally disconnected from France within the world I live in, but mine only in my fantasy history.

The only person in Britain who is aware of my being a Franco-American, and who understands historically what the names I've listed above connote, is Steven Runciman, who has said to me, his voice rising in pitch, 'North America should belong to *you*. You were dispossessed of what should be yours by the horrible William Pitt. And here you are, having made your home among the enemy.'

Thinking that we would introduce them, as if Nikos and I have taken on such a role in London that we can introduce people to one another whom we think would be of interest to one another, we invited Steven and Caro Hobhouse to dinner, and found it was as if they were relatives, knowing each other's family so familiarly they may have been distant cousins. Nikos and I simply listened.

Caro said that one of the pleasures of family gatherings, which seem to occur with them all bouncing about together in a large bed, is to sort out just how they are related.

And I must put this in: we thought Steven would like to meet the writer on food Claudia Roden, whose history seems to be the history of the whole of the Middle East. We asked them to a restaurant, and in conversation Steven said that the most noble name in the world is Cohen, but it must be a Ha-Cohen, and Claudia, smiling the kind of sad smile she has as if aware of all the history from which she has emerged, said, 'My grandfather was a Ha-Cohen.' He was chief rabbi in Aleppo, Syria.

My second novel, Slides, published, not to good notices.

Leave out my novels.

David Hockney drew the dust jacket for Slides, back and front, of delicate drawings of slides. He said that his assistant Mo, thinking they were in fact slides, tried to pick them up. In a bookshop, I found a copy of the novel, the dust jacket evidently stolen, the novel left behind.

———

Nikos told me that Miss Richards at their last session revealed to him that she was sorry to tell him she would be leaving England to go to live in Australia. If he was upset, he didn't show it, but I was annoyed that she had – as I saw it – rejected him.

I said, 'I never understood why you should have made yourself vulnerable in wanting to have analysis.'

He shrugged.

Could it be that I do not reach into him at the depth that is in him, a depth where I feel he is defeated, at the depth of his Greek history?

If I could revive him from that defeat, if I could!

———

I thought that in ending his analysis, Nikos would resume his life as before, but suddenly, when we were together on a Sunday night in our bed, the bedside light still lit, he said, aggressively, 'You never cared about my analysis, never now care how much I suffer the end of it.'

I said, 'When I suffer anxiety, you tell me it's nonsense, that I'm being self-indulgent.'

'You are,' he said.

'I am, and you've taught me that I am.'

I could see that his eyes were open and that he was listening intently to me.

'You taught me to see that my inner darkness means nothing because it refers only to me, and I just think of what is outside me, the darkness outside me. In a way, you've made me a good Communist, more aware of historical darkness than personal darkness. And now you tell me you have this inner darkness, which is yours alone, and you expect me to cater to all the aggression that results from it just because it's yours. No, I won't. I'm entirely supportive of you—'

He stopped me. 'No,' he said, 'you're not.'

'How can you say that? I am. I know I am. I'm as supportive of you as you are of me, which is, I know, total. But to be total doesn't mean to indulge you. And you know the difference. You have made me see the difference. You have no reason to be suffering.'

He said, quietly, 'Let's go to sleep,' and he reached out to shut off the light at his side of the bed, and when the room was dark he turned to me and put an arm over me and fell asleep.

———

For the Easter Resurrection services, we went to the Russian Orthodox Cathedral in Ennismore Gardens, as we've been before. Nikos does not want to go to the Greek Orthodox Cathedral in Moscow Road, he doesn't say why, but I sense in him the resentment of someone from a refugee family who never felt at home among Athenians, and in historical fact were never made to feel at home, even to having their own cemetery, the Second Cemetery, where Nikos' father is buried, all of them remaining among themselves as refugees, Constantinopoli, who call Istanbul Constantinople.

But, if Nikos feels there is some distance kept from him as a refugee by Athenian Greeks who form the closed provincial world around the Greek Orthodox Cathedral in Moscow Road, he keeps a much greater distance because he, as a refugee, feels he is superior to them. The refugee Greeks were – they are – superior, as made evident when, at the time of the Catastrophe, they had to move from Turkey to Greece and transformed provincial Athens into a cosmopolitan city with their much more evolved culture. The Greeks of the diaspora, the 'Oriental' Greeks, have much more knowledge of bureaucracy in business transactions for having worked in the bureaucratic class of Byzantium from long before Byzantium fell to the Turks, and, after the fall, for having functioned as tax collectors for the Sultans. This position of power and money allowed them to send their sons and daughters to be educated in Paris, Berlin, London, and so be much more in contact with Western Europe than the Athenian Greeks. Nikos tells me his mother, until she had to leave Constantinople, would never have considered even visiting the dusty, not Greek but, she said, Albanian town of Athens.

Distancing himself from the Greeks he feels superior to, Nikos for some years chose to go for the Easter Resurrection service to the Russian Cathedral. At these services, I liked carrying a lit candle and, after the archbishop shouted out, 'Christos anesti,' shouting out 'Alithos anesti' along with Nikos, those Greek words within a Russian liturgy resounding within Russian history, which multiple historical resonances I know Nikos enjoys as much as I do, perhaps he even more than I do.

(And here I make a connection with going with Nikos to the Christmas midnight Mass at the Roman Brompton Road Oratory and, standing behind a porphyry pillar because the church was too packed for us to have a view of the altar, I heard Latin being chanted, and, too, the Greek Kyrie Eleison, and with the smell of incense I felt I could be in ancient Rome. Too many connections, too many, and how can I deal with them except to let them occur?)

In the Russian Orthodox Cathedral, with our candles not yet lit for the Resurrection, we were standing near a young woman who stared up at the dome, her eyes concentrating as if at something she fixed on there, and suddenly she began to scream, a high, piercing scream, and a woman on the other side of her from us took her in her arms until she was quiet. The ceremony was being broadcast throughout the Soviet Union, so those devout there would have heard the scream and wondered what it was about. Nikos said we should leave. Back home, we set the table for the mageritza (that special Easter soup traditionally made from sheep's innards, but which Nikos, having become a vegetarian, made from vegetable stock and lots of onions and dill) and tsoureki (the Easter brioche with hard-boiled red eggs baked in it, bought the day before from a Greek bakery near the Greek Orthodox Cathedral, which we walked to, passing a house with a blue plaque on it commemorating Constantine Cavafy, who had lived there, and, and and – Where was I? Back home with Nikos for our Easter supper, the radio turned on low to a broadcast of the Mass and the chant still going on in the Russian Cathedral, and we heard the scream again and shortly after the siren of an ambulance, and Nikos turned the radio off, and we ate in silence.

———

Our rows. Almost all have to do with Nikos' need for order. I'm orderly too, but Nikos' need for order is far in excess of mine. He complains if, in the bathroom, I leave soap in the soap dish that becomes slimy, if in flossing my teeth I speckle the mirror, if I squeeze the toothpaste tube from the middle, if I do not lower the seat of the toilet bowl, if I do not hang the bath mat over the rim of the tub, if I do not turn on or off the light by the little wooden knob at the end of the cord but by the cord, if, if, if, oh, if I replace the roll of loo paper so that it rolls outwardly rather than, as he insisted, inwardly, against the wall.

Nikos listened when Steven Runciman told him that he has been in ducal houses, even princely houses, where the loo paper is always rolled outwardly, then said he always rolled the loo paper inwardly.

When I told Dee Wells, the wife of A. J. Ayer, about the rules in the bathroom, she exclaimed, 'Nikos is so anal-retentive, it's a wonder he needs a loo.'

Stephen has told us that what made it possible for us to live together domestically is that we were both orderly, which he is not, Natasha having to accept the way he simply lets his overcoat fall off from him onto the floor of the entry hall. Yes, I am orderly, but not to the extent that the socks have to be lined up in the drawer. I try to be amused by Nikos' fastidiousness, but when I shout that I will not have our lives reduced to the minutiae of order, he shouts back, 'I will not live in bedlam,' and I'm not amused.

And he never, ever apologizes, as if constitutionally incapable of apology.

When I arrived in Church Row, Ann told me that Adrian is dying of cancer of the brain.

I didn't make any pottery, but went directly to his study to see him. He stood, we embraced, and though he was weak he refused to sit. His skin looked gray and matt. Ann had warned me that he had very little concentration, but he seemed pleased to see me, however embarrassed he also seemed to be about his state. Finally, he sat at his desk, and for some reason laughed, in a totally expressionless way. Ann put a cup of tea on his desk, but he simply looked at it and said he wouldn't have any. He wouldn't because he couldn't lift the cup and he didn't want to ask for help. Ann held the cup up for him to drink. Again, he laughed, but again without expression. After he finished his tea, we talked a little. He said, 'I feel very calm.' Then he said he would like to be alone.

When I returned some ten days later, I found Adrian painting while Ann made a pot on her wheel. A large, loose, but finished painting was propped against the fireplace, and when I saw it I said, 'It's so beautiful.' He laughed, now expressing warmth and a curious detachment. Adrian has the ability to be both warm and detached at once, in the same way, I suppose, one can be both pleased by praise and indifferent to it. He immediately said, 'You must have it.' I said I couldn't. He said I must. I looked towards Ann, who said, yes, I must have it.

This was the first of the series he started after he was given pain-killers – pills that, he said, also made him 'very happy.'

He was, however, more confused than ever, and at moments he knew this. He said, 'I'm not really normal, you know.'

I took the painting away. It is of a cup and saucer and bottles as if almost dissolved in the loose, lyrical brushstrokes, brushstrokes so lightly applied that they appear to have been painted on air.

On my next visit, while Ann and I potted to Greek bouzouki

music Adrian painted in his studio at the top of the house. I
went up. He was hardly able to support the brush. He was painting bottles, and he wanted them arranged in a certain way, but
as he wasn't able to articulate his directives I couldn't understand how he wanted me to arrange the bottles. He'd point with
his brush and say something unintelligible, and I, feeling that I
should be able to understand, would place a bottle upright, or
on its side, but the arrangement was never what he wanted. I
said, Just say yes if I do the right thing, no if I do the wrong
thing, but this didn't work any better. He became impatient,
and said, 'It doesn't matter.' Then he seemed to become resigned.
He'd gone far from seeing objects in terms of his ideas of them;
in the last paintings – there were eleven of them – he had to take
objects as they were, beyond his control in every other way but
to paint them.

Do I understand Adrian's writing? I find it difficult to penetrate
through the dazzle of his metaphors and similes, and find I have,
not an understanding, but a 'sense' of his vision. I like to think he
uses the dazzle of his imagery, his metaphors and similes deliberately as one with the expression of his vision, not so much to
understand a work of art but to have the most vivid 'sense' of it.

No doubt I'm reading myself into Adrian's writing.

And so, too, the writing of Richard Wollheim – after reading his
Art and its Objects I look at a work of art as if it expands and
expands, not into an understanding of it, but into the 'sense' of it,
to mark a difference between understanding the meaning of something, which is difficult for me, and having a 'sense' of the meaning
of something, which is to me the most vivid appreciation of the
something I can have.

I have a 'sense' of what you mean, I say to Nikos, when he
explains a philosophical point about aesthetics, which was his
subject when he was a student at Harvard.

Why does the recollection come to me of Nikos telling me of
that time he was abandoned by a lover on the island of Poros and
he sat by the sea with the scent of lemon blossoms wafting from the

lemon groves on the distant mainland, the beauty of which was a consolation to him?

———

Nikos woke from a nightmare, shouting, and I woke. He said he dreamed that someone came into the room who was, he thought, me, and got into bed with him; he put his arms around the person and suddenly realized the person was not me, and this terrified him.

———

I recall that I was once amazed by Virginia Woolf's The Waves, and now wonder:

> The sun was sinking. The hard stone of the day was cracked and light poured through its splinters. Red and gold shot through the waves, in rapid running arrows, feathered with darkness. Erratically rays of light flashed and wandered, like signals from shrunken islands, or darts shot through laurel groves by shameless, laughing boys. But the waves, as they neared the shore, were robbed of light, and fell in one long concussion, like a wall falling, a wall of grey stone, unpierced by any chink of light.

I wrote this in response:

> She liked to use similes, and so she wrote of storm waves falling like walls, wall after wall crashing like the walls of a castle, the sunlight shot-arrows flashing through the air, and the seaweed sunken tattered robes, and the surf about the broken blocks of stone like clouds, clouds that come in to cover over the ruins and then go out to reveal the ruins, a reversed sky where the ruins float on ebbing and flowing clouds – And she paused to ask: Like and like and like and like? What is the likeness likeness likens itself to? And she put her pen down and closed her eyes.

Doubts about her use of metaphor and simile. Doubts about the use of metaphor and simile, which would never have occurred to Jane Austen as a way of enlivening writing which may otherwise be dead.

———

Stephen asked me if I would fetch the first edition of the two volumes of Du côté de chez Swann, left for him at reception at the Savoy Hotel by Pauline de Rothschild. I prepared myself to ask for a package left by 'the Baroness Pauline de Rothschild,' imagining that the receptionist would be in awe of me, he wondering who I was who was asking for a package left by the Baroness to be delivered to someone of the same world as she was. Of course he wasn't in awe, and indifferently handed me the package. Still, I was in awe of myself, and sitting in the Underground train with the package on my knees, I imagined the others in the carriage would know, simply by looking at me, that the package contained first editions of Proust from the Baroness de Rothschild which I was passing on to Stephen Spender, I participating in both their worlds by my connecting the two as a delivery boy. That I was carrying Proust, as if he himself were contained in a little coffin on my lap and his ghost hovered around it, seemed to me to expand the world outwardly into a world of literature that would be my world when I wrote it all down in my diary, creating an aura in which the entry in my diary would be read as Proustian. So here it is – my little Proustian episode.

———

A visit to Ann Stokes, she too preoccupied with Adrian to work. He will suddenly think he needs cigarettes and then goes out to buy them, Ann directly behind him; he pays for the cigarettes with a comb, and Ann, without his noticing, pays with cash, then she follows him back to the house with his cigarettes, though he does not smoke. Her face red, Ann stared at me with large eyes and I stared back.

A short time after, it seems, Ann Stokes had her annual pottery sale – her many-coloured pots and plates, and, too, ceramic birds and toads and fish spread out on tables and bookshelves and even an ironing board – and many people there, while, upstairs, Adrian was very ill in bed. Ann had arranged to have an intercom connected throughout the rooms where the sale was taking place in case Adrian should call her. Over the voices of the guests Adrian's breathing was heard, rather rough, and then, suddenly, very rough and rattling. A doctor was at the pottery sale, and he went up to Adrian and came down to say Adrian was dying. He asked Ann if she would want him taken to hospital, but Ann pleaded, no, he should die at home. Nikos and I were leaving with other guests, but Ann asked us to stay, a few close friends including Richard and Mary Day Wollheim, and Ann's sister Margaret Mellis, who was herself once married to Adrian, and Margaret's son Telfer by Adrian, and Philip, the son of Ann and Adrian, the sons both cousins and half-brothers. Ann, excited, thought we must be hungry, and over the telephone ordered tongue, and was upset that when the tongue arrived it was not salt, as she had asked for salt tongue. I felt it was very strange to be in the sitting room of the house, eating tongue and bread, while, continuing through the intercom, Adrian's always deepening rough and rattling breathing sounded loud in our silence. After a while, Nikos said we should go, and, embracing Ann and Margaret, we did. In the morning, we rang Ann, who said that Adrian died shortly after we left, and that she and her sister had spent the night together in bed speaking about their husband.

———

When I expressed to Richard Wollheim wonder at why sculptures on medieval cathedrals were placed so high no one could see them, he, atheist that I know him to be, said in a very matter-of-fact way, 'For the greater glory of God.'

———

Stephen says that to him to fall in love is to find himself hallucinated by another, and I understand this, if to be hallucinated by another is to be in a constant state of wonder about the other, to ask, over and over, who is this other? how is it that I am with this other? why am I with this other? These moments of heightened wonder occur when, lifting my eyes from a book I am reading, I see Nikos watering the plants in the sitting room, and I simply do not understand what it is in him and in me that makes me love him as I do. I feel the strain of that love as of my very heart straining to go out towards him, drawn by his presence at moments when he, as if so unaware of me he might be alone in the room, is concentrating on watering his plants. I put down my book and stare at him. This sense of hallucination in the wonder has, I think, nothing to do with any self-interested impulse, and not a sexual impulse, but is a more primitive impulse; and at these moments I am convinced by the love that religions, inspired by that primitive impulse, are meant to make central to their visions, but which love they so very, very rarely act on.

———

Through John and Hugh, who spend their winters in London as the unheated villa is too cold, we met Patrick Kinross, with whom they are guests, and he invited Nikos and me to drinks. He is known, most reputably, for his book on Atatürk, and he has also written a book on the Duke and Duchess of Windsor. He stayed with them in their house outside Paris and told this story: the Duchess called upstairs, 'David, luncheon is ready,' to which the Duke responded, 'Just a moment, darling, I have something on my mind,' which made her shout out, 'On your what?'

Among the other guests, all much older than Nikos and I, was Charlotte Bonham Carter, widow of Sir Edgar, who, blinking rapidly as she talked, mentioned T. E. Lawrence. I stopped her to ask, amazed at the possibility, if she had known Lawrence of Arabia. Blinking even more rapidly, she looked at me with a frown of annoyance and said, 'He used to come, and we'd see him; he used to go, and we didn't see him. Why do you ask?' I said, 'Well, can you imagine someone from far outside the world he inhabited excited to make contact with someone who was in contact with him?' She blinked even more rapidly and said, 'Yes, I can imagine that.'

I asked her who was the most interesting person she had met, and, blinking even more rapidly, she said, 'My dear, I think it must have been Puccini.'

Patrick Kinross told the story of visiting, as a young man, an old aunt who had been present at the assassination of President Abraham Lincoln. When he asked her, 'What was it like?' all she answered was, 'It was a great fuss.'

Some time later, I drove Charlotte Bonham Carter to the wedding of Deborah Rogers, my literary agent, and Michael Berkeley, composer, in Wales. In her old age, she has curvature of the spine, so had to lift her entire body to turn and look at me, which she did, always blinking, when she inquired, 'You're American, aren't you?' I said I was. Then she asked, rolling the R, 'Do you know the Roosevelts?' I said I didn't. 'How odd,' she said, 'I thought all Americans knew one another.'

No, I didn't know the Roosevelts, and, though it was part of my American history, I had never met anyone in America whose great-, or even great-great-aunt had been at President Lincoln's assassination. I do have friends in America, though I never think of them as all together connecting up to make a world, and I certainly never think of my family in this way. In England, it seems, if you meet one person, you find that within a short time – at a gallery opening, at a publisher's party to launch a book, at a private drinks or dinner party – you are connecting people to one another, especially in large, interconnecting families, with the deepening knowledge that they do all belong to a world that is larger than any one of them and that contains them all.

I've met Charlotte Bonham Carter any number of times (once at a lecture on stone anchors in the East Mediterranean where she sat next to me, she muttering from time to time, 'Fascinating,' and I wondering what I was doing at a lecture on stone anchors in the

East Mediterranean), but she never remembers who I am, though she always treats me matter-of-factly as someone to whom she would talk intimately about someone else whom she is intimate with, expecting me to know this person as well as she does. It hasn't taken me long to realize that the English are not reserved, but assume, even on a first meeting, the openness of telling me about a hysterectomy or about a daughter suffering from anorexia or a son who was being sent down from Cambridge for drugs. Lady Charlotte, as she is called though I learned she wasn't the daughter of a duke, a marquis, or an earl, and was perhaps called Lady Charlotte by people who didn't really know her but thought her too special to be anything but the daughter of a duke, a marquis, or an earl, whereas those who really did know her, such as John and Hugh, simply call her Charlotte, herself seems to imagine, with no sense at all of exclusiveness, that she and everyone else belongs to an England of country houses and a London of the Covent Garden Opera House, embassies, and the Royal Horticultural Hall.

Lady Charlotte is thought not to have known about the more intimate aspects of marriage on her wedding day, when she, arranging flowers on the altar, was asked who was to be married and responded, 'I am,' and when asked where she and her husband were to go on their honeymoon answered, 'I don't know about him, but I am going to Afghanistan.'

I asked her at one time about her travels, and she said, emphatically, 'I draw the line at Afghanistan.'

She sometimes visits John and Hugh in their villa outside Lucca, traveling by train and with a bag of hard-boiled eggs, sleeping in the train stations if her connections leave her in the waiting room to spend the night.

John told me that he and Hugh were in a restaurant with her, where she often made gestures to communicate with four men sitting at a table near by, and when asked who the men were she responded, 'I'm not sure, but I think the Amadeus String Quartet.'

Natasha Spender has lively stories to tell about her. Once, seeing her enter a reception and look about, Natasha, thinking she might be looking for someone she knew, went to her, and Charlotte put an index finger to her lips and said, 'Not a word, not a word, my dear, we can talk any time,' and passed her to meet people she hadn't met.

She is famous for appearing at intervals at performances, but during the performances themselves she is out at other events, even if this requires a change of clothing which she does in ladies' rooms, and at the interval of a musical evening she will say, 'Splendid, splendid, but I did think the brass was rather too loud,' to the total bemusement of the person she addresses because the performance was of a piano and violin duet.

She could only have evolved in England.

Whenever I am in the West End, I stop to look in at the shows galleries are putting on. I stopped in the Kasmin Gallery in Bond Street and found the entire large clear white space filled with one work by Anthony Caro, Prairie, a vast bright yellow sheet of metal supported as if magically at one corner so the vast bright yellow sheet of metal appeared to float. I was struck: this is a great work of art. This is sublime!

John Russell lives with Suzi Gablik. They give drinks parties where Nikos and I have met, oh, so many. Francis almost always comes. Suzi said that expecting nothing from Francis is a condition of one's friendship with him. At one drinks party, I found Francis standing by himself and went to speak to him. He was wearing tight gray trousers, a black turtleneck pullover, and another turtle-neck pullover on top of this, but this one white. I imagined his body as having very thin legs and a bulging belly. The sleeves of both pullovers were pushed up, showing his powerful forearms and red hands.

I knew it was risky – but I liked taking such risks with Francis

– but I tried to start a conversation by saying that the writer Jean Rhys had told me that she had flashes of religion. 'Does she, now?' Francis asked. Drunk myself, I asked him if he ever did. He laughed. 'Never, never never never never never.' I had heard him say this before, but, as before, I wanted to know what he was vulnerable to, and I asked him if he had any addiction. He didn't have any, he said. I said mine is sleep. 'Sleep?' he asked. 'Really?' I asked him, 'How much do you sleep?' He said, 'I get up every morning at seven o'clock.' 'I wish I could do that,' I said. He asked me, 'But don't you like consciousness, David? I love conscious life. I love being conscious.' He stuttered, but he didn't laugh.

————

We went to the opening of the Cecil Beaton show at the National Portrait Gallery, curated by Roy Strong, the director of the museum.

At the entrance was a photograph of a totally naked young man and woman, which announced that the National Portrait Gallery had opened itself up to the times, and there was an excitement in the dense gathering of the opening – yet, as if assumed among everyone that the opening had always been there privately but never quite announced publicly, as if the openness to sexual frankness had been a given among everyone there and only required an exhibition to make the inward given an outward given. So, no sense of shock, but of: yes, of course, of course. Yet, a sense of liberation in the of course.

Sitting on the top step of the flight just outside the exhibition was the most beautiful person I had ever seen, a young man wearing a silk bomber jacket embroidered on the back with a Japanese roaring lion, and standing around him, looking down at him, was a circle of admirers. Among them I saw Peter Schlesinger. I asked him, 'Who is that?' Peter whispered, 'His name is Eric Boman. He was a friend of Salvador Dalí and Marilyn Monroe.' I stared at this Eric Boman, who kept his eyes fixed on the steps below him.

———

For Easter we went for the Resurrection services at the Cypriot Orthodox church with Julia Hodgkin. She was amused that while the priest was at the altar a man was leaning on it as if they were having a business talk while the priest was officiating. There I saw Öçi's mother Mrs. Ullmann and his brother Tony, but I knew from the past that she was suspicious of me for my relationship with Öçi, so I stayed away even from asking how Öçi was in New York.

———

Ann Stokes, to supper, asked us what we thought of her joining a circus, as she had always longed to ride into a circus ring on the head of an elephant.

———

Having commissioned the historian Roy Strong to write a monograph on the paintings of Charles I on horseback by Van Dyck, Nikos went to Brighton where Roy Strong lives to talk about the book, and I went along with Nikos. We walked along the seafront. Roy was wearing knickerbockers with, I felt, the same aplomb with which, in the age of Charles I, he would have worn a wide-brimmed slouch hat, a lace collar, knee-breeches and silk stockings and shoes with pompoms. Roy appears to assume that all of British history is his, and he can, rightly, inhabit whatever period he chooses, and though I imagine him at ease in Elizabethan London, the elegance of early seventeenth-century British court life under Charles I would do, with poems, medals, eulogies, music, and such grand masques as Britannia Triumphans, all to end in the execution of Charles I by Oliver Cromwell.

Roy said he thinks of me as a Henry James character.

Nikos and I often have dinner parties in our small flat in Battersea, and often enough Francis Bacon comes. More often, Francis invites us out to restaurants, sometimes with as many as ten or twelve people around tables pushed together. At a restaurant, we met Francis' friends Dicky Chopping and Denis Wirth-Miller, both artists. Francis at restaurants is always as attentive to the waiters as he is to his friends, and whenever a waiter puts a bottle of wine on the table Francis hands him a pound note. I once saw him put a pound note in a bread basket that was being passed around by the people at the table. After, Nikos and I would drive Francis home to his studio flat in Reece Mews, in South Kensington, and wait for him to open his narrow door among the wide doors of the mews garages and climb his steep flight of stairs, sometimes stumbling and falling to his knees as he went up.

And we see him at drinks parties. At one party, he was introduced to Lee Miller, then Francis came to where Nikos and I were standing with Stephen and Natasha and said to us, laughing dryly, 'You mean, that's the Lee Miller whose photograph was taken by

Man Ray? I would have thought her beauty would have remained, but nothing of it has, has it?' We also laughed, too intimidated by Francis to stand up to him.

He had arrived drunk, and he was almost incomprehensible when he spoke. After Nikos had left our group because he wanted to but wouldn't stand up to Francis, Francis said to Stephen and Natasha and me – in reference to what, I didn't know, but I wondered if he was thinking of George – 'In every relationship there's always a cherished and a cherisher, always a cherished and a cherisher.' I said, 'I wonder if that's true. In my case – or, rather, in Nikos' and my case – I don't know who is the cherisher and who is the cherished.' 'Oh yes, you know,' Francis said, 'oh yes, and don't deny it. Don't deny being cherished. Don't deny it. Take it. Let yourself be cherished. You're the cherished one. And don't deny yourself being cherished.' Natasha said, 'But you don't understand, Francis. David is the cherisher.' Stephen said nothing. Francis lurched away with a jerk of his whole body, as if someone had suddenly called him away, and staggered from person to person.

Natasha left Stephen and me to talk with others, and Francis staggered back to us. Stephen asked him if he was working on something new, and Francis, loosely nodding his head, said, 'Yes. I'm doing paintings of two bodies locked together. Locked. Locked together.' He lost his balance whenever he paused to talk, but each time he regained his balance he repeated, 'Locked together, two bodies.' I said, 'Then they'll be love paintings.' He leaned towards me and almost fell onto me, his wine splashing from his glass. 'Yes,' he said, 'yes.' Then he stumbled backwards, his head up, and there suddenly came to his face a look of such terror that I laughed. I then realized that he was about to fall backwards, but before I could reach out to grab him he regained his balance and turned towards the wall and went to stand with his back against it. He mistook a door for the wall, however, and when he leaned against the door ajar it gave way, but, again, he righted himself just as I rushed to him to stop him from falling. Leaning now against the solid wall, he said, 'I want real tragedy.'

———

I am always aware of, even always in a daze of wonder about, the world I'm in. When Nikos and I were at the house of Patrick Kinross, I wondered why he, showing us into his sitting room – what I guess he calls his drawing room – stopped to stand still to admire, as he finally said, the proportions of the room, as if he had suddenly become aware of the proportions, which I too admired with the wonder of the room that appeared to float within its white proportions, the furniture and pictures suspended within the space.

And how could I not wonder, the other guests at dinner John Fleming and Hugh Honour, why the roast chicken, which Patrick had prepared, had so many feathers left on it, which, however, he seemed not at all to be aware of, nor John and Hugh, but which Nikos and I smiled about across the elegantly laid table?

Patrick seems always to be in a vague state of suspension.

———

Sorting out papers, as I often do, because Nikos and I keep everything from postcards and invitations to exhibitions to letters and drafts of fiction, I came across a story that Jean Rhys and I wrote together after the incident in which, both of us drunk in her hotel room, I used the lavatory then she, and –

He heard, 'Maurice!'

He went to the lavatory door and leaned close.

'Maurice!'

'Yes?'

'Help me, please.'

His hand on the door handle, he hesitated. He opened slowly but quickly closed the door when he saw Lucy Nicholson holding her frock over her raised knees, her feet off the floor, her large, loose knickers about her ankles, leaning sideways, stuck in the toilet.

604. ANDREA DEL CASTAGNO (c. 1420–1457) THE YOUTHFUL DAVID
(Widener Collection)

*Another messenger for Nikos
w.th love from Stephen, Jun 66*

The Youthful David by Andrea del Castagno, sent from Stephen Spender to Nikos with the
message, 'Another messenger for Nikos, with love from Stephen', June 1966. Nikos thought this
'messenger' by way of Stephen made inevitable our meeting each other.

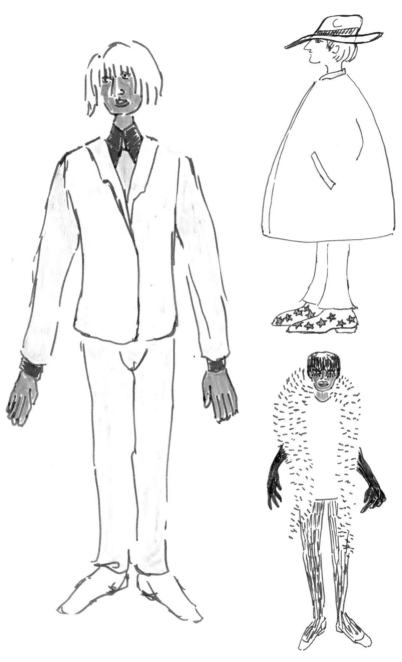

Saturday afternoon on the King's Road, 1966: a funfair at which people dressed for a different world… I sketched three interesting characters.

Patrick Procktor's watercolour of me and Stephen Spender, 1967. Very good of Stephen.

My watercolour of Nikos, San Andrea di Rovereto di Chiavari, 1968.

Three 'Exquisite Corpses' from many dinner parties Nikos and I gave for friends during the seventies, everyone clearly fixated on the inventive parts.

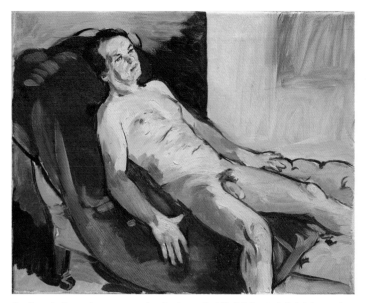

Sandra asked to paint my portrait – in the nude, if I didn't mind. I didn't mind. Then she suggested I come again and pose with another male model, very sexy, both of us nude. 'And you never know what will happen.' Dear, dear Sandra. Kitaj gave me the painting after Sandra died.

R. B. Kitaj's portrait of me, *David in Russia*. Nikos pointed out that the hands come from icons by Theophanis the Greek, mentor of Andre Rublev, the great Russian painter of icons. Kitaj didn't know this, but was very pleased, as his paintings are filled with references.

In the 1980s in London, while Keith Milow was fabricating a series of lead pieces, he heard of the death of Joseph Beuys, a mentor and an inspiration. Though the pieces were intended to be nameless memorials, as he worked on them they became charged, almost imprinted, with the presence Keith retained of having met the great man. This is one of those memorials. Lead, wood, putty, 1986.

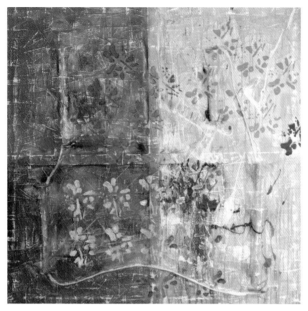

A note from Stephen Buckley: *There have been a number of paintings called FIELD over the years, none of them of a particular field, just as the flower stencil, first cut in 1963, is not of a particular flower. This flora universalis has made regular appearances over five decades in various paintings, always in colour.*

This was painted in 1972 by Adrian Stokes after an operation on his brain; he seemed to be painting on air. It is the first of eleven paintings from before he died. He gave me this, the art critic Lawrence Alloway was given the last, and the rest belong to the Tate.

He had forgot to put the toilet seat down.

Jean told me that if I ever found myself again in such a situation with a lady, I should place a glass of water and an aspirin beside her bed and leave quietly, and on telling the story later I must make it funny. As we did writing this story, giggling.

Dear Jean, now dead and cremated and ashes.

She once said to me: all of literature is a great lake, and there are rivers that feed the lake, such as Dostoyevsky and Tolstoy and Dickens and Balzac, and there are trickles such as Jean Rhys, but however little one must always believe in feeding the lake.

———

Peter Schlesinger has left David Hockney for Eric Boman, and David is very upset. The many people around David comfort him, and, slumped over, he puts a hand to his chin and sticks out his lower lip then says, 'Oh, I don't know.'

———

Jean Rhys once told me that she writes to let everything go, and I do often think, Let it go, let it all go, though I'm not sure what the 'all' is that I want to let go of.

———

We are often invited by Eva Neurath, the head of the publishing house Thames & Hudson, to drinks parties, to dinner parties, to the opera or to recitals.

She is not Jewish, but in Nazi Berlin she identified with Jewish students, and when they were expelled she herself left school. She was fourteen years old. She educated herself. She married a Jew and with him and a son left Germany. She speaks about the horrors both with gravity and – not a contradiction – almost a lightness of tone, sometimes with a delicate snort of laughter. She would never, she says, have become what she became if it hadn't been for that 'chap' in Germany, meaning Hitler.

Often interrupting her talk with a nasal 'Hum?' which, it seems, is a way of making sure one is keeping up with her, Eva recounts stories from her past life. If we are having a meal with her in her home, just the three of us in the basement, her stories will include her asking us to go to the wine cellar for another bottle of wine, and I think this is not as a sudden request but yet another turn in the multi-cornered story. When the story all comes together, it is like a whole world and she is aware of all the details of its history: from her childhood in Berlin, the detail of being accidentally struck in the eye with the nib of a pen, the detail of listening to her older sister play the piano in another room for Eva to guess which notes she was striking, the detail of her mother coming into her room to say goodnight before going off for the evening.

When she and her husband first arrived in London, Eva and her son lived in dim rooms, and she worked as a domestic; her husband was interned as an enemy alien on the Isle of Man. In the camp he became friendly with a German Jewish inmate, Walter Neurath, who had been living in England for some time. Working for the book 'packager' Adprint, Neurath had been responsible for a series, Britain in Pictures, which was seen as proof of his loyalty to Britain, and he was released. He was asked by Eva's husband, who remained interned, to help his wife and son, and Walter Neurath not only found Eva a job at Adprint, but started, in 1949, the publishing house Thames & Hudson with her. They married.

Eva is open with us, and she expects us to be open with her. She often asks Nikos and me about our relationship as lovers. 'I don't mean your sexual relationship. I mean your night-time relationship.' This amazed me until I knew that Eva is very attracted to Jungian analysis.

Nikos and I might be with her in the foyer of Covent Garden during an interval, all of us talking about the opera performance, when, suddenly, she will, with a quick, elegant movement of her wrist, grasp one's chin and, smiling, kiss one on the lips.

At an elaborate dinner party she gave, with many tables set in her dining room and sitting room, my place card had me sitting next to

Hattie (I think the spelling) Waugh, the daughter of Evelyn Waugh. She said to me, 'I hope I don't like you, as I have too many friends as it is,' which only someone brought up in a certain British culture could say, she not only not being offensive, but with a wit that I like to think I am British enough to be amused by.

———

Catharine Carver would want to be left out of this diary, but I can't leave her out. Editor at Chatto & Windus, she asked to read a novel I'd written in America, but was sorry to say it is unpublishable. Still, she takes an interest and reads what I've written and advises. A scout for Viking, Gwenda David, is waspish about Catharine liking her hot-water boiler to break down so she must bathe in cold water, but she did tell me that Catharine was/is the editor for writers such as Saul Bellow, John Berryman, e. e. cummings, Bernard Malamud, Elizabeth Bishop, Lionel Trilling, Katherine Anne Porter, Hannah Arendt, Flannery O'Connor. I know she is working closely with Leon Edel on a one-volume edition of his biography of Henry James. A while ago, Catharine rang me to say she would like to burn all the letters she had from whomever, and would I drive her out into the country to a field where she could make a pile and set it aflame? I answered that we would be arrested. I imagined the letters she wanted to burn would be from the writers whose work she had edited, and hoped that her not being able to make a pyre of them would deter her from destroying them in any less dramatic way. But she rang me a few days later to tell me she had thrown them all out into the rubbish.

Before she left America, she traveled to every state, then she left New York, where she was a publisher, to come to London, never to return to America.

All she ever said about her youth in America, without saying where in America, was that as a girl she once threw herself down a flight of stairs.

Nikos and I had a drinks party with an odd mixture, I suppose, but we like odd mixtures – including Catharine and Patrick Kinross,

who sat side by side on a sofa, she small and grey and he large and
red, Patrick smoking a cigar from which he flicked ashes onto
Catharine's head. Leaving, she asked, 'Who is that wonderful man?'
I now always think of Catharine as having ashes flicked on her head
and finding the abasement – wonderful!

———

And I must include Joe McCrindle – stocky Joe, American living
in London, rich, owns the Transatlantic Review, in which a short
story of mine was published, my first time published. Joe also
published in the Transatlantic Review the poem, 'Present Absent,'
that Stephen wrote when I was staying with him at Saint Jérôme.

Heathcote Williams is the editor. He intimidates me, if not
frightens me, for his startling good looks and startling bad behav-
iour, justified to himself, I think, as a Rimbaud qui essaie de
dérégler ses sens. In a way, I envy him.

In the basement flat that is the office of the Transatlantic Review,
I met B. S. Johnson, who appeared to me large and dark. He had a
novel he had just published, the pages unbound so they could be
arranged in different ways, the pages held in a box. It is called The
Unfortunates. Adamant, Johnson said he was not interested in the
creative imagination, no, but in describing a football match in itself,
for itself; or the work of fishermen in itself for itself. He said he
hated fiction. In his large dark presence I felt such a force of resentment towards the world for not recognizing his large dark presence.

When I heard he had killed himself in part for not being recognized, I thanked God that Nikos has always warned me about
resenting the world at large for non-recognition, has told me that
even the expectation of recognition is an egotistical self-indulgence.
What did B. S. Johnson expect from the world?

Many of the walls of Joe's large flat are hung, it seems from
ceiling to floor, with red-chalk drawings of male nudes.

He has massive drinks parties. If books do make a room, people
who are celebrated make a party, though they do not in London.
Once, I was surprised to see at one of Joe's drinks parties

Christopher Isherwood, standing alone with a drink, and I went to him. We talked about the revelation that Encounter magazine, of which Stephen was co-founder and editor, had· recently been revealed as being financed by the American C.I.A. Christopher Isherwood said he wondered why there was such an objection to the C.I.A. financing the magazine, as it was in fact a very good magazine. This, I think, would have made Stephen pause, but would have enraged Natasha, who took the betrayal of Stephen as personal, it seemed, to herself. To account for all of this episode would so overweigh this diary that it would fall flat, and, in any case, however much I try simply to account, the matter has been looked at by people involved, which I was not. Natasha has written, for the record, her account, as though she were the commanding conscience of Stephen.

It happens often enough at drinks parties in London that I remark it: the most 'celebrated' guest is left alone. I recall one book-launch party for Toni Morrison at which she seemed to be left by herself in the midst of other people talking, she standing with a warm glass of white wine, and I, thinking this was impolite, went to speak to her. Is it because the Brits think it would be a presumption to speak to the 'celebrated,' and, not wanting to risk that grave social sin, ignore the very person the party is given for? I feel embarrassed for the Brits that that person does seem to be ignored, so, not being a Brit (yet), I do presume. I saw, at one of Joe's drinks parties, L. P. Hartley, standing alone and looking about, and I thought, But it's socially wrong to leave him alone! so introduced myself and said I hoped to live long enough to see my past as another country, and this seemed to please him, and it pleased me to be able to speak to L. P. Hartley shortly before he died.

Joe's parties appear to fluster him terribly.

———

I see less and less of Rachel Ingalls, which I'm sorry for, but she seems not to want to see me. Both of us American, we have known each other since before we published, when we saw a lot of each other. We talked about writers and writing, especially about Ernest Hemingway.

Her first book, Theft, is a passionate retelling of the death of Jesus Christ, a great lament. In the novel, she reduced the settings to timeless images, such as rocks, prison bars, cups.

Whereas I am eager to meet critics who may, just by getting to know me, write in my favour, Rachel will not meet any, as she thinks that would be opportunistic and falsify her as a writer true to the writing.

Whatever the weather, Rachel always appears — or so I think of her — wearing gloves with buttons at the wrists and carrying a fold-up umbrella.

She has never invited me to where she lives, which I assume is one room, with a telephone in a passage outside. She requests that I do not ring her whenever, but send her a postcard to let her know just when I'll ring, and she sends back a postcard to confirm or not that she will answer. She may not be able to because she is writing or washing her hair.

Her style is of great clarity, and her subjects have become more and more strange, such as a young couple in a car lost in the countryside, the car attacked by a mass of man-eating frogs. It is the remarkable clarity of the writing that raises the dark subject to works of high literature.

I introduced her to Sonia Orwell, who invited us to tea and, as Sonia can do with flashing spontaneity, she took from a wall a painting that William Coldstream had done of her and gave it to Rachel.

She does not respond to my cards or, even, letters asking if I have offended her. Uncompromising as she is about standards, perhaps Rachel thinks that I have let go of standards.

————

As I read more of Victor Shklovsky I find more in his books that is meaningful to me, not only in the way I think of writing, but in my constant awareness of connections, for he was in love with Elsa Triolet.

And of course I am charmed by him into imagining Lili Brik:

Lili Brik loved things – earrings in the shape of golden flies and antique Russian earrings. She had a rope of pearls and was full of lovely nonsense, very old and very familiar to mankind. She knew how to be sad, feminine, capricious, proud, shallow, fickle, in love, clever in any way you like.

———

There are times while writing when I stop at a word and the word appears suddenly strange, an apparently simple word such as struggle, and I wonder not only about the origin of the word, if it is possible to think back at a time when the word was first used, but how the word has changed meaning over the centuries, accruing many different meanings. Such words are so one with their historically multiple etymologies that they appear, paradoxically, to be outside of time, timeless in time.

Idioms to me refer too much to the time in which they have appeared, so I don't use idioms.

This may have to do with Nikos' English, which is without contemporary idiom, is in a way purist for not being colloquial, and, of course, grammatically correct. I once asked him, 'Who do you love?' and he corrected me, 'Whom do you love?' And he seemed puzzled when I said that sounded pretentious, as if for him grammatical structure, as logic to thinking, is what language is essentially about.

He would never say, 'Someone has left their book on a chair.'

Nor would he ever say, 'Hopefully, the letter will arrive tomorrow,' or, 'He's too judgmental.'

Steven Runciman does not say 'healthy food,' which gives to food its own awareness about its health, but, instead, 'healthful' food.

———

At a gallery opening, I saw Ossie Clark, wearing, as he always seems to wear, a tight, sleeveless jersey knitted with many colours in a jigsaw pattern. He looked at me as if wondering if I recognized him enough for him to say hello, which surprised me as I had always felt he hardly recognized me and never made an effort to say hello. I noted how his long hair was greasy, his face pale and narrow and creased. I'd heard that he'd separated from Celia and that the business, badly mismanaged, had filed for bankruptcy. I'd also heard that he was deeply into hard drugs. He appeared isolated, perhaps even ashamed to be among people who had once gathered round him but who now left him alone, the past designer of frocks that appeared to float about the thin, long-legged models like large, light, fluttering wings.

At a dinner party of a rich Greek Nikos and I were invited to, he having reluctantly accepted because I said I wanted to find out about rich Greeks, I sat next to a woman who asked me if Nikos always takes off his shoes on entering our flat, and on my saying yes, he does, she simply smiled as if knowingly, she having put Nikos into a world she, a thoroughly Anglicized Greek, was ironically aware of; and the habit of Nikos taking off his shoes and putting on slippers before entering our flat (which he never insisted I do, but which habit I took on) became, to me, not a personal habit but a habit identifying the history of a culture. How could I have ever thought of wearing in our flat shoes that I had worn in the dirty street?

Anne Graham-Bell invited us to a dinner party. When I stepped out of the Underground train, I saw Nikos waiting for me on the platform. He was laughing. He had been in the same carriage as I, but at a far end, and, somewhat myopic, concentrated on someone at the other end he thought sexy – me!

Through Sonia, who told us how to answer a formal invitation, we were invited by the French ambassador to meet the writer Nathalie Sarraute, Sonia herself not attending. I arrived before Nikos, and found Marina Warner was seated next to me, and, as happens when I meet someone I know from a different context, I wondered through what connections she was there. I know her more from her novels than I know her in person, so I see her within the context of her novel The Skating Party rather than her lived life, always a strange way to see writers. As we were in the French Embassy, it seemed right that we should speak in French. The ambassador's wife came to me to ask when Mr. Stangos was to arrive, and I noted an empty place at the ambassador's table. I apologized, something must have delayed him, but, please, the luncheon must not be delayed. Across the table was, I recognized, Lee Miller, whom I'd seen at a drinks party at Suzi and John's flat. I kept hoping Nikos would arrive, but the chair at the ambassador's table remained empty. The dessert was a high, tapering configuration of profiteroles down which caramel dripped. After the meal, Marina introduced me to Lee Miller, who spoke to me as if she had always known me, which I imagined she did with everyone she met. She said she had to go to a department store to buy a clothes hamper, and would I like to go with her? I said I would, and thought it strange, very, to be in a department store with Lee Miller looking for a clothes hamper, she who had been photographed in Hitler's bathtub after the war, who had, a fashion photographer, gone into the death camps and taken photographs of the horrors, after which she stopped taking fashion photographs of bottles of perfume, who had been in the film Le Sang d'un poète by Jean Cocteau, had been painted by Picasso, had been married to Man Ray and an inspiration to the Surrealists, and was now married to Roland Penrose and devoted to cooking. At home, I rang Nikos, who said he really hadn't wanted to go to the luncheon, and would write a note of apology. I thought, well, we won't be invited again. I hadn't met Nathalie Sarraute, whose nouveaux romans Nikos admires more than I, for he is always keen on what he calls 'innovation,' and he will exclaim 'how innovative!'

about books, paintings, music, his exclamation not restricted to the contemporary, for he'll become even more excited in his appreciation of how 'innovative' Bach's music is.

———

For a week or so I've had the flu.

Nikos said he likes me to be a little ill so he can take care of me. But when he is ill, he doesn't want any care; he becomes impatient, and won't even stay in bed.

Stephen came to visit with a Picasso etching from the Vollard Suite, a monstrous, stony Minotaur raping (?) a delicately outlined woman, which he said he wanted me to have. As I have nothing, he said laughing, I should have this in case Nikos threw me out. He had taken it from the wall in his study where I had seen it in Loudoun Road.

Nikos said, 'But what if Natasha asks where it is? She'd be furious to find out we have it here, and rightly so.'

'She won't find out,' Stephen said. 'She knows I'm always turning in pictures to sell them to buy others. But there'll be hell to pay if she does find out. If she ever comes here, make sure you hide it.'

I thought, he obviously likes the possibility of her finding out.

I wonder if Stephen would become bored with us if we really became friendly with Natasha.

———

All that is left in my memory of a drinks party, as if I have reduced it in my memory to what most struck me in it, was seeing Christopher Isherwood among a number of people, and as I went towards him he, I thought, came towards me, but he didn't stop, he went on past me, all the while humming, his eyes staring out from beneath hanging lids and long drooping eyebrows.

Providence, Rhode Island

I am staying with my parents in my old parish home. While they are asleep, I look through the desk in the living room, through the pigeonholes where papers are kept, among them envelopes with clippings from the first haircuts of all my parents' seven sons, each envelope with the names of my brothers and me written on it by my mother in pencil. I also found many bits of paper on which my mother wrote in pencil sayings and fragments of poems that struck her while reading magazines and newspapers. This most struck me:

The realm of silence is large enough beyond the grave.

The winter afternoon is waning.

———

In London, I am constantly threatened by American darkness, which at moments comes over me portentously – comes over me, I feel, from outside, as if the vastest generalizations in America do exist outside, and the most vast is the darkness of 'everything' failing, of 'everything' just about to give way to 'nothing,' of 'everything' coming to an end. How dark American literature is, how fatalistic that America will fail, and the 'everything' promised will become nothing, that the end is always nigh.

When back in London, I will see through the surrounding large dark globe of America, see through it to the particulars of the London world about me, but there are those unaccountable moments when the globe becomes opaque and closes in on me, with both a sense of threat of its portent and a sense of the sublimity of its portent. The English live without it, and it is a relief to me to be among them; but, lacking that fatalistic, sublime dark, the English to me lack – what? – the spiritual, lack souls.

A difference between America and Britain: in New York, I would see people carrying placards warning against Armageddon, and in London I sometimes see a small man walking up and down Oxford Street carrying a placard warning the world against SITTING.

The constant impending threat in America of failing the written Constitution.

In Great Britain, no written constitution.

London

When I met the Briks in Paris, I wondered how they, Soviets, were able to visit Paris, as I thought Soviets were not given exit visas easily.

Recently, I've read that Osip Brik worked for Cheka. Boris Pasternak, who often visited the Briks, said he was terrified by Lili telling him to wait on dinner because Osja had not yet come back from the Cheka. Did he wear the long black leather overcoats and black leather cap? Did he participate in interrogations, in torture, in condemnations to death he knew were falsified? Did he believe that terror was the best way to govern?

And I think: there I was, in Paris, invited to dinner by the de Rothschilds, where I sat at the same table as Osip Brik, and even had my grand chair exchanged for his lesser chair in deference to him. Was it known that he worked for Cheka? Of course it was known, if not, as I believe, by Stephen, by the de Rothschilds.

In the same way that it is unbearable to be with a person who has been tattooed on entering a death camp and yet survived because her experience, as that of Katia Meneghello, is unbearable to any sane imagination, it is unbearable that I sat with a member of Cheka, because I cannot sanely imagine that Osip Brik's experience was the experience of a sane man. And yet, there he was, a man who seemed to me rather mild, perhaps, unlike his wife, shy.

I think this: that you have had to live through an experience,

even the historical ones about which everything seems to have
been exposed, to know what the experience in fact was to live
through.

I asked Nikos what he thought, and he raised his arms high and
dropped them, and turned away.

———

We are invited more and more by Natasha to dinner parties at
Loudoun Road.

She always has an anecdote to tell, and she tells each rounded
out with all the articulation her mouth and tongue allow, often
with glee in the telling. She had a career as a pianist until a double
mastectomy ended it. When she played at Wigmore Hall she, at
the keyboard, would from time to time look up to the apse over
the stage where a Dantesque figure writes on a long, flowing
scroll, the figure, Natasha thought, marking down every one of
her missed notes. She laughed. When she laughs, hardly more
than opening her mouth so the muscles of her cheeks rise, she
also appears to be thoughtful, frowning a little, as if wondering
why she is laughing.

She laughs at Stephen's anecdotes, méchant of him, she says, to
tell, but without that slight frown and thoughtfulness, she clearly
amused by him by the way her eyes shine looking at him. Somewhere in their relationship is, I think, his joking and her appreciation
of his joking, however méchant he is. She may exclaim, 'Oh,
Stephen, really!' but with delight as he laughs, delighted by his
joke.

For one dinner party, Sonia came early to help Natasha with
making a coulibiac, and from the kitchen, where they both were, I
heard from the dining table where I was sitting Sonia contesting
something that Natasha had done to undo her, Sonia's, work on
the coulibiac. I rang Natasha the next morning to thank her, and
she asked if I had noted Sonia's contention about the coulibiac, and
I said, well, yes, I had, and I felt that I was taken into Natasha's
confidence about her strained relationship with Sonia, which made

me feel confident in my relationship with Natasha. Whoever was most responsible for the coulibiac, it was very good.

———

Nikos did not like the way Penguin Books was going after the death of the founder, Allen Lane; he thought the emphasis was on being commercial not on upholding the standards.

He has gone to the privately owned Thames & Hudson, whose chairman – as she insists on being called – is Eva Neurath.

Nikos was invited to her house in Highgate for an interview before he was hired, and he came home to say they had had tea, beautifully laid among her beautiful Biedermeier furniture, on a table by her chair the poems of Heine, in German of course. She didn't talk with him about publishing, but the late quartets of Beethoven. Nikos was hired as a director.

At Thames & Hudson, Nikos's first impulse was to publish all the works of Adrian Stokes in three large volumes.

He has plans for books on David Hockney, Francis Bacon, Lucian Freud, Howard Hodgkin, Frank Auerbach . . . And he has contacted art historians to write books, among them the great expert on Cézanne, John Rewald, who is meant to be very, very difficult, but whom Nikos has charmed. Rewald has invited Nikos to stay with him in his castle in France. The castle, he told Nikos, has runnels over the main gate from which flaming oil was poured when in the Middle Ages an invading army tried to break through the closed gates; Rewald has kept them in case the self-justifying connoisseur of art Douglas Cooper ever dares to cross the drawbridge to try and enter before the doors close on him. Nikos does not like being a guest except with close friends.

The Mother of Feminist Art History, Linda Nochlin, greets Nikos with embraces and kisses, and has introduced to him her feminist disciple art historian Tamar Garb; together they gave Nikos a white yarmulke embroidered in silver, making him an honorary Jew as well as a feminist. Nikos has said that Jews, of all the other people in the world, just may be superior to the Greeks.

He will publish David Sylvester's interviews with Francis Bacon.

It is no surprise to Nikos that all the poets who were once keen to meet him when he was poetry editor at Penguin Books no longer have a vested interest. In fact, he took this as an of-course, perhaps a relief.

———

Somewhere in the writing of William James – whom I read as if to remain in contact with the American spirit that is everywhere in his writing (if in his writing the spirit isn't German!), for I am after all American – I came across an abstraction made concrete by his use of an example something like: when Peter and Paul are asleep together, Peter becomes Paul and Paul becomes Peter. I thought of Nikos and me, for whom sleeping together is perhaps where we are most attractive to each other, and where, after a row, everything that was contentious between us is resolved. What is that attraction?

Before we fall asleep together, he says a little prayer in Greek and makes the sign of the cross on me, and then he, as if this is his role, switches off the lamp on his side of the bed.

———

Stephen and I were on the crowded pavement among people coming out of the Aldwych Theatre after the performance of a play by Shakespeare (Henry V), and a man behind him in the crowd tapped his shoulder so Stephen turned round to the man and, beside him, a short, almost diminutive man with a long grey beard to whom the man introduced Stephen. As if lost in the crowd, Stephen simply reached out a hand to shake the hand of the short, almost diminutive man with the long grey beard, then Stephen turned away. I said, 'Stephen, that was Solzhenitsyn you shook hands with,' and Stephen frowned. 'Was it?' 'Yes.' He frowned more, with the expression of bemusement I've become familiar with, as though he couldn't quite believe that he had just shaken hands with someone who could only have existed on the world stage.

———

Because he had not seen his mother in Athens in years, and because the dictatorship is weakening, Nikos did go to visit his mother. While in Athens, he saw Chester Kallman at a kafenion where Chester spends most of the day, drinking, every day, bottles of ouzo, in the company of young men. Nikos said the young men were suspicious of him for what he might be after from Chester, whom they appeared to treat with protective affection. Nikos was expected to pay the bill.

Back from Athens, Nikos brought with him little tins – like paint tins – of gliko koutaliou, small oranges or strawberries or even rose petals preserved in a thick syrup which are meant to be eaten with a spoon, a specialty of the island of Chios. He also brought back a jar of almost solid but ductile white paste made from sugar and mastic, also from Chios, the basis of something of a ritual: a spoonful is plunged into a glass of cold water and left for a little to flavour the water, the spoonful of mastic is then licked or pulled out with one's teeth, and the water then drunk, called ypovrihio.

So I learn something about the past daily life of Nikos in Greece. As if nostalgic, he told me his aunt always set out on the dining-room table a starched white cloth and starched white napkins and small coffee cups and little crystal dishes with silver spoons and a crystal bowl of gliko koutaliou, all prepared for him on waking from his afternoon sleep, he to take a spoonful of gliko (strawberry, made by his mother once a year, the only time she goes into the kitchen), she then making coffee in a little pot, called a briki, over a burner, heavy rather bitter coffee to shock him awake. Perhaps it was I who felt the nostalgia, if it is possible to have nostalgia for a world never lived.

No doubt I romanticize Nikos' Greek life with these effects, but how can I not? And, yes, I romanticize Nikos' history, which is the history of gliko koutaliou from Chios, mastic from Chios, which island became famous and rich for sweets and gum from mastic trees in the Middle Ages, if not earlier.

And how much refers to the past life of his family in Constantinople? As a treat for me, he will prepare Kidonato, lamb with quince, which he says is Anatolian, or Chounkiar beyendi, lamb in a tomato sauce with a puré of aubergines made from the vegetable reduced outwardly to charcoal under a grill, the innards scooped out and squeezed and then cooked with milk and butter. And he talks of a pudding called Taouk kioktsou, chicken breasts pounded into a paste and boiled with milk and sugar. Surely, these, which may be merely picturesque to me, refer in him to a past deeper than his past, to layers and layers of civilization, if not civilizations.

He tells me that Turkish cuisine is really Byzantine.

And I see in his very features, which have an Oriental cast about his eyes, a past from so long past yet present in him that I imagine he in his very body dates back to a Mongol in a Byzantine Emperor's court and a lady in waiting to the Empress.

———

Separate from Nikos who was to come on his own from the publishing house, I went on my own to an opening of an exhibition at the Hayward Gallery, and, entering, I saw, standing facing me and talking to others, Pauline de Rothschild. I approached her to say hello and she turned her back to me. I thought she hadn't recognized me, or had had her attention taken away by someone behind her who had called her name and to whom she had turned. Her hair was in a long thin plait that fell between the delicate shoulderblades that jutted out through the thin black material of her dress. I went round to her side, where I spoke to people I knew to let her know, I supposed, that I privileged to be invited to the opening was able to engage familiarly with other privileged people also invited (this entirely because of Nikos, for he is invited as a publisher of books on art, and I as his partner), and, there at the side of Pauline de Roth-schild, I positioned myself so that if she glanced to her side she would see me. She did glance and she turned away again. And again, I thought, if I were to retain her attention even for a second she would recognize me and engage in talk, and I would remember with her that time in Paris when she entertained Louis Aragon and Elsa Triolet and Osip and Lili Brik, to relive a little an evening that had meant so much to me that I wrote it all down in my diary, amusing her with an anecdote or two. (I think I am getting rather good at telling anecdotes – never, however, as well as Natasha, who will tell one after the other in a vivid and well-rounded way, even though she, laughing, told me that a friend of hers driving with her to the South of France begged her, please, no more anecdotes.) I stepped round the group of people Pauline de Rothschild was among, now no longer talking to anyone, and I faced her, and she for a moment faced me and I nodded and she nodded, and she turned away, and I knew she did not want to engage in any way with me. Still, someone I knew standing by me asked, 'Who is that?' and I said, 'The Baroness Pauline de Rothschild,' as if I had just had an intimate conversation with her that ended with her inviting me to the Château Mouton. That she kept turning her back on me didn't offend me, and it didn't because I saw the scene – rather, see it now as I write about it – as literature, as Proustian literature, which surrounds the event with literary charm, for it was literature to me. Yet, why had she turned her back on me? What was there about me she didn't like? That there are people who don't like me does, I suppose, offend me, but, again, not much, no, not much.

When I was in Providence, I went one afternoon to the Rhode Island School of Design Museum to look at the classical torso there that I used to go study as a teenager and, within a world so far removed from Greece that Greece was certainly not aware of, revered Greece for having meaning in all the world.

About classical Greece, a Greek friend said, 'Modern Greece has nothing, but nothing, to do with classical Greece.'

Still, when Nikos props on his desk a postcard of the bronze charioteer from Delphi, standing still in his long chiton, his eyes staring far out, the horse reins a suspended tangle in his hands, I feel that the classical love of the beauty and the virtue and the honour made evident in this statue remains vitally meaningful, and, because Nikos has propped the postcard on his desk with special veneration, I feel that the statue is especially meaningful because Nikos is Greek. Nikos may be within a myth, a myth more meaningful to him than it is to me, for he is Greek, but in him the myth has to me, non-Greek, a great meaning.

Empedocles:

Don't try to see love, don't try to hear love, for love is a sphere of joy all about us, is all harmony inspiring harmony in the world, in which we do see, in which we do hear, in which all our senses are harmonious, and our deeds too.

———

Frank Kermode often stays with Nikos and me when he is in London for meetings, as he is now at King's College, Cambridge.

He got up before Nikos and me and went down to the kitchen to make coffee. I heard a big bang, and got up and went down to see Frank, staring out of the kitchen window, coffee grounds splattered everywhere and the Italian coffee pot exploded into two. He said, 'My father told me I would never be capable.'

He suggested to me that we write together a book to be called CONNECTIONS, which would connect all the characters of recorded history to one another, but the accounts had to be first-person accounts, forming, Frank thought, a daisy chain.

We have got this far:

CONNECTIONS:

King George III and Dr. Johnson Dr. Johnson and Boswell and Boswell and Rousseau and Boswell met Voltaire and Rousseau met Napoleon and Chateaubriand met Napoleon and Chateaubriand also met Louis XVI and Chateaubriand writes of meeting Washington in his memoirs and Lafayette writes of meeting Washington in his memoir and Mrs Catherine Macaulay met Washington and Washington left no account of meeting anyone . . . Napoleon met Goethe and Goethe and Beethoven met and Napoleon and Stendhal conversed outside the gates of Moscow and Goethe and Crabb Robinson met and Crabb Robinson Blake and Blake and Voltaire and Voltaire and Frederick the Great and Frederick the Great and Haydn and Frederick the Great and Casanova and Haydn and Mozart met Haydn and Beethoven and Haydn and Scarlatti and Beckford was taught the harpsichord by Mozart and Mozart and Maria Theresa met and Mozart met Fanny Burney, who met George III.

If I were knowledgeable enough, I would write a book about connections among writers that cross the borders of nations and their national identities and languages in order to see the more international influences of writers among themselves, such as Dickens on Dostoyevsky, Ruskin on Proust, Edgar Allen Poe on Baudelaire, Honoré de Balzac on Henry James, Gustave Flaubert on Franz Kafka, etc, etc, etc . . .

Waking and rising from bed before me, Nikos opened the curtains and said, 'Snow!' and I saw thin English snow falling, and I lay back in bed while he, as he likes, spent the morning alone, shaving, bathing, having his coffee and breakfast. Snow continued into the waning of the winter day, and I, at my desk, felt just enough of the effects of the winter afternoon to remember heavy, snow-bound New England winter afternoons – those paradoxically stark but deep afternoons that waned both outside and inside the house, in which details I fixed on as I walked restlessly from room to room appeared to take on a vividness and even a portentousness: the open book on an armchair, the tea mug on the kitchen table, the fluted, fringed lampshade of a floor lamp. I wonder if the deep but stark winter afternoons I remembered from when I was a boy make up the dimension of my awareness, the awareness in which details do become vivid and portentous, the awareness that so fixes my concentration on the details that they become, oh, meaningful! And so, away from my native New England, in England, in France, in Italy, in Greece, even there, I fix on details as if my awareness of them remains my native awareness, that deep but stark, stark but deep winter awareness that, in fact, defies any meaning, or, perhaps, any more meaning than the meaning of a winter afternoon.

This comes to me: that we are not only formed by our history but by our geography, and both history and geography together.

And this comes to me: the objects of my family house which I grew up with, objects that predated my birth, objects that had their presence in the house before I was present, objects that had, and in my memory have, more presence than I did, and do, objects that make me aware of how little actual presence I had, and have.

———

Sonia is not rich, but she often gives to friends who can't afford them gifts to help those friends live their lives as well as possible. When her friend the writer and very much bon vivant Cyril Connolly died, he left huge debts, and Sonia helped with letters of appeal to all her friends to raise money for his widow, Deirdre.

On the verso, Sonia wrote:

I've been so involved in this horror that I haven't been able to - ring you. The point is do you know anyone I could usefully send this to??? Any ideas would be marvellous. Please suggest as it is desperate. Love, S.

Nikos did send some suggestions, and, too, some money.

To the rumor after that Deirdre Connolly was using some of the money to buy champagne Sonia replied, in a rage, 'Of course she bought champagne.'

———

Some of Frank's anecdotes he loves to tell:

At a reception, Oscar Browning, the Cambridge don, accosted Tennyson and announced, 'I'm Browning.' Tennyson peered myopically at him for a while, then said, 'No, you're not,' and walked away.

Maupassant, on his only visit to London, was entertained by Henry James. According to an anecdote by Oscar Wilde, Maupassant, dining in a restaurant with James, pointed to a woman sitting at a nearby table and asked Henry to go over and bring her back to their table. James carefully explained that in England there was the matter of being properly introduced. Maupassant tried again. Pointing to another woman, he said, 'Surely you know her at least? Ah, if I could only speak English!' When James had refused, with full explanation, for about the fifth time, Maupassant was said to have remarked irritably, 'Really, you don't seem to know anyone in London.'

When Picasso came to London for the first time, he was invited by Roland Penrose, who, unable to meet him at Victoria Station, sent Victor Pasmore. Pasmore could not speak French, and Picasso no English. In Pasmore's car, they were silent for a long while, then Pasmore said, 'Je suis peintre.' Picasso paused, then said, 'Moi aussi.'

Frank laughs – his laugh always subdued – when asking the riddle
of the weasel and the stoat: how can you tell the difference between
a weasel and a stoat? The one is weasily distinguished and the other
is stoatally different.

————

In the past, the classics scholar Peter Levi would sometimes stay
with Stephen and Natasha, then Stephen found that Levi, having
the Oxbridge power, voted against him getting the Oxford Chair
of Poetry, which he may have rightly believed Stephen didn't
deserve, but, I think, he shouldn't have also presumed on a friendship with Stephen. A moral judgment which I shouldn't make, but
this turned me against him. He writes poetry himself – Pancakes
for the Queen of Babylon – copies of which he once gave to both
Nikos and me, perhaps hoping that Nikos would publish other
poems, but Nikos did not, which he told Stephen. Peter is good-
looking, quick, decisive, knowing, always distracted so that I feel
he is attentive to me only in passing, as when he said to me, 'You
are too pretty to be taken seriously,' then hurried away, as he always
seems to be in a hurry. A Jew who converted to the Roman Church
and became a Jesuit, he left the Order to marry the widow of Cyril
Connolly, Deirdre.

Which does make me wonder what is, or was, done with the
money Sonia raised to pay off Cyril Connolly's debts, apart from
his widow buying champagne. Nikos and I contributed some small
amount. I think Anne and Rodrigo contributed substantially.

————

Nikos and I were in a taxi with Suzi and John, and as the taxi went
round Hyde Park Corner, John said, forming the words with his
entire mouth to stop from stuttering, his eyes bright in his red
face, 'A man shouldn't live with a woman for more than seven
years.' I asked, 'How long have you been with Suzi?' John did stut-
ter when he answered, 'Seven years.' Suzi smiled a wide smile,

clearly thinking that John was talking in a general way that didn't apply to her. But she rang the next morning to say that John is leaving her to move to New York, where he will be art critic on the New York Times. Suzi depends on the I CHING for advice as to what to do now.

She makes collages made of images she cuts out of glossy picture books of jungles or rocky bare landscapes or animals or the natives of primitive tribes, dense collages that conjure up an alternate, magical world.

She so believes that art has lost the essential enchantment art must have, and talks of the re-enchantment of art.

Suzi lived for a while with René Magritte and his wife, during which time she gathered together her book on Magritte, the best book, John Golding has said, on the artist. Magritte gave Suzi a drawing of flying nib pens pursuing a man running down a street and Suzi gave the drawing to Jasper Johns in exchange for a small encaustic of the American flag in which Suzi's picture is imbedded. Suzi crosses many borders in the art world and at the crossroads is making a life of her own.

Lockerbie, Scotland

Nikos commissioned Steven Runciman to write a book on Mistra, the Byzantine capital in the Peloponnese. Steven asked him to stay in his castle in Scotland, Elshieshields, and I was asked along. We arrived in darkness at the Lockerbie train station, from which a driver took us into deeper darkness to what Steven called his house. There had been no restaurant car on the train, so we arrived hungry, and Steven served up plates of ham and salad in his study. 'I'm not going to give you water in your malt whiskey,' he said.

He showed us to our rooms, mine hung with paintings by his mid-eighteenth-century Scottish relatives John and Alexander Runciman – among those in the family who had 'gone in recklessly for the arts.'

There was no question that Nikos and I would share a room.

After breakfast – prepared by Steven, who walked up and down alongside the sideboard on which were a silver tea pot, a silver coffee pot, a silver water jug, silver toast-racks, and porcelain egg-coddlers – Nikos and I took a walk on flat country roads. We were late for elevenses. Steven had already had his coffee. He looked at us sternly, but he made another pot for us, waited for us to drink, then left us to go to his study.

Nikos joined me in my room, where we tried to read, but the cold was numbing, and not relieved by the electric fire on the hearth. From the windows was a view of high Scottish firs, in which rooks cawed: 'Car-car, car-car.'

Unable to bear the cold, Nikos said he would go out to look for a warm room, and returned after fifteen minutes, laughing. He had found a room with a fire, but shortly after he sat down before it, a door opened at the back of the room, a door made up of the spines of books to blend in with the shelves of books on either side, and Steven entered and said, seeing Nikos, 'You're not allowed in here.' This amused Nikos.

We were on time for luncheon. The paper napkins were printed with poems by Burns. Steven had prepared curried chicken livers. I salted the liver before tasting, and Steven leaned over the table towards me, as he does when he has something that you take to be personally addressed to you, and said, 'I don't invite guests who salt my food before tasting it to come back.'

'I'll try to be better behaved,' I said.

'It will help to know you'll try,' he said.

On the wood-panelled dining-room walls were large paintings by John and Alexander Runciman.

Nikos and Steven discussed the lack of interest that the West had had in Byzantium until, really, Steven inspired attention to those 1000 years of civilization.

Nikos suggested that the Phanariots kept Byzantium alive.

I had to ask who the Phanariots were.

'Are,' Nikos said.

Steven explained –

They are the Greeks of Constantinople who remained after the city fell to the Turks in 1453. By the sixteenth century, they were rich and influential, and even more so in the seventeenth century. They were called Phanariots because they lived in the Phanar, the Greek quarter of the city, a self-contained group, intermarrying and inter-quarrelling. The Ottoman Sultans appointed them Princes of Walachia and Moldavia in Romania, and from there they dominated Greek civilization from the late seventeenth century through the eighteenth, and maintained the great

Hellenic-Byzantine tradition. They had printing presses in Bucharest, discouraged in Constantinople.

Smiling, Nikos listened as Steven went on to me, 'They maintained the now defunct Big Idea to resuscitate Byzantium.'

'Resuscitate?' Nikos asked, offended.

'I am sorry,' Steven apologized to him. 'Their Big Idea was to get hold of the Ottoman Empire from within. The Phanariots existed as the aristocracy of Romania until the last world war.'

Nikos said, 'They've never been very welcome in Greece itself.'

'Because they were thought to be too grand and too pleased with themselves.'

'Koraïs disapproved of them.'

'That monster Koraïs.'

And so more explanation for me:

Adamantios Koraïs, a European Greek of the late eighteenth and early nineteenth century, was one of the instigators of Greek liberation from the Turks. 'Doing it safely from a flat in Paris,' Steven said. 'He was totally Westernized, and had hardly ever been to Greece. He visited once or twice Chios, where his family were from. Like all Europeans of the time, he saw Greece purely in classical terms. After all, the Turks had occupied what we now know as Greece for four hundred years. The Greeks there hadn't thought of classical times at least for that long. It was the Orthodox Church that kept everyone aware of Byzantium during the Ottoman Occupation, because the Church was functioning all during that time. Koraïs disapproved of Byzantium, disapproved of the Orthodox Church, disapproved of Greeks of his day. He disapproved because of Gibbon. Gibbon thought the whole of Byzantium decadent. And Gibbon was the god of Koraïs. He thought all Greeks should be like the classical heroes. I can't think why people praise him, except that he did leave a very good library on Chios. About the only good thing he did. He was basically responsible for Katharevousa. Just think of all that poetry written in a language now disclaimed. It's the great disaster of Greek literature written in Katharevousa.'

'Oh, I know,' Nikos said.

'Of course, Koraïs was European, and no European of that time thought of Greece as anything but classical. Think of Byron.'

'And Greeks welcomed the myth of ancient Greece imposed on them by Europe. They wanted to be European too.'

'Would you say that is still true?'

'Greece wanting to be European? Yes.'

'They repudiated Byzantium, these Europeanized Greeks. Koraïs disapproved, and they, ashamed, disapproved.'

'But so much of the recent – well, recent in your lifetime – revival of Byzantium is due to you.'

'I hope I played a little part. I think I made Greeks a little more aware of Byzantium than they had been. When I first started, and even after the last world war, when I was living in Greece, it was thought somewhat odd to be interested in Byzantium. It was certainly not fashionable.'

'It became fashionable among Greeks because a foreigner took it up,' Nikos said.

'How the Greeks explained the survival of Hellenism when they took out pretty much all of the Byzantine centuries, and took out entirely the Turkish domination – well, how they did it was not historical. My book The Great Church in Captivity was one of the first to deal with Greece under the Turks – a very necessary link in Greek history.'

Nikos simply nodded, as he was not going to disagree with Steven.

'In some ways I regret the passing of the Ottoman Empire,' Steven said.

I asked, 'Why is that?'

'Because I'm the Grand Orator of the Great Church of Constantinople, which in Ottoman times would have entitled me to be a prince. Alas, the Ottoman Empire has fallen.'

Steven stuck out his lower lip and made a face as of someone looking down at another from a great height.

Maussane

We are in Provence staying with Stephen and Natasha.

It was six years ago that I was last here, alone with Stephen, which I found out later upset Natasha very much. Now she asks me if I saw this or that when I was here.

She has been tremendously hospitable. Today she drove Stephen, Nikos and me up to the Ardèche Gorge, a very long way, for a picnic, prepared and packed by Natasha in a basket with plates and knives and forks and napkins. We've just got back, and it's late, but while Nikos sleeps I, in the bed next to him in the guest room, want to describe the day, which was so much like a dream I want to get it down before, like a dream, it fades.

The mistral is blowing outside.

We stopped at various belvederes on the way for views of the gorge, the river flat and black and shining far below between the steep white rocky banks. From one belvedere, Nikos spotted some bathers far below in the river, and we decided to go down to the river bank to have our picnic lunch. We walked down and down a path, through woods still filled at this late date with purple wild flowers, Stephen's untied shoelaces getting tangled in the branches of small bushes, then down rocky places, all of us laughing, until we came to the broad flat stone bank of the river, like a number of smooth stone platforms that seemed to float in strata one above the other by the side of the river, green and flowing over and around boulders out in the current. Some people were swimming in the river, some canoeing. I put down the basket I was carrying and Nikos the rug he was carrying, and the four of us went to look out at the river, and just then there swam toward us three youths, their bodies green in the green water, who rose up onto a stone platform below us, naked. Their hair was long and wet. Touching their genitals, they stood in the sunlight to dry themselves, then sat on the rock.

Natasha turned away to go back to the picnic basket and unpack it, and I quickly followed her to help. Nikos came, too, to spread out the rug. Only Stephen remained where he'd been, and sat on the edge of the platform and took out his spectacles from his shirt pocket and put them on to stare down at the boys.

Natasha called Stephen to eat, and all the while we had the picnic the boys remained on the rock below us. Natasha and Nikos and I pretended that they were not there and didn't look toward them, but Stephen kept his spectacles on and didn't stop looking at them, smiling. I heard them speaking German, and I thought that they had put a spell over us and were tempting us to acknowledge them, and, in acknowledging them, something would happen to us that Natasha and Nikos and I must not acknowledge. And yet I was, as much as I pretended not to be, always aware of them while Natasha and Nikos and I talked and laughed about anything but where we were. I didn't even focus on them closely enough to find out if they were in fact attractive, but just my awareness of them naked and near us gave to that river, to the rocks, the trees, the entire gorge a sense of sexual potency that was all the more potent to me for being unfocused. Stephen alone acknowledged them. The spell they cast lasted long after we had finished our picnic and walked back up the path to the car.

I told myself I knew what Nikos' and my reactions to the boys were, and there was no doubt about Stephen's reaction, but I had no idea what Natasha's reaction was.

She drove very fast, often all of us in silence, but she stopped again at different spots so we could get out to see the gorge, which had now become enchanted.

Then Natasha drove through beautiful countryside, past beautiful little villages on the sides of green hills, to Orgnac, where we stopped to see the grotto. Natasha stayed in the car to rest while Stephen, Nikos and I went down, giggling and now able to talk freely about the German boys, into an enormous space of stalactites and stalagmites, the air damp and feverishly cold. We were with a group, and before the tour the group's photograph was taken, then we went down deeper and deeper, down long flights of cement stairs, into a surreal world. Stephen and Nikos, however, were bored, and Stephen said, 'I always feel that what I imagine these places to be like is always better than what they in fact are.' Perhaps he was right, but it was strange enough that when we came out into the sunlight and flat ground I had the strong feeling that I had just woken up from a dream. Stephen had bought and given to us a copy of the group photograph.

And then I felt I went right back into the dream as Natasha drove us on, through Barjac, through small towns like Tharaux and Rochegude, and by the time we got to Uzès it was dark. We had dinner there, and on the way back to Maussane we saw, the moon shining through one arch, the Pont du Gard, seeming to float like a dream image in vast blackness. We saw the castle at Beaucaire, the medieval dungeon at Tarascon, the Roman triumphal arch and mausoleum at Saint Rémy.

Now I will go to sleep.

———

When I got up, Stephen was having breakfast and I joined him. Natasha and Nikos were out in the garden, working. The mistral was still blowing, and from the breakfast table we could see them, through the French doors, their clothes and hair blown out.

I said to Stephen, 'Those boys we saw yesterday in the Ardèche River, they were Rhine Maidens.'

I had thought this would be our joke, which we might share with Nikos later, but keep from Natasha because she would not find it amusing, but Stephen, excited, said, 'That's wonderful!' and he immediately got up and went out into the garden and called, 'Natasha! Natasha!' She and Nikos stopped working, and 'Yes?' she called back. Stephen shouted in the wind, 'Those boys we saw in the river, David says they were the Rhine Maidens.' I saw Natasha laugh and say something to Nikos, who smiled, and I thought that the spell the boys had cast on us all was broken.

Natasha, Nikos and I walked through the valley of the Alpilles to pick blackberries. The mistral was blowing harder than ever, and sometimes pushed us forward, sometimes drew us backward. Tree branches and cane thrashed. The light was bright and pure, as were the smells: smells of lavender and rosemary and mint and thyme and fennel and juniper, bits of which we picked off as we walked along. The smell of lavender or rosemary or any other wild herb seemed, as I breathed it in deeply, to hollow out, as penetratingly as the smell of ammonia, a great dark space behind my sinuses and the space filled up with the scent, so pungent that I'm able to recall the smell long after having dropped the twig of lavender or rosemary.

It was very curious, the three of us walking along. I kept wondering what our relationships were, Natasha's to Nikos and me, ours to her, and, even, Nikos' to me and mine to him. What, I wondered, did we really think of one another as we walked along together? Nikos picked almonds and broke them open on the paved road with a stone, Natasha picked thyme, I found a snake's shed skin tangled in grass – little events which themselves seemed very strange to me.

When, later, I was alone with Natasha in the house, both Stephen and Nikos in their rooms reading, she told me about her childhood: that she was an illegitimate baby, her mother an actress, her father a Welshman, brought up by a working-class foster mother, finally taken back by her own mother.

After dinner, which Nikos prepared, the four of us worked in the garden. The moonlight was bright, the stars dense, the Milky Way showing like a thin, luminous mist, the mistral still blowing strong, and the rocky hills of the Alpilles beyond the garden looked to be wild and to be moving. We transplanted irises. Stephen would simply dig a hole and stuff in all the irises he could fit in, then stomp the earth in around them. His white hair flying about, he would then ask, 'Is that all right, Natasha?' She would answer, 'It's perfect, darling,' and when he'd go for more irises she'd smile at Nikos and me.

I think he was worried about having Nikos and me here before we arrived, but he has relaxed. However, he still seems particularly to want Natasha to like Nikos, because whenever Nikos does anything or even says anything, Stephen draws Natasha's attention to it as if hoping to make her see how helpful or how intelligent he is. Natasha is always appreciative.

He has three kittens he has become very attached to. He feeds them over and over all day and keeps trying to pet them, but they run away.

London

Nikos keeps adding to the poem he showed me when we first met, 'Pure Reason.' I have never asked him whom the poem was initially meant for, someone he loved and someone whom I don't want to know about, because I want that someone to be a vague presence that Nikos is filling out, perhaps, after all, with me. The additional layers consist of an investigation into what love means, and Nikos has looked into our love for each other with a critical eye, at times severe:

> Disjunction has triumphed. Now each on our own, we muse about our pure craving . . . We have failed. Each of us keeps to himself.

Reading this, I'm shocked, and wonder what happened between us to make him write this.

Then, after many considerations, many of them when he is alone, the revelation comes to him: love is a category of the mind, an absolute.

> Once the centre is fixed we can allow the antinomies to revolve around it, to resolve themselves as if by magic, and fabulous marriages will take place among them.

———

Conversations with Frank (his heavy-framed spectacles too big for his pale face, his longish hair in wisps, preoccupied with keeping his pipe lit) seem to be incidental. It is as if he, well known among his friends to be self-deprecating, wants at best to keep his comments light-spirited, yet he touches lightly on some of the major issues of literature. He never in these conversations refers to any of his books, but it is in his books that the issues, these too seemingly incidental to him, are made so vital. And the one that strikes me personally as being most vital is The Genesis of Secrecy.

> If there is one belief (however the facts resist it) that unites us all . . . it is the conviction that somehow, in some occult fashion, if we could only detect it, everything will be found to hang together.

(What a Jamesian expression that: to hang together!)

How might this be done? By halting the movement of the senses, or by trying to – which I take to mean: by fixing on what Frank calls an immediate interpretation to focus in the blur of sense for one central sense about which the infinite chaos of objects will come together as a temporary whole.

> . . . the shrine of the single sense.

(This is Wallace Stevens.)

I remark: Frank does not use the word idea, but 'sense'.

The very last sentence of the final chapter ends: 'our sole hope and pleasure is in the perception of a momentary radiance, before the door of disappointment is finally shut on us.'

As for what the book reveals about Frank himself – he never assumes it would be possible for him to be a 'spiritual insider,' and yet remaining a 'carnal outsider' doesn't give him a 'hold' to see 'inside.' He is a 'carnal' working-class man from the Island of Man, an outsider to the rest of the world, but being such a 'carnal outsider' doesn't give him an identity enough, a 'hold' enough, to reject the identity in order to free himself and find his way among the 'spiritual insiders,' where, however, he wants to be. So he is neither outside nor inside.

Anita told me that Frank deliberately changed his Manx accent into what he thinks a more conventional English accent. She also told me that, having been rejected by Oxbridge and so educated at Leeds instead, he always felt like an outsider, but an outsider who wanted to get inside, which outside was, for him the one most open to him, that of literature. As much of a 'spiritual insider' as Frank is, and he is considered to be very much one, he himself does not consider himself to be one, not really. He does not feel entitled.

What does Frank want?

Frank is in 'love' with literature, in which he finds his greatest fulfillment, but the moments of fulfillment are only held for as long as the radiance lasts against the overwhelming threat of the unfulfilled. The spiritual is too inconstant to be anything but a disappointment.

I honestly feel there is a lot of Frank as a person in this. I remember what the moral philosopher Bernard Williams once said about him: that Frank can't bear too much feeling, and shuts the door on it when it threatens him.

Only once did he tell me he had an experience that had a 'sense of meaning': he was in Japan, and was asked to place a branch on an altar, and as he did that 'sense' came to him. He told me this simply, and then went silent. He remembered the 'sense,' was even able to refer to the 'sense,' but it passed.

In his dedication to Nikos and me on the flyleaf of The Genesis of Secrecy, Frank wrote, 'Keep the carnal outsiders outside . . .'

———

Alone, Suzi continues to give drinks parties, and Francis, faithful to Suzi, comes. After one party, when most people had gone, Francis said to me, 'Let's go to dinner – you, Nikos, Suzi, me, we'll go to dinner.'

At the restaurant, Greek, Nikos said, reading the menu, 'They have grilled gray mullet. That's what I'll have.' Francis said, 'That's what I'll have, too. Grilled gray mullet. I love that. I'm a simple person. Aren't I a simple person? Aren't I, Suzi?' Suzi smiled and reached across the table and squeezed one of his hands. Nikos asked him, 'What do you mean by simple?' He answered, 'I'm direct and I'm obvious. I've had an appalling life. I've had a very unhappy life. I don't think about it. There it is. That's simple.'

Suzi asked him, 'You've never been happy?'

'Once or twice,' he said. 'When I was young, in moments of ecstasy. Now I'm too old. I don't think about it, about happiness. There are many things I don't think about. I've done horrible things in my life, horrible. There they are. I don't think about them. I'm too old.'

His dyed hair, with, it appeared, a hair cream to make it smooth and keep it starkly in place, was combed against his head, with some stiff strands carefully arranged down over his forehead. He said, 'I've had a horrible life, a tragic life.' He picked up a small pickle from a white plate and ate it, picked up another one, a large one, ate it, picked up another one, a large one, ate it, picked up another and put it into his mouth, and as if the taste had only now occurred to him, he said, 'These pickles are horribly sour.' He didn't laugh but everyone else did. He said, 'I'm a very simple person who's had an appalling and tragic life.'

Nikos said, 'What's been so appalling? You've never been seriously ill, you've never had to worry about money.'

Francis said, 'You're right. I was pretty when I was young. Old men liked me. One old man, an old Greek – I even remember his name – fell in love with me, gave me money, and I used the money to paint. I lived off old men. I always had a clear idea of what I wanted to do. I wanted to be exceptional. I wanted to do exceptional work. I just took money. I was an old whore. I still am. An older whore. A lucky old whore.'

A strange sensation passed through me. I sat back and tears came into my eyes.

A waiter put a gray mullet in front of Francis and he asked, 'What's this?' 'Your grilled gray mullet,' Nikos said. 'I hate this,' Francis said, 'I can't eat it. I couldn't get a forkful down me (sic) throat.'

Nikos asked Francis, 'What makes your life tragic?'

'I've been in love, and love is tragic.'

'Love can make you happy,' Nikos said.

Francis said, 'I was in love with someone who killed himself. That made our love tragic.'

———

When I told Sonia about the deaths of my parents, she didn't react, just stared at me, her eyes, within puffy lids, hard. Then, after a moment she said, still staring hard at me with bloodshot eyes, 'Now there is nothing between you and eternity.'

———

In what way am I essentially American? Though I have dismissed Henry James as a fairytale European, I go back to him as an American, and I go back to him for what I believe an essentially American awareness that has survived in me for the simple fact that I was born and brought up in America –

I counted the use of the word 'everything' over eighty-five times in The Wings of the Dove, which I have recently reread after many years. For example:

'I want everything at once and together –'

'There was more to come – everything.'

'I want the whole thing.'

'It gains you time.' / 'Time for what?' / 'For everything.'

'It makes everything fit.' / 'Everything.' / The word, for a little, held the air, and he might have seemed the while to be looking, by no means dimly now, at all it stood for.

'But a denial, when it comes to that – confound the whole thing, don't you see! – of exactly what?' It was as if he were hoping she would narrow; but she in fact enlarged. 'Of everything.'

Everything had never yet seemed to him so incalculably much. 'Oh!' he simply moaned into the gloom.

'He has done everything.' / 'Oh, everything! Everything's nothing.'

The word, repeated so often and in so many contexts, appeared to me to attract the whole novel into itself. Was 'everything' money? Was 'everything' life? Was 'everything' a horror? Was 'everything' a great and final fulfillment? What was 'everything' in itself? (As Ezra Pound wrote: 'Henry James was aware of the spherical form of the planet . . .') The awareness of 'everything,' the possession to connect 'everything' into a whole, the need to have everything – isn't that essentially American, and isn't my essential, impulsive American awareness to sustain that 'everything' within one spherical globe?

When I recall myself, a college student in Boston, walking around Louisburg Square, the Hub of the Hub of the Yankee Transcendentalist Universe, I, in my Ivy League suit, desiring 'everything . . .'

In London, this desire is mitigated by the particulars that life here is essentially made of, particulars so particular they belie the desire for 'everything,' which is, of course, a spiritual desire, but in London to be kept to myself, my secret.

Nikos, from whom I have no secrets, is aware in me of that desire.

———

Suzi gave a dinner party for Sonia, Francis, Nikos and me. Francis didn't drink, and put his hand over his glass whenever Suzi was about to pour wine into it. He didn't say much all evening. He looked sad – polite and attentive but making an effort to be so.

We talked about people becoming dependent on others, and Francis said, 'George became dependent on me. If he hadn't, he'd probably be alive now. He was a thief, an inept thief, always getting caught, when I met him. He'd probably be in jail and alive now if he hadn't met me. But he did, he drank himself into a mad state and, because of me, killed himself.'

Sonia said, aggressively, 'He didn't kill himself. I read to you the medical report, in English. His death was accidental.'

'He did,' Francis said, 'he killed himself.'

———

I thought of Frank Kermode when I read the following:

> We count and name whatever lies upon the special lines we
> trace, whilst the other things and the untraced lines are neither
> named nor counted. There are in reality infinitely more things
> 'unadapted' to each other in this world than there are things
> 'adapted'; infinitely more things with irregular relations than
> with regular relations between them. But we look for the
> regular kind of thing exclusively, and ingeniously discover and
> preserve it in our memory. It accumulates with other regular
> kinds, until the collection of them fills our encyclopedias. Yet
> all the while between and around them is an infinite anony-
> mous chaos of objects that no one ever thought of together,
> of relations that never yet attracted our attention.
>
> William James, The Varieties of Religious Experience

When I quoted this to Anita, she sat back, as though a revelation
had occurred to her, and she told me that when Frank sets himself
to read a novelist it is to discern the untraced lines, the connections
that the text makes but that haven't yet been made by another
critic. He uses the word 'occult' a lot, trying to trace lines that form
a pattern in the details. It is natural that Frank should turn to the
Bible, that most occult of texts. What he longs to do is write a
book about religious heresies.

Interesting, Anita's telling me that Frank has lost interest in the
poetry of W. B. Yeats for being too obvious, and has instead taken
on the more occult poetry of Wallace Stevens.

The title, The Genesis of Secrecy, was Anita's idea.

It is odd to go to her for an elucidation of Frank's work, which
he would never elucidate.

———

Often, when we have dinner parties for friends, we play the game of Exquisite Corpses – that is, a sheet of paper is folded into four or five parts, one person draws a head and folds it over so the next person can't see it and this person draws the shoulders and torso, which is folded over so as not to be seen, and the next person draws the thighs and genitals, and on and on until a whole figure is drawn, which is then revealed when the folded sheet of paper is unfolded. There have been evenings when we were howling with laughter.

So far, these are the friends who have played the game with Nikos and me:

Mark Lancaster, Andrew Lord, Keith Milow, Stephen Spender, Suzi Gablik, Stephen Buckley, James Joll, Tony Stokes, Teresa Gleadowe, Stephenie Bergman, Gregory Evans, David Hockney, Barry Flanagan, Sue Flanagan, Jan Hashey, Anne Wollheim, John Golding, Frank Kermode, Keith Walker, Michael Craig-Martin, Antoinette Godkin, Maggi Hambling.

———

About Patrick Kinross – he goes to North Africa for paid sex with young men (which Nikos seems to accept as what is done between older and younger men, and he laughs), and, after a recent tryst there, in London became afflicted with a disease that can't be diagnosed that wastes him away, so he is becoming thinner and thinner.

I suddenly recall Patrick opening the door to Nikos and me and, as I saw, noting that I had a small wound on my forehead, and this made him smile in a way I thought knowing, as if the small wound, which was caused by my bumping my forehead against a low lintel, signaled to him an activity, shared by Nikos, which he indulged in and that involved wounding.

From time to time, hinted at and then withdrawn, a suggestion opens up of a world Nikos and I know nothing about, that of sado-masochism, a world that seems as closed as the world of homosexuality once was, but, as once happened among homosexuals, hinted at and the hint withdrawn if the hint is not taken up. My impression is that the world includes all sexes, as if sado-masochism is a sex in itself, in which wounding and being wounded identifies the sex. I find myself wondering about so-and-so or so-and-so if he or she is of that sex, which keeps itself closed, but the members of which may be among my close friends. And I find myself not expressing horror at one person inflicting pain on another for pleasure, in case someone who is a friend is far from horrified – as, I suppose, a heterosexual may hold back from saying anything against homosexuality which he suspects in a friend he loves.

———

More and more, Nikos' memories become mine. I feel I was with him when he was a child and his family during the summer they moved from Athens to what was then the countryside in Kifisia and he was allowed one white balloon to play with. I think his memories have become more important to me than my own because I imagine I can possess them in a way I can't possess my own, he someone I view from the outside, and so, outside of me, viewed by me as more contained in himself than the uncontainable thoughts and feelings that I have inside of me. Yes, I would have to be him to make all the connections among the memories he recalls for them to be mine, all his memories beyond me. Still I go on to record his memories, and perhaps one day the complex context of all my own massively posses-sive feelings and thoughts about him will go and he will remain, himself, apart from me in this writing, on his own.

———

Stephen gave me a copy of his short stories and novella, The Burn-ing Cactus, which he asked me to 'edit.' I took him at his word, and did just that, limiting myself to one story, 'The Dead Island,' in which I crossed out lines and whole paragraphs to tighten the text, and what I mostly crossed out were metaphors and similes:

The sea was silent and brittle like smashed glass. The water

looked so clear that it seemed like varnish adding colour and
translucency to shoals of darting fish . . . She paused in her
walk and listened closely to the birds' song bursting from the
packed bushes, like white satin streamers against the cork-
screwing cypresses . . .

It seems to me that Stephen relies on metaphors and similes to nail
down impressions he is otherwise unsure of nailing, as if the simple
The sea was silent . . . or She saw through the clear sea water shoals
of darting fish . . . or She paused in her walk and listened to the birds'
song in the cypresses . . . do not flash in the mind with the vividness
metaphors and similes should give them. I want to say to him that it
is not that I don't believe in the vivifying effects of metaphors and
similes, but that I believe they are such mysterious workings of the
imagination that they are miracles, and so should be used with all the
respect miracles demand, perhaps one a book, and used as the key to
unlock and reveal the meaning of the book. (As Frank does when he
uses 'a ghost of a cup of tea' to unlock and reveal an inner meaning
of Conrad's Under Western Eyes, and I wonder if this image of a
'ghost of a cup of tea' is what Frank would consider a 'shrine of the
single sense' in which an 'immediate interpretation' is sustained for as
long as any interpretation can be sustained.) I didn't go on about the
deepening doubt I have that literature is too dependent on metaphor
and simile, as if uncertain about anything but the use of imagery to
sustain itself. I gave the book to Stephen and he thanked me, but he
has not mentioned it to me. He did, however, tell Nikos that he was
impressed by what I had done, and Nikos passed this on to me, and,
oddly, I was embarrassed and would have preferred Stephen not telling Nikos, who he knew would tell me. But perhaps Stephen, too,
was embarrassed that I should edit his stories.

———

I recall David Sylvester coming to dinner, where, as usual, he
pushed back his chair to think about something that had been said,
to think a long while. He said, 'I'm trying to think . . .' and

everyone else at the table stopped to listen, and after a very long pause David said, 'I'm trying to think why . . .' and there was another long pause before David said, 'I'm trying to think why Cimabue is a greater artist than Fragonard.'

—————

Nikos is more interested in writing poetry than being an editor, which poetry he allows only me to read. In his poetry the most abstract ideas are plangent, as in this, in which not one image occurs, but which expands into a sensitive plangent sense within the idea:

THE DEFINITION OF GOOD

Stripped finally of the 'bare essentials'
he had achieved a 'luminous simplicity'.
Removing one by one the layers of all that was 'superfluous',
down to the 'hard core',
divested of all 'attributes',
aspiring to a 'simple idea',
he strived to 're-define reality'.

Simplification, his aim, was a mere pose, we said.
Therefore, we concluded, he lied.
And yet, to him his pose was how he saw himself.
This was how he was . . .
He saw himself engrossed in, obsessed even
by the 'process of simplification', or 'self-simplification'.
What did this 'mean'? What did it mean to him, to us?
To him it meant arriving, through this process,
at some simple 'truth', a 'unit'
that could not possibly be simplified any further.
But this was vague – or so it seemed to us.
To us, 'simplification' meant, really, a dangerous, a suspect
obsessive drive to 'reduce' things, himself,
to what we called, in a derogatory sense, 'over-
    simplification'.

That is, to us it meant, again, lying of sorts. To him?
The fact is he believed in this 'good', whereas we didn't.
We neither 'believed' nor understood what 'good' means.

———

Though it is impossible to ring Lucian Freud – contact with him can only be made through his solicitor – he often rings Nikos at home, at any hour, to insist, say, that there be no page numbers wherever a reproduction of his work appears. Nikos asks how a reference could then be made to a specific work, but Freud remains adamant, so there are no page numbers where his works are reproduced.

Stephen Spender calls Freud evil, and recounts the story of a book dummy that they once did together, Stephen writing and Freud drawing, which Stephen had but which Freud stole. He is also known to lie, and worse. Does he think that after his death none of this will be revealed? Better, I think, to reveal all when alive.

———

Costas Tachtsis, Nikos has heard, was murdered in Athens, where he had had more of a money-making career among certain men than he did as a writer among readers. Fed up with how little his novel The Third Wedding was selling, he went out into the street and sold copies as a hawker. It was known that he kept a diary, recording the names of the men who came to his flat, but the only object stolen from his flat was the diary. The rumour, Nikos was told, is that his murderer has found pre-planned refuge in a monastery on Mount Athos, the Greek peninsula of monasteries where no women are allowed. Eulogizing him on his death, Melina Mercouri, now minister for culture, made a statement about Costas, that he was the best Greek novelist after Kazantzakis.

———

No doubt partly to get into her good graces, which I am eager to do, and also because I find her fascinating, I offered Natasha to help her in her garden in Loudoun Road, which help she accepted. But first lunch, where she told me a lot about her youth, much of which she had told me when we were in the South of France. Her mother, Ray Litvin, is alive still, and I gather lives in a flat whose rent is paid for by Stephen. I may get the sequence somewhat wrong, but the episodes from Natasha's life stand out. She had told me that she was illegitimate, the daughter of a music critic. She was sent as a baby to a home where she was restricted to a high chair, and all she could say when her mother visited her with a friend was 'Gwen, down, down,' referring to herself as Gwen; this alarmed her mother's friend, who suggested that Natasha be put in fostering care in a working-class family, where the mother, however strict, used to hold Natasha on her lap and close to her, the only reason, Natasha said with a short laugh, she is in any way sane. There was no recrimination in what she recounted, but everything sustained on a level of fact, and I wondered why she was telling me such intimate facts. Unknown to her, her father did arrange for Natasha to have what she called her other family, upper-middle class and wealthy, where she would spend periods and where she was encouraged in her gift of playing the piano. Her mother, an actress, became deaf, and blamed Natasha, whom she brought home – I think to a flat in Primrose Hill – and at eleven years old her mother instructed her to take a number such and such a bus and get off at such and such a stop and ring the bell at such and such an address, and the man who would answer would be her father, from whom she must ask for £15. Natasha did, and her father almost immediately engaged her in talk about music, which led to Natasha playing the piano for him. Whether or not she was given £15, I'm not sure Natasha said. Living with her mother, with no money, Natasha would sometimes go out on a walk for hours, distracted, then would look about with the realization that she had no idea where she was, but would then have to walk back. (This distraction, a sudden blankness, often comes over Natasha's face, even while she is talking, as if a sudden shock occurs to her.) She managed to continue with her piano, and at sixteen won a scholarship to the Royal College of Music. Years later, she found herself in a train compartment with Sybil Thorndike, and mentioned that her birth had caused her mother to go deaf and therefore ruin her career as an actress, and Sybil Thorndike said, 'But, Natasha, your mother was always deaf.'

In her late age, Natasha's mother has taken to painting, as instructed by Maggi Hambling; the garden shed is filled with her paintings.

Stephen, it seems, just about tolerates her.

Out in the front garden, I mostly dug and pulled up long tangled roots, while Natasha appeared not quite to know why she was there, but watched me.

She said, suddenly: when she opens a drawer and finds a photograph of a young man she does not know, obviously taken by Stephen, her heart crashes to her feet; but then she closes the drawer, thinking, he is not doing it to hurt her.

About W. H. Auden, Natasha told me she once confronted him with the moral problem of his sexuality and his calling himself an Anglican, to which he replied, 'I sin. There it is, I'm a sinner.'

———

A description:

Nikos and I on the Spanish island of Minorca for a summer holiday – the sun so bright it appeared to be black, but bright black as in a bright night, and the moonlit night appeared to shine with the blue light of day, and there was a sense of such freedom in the strangeness of it all.

Dry stalks of plants were covered with snails, and the stone walls along burnt-out fields looked like walls of skulls, and in the burnt-out fields were rough cactus.

Nikos took a film of me standing naked in the landscape.

———

What could be more relevant to today than this?

Do we learn with one part of us, feel angry with another, and desire the pleasures of eating and sex with another? Or do we employ our mind as a whole when our energies are employed in any of these ways?

Plato

———

Sebastian Walker (Sebbie), who has begun publishing pre-literate books for children (I asked him, 'Have you become a millionaire, Sebbie?' to which he replied with half-closed bulging eyes, 'Multi'), sponsored an evening of piano played by Alfred Brendel in the Middle Temple.

Nikos declined the invitation.

I went with Julia Hodgkin, she in a simple black evening frock and carrying a small black reticule covered with black sequins and

I in black tie. The taxi driver, leaving us off, asked, 'Important do
this evening?'

The Middle Temple has stone-paved passages with polished
wood-paneled walls and portraits of men in old frames. Just within
the entrance was a round table with cards with names written on
them arranged in circles to indicate at what tables and in what
rooms people would sit for supper, then down a wooden staircase
with a thick wooden banister and a red runner patterned with large
blue flowers out into a garden where men and women in evening
dress were gathered along a stone parapet, a wide, deep lawn
extending beyond the parapet. A waiter came to offer us flutes of
champagne from a silver tray.

I heard someone near by say, 'Really, Sebbie only gives a do like
this to be able to invite the royals.'

'We'd better go up to the recital hall,' Julia said. 'The seats are
unreserved.'

The hall is large, with a groined ceiling and high, wood-
paneled walls. Along a high shelf all round the hall are placed
breastplates and helmets, and painted on every wooden panel is a
coat of arms.

Julia and I sat behind Stephen and Natasha Spender. I leaned
forward to say hello to him, and he turned to me as if with a shock
and asked, 'What are you doing here?'

I smiled.

He said, 'You're wearing a clip-on bow tie.'

I put a hand over my tie.

Natasha didn't turn to me.

Alfred Brendel came in, sat at the grand piano, adjusted the
height of the stool by turning knobs on either end, and then held
his fingers over the keys for a moment before he struck the first
chord. All the while he played, people in the audience coughed.

Julia and I sat at a table among barristers and their wives. Napkins
falling to the floor from laps, everyone rose when the royals, the
Duke and Duchess of York, she at one table and he at another, got
up. The Duchess, her eyes wide and staring apparently at nothing,

walked through the standing guests, and, still apparently without seeing anything as she stared out, stopped for a second before a woman and smiled a smile that seemed to float out from her face and have nothing to do with her. The woman curtsied. Then, as soon as the royals had left, the guests dispersed, as if in a hurry to get away.

I heard this conversation:

'I was a long way from being seated at the best table.'

'What was the best?'

'With the Duchess.'

'And the second best?'

'With the Duke.'

'I would put our table at, say, fifth best.'

'Not too bad.'

I did not see Stephen and Natasha leaving.

———

Vera Russell asked Nikos to choose poems by Auden to be included in a large book of etchings by Henry Moore, and Vera arranged for Nikos to accompany Auden to Henry Moore's estate. Entering, all Auden said was, 'You must be a millionaire,' and lit up a cigarette, then, as if to himself, wondered why poets are not millionaires, and then consoled himself with the thought that when an artist does go into a slump he never rises from the slump, as though poets never go into slumps from which they never rise. What this had to do with Henry Moore, who clearly is not in a slump, Nikos had no idea, nor, he thought, did Henry Moore, who simply stared at Auden smoking his cigarette, his large, deeply wrinkled jaw thrust out, the bangs of his hair falling over his deeply wrinkled forehead. He showed no interest in Henry Moore's work, nor in the book. He was mostly silent at the meal of ribs of beef, which he ate, grease dripping down his chin, 'ravenously' Nikos said, after which he said, 'Well, I prefer mutton.' Nikos was very amused by this, and admiring of the total self-containment of Auden, as total as a monument so aware of its own monumentality that it is indifferent to spectators. Yet, perhaps because he was somewhat aware of his duties as a guest, he did talk, in his monotoned, gravelly voice, not so much to communicate as to express his many opinions about his many subjects, everyone else simply listening, as of course one does simply listen when a monument speaks.

Nikos told me he recounted to Stephen the visit and Auden's behavior, and Stephen, opening and closing his lips as if to suppress a smile and frowning a little, appeared to be thinking, More evidence of the personal monstrousness of Auden.

———

Marina Warner is often a guest at Sebbie's. She is an editor for Vogue magazine, or so I imagine, as her elegance makes her appear to be familiar with that world; but, too, when I hear her talking so knowledgeably with Dawn Ades about art history, also at Sebbie's, I imagine that the academic world is where she most fits in. Perhaps she lives one world within the other. She wears her spectacles at the tip of her nose.

Nikos was the first to publish Dawn, her book Photomontage.

———

We see a lot of Francis, who invited us to the Colony Room, which he calls Muriel's because it is run by Muriel Belcher, a close friend whom he paints. Up a flight of old stairs, the walls painted dark green where the plaster hasn't fallen away, we went into a small room with a filthy gray carpet, dirty pale-green walls, empty bottles under the chairs, and on the floor a large tin tub filled with ice and green bottles. The first time we went there, a mirrored door at the other side of the room opened and in came a man with loosely curled hair, spectacles, and a black-and-gold scarf about his neck. He was supporting an old woman in a lank gray dress. The man helped the woman to a stool at the end of the bar, near the entrance, and Francis introduced Nikos and me to her, Muriel, and to the man, Ian Board. Muriel's hair was long and thin and pulled tight over her skull so her scalp showed. Her face was long, wrinkled, slack; her mouth was always open, and her teeth made me think of her skull. Her gums were bleeding so she held a handkerchief to her mouth. She didn't look at us so much as tilt her head and throw an approximate glance at us. Francis said, 'Isn't she beautiful?' We said yes. Francis ordered champagne from the barman, whom he introduced us to. His name was David. Then Francis introduced us to the pianist, a young handsome man named Felicity, then Francis ordered a brandy-and-soda for Felicity from David. Francis, Muriel, Ian, Nikos and I talked about sex. Francis said, 'I hate sex in the morning.' 'When do you like it?' I asked. He said, 'Between three and four in the afternoon, with sunlight blazing through the windows.' I said, 'Nikos and I like it any time.' Muriel tapped me across the cheek with the back of a twisted hand and said, 'You old cunt.' Nikos said, 'You tell him.' Ian said to Nikos and me, 'You should come often, darlings.'

———

David Hockney comes to our flat, lounges on a chaise longue and answers questions Nikos asks him, which answers are recorded; Nikos has the tapes typed out then cuts himself out and arranges the text so it forms a narrative for a book. David has lively anecdotes to tell: how, on his first trip to Switzerland, he had looked forward to seeing the mountains, wanting to make a painting of them in 'Gothic gloom,' which he loves as much as Mediterranean or Californian; but, unfortunately, he didn't see the mountains as he was in the back of a little van and thought it polite not to ask to sit in the front as this was the first time his friend had been to Europe, a shame, as he had so wanted to paint the mountains; yet, when he returned to London he did do a painting with made-up mountains, called Flight into Italy – Swiss Landscape. He laughs a high bright laugh when he tells such anecdotes, and I hear them wishing I too had been in the back of a van unable to see the mountains and then be able to tell an anecdote about being in the back of a van and unable to see mountains.

———

We asked Stephen and Francis to dinner. As if he had all the time in the world, Francis arrived before Stephen. In the living room, I asked him to sit, but he said, 'No, I'll stand. I like being uncomfortable.'

At our small, oval dining table in a bedroom, Stephen asked Francis, 'How old are you?' Francis said, 'I was born October 28, 1909, so I'm sixty-eight.' 'And I was born February 28, 1909,' Stephen said. 'So I'm six months older than you,' Francis said. 'Six months younger,' Stephen said. Francis looked puzzled. 'Oh yes,' he said. Stephen said, 'And you were in Berlin while I was there. I wonder why we didn't meet.' 'We probably went to different places,' Francis said; 'I used to be in the clubs all the time.' 'So was I,' Stephen said. 'Then we were probably in the same club at the same time,' Francis said.

'How did you get to Berlin?' I asked Francis.

He seemed to like being asked questions about his life. 'Oh,' he said, 'my father found me wearing my mother's underclothes, and to put me right he sent me to a friend – like my father, a horse trainer. This was in Ireland. I left home to go with my father's friend, who took me to Berlin. He was very rich and we stayed in a grand hotel. That was the first time I had sex with anyone. From there, I went to Paris. My mother sent me three pounds a week. I never really went back to Ireland.'

———

Natasha's mother has died. She spent her last days in Loudoun Road. After she died, Natasha was very apprehensive about reading her letters to her mother, worried that they would be filled with reproaches; but she found reading them that they were written with tenderness and love, and this came to her as a great moral relief.

I recall Stephen once telling me that he and Natasha were in Germany just after the war, on a train; Natasha insisted that they change their pounds on the black market, and Stephen said, no, he'd rather the official rate, which made Natasha react by threatening to throw herself off the train and kill herself if he didn't agree with her. I wonder if she does sometimes assert her will by threatening to kill herself. But how could I imagine this to be heroic, which I do? Leave aside whether or not Stephen was more admirable than Natasha in wanting to exchange pounds at the official rate (it is very much in Stephen to want to do this), I see her threat to kill herself as a way to assert her will within the whole of her past life, a past life she had to will herself to survive, and which she continues to will herself to survive.

I've heard people say about Natasha that the best they can do is tolerate her because of Stephen, who suffers her will. These people, I feel, don't see what an heroic struggle it is for Natasha simply to will herself to live, helpless as she is against a past life that she could easily have not survived.

I once asked her if she was happy, and she said, 'That is something I never consider.'

She told me that there was a trying time when, inspired by the Farm Street Jesuit Martin D'Arcy, she thought of converting to the Roman Catholic Church, and read a good deal of theology about relinquishing one's will to the will of God.

———

After the death of W. H. Auden, whose funeral service she went to in Kirchstetten in the countryside of Austria, Sonia seems to have taken on caring for Chester Kallman, whom she invited Nikos and me to meet at a dinner party. He appears to have become Auden, in manners and speech, his features as pendulous as Auden's.

He lives in Athens, no doubt at Auden's expense, and while Sonia was downstairs in the kitchen preparing a meal he told us that what he likes to do with Greek boys is have bubble baths with them, and I had the horrific vision of him, hump-backed and hump-stomached, in a large bath of three or more boys cavorting among foam and rising bubbles.

A few days later he sent us a poem he had written on the death of a young Greek lover, a tender poem:

How, darling, this innocent grief
Must irk you, more
Even than those outraged, mute
Or pleading jealousies, though now
This you are too pitiless to refute,
Making me all you disapprove:
Selfishly sodden, selfless, dirtier, a prodigal
Discredit to our renewed belief in love:
And addressing the dead! You'd laugh.
Yet I can't imagine you dead
As I know you are and somehow
Hold this one indulgence you allow,
You who allowed me so much life.

This was translated into Greek by Costas Tachtsis. I didn't know
that he and Chester Kallman knew each other, but more and more
I expect people I meet to have themselves met one another.

––––––

The time came for Nikos and me to move from Battersea into
central London, partly because he had a long way to go to his office
at Thames & Hudson, and partly because we had enough money
now to move to a bigger flat in what I at least thought a nicer area
of London. Nikos liked Battersea, liked the working-class shops
and, too, the park just across Prince of Wales Drive, where we had
picnics with friends. And, too, he said it was there that we created
our lives together, painted the walls, bought furniture (some given
to us by Johnny Craxton), hung our pictures, sewed curtains, and
where, in our small sitting room we had so many drinks parties,
and where in our smaller dining room we had so many dinner
parties.

Between the time we sold the flat in Battersea and were able to
move into the one in Montagu Square, more or less around the
corner from where we had met in Wyndham Place, we stayed in

the pied-à-terre of Nikos' cousin in Ovington Square, which to Nikos was like being homeless. This panicked him.

He is always anticipating a catastrophe.

He asks, Does he have cancer? No, I answer.

Does he have a bad heart? No, I answer.

Will he lose his job? No, I answer.

Will the flat we're supposed to move into be taken away from us? No.

Will his kitties die? No.

(He now has two cats, Jasmine and an offspring called Mustafa.)

His uncertainty, often parodied by himself and made into a joke, fills me with affection for him and the desire to reassure him.

But to truly reassure him would be to go back into his past and relieve him of the fear of belonging to a refugee family; his uncertainty, his sense of impending catastrophe, are in his history. I would like to undo his history, but cannot.

In Montagu Square, we now live in a Georgian house, the top maisonette, overlooking a garden in the square. We have a key to the garden. The area of the house has black iron railings about it, and the front door, wide and shiny black, has a bright brass knob. We have had our furniture removed from Battersea, hung our pictures, organized books in especially built bookshelves, and each of us has a study. We have our bed from Battersea, the bed that means so much to Nikos, as if that, where we sleep night after night together, where we make love, is where our lives together are most our lives together.

I sometimes dare to think Nikos is happy.

He longs, he says, to stay in – no drinks parties, no dinner parties, neither ones we give nor ones we are invited out to.

He says, 'Please, no socializing.'

I should put in that since we last lived in Wyndham Place, the neighbourhood has changed, and where there was once a greengrocer where you could not buy green peppers because such a vegetable was too foreign, there is now a Lebanese grocery where vegetables and fruit are on sale that are totally foreign to us (thinking they were bananas, Nikos bought plantains), and where Nikos can buy Greek pasturma, halumi, feta cheese. The grocery is open on Sunday, as are all the grand department stores in Oxford Street.

I forgot to put in that we now lived next to where Trollope lived and died.

The story is: he was working on a novel but was so disturbed by a man playing hurdy-gurdy in the square, he raised the sash, leaned out, shouted that that abomination must stop, and had an apoplexy and died.

———

A Sunday afternoon, Nikos and I walked about Hyde Park, and I was reminded of the times we used to walk there when we lived in Wyndham Place. I remembered how anxious I was, and how Nikos would say, 'Now breathe in deeply, and look closely at what's around you.' The flowers in the parterres we walked along appeared to me dead. Now, walking along the same parterres, the flowers appeared brightly alive. I wondered about the difference between then and now. Perhaps we were closer then, not despite, but because of my mental illness, for it was an illness, and Nikos cured me.

———

It is only at odd moments that I feel this flat is home. Nikos said he feels the same, that he imagines he is a guest in someone else's flat. Then he said something that struck me as being true for myself as well as for him: that he doesn't feel he belongs in such a posh, upper-middle-class neighbourhood. I can understand why I feel this, but he, used to his own upper-middle-class culture, should feel comfortable here, if somewhat disdainful. When we lived in Battersea and came into more central London on walks and passed through the kind of neighbourhood we now live in, Nikos, look- ing through the windows of elegant houses, would ask, 'Why can't we live in such a place?' as if it were not simply a question of money but that we were not allowed. Again, I understand this in myself, but in Nikos I can only think his having felt more comfortable in working-class Battersea (where he liked to go to Clapham Junction to the working-class department store Arding & Hobbs for his socks and underwear), was because he felt he was not entitled to live in what friends now say is a 'posh' place, his sense of class in fact weak from coming from a refugee family who, though upper-middle class from Constantinople, were not accepted into middle-class Athens, so Nikos grew up feeling déclassé.

We keep saying we want to be quiet in our new flat, but we see many, many people.

I repeat once again the observation I have made over and over about our similarities and differences. If I am discontent, I blame myself (at a drinks party, I drank too much so have a hangover), whereas Nikos, discontent, blames the world (if people did not invite him out to a drinks party he wouldn't drink so wouldn't suffer a hangover, and he thereby puts the blame, not on himself, but on others inviting him out!).

———

Sue Flanagan came to tea. She talked about herself and Barry. Barry, living away, wants a divorce, Sue doesn't. I asked, 'How can you know what Barry wants, given how convoluted his talk is?' Sue said, 'That's because he didn't learn to speak until he was eight or nine, but I understood him, he wants a divorce.' 'Why?' 'He says he is in love with someone else.' 'Are you sure that's what he said?' Sue did laugh a quiet laugh. I told Sue that in fact I had met the woman, Ann, some time before at a drinks party, and she had said that she understands Barry and that with her he is perfectly clear when he talks, which she thought had to be a sign that something was going well between them. Sue said, 'She's a liar. I do understand Barry, I do.' And I wondered about two women contesting their love for a man because they understood, one better than the other, what Barry meant by – as I recall him saying to me – 'It's a melon thrown at me from a truck driving at a hundred miles an hour.'

———

That Nikos and I arrange books together, that we shop together, go to a recital together, makes these banal activities aspects of our relationship, imbues these activities with the multi-dimensional and in doing so imbues our relationship with the multi-dimensional. Our relationship needs these activities, I realize, in that the degree that they come alive in our performing them together is the degree that our relationship comes alive.

Nikos has gone to bed. Now I'll go to bed.

I said to him today, 'I really love this flat,' and he said, 'I do too.'

―――――

I am alone in our flat, and I try not to think of anything but what is immediately about me, as I feel anxious in his absence and don't want the anxiety to take hold of me, which it so easily can do when I am alone.

I love London. In the morning, I went out to walk about the neighborhood, and everything appeared so vivid, as if I were seeing everything for the first time. The weather was gray and wet, and I loved this, too.

New Year's Eve, Roxy and I gave a party.

Roxy: 'I awoke one morning with the horrors, you know them, having an unstructured life, no job, just the round of parties, openings and movies, and realizing I'm not in love with the boyfriend, nor he with me, quel sadness, so I went back to bed for the rest of the day, sleeping heavily and now, a week later, I still feel dozy. But we shall have a wonderful party on New Year's Eve. Do you think sandwiches and Christmas cake and tequila, or something more traditional like blinis and glasses of stout? Mr. Keogh from Dublin says the best poured glass of stout in London is to be had at the Catholic Martyrs Club in Aldgate.'

Frank and Anita, that day back from Jerusalem, came to the party. Natasha, who had been so adamant on saving Frank's first marriage to Maureen and so alienated herself from Anita, came, and was, as she would have said, on her 'best behavior' with Anita, and was affectionate towards me. Stephen is in New York. The poet Al Alvarez and the child psychiatrist Anne Alvarez came. Suzi. Sue Flanagan (she has split up from Barry). Joe and Jos Tilson. Old friends, old friends! In the Greek manner, I opened the windows at midnight, as we all drank sparkling wine, to let the old year out and the new year in.

The day after, to Sylvia's for supper. She said, 'You're in a very lively state. I wonder if, however much you love it, London will pull you down.'

'But I'm in a lively state because I am in London,' I said.

I feel loving towards everyone.

———

John Fleming, staying with us in Montagu Square, told us this, which we hadn't known: one of the previous occupants of the house, married and with children and living in the country, would come up to London from time to time to stay in the flat and from there go to Piccadilly Circus and the arcade of flashing pinball machines and pick up boys and bring them back, one time a boy scout who went to the police, so the man was arrested. Charlotte Bonham Carter, hearing of this, shouted, 'Those terrible, terrible boy scouts, they should be disbanded.'

———

In what he calls the bottomless pit in the basement of Loudoun Road, where years of accumulations are stored, Stephen found an envelope with old photograph negatives which he had printed and which, to his surprise, revealed in black and white people he had known in Berlin. They include Stephen (taken by his brother Humphrey) and Christopher and his boyfriend and the original Sally Bowles, in fact Jean Ross, she standing full square in a loose smock and loose slacks and ballet slippers, a beret tipped to one side on her head, and she looking out at the camera with large dark eyes. Stephen gave us a set. The photographs taken in Weimar Berlin appeared to me to be representative of all of Weimar Berlin, as if all of that period of history was consciously being lived by those photographed – whereas, as I heard Christopher once say to Stephen, the boy in the photograph is not thinking of history but of a suit he hopes Stephen will give him, while Stephen is worried that he won't have the money to buy the suit. Really, photographs, if seen as taken, not within history, but within the moment, demythologize history, and there is every reason to demythologize history when it is as romanticized as Weimar Germany.

———

We were, Nikos and I, collating the dates in our agendas, which we do every Sunday as it sometimes happens that he has written in a date when I haven't, or vice versa, and we double date. I saw that he had written down, for lunch, Paul.

I asked, 'Paul who?'

He laughed. He said, 'My old friend Paul.'

'You didn't tell me you were having lunch with him.'

'If I didn't, it was because I didn't think it was important enough to.'

'Of course it's important. He loved you and you made love together. Of course it's important. And you were keeping it from me.'

'I wasn't.'

'It doesn't matter.'

'You don't believe me.'

'No, but it doesn't matter. It's not important.'

'Of course it's important that you should believe me.'

This went on for a while, then I came up to my study and my desk to work, and he came in.

He said, 'You've got to trust me.'

'I don't, not entirely. You've destroyed letters in the past then conveniently forgotten what was in them so I wouldn't know. Of course you've hidden things from me. But I have to recognize that you did this just so I wouldn't be hurt. I accept that.'

'You've got to trust me. I do tell you the truth.'

'I don't quite believe you.'

He went out.

Later, I went downstairs to find out what he was doing. We are always checking on what each other is doing, as out of curiosity. I found him in the kitchen preparing supper for John G. and James J. We hugged each other, then laughed. I left him, as he wanted to prepare the supper, and I went back to my desk, thinking, It doesn't matter.

———

Our downstairs neighbours in 38 Montagu Square are Joseph and Ruth Bromberg.

Joseph is originally from Russia, from a family of furriers; he grew up in Berlin. As a boy, he was taught tennis by Vladimir Nabokov, a relative through marriage to his wife Vera. Joseph said that, really, Nabokov would let him and his brother play in whatever way while he sat on a bench on the side of the court and read. Ruth was from Nuremberg, where Jews were allowed to own land, she from a family of gentlemen farmers, her father even calling himself, as a descendant, the Third, which is not Jewish. He and his family escaped by way of Cuba, she by way of going east, to Japan, to San Francisco, to New York. They met in New York.

She stayed with an aunt who did not like her, and restricted even her food, so that Ruth with all of ten cents bought apples which she had to hide in her room until her aunt, coming in, sniffed and said, 'I smell apples,' and Ruth had to give them up.

Ruth remembers walking down Broadway with her bobby socks and pleated skirt and hearing a man call out, 'There goes an American girl!'

After they married, Ruth's aunt said to her, 'So you've married a kike.' He was from Russia and she from Germany.

From Milan, where they lived for thirty years, Joseph working his way up to head of a furrier company, they moved to London, where their son Michael, after unsuccessful treatment for leukemia, died, a young man. His absence is also his presence in their flat.

Ruth is completely autodidact, especially in old master prints.

She completed the catalogue raisonné of Canaletto prints, and is now working on the catalogue raisonné of Walter Sickert prints, of which they buy as many as they can for her to study them closely. Nikos and I proofread her entries.

She says we are all family.

They invite Nikos and me to grand restaurants, and we invite them to less grand. Or they invite us to dinner parties, catered, with other guests from the world of art historians and museum curators, as the Brombergs have endowed a fellowship in their son's name for research in prints, and, too, they often donate money and works to the Print Department of the British Museum.

Ruth sits to Frank Auerbach every Wednesday. Every Tuesday, she has her hair done at a hairdresser in preparation. From time to time, Frank, as a gesture of thanks, gives Ruth a portrait he has painted of her. Each time a new one is given, all the pictures have to be rearranged, and, when Nikos and I visit, Ruth looks down at us from many different angles with contorted faces, but always with a rather comic smile applied, it appears, almost as an afterthought with a quick stroke of the brush.

Because he hardly ever goes out, very occasionally Frank and his wife Julia come to dinner at the Brombergs', and Nikos and I are invited.

This amazed me:

Joseph said that the most powerful image in the Western world is the image of Jesus Christ crucified on the cross. I still hear him saying, as if in awe, 'He gave up his life for the salvation of humankind.' He asked Frank what he thought, and Frank, in a low voice, said, yes, there is no more powerful image in the Western world.

Sometimes, when I am alone with Joseph, he will tell me stories that he does not want Ruth to hear, they would upset her; and I weep.

———

We commissioned Keith to do a work for us, one to fit into a narrow space in our new flat, but, Keith being Keith, he brought to the flat a work so large it has to take up an entire alcove where there was once a fireplace. It dominates the room, and it dominates with grandeur: it is made out of sheets of lead folded over wooden frames so that each frame is the size of a building block, the lead blocks layered to form a wide, high, semi-circular wall, rather like the stone wall within a medieval tower, between the blocks non-drying putty that drips oil onto the lead. The whole is majestic and has the quality that Keith says he wants in his work: classical.

A comment about Keith's work –

He uses raw, perhaps what he considers essential, materials – lead, resin, cement, plywood, copper, sheets of plastic – and with them structures works that themselves stand for essentials in, say, the essential shapes of tondo, cross, cenotaph, different stylized architectural forms, all essentially timeless, majestic, classical, and all with an intellectual 'edge' to them that defines them with clarity.

We also have a large cross by Keith, made of cement and resin, one vertical half of the cross flat and the other vertical half at a slant, the whole giving the impression of a Greek kouros with one leg rigidly straight and the other taking a step forward, and, again, there is classical grandness to it.

And we have other works by Keith, some we have bought, some he has given to us.

One of our pleasures is to acquire a work of art and then spend all weekend rearranging the hanging of all the pictures.

What we have: paintings by Adrian Stokes, paintings by Stephen Buckley, a painting and prints by Mark Lancaster, two etchings by Frank Auerbach, a cut-out tin piece by Julian Opie, a painting by Lisa Milroy, prints by Joe Tilson, prints and a small painting of me by R. B. Kitaj, an etching by Lucian Freud, etchings and drawings and a small painting by David Hockney, a drawing by Sandra Fisher, drawings and a sculpture by Barry Flanagan, a pastel by John Golding, drawings by Michael Craig-Martin, drawings and a water-color by Patrick Procktor, a stone tondo by Stephen Cox, a large pastel by Jan Hashey, a print by Howard Hodgkin –

David Sylvester will ring up to ask if a sentence he has written sounds right, and, with long pauses, he will be on the telephone for hours, getting the sentence right. The people he rings talk among themselves, perhaps with a degree of complaint, about those long conversations, but no one would want to be left out. And it is certainly a sign of belonging to a circle to be invited to dinner by David to his house (bought by his selling a painting that Francis Bacon gave him, which Francis did not seem to mind), the house like a private museum, all dominated, it seems, by an immense sandstone Egyptian pharaoh standing within a bay of windows, outside the windows a screen of high reeds. You ask if you may look about the house, and David, not saying anything, stares so intensely at you that you wonder if you shouldn't have asked, but that's the way with David, he doesn't say yes or no, he simply stares. The house has bare wooden floors painted a carefully chosen slightly mottled, pale grey-blue, with only fragments of rugs here and there, and from room to room, each object given space to set it off, you see a Kerala canoe, battered Roman busts on marble columns, an African Nupe stool, a Neolithic pottery jar, a drawing by Joan Miró, a Regency card table, a lute, a large painting by William Turnbull, an Indian sandstone female torso, etchings by Picasso, an Italian walnut wardrobe, drawings by Giacometti. You say, 'David, this is all wonderful,' and again David stares at you, then finally says, 'But I don't have one major work,' and you feel a little badly for him that he doesn't.

The evening will have been as carefully arranged as the furniture and pictures and antiquities in his house, and you always have the sense of the privilege of being invited, though, at the glass-topped table, David will listen with acute attention to what you say, staring at you, one eye drifting off to the side as if with the strain of his attention, and after saying what you think of as at best incidental, if not stupid, David will seem to think a long while about it, then say, portentously, 'That is very profound.'

Nikos and I were invited to a dinner party at his house, Marina Warner also invited, and Sarah Whitfield, from the house next door, a partner to David, who in fact prepared the meal, the menu chosen by David. Suddenly, David got up from the dining table and went out then came back with a picture which he handed to me across the table, saying, 'The only gift worth giving is a gift it hurts to give,' and I reached out for a colourful drawing by Stephen Tennant of an ancient Greek goddess among white roses, a fantasy cover for a book of poems by Stephen Spender. It was as though David were giving me a world of associations, and I realized that David himself lived in that world, was himself a world of associations.

During a weekend when I was away, Nikos saw Dawn Ades, and, he told me when I returned, they had asked each other whom they would like to sleep with, just lay next to and sleep, and Nikos said, 'David Sylvester,' and Dawn said to Nikos, 'You!'

———

Pleading with me when I feel I have failed as a writer, Nikos asks me, 'Isn't my love for you enough?' and I become weak and want to fall on the floor.

———

A sun-filled Saturday, edged with blossoming daffodils. Suzi came to lunch, then we sat in the sun on the roof, Nikos repotting some plants there. After Suzi left, Nikos and I had a nap. We will have drinks with the Brombergs, then all go together to our local church – Saint Mary's – to hear Bach's Saint Matthew Passion.

If no one had ever conceived of eternity, of timelessness, which we long for, especially on a day like this, perhaps we wouldn't mind the day passing because we would not imagine anything different. But the fact is we do imagine. As we'll never realize what we imagine, I wonder if imagination is our greatest curse.

———

When I rang Stephen and Natasha to invite them to dinner, they both answered on separate telephones, as they often do, so there is a three-way conversation. Stephen said, alas, they couldn't come because they were to take an American professor to the theatre, as he'd entertained them when they were in Nashville, Tennessee. Natasha asked Stephen, 'Where will we take him to dinner after the theatre?' and she and Stephen had a little discussion as to what restaurant they'd go to while I listened in, then Stephen said to me, 'I have an idea – if I buy some meat pies and wine, can we come to you and Nikos after the theater?' and I, feeling small because I hadn't suggested this first, said, 'Of course you must come here, and don't bring anything, as I'll make a stew of some kind that will keep,' and they were filled with thanks. Natasha said, 'Thank you v. v. v. much.'

Nikos was pleased.

The next day, Stephen rang and said, 'Honestly, Natasha shouldn't have agreed to your offer to entertain us all. I feel she takes advantage of her friends.' I thought back at our conversation, wondering if I had remembered correctly, but was pretty sure I had: Stephen had proposed coming to us.

I also asked Melvyn Bragg and Cate Haste, to whom I'd explained that Stephen and Natasha would come late; they arrived about 10.00, and they and Nikos and I drank wine and talked, I wondering when Stephen and Natasha would come.

They arrived late, about 11.30. Stephen had a basket of three bottles of good wine. We sat around the sitting room and ate off our laps as there was not enough room at our dining table. The professor hardly spoke, hardly ate the food I served him. We others talked about the campaign to retake the Falkland Islands, which everyone agreed was a mistake. It was, as Natasha would say, a jolly good evening, or so I thought; she was especially lively and talkative. Then everyone got up to leave, and as Melvyn and Cate were saying goodbye, I saw Natasha looking at a picture in the sitting room, and I suddenly thought: My God, the Picasso etching!

I've mentioned the etching in here: Stephen gave it to me in case Nikos threw me out, so I'd have something to rely on. At that time, he also gave one to David Hockney as a gesture of thanks for all the drawings and etchings David has given to him. Shortly after, he and Natasha were at David's studio, and Natasha, seeing the Picasso, said, 'Oh, we have one just like that,' and David said, 'Stephen gave it to me.'

There are many stories of Stephen giving precious possessions away without telling Natasha, the most dramatic story being: Stephen gave to Natasha a special bound copy of World within World, his autobiography, which some years later Cyril Connolly saw in their house and asked for, and Stephen simply gave to Cyril what he had given to Natasha as a wedding gift; when Natasha, perhaps one day looking for it and not finding it, asked Stephen where it was, he told her he had given it to Cyril, and she went into a state; Stephen asked Cyril, explaining the situation to him, if he'd give the book back and Cyril said no, and from then on Natasha wouldn't speak to him.

When Natasha was told by David H. that Stephen had given the Picasso etching to him, she went into a state – at home, of course, alone with Stephen. Stephen had told me this story and admonished me, 'For God's sake, don't let Natasha know you have that Picasso. It's an atomic bomb!' How he explained its disappearance from the house I didn't know. Each time Natasha came to the house, I had to remember to take down the etching and replace it with something innocuous, say a drawing by Johnny Craxton. Sometimes I remembered to change it only minutes before she arrived. This evening, I forgot.

When I saw her studying the etching, I quickly went to her, not knowing what to say. She said, 'That's nice,' and I said, 'But that's yours.' 'Oh,' she said, 'is it?' I said, 'We have many pictures that belong to you.' 'Oh yes?' she said. I didn't know what else to say, and looked across the room towards Stephen, who gave me one of his looks of combined anger and defeat. They left with the American professor, Natasha hardly saying goodnight.

Nikos said, 'Well, you'll simply return the etching.'

It took me a long time to fall asleep.

As I'd anticipated, Stephen rang me in the morning. I

apologized for what had happened, and he said, 'No, don't worry. Natasha didn't mention a thing about it.' We talked more, and I heard the second receiver being lifted and Natasha listened for a moment before Stephen asked, 'Natasha?' and she said, 'Oh, I'm sorry,' and hung up. I said to Stephen, 'I feel awful about that Picasso. Supposing I had given one that Nikos and I owned to a young man without telling him and he found out, of course he'd be angry. I'm amazed that Natasha isn't. You must have it back.' He said, 'Well, if she asks for it, perhaps. But no one is going to sell it. There it is. Why shouldn't you be enjoying it?' 'No,' I insisted, 'Nikos says I must give it back.'

———

Vera Russell is writing her memoirs. In conversation, she will say, 'Henry told me . . .' and one has to know this is Henry Moore, or 'Sam told me . . .' and this is Samuel Beckett, or 'Joyce once told me . . .' and you think this must be James Joyce, or 'Igor . . .' and who else could this be but Igor Stravinsky, or 'Serge . . .' and, yes, Serge Diaghilev, and 'Valéry' had to be none other than Paul Valéry, but when she mentioned that 'Albert once said . . .' I was hard put to know that this was her friend Albert Schweitzer. As she has no money, she rang the dealer in books and papers George Lawson to ask him to come round to see the letters she'd saved and to give an estimate of their value. George came back saying, 'It's absolutely true – Vera has known everybody.' Her memoirs, which require the help of a research assistant, are already four volumes long. We had lunch in a restaurant in Hyde Park, where she said, 'I'll have a big steak. I need strength.'

She said to me, 'Henry told me that he believes the word is more powerful than the image. Writing matters more than painting or sculpture.'

'That's reassuring to me,' I said.

'I have known Henry for fifty years,' she said, 'and worked with him for twenty-five.'

The impression (and I rely on the word: impression) is that Henry could not have achieved what he did without her.

'When I was placing Henry's –' and here she identified a huge sculpture – 'in the landscape of Yorkshire –' and I imagined Vera hefting the huge piece and placing it on a hill, or in a dale.

I shouldn't be making fun of her.

She showed me her essay on Henry Moore. 'I wrote this five times. I wanted to write something about him that hasn't been written before.' The essay is filled with wonderful non-sequiturs. 'Because I am a revolution baby' (she was born during the Russian Revolution in Moscow and can remember, she says, looking out the window and seeing the Revolution happening) 'I understand Henry Moore's art –' No, this isn't right. I am making fun of her.

Once, she showed me a reproduction of a painting by Francis of a grotesque figure with a leg in a large plaster cast, and Vera said, 'That's me.'

———

Francis invited Nikos and me and Stephen to meet his new friend, Bill. We hadn't known he had a friend since George. Bill is an electrician. Sonia says telephone engineer. He is a broad, very handsome man who wants to become a policeman in New York but who is intelligent enough to know that he really only wants to satisfy a fantasy he has about New York cops. His life, it seems, is devoted to satisfying his sexual fantasies. He's been all over the United States, and Canada too, and he can tell you where the best bars are, and where men like one thing or another. Because of his looks, he said that every time he goes into a queer club in America the bouncer will say to him, 'You do realize, sir, that this is a club for homosexuals?' He loves asking policemen in the street for the way to bars and clubs that, he said smiling, they of course know are queer. Bill's smile is wide and clean and very white.

After dinner at Langan's Brasserie, for which Francis insisted on paying, we all got into a taxi to go to a club in Leicester Square called Adam's. The taxi stopped and started, stopped and started in the Friday late-night traffic in the West End. Once we got to

Leicester Square, Stephen said he thought he'd go home – it was still early enough to catch the tube.

Adam's is a large, crowded club with gold chandeliers and gold-framed mirrors, and is so dark and filled with smoke we could hardly see. Francis, Bill, Nikos and I stood by the bar. Francis kept giving Bill twenty-pound notes to buy bottles of champagne. We talked a lot about sex. Bill said he liked to be fucked, fist-fucked, and he also liked, from time to time, 'G.B.H.' Nikos asked, 'What's that?' 'Grievous bodily harm,' Bill said, and smiled his bright smile. 'And you've had it?' Francis asked him. 'Only a couple of times,' Bill answered. 'Real welts and wheals?' Francis asked. 'Oh yes,' Bill answered; 'I enjoy it but it has to be done by someone you like. And there's always the danger that they won't be able to stop when you want them to.' 'Well,' Francis said, 'I like G.B.H. now and then. I had a friend – he finally killed himself – who had a collection of whips he kept at my place. A while ago, I took someone there who said he was interested in whips, and I showed him the collection.' Francis laughed. 'Well, I undressed and got on my fish-net stockings –' 'Black?' Nikos asked. 'Of course black, stupid,' Francis said. 'And he started to beat me. But he got carried away. He wouldn't stop. I'm a total coward. In nothing but my black fish-net stockings, I ran out into Reece Mews.' He laughed a loud laugh.

A tall, blond man came up to us and asked, 'Who are you all? You all look so interesting, so glum.' Not even Francis spoke to him. He asked Nikos and me, 'Do you two live together?' 'Why do you think that?' I asked. 'I can tell,' he said. A friend behind him said, 'Come on, let's go, they look creepy.'

We were in the club until three-thirty. Nikos and I left only when Francis said he'd leave. Bill remained with a fellow who looked like a bearded Greek priest.

Outside, Francis said, 'Bill and I spent four days together and discovered we're incompatible because we both like the same thing. But we've remained friends.'

I ran around the square trying to find a taxi, but none would stop for me though their lights were lit. Francis, who hadn't moved, simply put up a hand and a limousine, not a taxi, stopped in front of him. A young man rolled down the window and said, 'You look like three cold gentlemen. I'll drive you wherever you want to go.' Francis got in beside him, Nikos and I in the back. The driver asked, 'Now, what have you been doing up at this hour when all honest people are in bed?' Francis answered, with that short, shrugging laugh he has, 'Not being honest.' He asked the driver his name. 'George,' the driver said; 'and what's your name?' 'Francis.' 'Is that Mr. Francis?' 'Mr., Mrs., Miss – however you like it,' Francis said. The driver left Nikos and me off first.

———

I asked R. B. Kitaj what he thinks of Francis' painting, and he wrote me, on many postcards, his favourite form of communicating:

For me, Bacon is not a great painter like Matisse or Picasso. He is a narrower talent, and he seems to have refused to draw, but from my perspective he is the best, most original and engaging painter . . . I cherish unusual paintings and, boy oh boy, are they rare and hard to achieve! Bacon keeps doing them . . . Of course it's all a matter of taste, so I don't wish to argue Bacon with those who are turned off by him, including brilliant friends of mine . . . But I do think he sings the song of himself. His pictures are every bit as elegant as the high American abstraction, but he engages his urbane nihilism to one's one neurotic unease and achieved a psychological bloody pitch which almost always holds my attention.

———

A conversation with David Sylvester. He wondered if Yeats, great a poet as he was, failed to be the greatest because he lacked 'helplessness.' Nikos said that Yeats is limited because he is, however subtle, rhetorical – his poetry is constrained by its complicated intentions.

I said I wonder if this applied to Francis' paintings, but with an essential difference: he himself is aware of the constraint of intention and tries, with more than will power, with passion, to go beyond intention and give his work 'helplessness.' I wondered if Francis in fact succeeds, if there is too much intention in his attempt to give himself up to the unintentional, even by throwing paint on the canvas then to work it into a figure. Nikos smiled and said nothing, but, as he always does, David looked at me for a very long time, and after a very long time he slowly, carefully said, 'That is very interesting,' as if he himself had not thought, among many, of such an obvious comment about the works of Francis Bacon.

When I think of 'helplessness' in writing, I think of Victor Shklovsky, who started out a novel with an intention but at the end he found he had written a novel completely different from what he had intended it to be, a novel that had occurred and expanded beyond his intention; so, when he started a new novel, he gave in helplessly to whatever novel would occur, that novel expanding as if on its own intentions beyond his, and he did this by writing whatever came to him, however seemingly disconnected, taking it on faith that everything in the end would connect, but not as he had thought. The unintended is truer than what is intended, because – and this I wonder at – what can't be helped is truer than what can be helped, what is allowed to happen is truer than what one tries to make happen, what one gives in to is truer than what one imposes oneself upon.

But what is the unintended that expands on its own, to which the writer and the artist give themselves up helplessly? What expands beyond intention? What is it that we can only ever have a 'sense' of, can never give a rhetorical name to? What? We can't say, but it is in us – it strains in us, it strains with a longing in us – to want to say what it is, to release it, to see it formed out there around us into – what? – a bright globe of everything, everything, everything all together held in that one great globe, is that all I can imagine of what it is?

———

Paul Levy (writer on all forms of culture, including cuisine) and Penny Marcus (editor) give large parties in and outside their large stone house in Oxfordshire, parties during which the guests seem to fall in love, sometimes in the barn in the straw, or guests fall out of love, in no place in particular. Usually, the party takes place in the garden, as if in the midst of greenery diffused into the green air, where there is a site-specific rock sculpture by Barry Flanagan. And there is a long table covered with a white cloth and food and bottles, though the guests more often than not wander about, attaching and detaching, and so I attached myself to Beryl Bainbridge (novelist) and asked her if Maggie Drabble (novelist) and Michael Holroyd (biographer) – standing side by side near a brick wall against which was an espalier apple tree, he a tall man slightly stooped and she, shorter, her shoulders thrown back and her chin, as if she were at attention, held in – are a couple, to which Beryl, at first testing the elasticity of her mouth by twisting it about so her nose swerved, answered, confidentially, 'If I tell you nothing,' which left me to go to Maggie and Michael to ask them nothing but say how lovely to see them, they both nodding and smiling.

Maggie said, 'Come to me for lunch, then we'll go to Michael's later for tea.'

———

In Paul and Penny's sitting room, over the mantelpiece, is a painting of Paul by Howard Hodgkin, which does look like Paul, round and multi-coloured. During the party, he, his hands out and twiddling his fingers, goes from guest to guest, while Penny sits still.

In China, Paul, who is what is called a 'foodie,' that is someone who is interested in and writes about even the most exotic cuisines, went to the market where caged dogs are sold for their meat, but the cages were empty. He was told that though the Chinese eat dog, they do have pet dogs they love.

———

Dinner at the Glenconners', in London from Corfu for the winter. Vidia Naipaul and his wife Pat were there.

The Naipauls have, for twelve years, lived in the gatehouse of the house Christopher's brother Stephen inhabits in Wiltshire. They have never seen him but once, when, across a lawn, they gently waved to one another.

Stephen Tennant stays in bed all day, all winter, spring, autumn. His bed is covered with objects, mostly dolls, so he can't move. Only in the summer does he get out of bed to go down to the west lawn to sit for an hour. He wears jewelry and make-up. And from time to time he does drawings, of flowers and French sailors.

Christopher said, 'It is wonderful that he's never bored.'

When he's in London, Christopher goes to Wiltshire to see him. He spends twenty minutes by his brother's bed, then his brother says, 'I'm really rather tired,' and Christopher goes down to the kitchen to have a meal with the housekeeper and her husband, whose company he loves, then he returns to London. He never spends the night; the beds are too damp. Clearly, Christopher is supporting his brother Stephen and would never pass a judgment on him, but say, 'He's wonderful.'

Christopher said, 'Nothing really matters, you see. I'm not a believer, really, but I'm sure the workings of the universe are on such a grand scale that what we consider important isn't. There is no reason to be upset by anything. I'm a very happy man.'

———

I asked John Golding if his being an historian in any way influenced him, or, perhaps, hindered him for the self-consciousness that history might have imposed on him, and he said, No, not at all, he was able to work in direct contact with the painting. Yet, John, in writing, say, about Malevich (in an essay contained in a book that Nikos was responsible for Thames & Hudson publishing, Paths to the Absolute), will include an appreciation of art by Hegel that he supposes was an appreciation of art by Malevich: 'Hegel's view of evolution, as propounded in the 1820s, is that in which spirit detaches itself from nature and achieves total freedom, thus becoming "pure universal form . . . in which the spiritual essence attains the consciousness and feeling of itself." It was this state of advanced spirituality that Malevich felt had at last been brought to a conclusion by himself.' Malevich's work became 'frankly mystical.' There is not a hint of irony in John's attributing the spiritual, the mystical, to Malevich, none. But he would not, ever, attribute the same words to his own work, which, in conversation, he described as being influenced by Adrian Stokes' view of the body, as in Adrian's essay 'Reflections on the Body.' (I once told Adrian how wonderful I thought that title, which made him look at me with bemusement, for I had seen in the title a wet body on which light was reflected.) I said to John, 'I don't at all see the body in your paintings,' which consist of very abstract planes of colour that, on looking for a long while at them, appear to take on dimensions, one plane receding and another plane coming forward, and he said, after a long pause, 'Well, the spirit,' and I pointed at him and said, 'I've got you,' and laughed, and he laughed a little, grudgingly.

There is a divide between the appreciation of art allowed by a critic, which appreciation can make use of transcendent words, and the view an artist (most of the artists of today, who seem to deny the transcendent, or at least refuse to admit it) has of his/her own work.

I think of the white-on-white paintings of Robert Ryman, about which he will only say that they are white-on-white paintings, as if to deny he has any intention in painting them than that they should consist of white-on-white paint, so that everything unintended beyond his intention is left to the art critic to admire – which admiration, however, I can only think Ryman reads with the thought, yes, yes, that's what my work is all about, but I would never say so. At the exhibition of his work at the Tate, I thought: But he's wrong not to admit that his paintings have transcendence, because they do have transcendence. I asked him to sign the catalogue, which he did reluctantly, as if that would be to give too much of himself away.

———

After I've been to a dinner party where I've heard a remarkable story – one of those stories that belies the reserve of the English – I, at my desk, write out the story with the idea of using it as the basis of fiction. I wrote out the following some time ago, long enough that I forget (just as well) who gave the dinner party and whom (better) the story was about.

She went to Ghana where she fell in love with an African, became pregnant, came back to England, near Salisbury, went into a wood, nine months pregnant, and tried to kill herself by slitting her wrists, made a mess of it, woke up covered in blood, staggered out to a road, was picked up by a farmer who took her to hospital where her baby was born, took baby to Ghana, a boy, drowned it and gave the dead body to the father, a tribal chief who in his grief went off into the jungle, but came back to try to help his imprisoned, mad wife, swearing to a judge that the baby had died a cot death, so she, free, returned to England, her mother bought her a slum house in Brixton, where she now lives alone, and where her husband comes from Ghana once a year to visit her.

Coming across this, I thought, but there is no way I can turn it into fiction, and put it into my diary as a story in the history, not only of this woman, but of Great Britain − of colonial Great Britain, about which I know so little, my ignorance very much a gap in my ever becoming British.

I think of John Osborne's play at the Royal Court Theatre, West of Suez, and a scene in which all the actors sit on canvas lawn chairs in a circle and announce where each was born, not one in Great Britain, and I felt a circle of loneliness among them, all of them displaced, dissatisfied, even defeated, and yet nostalgic for a lost world. What I don't understand is the residue of colonial times, in which, it seems to me, the above tragedy occurred, as if the nostalgic were deep in the post-colonial conscience, but not the tragic. For all that I recall, the above story might have been recounted with irony, a British affectation I often find difficult to appreciate when I hear someone British dealing with tragedy, and which Nikos disdains. I remember the story above was told with amusement, and, yes, it was told by someone of the upper classes, among whom I can hear the dictum: we do not take ourselves seriously.

———

Harold Acton rang. He had got, he said, our number from Eva Neurath, whom he sees in Florence. Nikos is not interested, but indulges my interest – my fascination! I invited him to supper. How could I not be fascinated by Acton for the worlds he is connected to? Nikos suggested we invite Howard Hodgkin. Acton arrived in a three-piece grey suit, elegant, and he was all elegant declamations about our flat, our food, ourselves, with something of a Chinese elegance. He and Howard had more connections to make than Nikos and I with him, for Howard is well connected. In our flat, I saw, as if visible about Acton, his villa and gardens, and what amused me was his complaining about the responsibilities of the villa and garden. 'Oh, it is a prison, a prison. I hardly dare leave it for what may happen while I'm away, the staff not to be trusted, no, not to be trusted. And how can I afford to keep the staff?' He made elegant gestures with his hands and said, 'There should be a charity for destitute millionaires,' and smiled. After he left, Nikos asked, 'Why did he want to see us?' I said, 'I have no idea.' Howard stayed on and we talked about the artists we know, he praising the work of Stephen Buckley.

A few days later, a thank-you letter: 'Much love to you both, Yours ever, Harold, hoping to see you in Florence.'

How can I not be impressed by this? – though I admire Nikos, keeping an ideological distance, for not being impressed, though he was very courteous towards Acton.

———

Strange, violent dreams about Nikos. Here is one: he, in the centre of a room, is fashioning a work of art out of variously shaped blocks of wood, and pays no attention to me, so I, angry, throw things at him and his work of art; he remains indifferent, his indifference calculated; he is resentful of me, will have nothing to do with me, though I have no idea why he is resentful, why he won't have anything to do with me, and my anger turns to rage. What I wonder is: who is this Nikos in my dreams, a Nikos who reoccurs in my dreams, and who is completely unlike the Nikos I know and love? In life, Nikos is never indifferent to me, never even suggests rejecting me. Why, in my dreams, does he reject me so often?

———

I am always, if less and less, surprised by the way the sexualities of people in London appear to be incidental to friendship. So, I think of Stephen Buckley, who has all the seductive good looks of a young man who rather enjoys the friendships of other young men – in particular, Mark Lancaster – who are seduced by his good looks. That Stephen has girlfriends – in particular, Stevie – in no way diminishes his friendship with those others who have flirtatious feelings for him. Stevie became pregnant by Stephen, and gave birth to a daughter. I went to visit her in hospital with a large pot of blue hydrangeas, but I couldn't recall her maiden name, which, as she and Stephen were not yet married, she still went by, so I had to go along the beds looking for Stevie, who waved to me. They married some time after.

With pleasure, I thought this was rather bohemian of them.

———

If I were to try to create a British character, how would I characterize him/her? Would I centre on someone I know somewhat – say, A. J. Ayer who represents Logical Positivism as a thoroughly British mode of thinking? I see him from time to time at the Spenders', and once had an amusing talk with him about the Assumption of the Blessed Virgin Mother, trying to establish the date of her bodily assumption and the speed at which she was assumed into heaven, whereby we would be able to calculate where in the universe she is, and, if she had reached heaven, where in the universe heaven is. His wife Dee said he visits the Jesuits in Farm Street to talk about Scholastic philosophy, which talk I would very much like to hear, Ayer against Aquinas! Dee told me that e. e. cummings, a friend, described Ayer as having a stainless-steel mind. How would I be able to give a character based on Ayer a soul? And by soul I mean: what can't be made logically positivist, what is beyond intention. Would such a character in a novel be interesting? Doesn't Ayer's Logical Positivism reduce the novel to, at best, social life? Could I possibly create a British character with a soul, a soul in an agony that embarrasses him for being an agony, so a soul he must deny as an indulgence for not being positively logical? And whom would that be based upon?

Could it be Stephen Spender?

I would never try to engage Freddie Ayer in a conversation that had any hint of being serious, but I would like to ask him, in a joking way, if what is called an idea is no more logically positive than a vague 'sense' of having something to think about, in which vagueness we imagine we think logically, especially when we think we are thinking logically? The joke would be that, as I am not good at logic, better do away with it all as illogical. The closest to making a reference to his own philosophy – if it can be called that – is my hearing Ayer say, with a gesture as of cancelling it out of the air, that the end of Wittgenstein's Tractatus, when Wittgenstein states that the mystical shows itself, is rubbish. It is just this affirmation of the mystical that appeals to me in Wittgenstein, but I laughed at Ayer's affirmation that it is rubbish, thinking to myself: yes, it is rubbish, and everything that has its appeal for being imagined mystical is rubbish. This reassurance lasted only as long as I was with Ayer.

To listen to Dee talk about her past is to be entertained by a whole life, at least in her telling, of entertainment. Just this: when young, living in Paris, she became infatuated with a man from Oklahoma, a man whom she was warned against because he lived in a hotel known for – a nod of the head – men like that. Queer?

Impossible! No man from Oklahoma could be queer! She invited him for supper, calculated the drink to get him drunk but not too drunk, but drunk enough that – oh dear! – he missed the last Métro back to his hotel, so he'd have to spend the night.

———

A long walk with Anthony Page through Hyde Park, he telling me about directing in the presence of Samuel Beckett at the Royal Court Theatre in Sloane Square. About directing, Anthony told me this:

'The first thing is to know the text of the author you're directing as well as you can. What the conscious structure of the piece is, how thoughts and lines connect with each other.

'My ideal is that the actors should come knowing their lines when we start rehearsing. They will make any excuse to avoid this but it gives you the equivalent of at least ten days' extra rehearsal when you have a month.

'Noël Coward and my teacher Sandy Meisner both felt very strongly indeed about this. Meisner said that rehearsing without knowing your lines was like acting with a grand piano on your back and for me from the very beginning of rehearsal the actors should start working on their relationships with the other characters, their objectives and so forth. Very difficult if you're reading or feeling for lines.

'The director is largely responsible for the atmosphere at rehearsals and he needs daring actors who are in touch with their instincts. He needs to keep the objective balance and structure of the play in his mind, at the same time encouraging fun and freedom and improvisation. Unintellectual instincts are often what make the most magical side of a production. This freedom should be retained right through the run of the play.

'I hate productions which are too choreographed, self-conscious – too obviously directed. Better by far if the direction is invisible, unnoticed – and if the action seems every time to be happening for the first time ever before the audience's eyes.

'If a play has been rehearsed and its foundations laid in this way it can continue to develop and to grow in truth and strength for the whole run. Once it's in front of an audience, who reveal new things to the actors, the job of the director is rather like gardening. New growths spring up – often by instinct – and may need to be watered – by making the actors aware of them. Also inevitably there are weeds, temptations to cheapen, which must be got rid of.

'Ideally a director should visit a production – at least for part of the performance – every two weeks or so. And give notes to the cast. Probably written down. Actors often aren't too happy with notes once a play has opened and if they can read them it gives them a chance to ponder, and try them out and not to forget them, if they agree with them.'

———

Nikos and I have seen such extraordinary productions in the theatre, most notably the plays of D. H. Lawrence, and among these the Widowing of Mrs. Holroyd, with its scene of the widow washing the dead body of her husband, killed in a mine, and keening over his body. I thought: yes, for all that D. H. Lawrence intended too much in his writing – what his friend Bertrand Russell condemned as a philosophy of 'blood-consciousness' that led straight to Auschwitz, and that Virginia Woolf derided, too, as philosophy, which she did not want in a novel (she wanted 'no preaching: things in themselves: the sentence in itself beautiful . . .') – for all that D. H. Lawrence intended in his writing, the unintended, beyond his philosophy, has more of a soul than any of his contemporaries, especially the Bloomsbury writers, and especially Virginia Woolf, could ever have been capable of expanding upon in their writing.

———

To Stephen and Stevie Buckley to supper at the long, wide refectory table from King's College, Cambridge, from when Stephen was artist in residence there. The architect Max Gordon was at the table, and Stephenie and Roxy, and Suzi. Nikos talked of some good reviews I've had. I said, 'Nikos tells me I have become terribly immodest.' No one said anything, not even Nikos. I said, 'Well, I see no one is denying that I am.' They all laughed. Stephen said, 'You can always count on your friends.'

Suzi sat next to me at the end of the table. She asked me, 'Do you believe in God?' 'No,' I said. She said, 'I find it difficult to understand how anyone cannot believe in God.' I said, 'I find it difficult to believe how anyone can.'

A little while later, Stephen described how he, as a student, was visited regularly by a ghost which stood silently by his bed.

Suzi asked, 'How did it manifest itself?'

'By its silent presence.'

'Was it a man or a woman?'

Stephen said, 'I couldn't tell.'

I am amazed when I find close friends believe in what I find unbelievable. It makes those friends, whom I consider familiar, to be totally unfamiliar, and more interesting than before.

We drove Max to his flat in Mayfair.

He talked about Jennifer Bartlett. 'She's really a dumb artist. She knows nothing about technique. In fact, she's an appalling technician. When she succeeds technically, it's by sheer accident. But she has something that goes beyond technique, and when she's able to realize that her work is sensational.'

———

From the time I last saw them until recently, Maggie D. and Michael H. have married, but they still live separately.

The sitting room of Maggie's terrace house in Hampstead has large, deep armchairs and a sofa, and the wallpaper is a dark red William Morris pattern with simplified, overlapping leaves or feathers, I can't recall which, though I do like to get the details right. At the other end of the room was a guitar on the floor leaning against a wall, and a black, perhaps lacquered grand piano painted with Chinese scenes about its curved body, a glass of bluebells on it, and beyond it glass doors out to what looked an overgrown garden whose large-leafed plants pressed against the lower panes. On a wall across from the piano are bookshelves, floor to ceiling, but books were strewn about everywhere. Once again, I try to see such details as referring to something more.

We talked about London.

I said I never feel that, in the multi-roomed houses of London, I understand what all the furniture, the pictures, the books, the bibelots, the teapot and cups and saucers mean. My incomprehension makes me feel I'm not in London.

Maggie said, 'But I don't feel I'm inside either. I'm not from London, I'm from Yorkshire, and that makes me a foreigner in London. I didn't know anyone here until I came, after I graduated from Cambridge. I certainly didn't know any writers. I was the first writer I'd ever met.' She spoke calmly, sitting straight, her hands, palms down, on her knees, her fingers straight. She asked Michael, 'You don't feel you're a part of London, either, do you?'

Rising from a slouch, he said, 'No, no. I'm hardly English. My father was half Irish and my mother Swedish. And I grew up everywhere. I recall a time when I was a boy waking up in a wet, cold place, and not knowing where I was, and being told I was in Vienna.'

'Why Vienna?' I asked.

'I'm not sure why. My parents divorced and remarried again and again, and I'd spend time with my father and my stepmothers and with my mother and stepfathers in different places. One stepfather was Hungarian, another French. I was all over the place. The closest I got to proper English life was when I stayed with my grandparents, my father's parents, in the country here. When I came to London, finally, I felt I didn't know anyone. I still feel I don't, really.'

Brushing her bobbed hair back over an ear, Maggie said quietly, 'Your childhood was a muddle.'

'Yes, a muddle.'

Michael's face looks as if he usually wears spectacles that he at

some point in contemplating the world took off, and he wonders
where he has put them. 'It may have been Venice,' he said, 'the
cold, wet place I woke up in.'

I said, 'I'm very surprised. I thought you'd both feel very much
at home in London.'

'No, no,' Maggie said.

And I said, 'Well, if you two don't feel at home in London, what
can I feel?'

While Maggie prepared a hollandaise sauce in the kitchen,
Michael and I had gin and tonics in the sitting room.

He said, 'They're very demanding, the people I write biogra-
phies about.'

'Because they demand you get in the whole world each one
lived in?'

'The whole world.'

'But writing biography is like writing fiction, isn't it?' I asked.
'Trying to realize characters, trying to realize the worlds of the
characters, which, after all, exist in the writing.'

'If only one didn't have to verify all the facts,' Michael answered.

In a shiny apron, Maggie appeared to say lunch (or did she say
'luncheon'?) was ready – steamed salmon and boiled potatoes and
the bright hollandaise sauce. Michael opened a bottle of white
wine. The table was set near windows, the outside plants pressing
against the panes.

Again, we talked about London, or I wanted to talk about
London, as I always do. We talked mainly about writers from the
past, and the talk gave way to Bloomsbury and the survivors, such
as Henrietta Garnett, the grandniece of Virginia Woolf, who had
just published a novel – which, in fact, Henrietta had shown me
and which she wanted to call Catherine's Bidet, but published is
called, I think, Family Skeletons, and this made me feel I may be a
little more involved in London than Maggie and Michael.

Then talk about recycling of rubbish, which we were all for, and
as anyone with any common sense would be for. I suddenly looked
at Maggie and, as if an insight had come to me about her, I said,

'You appear to be, but you're not at all commonsensical, are you?' She has a way of jerking back her head so her hair, with long bangs, swings forward about her cheeks. She said, 'No, I'm not. How did you guess?'

As we were leaving to go to Michael's apartment, he and Maggie with bags and books, she asked him, 'Do you have chapter sixteen?' He opened his red plastic carrier bag and answered, 'Yes.' 'Whose chapter sixteen?' I asked. 'Michael's,' Maggie said. 'He keeps a copy of everything he writes on top of my wardrobe for safekeeping. I don't keep a copy of what I write, the typescript is all it is.'

Michael's apartment is in Ladbroke Grove, where, Maggie said, the air is less salubrious than in Hampstead. She said this in such a careful way, her chin jutted out, I thought she was being ironical, but wasn't sure.

Michael's wide sitting room is muted yellow, and three busts – of Augustus John, Lytton Strachey, and Bernard Shaw – all larger than life, keep strange company with one another, all looking away from one another. Everything neat, the books if not placed in their proper places on shelves stacked in piles.

When I thought of asking them why they live separately, I thought, no, don't, and I felt I had been long enough in London to know what to ask and what not to ask. Asking would have been like asking them to justify their marital relationship, and to ask anyone to justify his or her life is never, ever done. But I did say that, given all relationships are necessary but impossible, it is a very sensible arrangement, thinking to myself at the same time that, as the English would of course say to themselves about the arrangement, it was really too peculiar.

Maggie smiled, and with a fine irony said, 'Very sensible.'

Tea in Michael's garden, and talk about Margaret Thatcher and the threat to freedom of expression, which should be considered violations of human rights. And the absurdity of her claiming that Socialism is dead! Maggie said this is her basic belief: that the State is responsible for the ill, the old, the out of work and poor, and students, and, yes, we pay our taxes for this responsibility of the

State. But Thatcherite Britain couldn't last, Michael said, which he thought is already beginning to crack. Looking at the ground, Maggie said, 'I'm not so sure.' Michael raised his hands and said, 'Of course, I don't know.'

Maggie, in a canvas chair, dropped her wooden clogs and folded her legs under her, and the long afternoon light shone on her smooth face. Contradicting what they had said when I first came about not feeling they are part of London, we talked of people we know, people we meet over and over again in different contexts, at concerts or plays or openings of exhibitions or book-launch parties or dinner or drinks parties, and I felt that particular charm of being with friends with whom idle talk about other friends, or even talk about flowers, can seem the most intimate talk you've ever known.

Michael told a story about being driven by Charlotte Bonham Carter in her motor car, she often swerving to drive on the left side of the road.

———

I recognize this about Nikos: though he is constitutionally incapable of apologizing, as if it is a deep Greek trait never to blame oneself but always another, when he knows he has been unfair to me by blaming me for, oh, never mind what, he will press his forehead against mine for a long while and smile, and I always smile in return.

———

Stephen Buckley's wife, Stevie, was among a number to hold a jumble sale of whatever they no longer wanted but thought could be interesting to others – old tea caddies, stoneware bottles, crocheted antimacassars – the sale organized in the loft-like post-industrial space overlooking the Thames, near Tower Bridge, where some artists have their studios. We added to Stevie's stall whatever we no longer wanted, whatever was now irrelevant to our lives together, and among these were the sailor's trousers dyed bright yellow that I once bought for Nikos on a Saturday afternoon on the King's Road, then when the King's Road was as if a road into a world in which people dressed for a different world and, too, fell in love and had sex in a different world. Though I had bought the trousers for Nikos, he'd never worn them. In the loft I saw a boy, the son of an artist and his wife, study the yellow trousers with an attentiveness that could only have been inspired by fantasy, though his fantasy was all his. I said to Nikos, 'Give him the trousers, just give them to him,' and Nikos was amused to give them to the boy, who took them away to wear in whatever he fancied his world to be.

———

Francis told us he has a new friend he wants us to meet. His name is John, John Edwards, and he runs a pub in the East End. On a Sunday morning, Nikos and I drove Francis there. John has black curly hair and wore a smart grey-flannel suit. Nikos and I were in jeans. We had drinks in the saloon, where young men were playing snooker. John's boyfriend Philip was among them. A pretty, blond young man with pimples along his jaw, he couldn't go more than a mile from the pub, as he'd been convicted of a crime and was awaiting sentencing. After some drinks, we all went to another pub, which closed while we were there, but we stayed on behind the locked doors and met a number of middle-aged Cockney queens and their boyfriends. They and John and Philip and Francis and Nikos and I, about twelve of us, went out for late lunch at a Chinese restaurant, all of us about a large round table. One bleached-blond queen said to Francis, 'So you paint pictures, do you, Francis? Excuse my ignorance, but what kind of pictures do you paint?' This was all said in East End Cockney. Francis said, 'Well, it's difficult to say.' 'Like, do you paint landscapes or people?' 'Sometimes landscapes, sometimes people.' 'Do you paint pictures of dogs, Francis?' someone else asked; 'I like pictures of dogs myself.' 'I used to paint dogs years ago. I don't any more.' 'What do you do with your paintings, then? Do you show them on the railings along the park in Bayswater? I seen paintings, on a Sunday, all along the railings.' Francis, laughing, said, 'I haven't come to that yet. I might soon.' John said, 'His paintings are fucking awful. He can't even draw as good as that Piss-casso, and fucking awful he was, too.' 'Right,' Francis said, 'I can't.' John said, 'Ask him to paint a picture of you, it don't look anything like you, all a mess.' 'That's right,' Francis said, 'I couldn't do a portrait that looks like anyone to save my life.'

In the car, riding back through the East End, Francis said, 'I feel an idiot among them. I feel they know so much more than I do.'

'What?' Nikos asked.

'I don't know,' Francis answered.

Nikos, not feeling well – which is rare of him – stayed home from work. In the afternoon I asked him if he was better, and he said, 'Yes, because you've taken care of me.' This surprised and pleased me because he usually doesn't like being cared for

---

After her death, Francis wanted to talk to me about Sonia. I went to his mews flat in Reece Mews about midday. He said he wasn't working for a few days. We drank three or four of what he called Dead Dogs, I think. I asked him if Sonia had ever attacked him, as she had attacked almost everyone. He thought for a long time. There is something comical about him when he is thoughtful: his expression is almost a parody of thoughtfulness, one eye low, the other high. He is looking more and more like one of his paintings.

He said, 'I don't know, really. I think it may be because I was introduced to Sonia by the art collector Peter Watson, whom she was desperately in love with. Of course, he was queer. He was a marvelously good-looking man, and intelligent, and rich. He had all the qualities Sonia needed in a man to fall in love with him, especially his being queer.' Francis said this with a barking laugh. 'Perhaps she never attacked me because she associated me with Peter in some way, and she would never attack Peter.'

'I wonder,' I said; 'I suspect she never attacked you because she was frightened of you.'

'Frightened of me? Why?'

'Because Sonia was frightened of people – or at least was in awe of people – whom she thought had succeeded totally in their creativity. She believed you have.'

Now he shrugged and again laughed, now a high laugh. 'Did she? I can't see why she should have believed that. I'm not a success.'

I said, 'Sonia had a great deal of respect for creativity.'

'I think she did,' Francis said; 'I think she wanted very much to be creative, and even tried, but she failed. You know, she was sent by the Observer's editor David Astor to Israel to interview General Dayan, and she went with great enthusiasm, but when she got back her piece on Dayan was found to be unpublishable. She simply didn't have the talent.'

'I wonder if her realization that she had no talent changed her. I've often wondered what changed her from the charming, bright, young woman everyone thought she was to the dark woman I knew her to be.'

Francis said, 'Drink.'

'Yes, but why did she drink?'

'I think you're right – one of the reasons, perhaps the central reason, was that she wanted to be creative, and knew she couldn't be. And once she knew she couldn't, once she denied it totally in herself, she was in awe of it in others.'

Odd, I thought, that Francis could take what I had said and repeat it in a way that seemed to be original with him.

I repeated, 'Only those others she thought had really succeeded in realizing their creativity, which were not many.'

'Not that she knew much about books or paintings or music. She read a lot, but, as far as I heard when she spoke about the arts, all her ideas were received.'

'About books, I think her enthusiasm was great, and her enthusiasm about certain writers – I remember her praising Victor Hugo – was inspiring – she made me want to read Victor Hugo. But she didn't know much about painting and music.'

'Nothing.'

'And yet, and yet,' I said, drunk enough to repeat myself, 'she had this tremendous respect for all creativity. She thought it was what she most wanted but didn't have. She wanted to possess it in others, but couldn't. At times, she imagined that if she couldn't be creative herself she could understand creativity, especially writing. I remember her once talking to Jean Rhys and me about a writer's intention, and Jean and I both said, "No, it's not that way," meaning there is much more to writing than what the writer intends, much more, much much more, and Sonia looked very puzzled – puzzled and hurt – and said, "Tiens, that goes to show I know nothing about writing."'

Francis said, 'Nothing about what happens.'

I asked, 'Do you think she was a pessimistic person?'

Francis answered, 'Totally, totally pessimistic. You see, I am at least optimistic in the moment –'

'When you're painting?'

'When I'm painting.'

'Because to create is to be optimistic. Sonia didn't have that. At least that's what I imagine.'

'As much as one can be right in anything one imagines,' Francis said, 'I think you're right. I think you are.'

We were sitting at the bare table before the windows at the end of the long narrow room which is his living room and bedroom; bare bulbs hung from the ceiling, and though the electric fire was lit, there was a chill.

John Edwards came. We went out for lunch. We drank three bottles of wine. I was very drunk. After, we got into a taxi to go to the Colony, where Francis ordered a bottle of champagne. I can't recall what the three of us talked about. For a while, we talked to a short, dark, bull-like man who spends four months working in an Arab country running a power station, then four weeks in London, over and over; he has done this for fifteen years. Very friendly, he invited us all to Sunday lunch: roast lamb. Francis said, 'We'll come. That'll be lovely. We love roast lamb.' The man left. I asked Francis, 'Where are we supposed to meet him?' 'I have no idea,' Francis said, and laughed. He ordered another bottle of champagne.

One glass more, and I knew I was going to be sick. I said I had to go. Francis helped me down to the street, asking if I'd be all right. Yes, I said, but I would be all right only if I kept moving, so crossed streets if the little man was red. In the bathroom, I lay on the floor, naked, and from time to time vomited into the toilet.

When Nikos returned from his office he found me on the floor. He had planned on taking me and Stephen out to dinner. I said, 'I can't go out.' Stephen arrived. I fell asleep on the bathroom floor. Whenever I woke, I heard Nikos and Stephen downstairs talking while they ate an improvised meal Nikos prepared.

It took me a couple of days to recover.

———

I have never asked Francis what he thinks of Minimalist Art, that of Robert Ryman, Agnes Martin, Donald Judd, Dan Flavin, Richard Serra, which Nikos and I have seen most prominently displayed in the privately owned Saatchi Gallery in Boundary Road. (I have to interject here that when I told Stephen S. about the Boundary Road Gallery, he frowned as if what I knew, which he had not heard about from more authoritative sources, could not really be serious. I resented this a little, and told Nikos as much; Nikos, unabashed, then told Stephen, who told Nikos that, yes, he could only take seriously people of his own generation, and found it difficult to take seriously younger people.) No doubt Francis would stick out his lower lip and say, as he says about the Abstract Sublime (a term David Sylvester prefers to the Abstract Expressionists), that it is all wallpaper. Sometimes, studying a painting by Francis, I eliminate with a hand the figure if I can, and see in itself the space in which the figure appears, space delineated by lines that stand out from the flat backgrounds, space that seems to me the essence of his pictures, the figures the accidents. But this is getting too close to opinion, which I won't allow myself. To go back to the Boundary Road Gallery. The Saatchis never appear at the openings of the exhibitions there, so, at those amazing openings, those invited are aware of them with more amazement at what they have accomplished than if they were there. I've met them, Charles and Doris, at Stephen and Stevie Buckley's house, and, talking to Doris, I had more than an impression that it was she who determines the exhibitions in their gallery, especially the works of the American Minimalists, against whose works I see her, her very pale hair half covering a pale, delicately angular face, precise, her demeanour itself apparently minimalist.

The photograph of her by Robert Mapplethorpe shows this.

Doris Saatchi, 1983 Copyright © The Robert Mapplethorpe Foundation. Courtesy Art + Commerce

About Robert Mapplethorpe, Doris said he is a very gentle man.

The Boundary Road Gallery was designed by Max Gordon.

Max gives the impression of not only knowing everyone intimately but of being an influence in their lives, such as his promoting the work of Lisa Milroy to the Saatchis, Max particularly keen on Lisa's paintings of piles of folded shirts, for Max collects shirts which he keeps in piles in drawers. His flat, designed by himself to be all white space, appears meant to be a space for the art he collects. It amuses him to point to the floor at a very tiny house in bronze, or perhaps iron, by Joel Shapiro, the size of it made all the more meaningful spatially in the space of the room. Max is very much in contact with New York artists such as Joel Shapiro and Ellen Phelan and Jennifer Bartlett. Max also collects narrow boxes that tubes of toothpaste are sold in, his prize a box with the brand name Craig-Martin.

He urged Jennifer Bartlett to give the name Rhapsody to a large work of art, many white enamel plates covered with different-coloured dots and dashes that cover whole walls, which the Metropolitan Museum of Art in New York have bought.

———

Learning to be English –

I received a notice from H.M. Inland Revenue to inform me that I had overpaid my tax for two years and I would soon be getting a 'check' (American) to the amount of £1,517.08. I have learned that in England such things take a long time. I waited a few months, then thought I would notify the Inland Revenue that I hadn't got it, as I had asked at my bank if it had been deposited.

A handwritten note came back a couple of weeks later expressing surprise. The cheque (British) should have been sent. The note was signed by a Mr. Ridge, with his telephone number and extension.

A soft-voiced man, he said he didn't at all mind my ringing him. I gave him my reference number. 'That's just what I wanted,' he said, then added, 'Now let me see if I can find your file.' He came back and said he was terribly sorry, he couldn't find my file, but they did have a system whereby lost files were eventually 'kicked up.' I asked him if he minded my ringing him again in a week's time, and he said not at all.

My file still hadn't been kicked up by the time I rang again.

Mr. Ridge said, 'You can't imagine the confusion here.'

I said I would ring again in a week, and by then my file was found. Mr. Ridge had placed it on his desk in anticipation of my ringing him. The problem seemed to be what had happened to the cheque. He couldn't issue a new one without finding out what happened to the old. Had it been cashed? And if it had, who had cashed it? This he couldn't find out himself, but would have to alert the Computer Centre in Worthing to do so. He would write to them that very day.

He hadn't heard from Worthing when I rang him a week later. He couldn't understand why. Never for a moment did I doubt that Mr. Ridge had in fact written. We decided between us that we would give them another week. We did, and they still hadn't responded. Mr. Ridge would write to them again, and he would mark his letter urgent.

When I rang a week later, as usual on a Wednesday, I was told that Mr. Ridge was on sick leave for two days. I said I'd ring again on Friday, and the receptionist said I would have a much better chance of getting Mr. Ridge on Monday.

Monday morning, Mr. Ridge, recovered, was back at his desk, but he hadn't yet sorted out the morning's post, so he wouldn't be able to tell me till the afternoon if Worthing had responded, though, as far as he knew, Worthing hadn't responded to his letter marked urgent while he was on sick leave.

I rang him at 3.00, but Mr. Ridge was still out to lunch. I rang at 4.00 and found that Mr. Ridge had gone home.

I rang the next morning. He explained that, as he hadn't had any word from Worthing, he hadn't wanted to disturb me, but, perhaps, today there would be a notice from Worthing. I asked him what was a good time to ring him in the afternoon, and he said 3.30. But Worthing hadn't sent him the information he had so urgently requested.

He said, 'You could threaten to write to your M.P. That always gets them going.'

'I hadn't thought of that,' I said, not wanting him to know that, as a non-voting foreigner, I didn't have a Member of Parliament to whom I could threaten to write. 'But I wonder if, in the meantime, we might give Worthing another chance by in fact telephoning them and speaking to them directly.'

'That is a possibility,' he said.

He rang me that afternoon to tell me he'd spoken with Worthing. I would appreciate that they were in the process of transferring one tax district from another (indeed, I had had a notice about a year before that my tax district had been changed to Willesden from I can't recall what previous district) and the information I requested was not yet on the computer. He suggested I ring in two weeks.

I'd be happy to know, he told me when I next spoke to him, that the information was on the computer, but the computer would take forty-eight hours to come up with it. This was Friday, and he wasn't sure the computer worked over the weekend.

Each time I spoke with him, he reiterated the problem: he could not issue a new cheque until it was clear that the previous one hadn't been cashed. He said, 'There is a possibility, you see, that you might have cashed it.'

I had a moment of English doubt. Had I, without remembering, cashed it? But for the first time I became irritated, angry even, that he should be making me doubt myself.

I said, 'Of course I didn't cash it.'

'Of course you didn't,' he said.

When I next rang him, the computer still hadn't come up with the information. Mr. Ridge had done everything he could, and was going on holiday for three weeks.

I said, 'This has to be settled before you go.'

He would do everything he possibly could, but if he couldn't bring the business to a satisfactory conclusion before he left, he would leave it in the hands of Miss June, his colleague, to whom he would explain the situation.

Miss June startled me by saying she had not yet 'gotten' information from Worthing, and I was worried that that Americanism (however old English it is meant to be) indicated American infiltration into the Inland Revenue. She was understanding, and said she would keep ringing Worthing until she had the reply she wanted. We spoke every day, I often ringing her, she sometimes ringing me. Whispering, she told me, just between us, that Worthing was in a terrible state, but she would keep trying.

I did get the cheque (British).

———

Thinking about Sonia –

Sonia rejected God, any God, with a force that would have destroyed God had God existed. A cigarette in one hand and a glass of wine in the other, her ash blonde and grey hair shaking as she, frowning deeply, shook her head from side to side, she would rage, rage, not only against any belief in God, which she found totally uninteresting, but against God Himself for ever having supposed He existed, for ever having supposed He was of any interest to anyone. He had never existed, and he was of no, but absolutely no, interest.

I knew that if I asked Sonia if anything at all was left of her once having believed in God, she would have answered, 'Don't be so stupid. Of course not.' But Sonia remained a passionately negative Catholic, a kind of passionately negative Catholic missionary to friends who doubted: there is no transcendence, no redemption, no realization of any promises made by Catholicism or any other religion. She considered herself a realist. And she was, and the greatest expression of her realism was her pretty dining-room table.

Sonia said to me, 'Our both being Catholic is our secret.'

———

There was a time in my life when I believed the Roman Catholic Church, under the absolute dictatorship of the Vatican that I was brought up not to question, portraits of Pope Pius XII hanging in our church and school rooms as the supreme authority over morality, dictated to me whom I could love, and what the expression of that love could be. Imagine. The residue of that belief has gone, gone, gone, and so dated it is not of any interest to me. What the residue of my religion that remains is – oh!

———

If she is to be away, Natasha will ring us and ask us, please, to take care of Stephen. Often, we will be just the three of us for a meal, and I will mentally draw back from the conversation and look at Stephen and wonder how it happened that he is with us, this person who connects us to people from the past who survive in cultural history, this witness to so much history, our closest friend. How can we not be attentive when he recounts bringing T. S. Eliot and Igor Stravinsky together, Eliot complaining that his blood was too thin and Stravinsky bragging that his blood was thick enough to form rubies? And his laugh, his high, bright laugh when he tells a story that Natasha calls méchant, his face beaming red, how can we not be as amused as he is? And how he turns self-deprecation into something to laugh at, as when he told us he had been to a dinner party in some Mid-Western American city where he sat next to a woman who asked his name, she reacting dismissively when he told her with: the only Stephen Spender she had heard about, a poet, was dead. At moments, his large body appears to be too large for him to support it, and he slumps a little, as he appears, too, to slump in spirit, but only for a moment, because he would say he has had a good life, a very good life. He may hint that it is only because of his connections that he has had the recognition he has had as a poet, but he goes on writing his poems, and from time to time shows us a draft – rather, shows it to Nikos, and if Nikos suggests a change in one line Stephen will rewrite the entire poem.

———

Max Gordon invited Nikos and me to the Albert Hall for a performance of music by John Cage. After, he said we should go backstage, and Nikos and I, assuming that Max was friendly with Cage, went with him to the entrance to the backstage, where, however, a guard stopped us and said we were not allowed in. Max simply walked past him. Nikos and I held back. The guard, who was stunned by Max simply walking past him, stepped aside, and Max, beyond him, gestured us to follow him. We did, into a wide, curving corridor with many closed doors along it. Max opened door after door, until he opened a door onto a room where, it appeared to me, at a far distance were John Cage and the pianist and composer David Tudor and others, who stared at us clearly without knowing who Max was and who we were. Again, Max told us to follow him in, but Nikos and I held back and said we'd rather not, and left. The next day Max rang to say we should have stayed on, he had joined the group and with them gone to a restaurant for a meal.

———

I have been reading the diary of Virginia Woolf. As fascinated as I was by the people who I imagined would appear in the diary before I started to read, I find that as I read my fascination diminishes and I see, not a world, but a room with blank windowless walls and a low ceiling, Virginia's own room where she is locked in, locked in with people whom she gives no space to move about, to talk to one another, to be themselves; and she won't let them escape her severe judgments of them. I think: I would not have wanted to be locked in that room.

———

Steven Runciman at dinner:

'Here is an anecdote for you from my stay in Jerusalem in 1913. I was staying at Government House, where my fellow guest was the late Lord Athlone and his wife, the late Princess Alice – Victoria's last-surviving granddaughter. There was a British regiment in Jerusalem, and the colonel of the regiment, a certain Colonel Montgomery, used to come to dine at Government House. He lectured us on our unnecessary luxuries. He was priggish, and we all loathed him. It so happened that at one of the ceremonies of the Church of the Holy Sepulcher, I was next to Princess Alice in the gallery; we looked down, and there was Colonel Montgomery's bald patch just below, which prompted Princess Alice to say, "See if we can hit him with some wax," so I tilted my candle, as she did, and she was a better marksman than I . . . She wrote later in her memoirs about being in disgrace with the future Lord Montgomery for accidentally dropping wax on him. I reproved her, and she said, "I know, my dear, but I didn't think it would do to say I did it deliberately." "You've been a coward," I said, "you've put history wrong." She giggled. I met her after the war, and she said to me, "Do you remember when we dropped wax on Field Marshal Montgomery?" And that was the first time I realized that the odious colonel was the odious field marshal.'

Mary McCarthy wanted to have, not a service, but a gathering at which friends would speak about Sonia. The writer Francis Wyndham rang to ask me if I would be the compere, as he did not want to be, and I agreed – agreed, no doubt, because the position gave me some prominence in London. The gathering was in a stark hall with rows of folding chairs and a simple table. A song was sung to a guitar, a poem was recited, and I read from my diary an account of Sonia staying with me in Italy. Nikos told me later that the critic and editor John Gross, in the audience, seemed to be scowling at my presuming to speak about Sonia. Then Mary McCarthy spoke, her rectangular smile held rectangular and exposing her teeth as she spoke, and what she said about Sonia didn't seem complimentary, except her comparing Sonia's pure English looks to a portrait painting by Reynolds. I'm very pleased that, a few days later, I had a postcard from Miriam Gross, John's journalist wife: 'I thought your diary was marvellous – it evoked Sonia with terrific accuracy and vividness.' This makes me feel I in some way belong in London.

I asked Gregory Evans, David Hockney's assistant, how often it happens that he and David don't know all the people they are entertaining in a restaurant, and Gregory said, 'Oh, all the time.' Among the people at a table in a restaurant, David presiding (and as always paying in the end), was a delicate youth with golden eyelashes and golden hair. I later asked David who he was, and David said, 'Ian Falconer,' and David said, 'He's in love with me. He wants to come to California to stay with me and study art with me. But I'm intimidated by him because he's so beautiful. I'm always intimidated by beautiful boys, and can hardly speak to them.' I said, 'I used to feel that way. Since I've been with Nikos, I don't any longer.'

Some days later, Nikos and I went to the Mughul Exhibition at the Victoria and Albert Museum, where we met, by arrangement, Ian, and the three of us stood together in the wonderfully decorated tent of panels of Indian chintz, the panels decorated with small vases at the bottom from which expand and expand and expand flowers that cover the panels, and on the tent's roof more flowers, so we were in a bower of flowers. After an hour, we went together to David H.'s studio. David, with so many demands made on him, had to leave, and Nikos and I stayed on with Ian, whom Nikos flirted with. Later, Nikos said, laughing, 'I wouldn't mind making love with Ian.' Well, he is very beautiful. I said, 'Nor would I.'

———

It used to be that when Nikos and I had a row, I would say, 'We've got to talk about this,' to which he'd respond, 'No, we're not, I'm not going to indulge you in your American introspection.' We would be silent towards each other for a while, then I'd think, Well, I know he loves me, and conversation would be resumed.

I don't introspect in my diary. Nor, I hope, do I express opinions.

As an aside: Steven Runciman recounted his having invited the Queen Mother to his club, the Athenaeum, when she asked him what men did in their clubs. He booked a room and invited what he called other queens, as the Queen Mother likes queens. After their meal, he showed her about, and noted, as they entered the large common room, men in their deep armchairs lower their newspapers and frown at the sight of a woman, until, that is, they recognized who she was, and, my God, they stood to attention! I asked him, 'What is she like?' to which he answered, 'She is not introspective.'

I think I am not, after all, an introspective person, and it's because I'm not that I so easily accept that Nikos will not talk about our rows. Perhaps I feel that our love for each other is in some way objective, and contains us as a great globe, and has love's own will.

———

From Frank's An Appetite for Poetry, this:

> We understand a whole by means of its parts, and the parts by means of the whole. But this 'circle' seems to imply that we can understand nothing – the whole is made of parts we cannot understand until it exists, and we cannot see the whole without understanding the parts. Something, therefore, must happen, some intuition by which we break out of the situation – a leap, a divination . . . whereby we are enabled to understand both part and whole.

———

A novel, The Family, has been published. I call it a novel, but it is entirely autobiographical, and a lot of it comes directly from my diary.

The residue of my religion – what is left is not belief, no, but a constant awareness of a way of thinking and feeling. What awareness? It is the awareness inculcated in me by my religion, the essential teaching of which was: the reason why we are on this earth is to suffer in order to earn our places in heaven to be with God for all eternity.

As a boy, I had no choice but to believe. Again and again, I recall how, in my parochial primary school, I and all the first-grade students standing by our scratched and ink-stained desks were taught by a nun to make the sign of the cross. The nun, rigid in her black robes, faced the class and, slowly repeating the gestures over and over, demonstrated on her body the sign that the students were to repeat on their bodies. But I couldn't do it. I was so aware of myself in the glaring ring of my concentration I became uncoordinated and wasn't able to tell my right from my left, my forehead from my chest. The nun had to take my right hand and guide the tips of the fingers first to my forehead, then to the middle of my chest, then to the left shoulder and across to the right. The nun nailed to my small body the sign of the suffering of my Savior, the Savior whose suffering gave meaning to my suffering, to all the world's suffering, because it was by suffering that I and the world would be raised into heaven to be with God eternally. Our deepest love was for God in eternity, and our deepest longing was to be with God in eternity.

No, I do not believe in God, but the love and the longing remain – remain, however, love and longing that cannot be fulfilled, because there is no God in eternity.

Sometimes I feel that everything I see, hear, smell, taste, touch I do in that awareness, so that even the sight of a glass of water on a sunlit windowsill will fill me with the awareness of something promised in the glass of water on the sunlit windowsill, something that I sense so profoundly is there to be fulfilled, but can't be fulfilled.

Walking along Oxford Street among the crowds, that awareness comes over me about everyone I walk along with or pass, that awareness of so many of us aware of what we love and long for, but what we can't have, because it is beyond having.

When I am with Stephen Spender, I may suddenly see in him a large, awkward man who wants to fulfill so much more than he knows he can fulfill, and a feeling of tenderness comes to me for him.

Even with Nikos – say, sitting next to him at the Wigmore Hall for a recital of Bach's Well-Tempered Clavier, he so attentive to the music and I trying to be attentive – a loneliness will occur to me that isolates me, a feeling that as much as I love him and long to be with him, the love and the longing will never be fulfilled, not fully, because it can't be.

That awareness is the dimension in which I wrote the novel, The Family. The awareness I retain most of my family is the love and the longing that surrounded us all – the love and the longing inculcated in all of us, mother and father and seven sons, by the enclosing religion of a small, working-class, French-speaking parish in Yankee New England, a parish that might have been enclosed by a palisade – and within that surrounding awareness the memory of my father coming home to say he had been fired from the factory, the memory of my mother in a daze after shock treatment, the memory of my hysterical self shouting that I'll kill myself, memory after memory after memory, and all, again, within a surrounding awareness that made us helpless, and because helpless innocent, and because innocent vulnerable to a world promised to us in our suffering, suffering that would earn us our places with God in eternity.

It ends with a prayer.

Pray to God the Father
  To the Holy Spirit
  To the Son
  To the Virgin Mother
  To all those, in their strange high country, in their large bright house, pray for the small dark house in this low country.

Catharine Carver worked closely on editing the novel, but did not want any acknowledgment.

Stephen is enthusiastic about the novel, as if for him I have finally situated the characters in the world.

It especially pleases me that Sonia Orwell said, 'Enfin, you've written a novel I can take seriously.'

Frank Kermode gave it a nice quote.

Nikos said, 'The suffering of your family.'

Jennifer Bartlett is in London to design the dining room, in tiles she paints, for Doris and Charles Saatchi. We went together to the Saatchi house, which is attached to another house used for their collection of modern art, including a huge John Chamberlain crushed-automobile sculpture standing alone in one room. Doris prepared tea for us while Charles, hardly greeting us, played back-gammon with his brother Maurice, of Saatchi & Saatchi, meant to be responsible for Margaret Thatcher being elected as Prime Minis-ter with the slogan: Labour isn't working. Doris moves slowly, with the grace of a ballet dancer, and as carefully.

Left alone, Jennifer and I lay on a bed and talked and talked, often shifting positions. She prefers lying down to standing.

———

Invited by Tony Stokes, Jennifer gave a reading at Garage from her book, The History of the Universe, in which she recounts, in a flat tone, recollections from her life:

> I went to swimming lessons at the bay. The lifeguard wore red trunks, the water was blue, the sky was blue.

In that same flat tone, she recounted very intimate facts about her life.

In the book are written portraits of her friends, including Jan Hashey, her pseudonym Meredith Ridge Slade-Ryan, and Michael Craig-Martin, his pseudonym Robin Slade-Ryan ('In Corsham, Wiltshire, England, Robin and Meredith fell in love with the same student, Brian, a young boy committed to an extreme evangelical faith which involved speaking in tongues and being moved by the spirit'); also of Keith Milow as Gavin Frazer; then there is the woman Maggi Hambling ('He lived for some time with a woman who became a lesbian'), and I, Daniel Francoeur, the name I use for myself in The Family ('During college Daniel woke up, looked out the window and even if the day was fine thought of suicide. In London, Daniel was cured of an ulcer by acupuncture. During the course of the cure he went mad, beat his hands against the head-board of the bed, wept, screamed, shook, shouted. Since then he hasn't been seriously depressed. Andreas, who is a poet and works in a publishing house, took care of him').

The epigraph of the book is from Gertrude Stein: 'She was more interested in birds than flowers although she wasn't really interested in birds.'

Jennifer would like to meet Francis Bacon, but I'm not sure Francis would get on with her.

Needless to say, Nikos has no interest in all of this, but allows me my interest and, yes, amusement, and, yes, more than amusement in the charm I feel when I am with Jennifer.

© Eric Boman

Nikos has made me aware of the critical works of the French decon-structuralists, Piaget, Foucault, Lacan, Derrida, and especially of Roland Barthes whose books take up a length of shelf space in his library. I pick up a book, read here and there, and pick out a word that seems charged with meaning for me, then I close the book. Such a word is 'syncretistic.' Out of its original context, I use the word 'syncretistic' in conversation with Nikos, and he asks me what I mean, and I suggest the meaning is in connections that all come together in a way that Frank means by 'divination,' and Nikos, smiling, asks me, a little devilishly, what I mean by divination, and I try to give 'divination' a definition that I trust Nikos will understand in the way he understands me, and I answer, 'That there is an impulse in the mind to make everything connect,' and he smiles more and looks at me as if I were a student whose naïveté he is touched by.

————

The BBC producer and interviewer and critic Julian Jebb asked me to drinks, or so I thought, and as I was sure he wouldn't mind – also, to show her off to him and a friend of mine he would not have suspected I had so he would have been surprised and intrigued – I brought along Jennifer. Julian welcomed us as if he had been expecting us. Jennifer and I joked lightly with each other more, I felt, than we talked to Julian, she and I as though lolling together in the talk. In fact, Jennifer does have a way of lolling, even when sitting on a chair, and often she will slip off the chair and loll on the floor, her head propped up by her elbow against the floor and her hand to her cheek, and then, that too taxing, she will lie flat on the floor, but go on talking. I felt Julian liked her, but was bemused, and all the more bemused when I said we had to go, for he said I had been invited to dinner with Vidia and Pat Naipaul. Apologies, of course embarrassed apologies, but Julian insisted, all was prepared. Jennifer sat back on the chair when the bell rang and Julian went to open to the Naipauls.

I wanted them all to wonder what I was doing with her and what she was doing with me as a couple, which I wasn't sure of myself.

Julian said he had to go to court for not having paid his bills, but he couldn't, he simply couldn't, open brown envelopes with narrow windows in them that show his name and address.

————

I should write about our evening out with Francis and Stephen. I should, and yet I don't want to. Why? When Nikos and I were driving Stephen back to Loudoun Road after, Stephen asked, 'Will you write about this evening in your diary? It was very strange.' 'Yes,' I said, 'of course I will.' The evening was strange, but I think the strangeness can't be accounted for.

As usual, we all met at Francis' flat in Reece Mews. John Edwards was there (his friend Philip is still in prison for raping a woman at knifepoint, and John misses him terribly) and a young, thin, beautiful man named Roc. Whereas John, who is working class from the East End, was dressed in a smart gray suit with a white shirt and a dark silk tie and smelled cleanly of cologne, Roc, who is upper class and from a very rich family, was dressed in a black motorcycle jacket too big for him, shabby, tight corduroy trousers, and old, narrow and pointed black suede shoes, and he did not give the impression that he was altogether clean. It took me a while to recall that I had met Roc before at a big party given by Rodrigo and Anne Moynihan, and that he is Roc Sandford, the son of the writer Nell Dunn. In Francis' narrow sitting room–bedroom with the large, smashed mirror held together with duct tape, in front of which, Francis likes to say, someone tried to kill him by throwing an ashtray at him that missed, we drank champagne. Francis showed us the only work of art by another artist he owns: done by a Royal College of Art student, a girl, a sewn portrait of her mother, so the nose, made out of canvas, was sewn on, and the open mouth and tongue and teeth, and eyes and eyelashes, and even the hair, were all sewn onto the canvas, the hair, Francis said, the hair of the artist's mother. He said it was the only good work of art he had seen by a living artist in a long while, and he had bought it. After he showed it to us, he propped it against a wall, in a corner. We all said it was extraordinary; we didn't know what else to say about it. We drank two bottles of champagne and then went to an Italian restaurant round the corner, a basement restaurant, where we all sat at a long table. I sat across from Roc. I realized I had as much difficulty understanding Roc's upper-class accent as I did John's Cockney. I asked him what he did, and it seemed to me improbable that he does what he said he does: runs a large farm, a family farm, on Majorca. He flies between Majorca and London often, but he isn't happy in Majorca and wants to stay in London, though he doesn't know what he'll do here. He looked at me deeply in the eyes, then, suddenly, he slumped back and put his hands over his eyes, and I wondered if he had passed out or had a fit of depression. No one took any notice of him, and I joined the conversation of the others, which was about John's friend in prison and how cruel it was to keep him in prison for so long. Francis said, 'It's criminal.' Roc appeared to revive, and drank more, and when the waiters came he asked for all the food to be heaped on his plate, so he had a mixture of pasta, beans, boiled potatoes, roast potatoes, cannelloni, and on top a big gob of mustard. While he ate, the rest of us talked, then, again suddenly, he slumped back and put his hands over his eyes, and when he lowered his hands he smiled at me and said he'd just had a little sleep.

When we got out of the restaurant, Roc invited us all to his flat in Soho for vodka. Francis said he'd go home, and the rest of us, Stephen (who appeared bigger and less coordinated than ever), John, Nikos and I, and Roc, left Francis in the street and went by Nikos' and my car to Roc's flat in Brewer Street. The flat is the top floor in a building among porno film houses, the lights of which flashed through the curtainless windows. The flat appeared to be in the process of being torn apart, with exposed wall struts, and rubbish. One room, the bedroom only because there was a mattress on the floor and clothes thrown about, though there was also a mattress on the floor of the sitting room, the sitting room only because of some broken chairs and a big record player.

I sat with John by a wood fire, the only light in the room – Roc appeared to be burning bits of table he'd smashed – and we talked, though I wasn't sure I understood, about Francis. He loves Francis, and Francis is helping him to buy a pub, but their relationship is non-sexual; he feels he can do Francis a favour, however, by making sure his friends don't nick him, so at least Francis is safe in a world of thieves.

On the mattress on the floor were Stephen, Nikos and Roc, reclining and laughing. John asked me if I thought Stephen would write a poem for Philip to give to him in prison – John can't write at all – to tell Philip how much he loves him, and I said I'd ask Stephen, and did, but Stephen appeared very puzzled, as if he didn't understand the request, or perhaps he didn't want to write the poem. He said to John, 'I'd love to, I really would, but it takes a very long time to write a poem.' 'I understand,' John said.

Then a door opened and a girl came in. Her hair was bunched up at the top of her head and fell in front of her face; her black eyes, through the hair, appeared startled. Seeing her, Stephen said, 'I must go.'

John, Nikos, Roc, I pulled him up onto his feet; he was unsteady, and I worried that he might fall back. Roc showed us all out. On the street, Stephen asked, 'Who was that ugly girl? She ruined everything.' Nikos said, 'Pity her if she's Roc's girlfriend.' John kissed us, over and over, and left us to go to clubs.

On our way to Loudoun Road to leave Stephen off, we were stopped in Portland Place by a policeman who held out a hand. There were many policemen about. The one who stopped us looked in, then waved us on, and I said, 'I guess we look proper.' I imagined the policeman thought Stephen looked like a minister of some kind. Stephen kept repeating, 'How strange it's been. How strange.'

———

Another Easter, and we wondered where we would go for the service, and decided on the Ethiopian Orthodox Church, Saint Mary of Debre Tsion in Battersea, where we went with Doris Saatchi, now divorced from Charles Saatchi. We had to take off our shoes and place them in large pigeonholes, and as the nave was filled we climbed up to a gallery to look down at the service of priests in white and gold robes chanting and acolytes beating drums, one acolyte carrying a large white umbrella with a long fringe about the edge. The congregation, almost all in white, stood to pray with their hands held out. First the men advanced for communion, each given a little cloth with which to wipe his mouth and then throw onto a growing pile; then the women. Near us in the gallery was a man, who appeared to be English, dressed as a woman in a long, sleeveless shift and golden bracelets on his bare arms, he talking animatedly with Ethiopians around him. Nikos was disappointed because there was no moment of resurrection, which we had all imagined would happen with the loud beating of drums but didn't, and people began to leave before the Mass finished, and we left too. The three of us went to our flat for the traditional Greek Easter supper, which, however, was out of the cultural context that used to give it meaning.

What was most strange about the service was that it did not seem strange at all, not even the presence in the church of the man dressed as a woman.

More and more, I like to think that keeping a diary has to do, not with the writer, but within the historical time that the diary is written. And if there should be any deep structure to that time, the structure would be in the diary. A diary, which is supposed to be the most personal of all forms of literary expression, really is the most impersonal, having to do not so much with the writer but the times in which the writer lives.

In London and staying with us, John and Hugh invited us to meet Douglas Cooper. John likes to give us a little biography of people he thinks we'd find interesting, or, perhaps, who'd find us interesting, and told us that Douglas Cooper is a close friend of Picasso and a collector of his works which hang in his grand chateau in France, and who, during the war, was particularly adept at interrogating young German soldiers, terrifying them with his command of German, so that Nikos and I were prepared for the entrance of a large man with a large-brimmed Texan hat coming towards the restaurant table and more or less shouting, in what sounded like a Texan accent, that paintings by Picasso had been stolen from his chateau, but had been found in Switzerland.

He took no interest at all in Nikos and me, which we thought just as well.

Nikos did not mention that he publishes the books of John Rewald.

After Cooper left, John and Hugh said there was some suspicion that the paintings were not stolen but spirited away to get them into Switzerland and out from under a French ruling that they must remain in France.

————

We had not seen Patrick Procktor for a while, then, out doing Saturday shopping, came across him in carpet slippers walking his dachshund and looking very thin and wan. He asked us to join him in a pub, and though Nikos was reluctant I agreed and at the pub realized that Patrick was already drunk. He spoke nasally, sometimes snorting with brief snorts of laughter, his head held high enough to look down at us.

He seemed to sum up his life by recounting the meals he and his son Christopher have every day, grilled sausages, and I saw a grill dripping with grease. When I asked him what he is working on, he raised his head even higher and swung it away and looked into the distance, and I knew he has stopped painting. Nikos wanted to leave, and I thought that this would most likely be the last time we saw Patrick.

————

Steven Runciman to supper, always with eggs from his hens from his castle in Scotland, and always with amazing anecdotes.

I can't resist including some of his anecdotes:

'Virginia Woolf never forgave Ottoline Morrell for not introducing her to her half-brother the Duke of Portland, because

Virginia aspired to know the royals. Virginia Woolf dressed out of the acting box.'

'My father was a friend of Maynard Keynes, who introduced me into the fringes of Bloomsbury. Lytton Strachey, of whom I was very fond, was very kind and very entertaining to the callow under-graduate I then was, at Trinity, though I knew more people at King's. I met Lady Ottoline Morrell when we were doing a cure together for rheumatism at Tunbridge Wells. She had her Thursday-afternoon tea parties to which guests had to be specially invited, but I could come any Thursday as long as I let her know beforehand. This was in case she was away, or in case something else had come up, and that was fair enough, I thought. At her tea parties, one met every sort of person. There I met and disliked Yeats. Ottoline thought it would be lovely for the poet of Byzan-tium to talk to the student of Byzantium, but Yeats didn't think that was at all lovely. He didn't want to talk to anyone who knew about Byzantium. Sturge Moore, one of whose poems, "The Gazelles," appears often in anthologies, haunted Ottoline's. He was a brother of G. E. Moore, the philosopher, but, unlike his brother, had a slightly common voice. He was terribly jealous of Yeats, because he knew he would never achieve his eminence. Sitting next to me at Ottoline's, he kept saying to me, "That man Yeats, why does he put so much gold in his poetry? You can't read a line of Yeats without there being gold in it. You go and ask him why he puts so much gold in his poetry." I was nagged into moving over to Yeats and getting the conversation around to gold. Yeats looked at me coldly and said, "Gold is beauty."'

Lockerbie, Scotland

But how can I leave Steven with so little to account for such a presence in our lives? Again and again, I'm overwhelmed in this diary with what I want to account for and what it would take me volumes and volumes to account for.

Steven has allowed me to write a profile of him for the New Yorker, and I've stayed at Elshieshields for some days. When I was not recording him with a microphone, I would, each evening, write out what I remembered of our conversations.

Steven does not allow anyone into his kitchen but himself, not even his staff to do the washing-up, as he thought anyone but himself would chip his china. He does the cooking while I wait in the dining room, in the basement of the castle. The plate before me was illustrated, in sepia, with a scene of a Jesuit in a canoe, two Indians paddling him through rapids. I didn't presume to go for the bowls of soup that appeared on the shelf of the hatch to the kitchen, not sure what was right and what not, but waited until Steven came out of the kitchen and himself brought the bowls of soup to the table. Before placing the bowl on the plate set before me, Steven said, 'I chose that with its scene specifically to refer to your ancestry.'

He said, 'I have told you that you are, in Britain, among the enemy. You are aware, are you not, that you will join the enemy by becoming British? Do think carefully before you do.'

'That has occurred to me.'

'On several counts – the British enemy for dispossessing you of La Nouvelle France, which in war they won, and for going to war with your American colonials to stop the American Revolution, which war they lost. But, being French of a long and, I dare say, distinguished American history, perhaps you don't quite think of the British colonials as your ancestors.'

'No, I never did quite think of the colonials as my ancestors. In my French-Canadian-American parochial school in New England, an attempt was made to integrate us into Yankee America by emphasizing the role played by Lafayette in the American Revolution, but I was never really proud of Lafayette as one of us, representing us. He was an honorary Yankee.'

'Whom do you honour in your history?'

'No one, no one I can think of.'

'Would your parents have had a sense of their history? Would they have known about the defeat of the French on the Plains of Abraham in Quebec by the British, a turning-point in North American history? If the French under Montcalm had succeeded in repulsing the British under Wolfe, the British colonials would not have assumed the security they needed to expand into French territory, and La Nouvelle France would still claim most of the continent. I do enjoy speculating about what would have happened in history if wars had been won by the opposing forces. Alas, I must stick to the facts.'

'My parents wouldn't have known about the Plains of Abraham. Their sense of history was very limited, and perhaps went no further back than to their own parents and their emigration from farms in French Canada to work in the textile mills of Yankee New England.'

'They wouldn't have known about the Jesuits and the Indians?'

'Only in that my father was a quarter-breed Blackfoot Indian, his grandmother lost, as it were, in the forests of North America along with the Jesuits who braved rapids to reach them to convert them. I was brought up with almost no sense of my own native history.'

Steven suddenly said, 'I see you eyeing the bottle of wine.'

'I did happen to glance at it.'

'Wine is not drunk with the soup.'

'I admit that I do have a lot to learn.'

'If you were familiar to the household, you would be allowed to add a dash of sherry to your soup, but I think that would be too familiar of you as a guest.'

'I wouldn't dare.'

Steven took the soup bowls into the kitchen, and I waited, studying the scene on the plate of my ancestry, and a deep loneliness in my isolation surrounded me like the shadows that encircled the dimly lit room.

The panel to the hatch rose, and there appeared on the shelf an elaborate tureen.

'What,' Steven asked, lifting the cover of the tureen to reveal kedgeree, 'do you know of the battle of Ain Jalud?'

'I wouldn't try to fake even guessing.'

'The most important battle in the Western world, and you know nothing of it?'

'You won't tell me?'

'I am ashamed of you for not knowing, but you must learn, as you say. The battle of Ain Jalud occurred September 2, 1260, between the Muslim Marmelukes of Egypt and the Mongols under the Christian general Kitbuqa. Had the Mongols won, Islam might have crumbled in the whole Turkish Crescent and possibly the Turks might have become Christian. As it was, the Muslims won and punished the native Christians for their friendship with the Mongols. And the Mongols in the Near East eventually turned Muslim.'

'I didn't know.'

'Again, my failing as a proper historian – I speculate too much on what might have happened if, the if always suggesting a fantasy of an entirely different world.'

'You fantasize about history?'

'About a world that might have been, yes, I do.'

'A better world?'

'A different world.'

'Different in what way? More to your liking?'

'As much as I must stick to the facts, I am all too human in wanting a world more to my liking.'

'Which would be?'

'Dear boy, you do have an American way of asking questions that are too personal. If you are to become truly British, you must understand that we British do not indulge in the personal, which is of little interest even to oneself. What is of interest I leave for you to find out.'

'Manners?' I asked.

'Well, you are astute.'

'I can claim to have been brought up to be polite, to hold the door open for women, to stand when a woman enters the room, to walk along the outside of the pavement if I am escorting a woman. But this is rudimentary.'

'You have been brought up well, and have the basics. As for British manners, you have more to learn. Where, for example, would you place the pudding – "pudding" being an acceptable term except for fruit salad – fork and spoon?'

'At the sides, always at the sides,' I said, seeing where they were placed at either side of his plate.

'What about fish knives and forks?'

'You tell me.'

'I was once in Bucharest with my mother at the Jockey Club there – we were on a cruise in the family yacht – and we heard a woman at the other side of the dining room shout out, "Take this fish knife and fork away. What do you think I am?" We never had them at home. In later life, I was given a set as a gift, and gave them away, but, on reconsidering, I thought that after all they are rather useful, so I bought a set. One must adapt to the changes – we are no longer in an era when knife boys must clean the knives of those who could not afford silver, distinguishing, all too undemocratically, the lower classes from the upper. Fish knives and forks are a sign of a democratic spirit, in a rather conservative way.'

'What about placement cards?'

'Perfectly acceptable, but the full title must be written, and they must never be the vulgar stand-up kind, but must lie flat on the plate.'

'Finger bowls?'

'Also perfectly acceptable, except when you have royalty.'

'Why?'

'The royal would be offended if someone passed a glass over the fingerbowl, reminding him or her of Bonnie Prince Charlie having to cross the water to escape death. I must say, I was once derided by Lady Holmes for being such a stickler about not having finger bowls when royals come to a meal, she insisting that it would do simply to put one's hand over the bowl when raising one's glass.'

'I'll remember that.'

Steven thought. 'Odd, I must say, that the British should have put up a statue of George Washington in Trafalgar Square – a traitor.'

———

The next day, in his drawing room, I recorded Steven talking.

Propped in a corner were a Regency table harp, a Javanese one-stringed instrument, and a nose flute from Borneo, and a hubble-bubble, a water pipe of green glass with simple flowers painted on it.

I asked Steven about the hubble-bubble.

'Do you really want to hear?' He seemed a little annoyed.

'Please.'

The September sunlight on the lawn, seen through glass doors, was low and long. Steven sat at the edge of his chair, his thin legs turned to the side, as if the room did not have enough space for him. He didn't look at me, but at the walls of the room, and he smoked a cigarillo.

He started with a faint growl.

From the recording:

'When I was in Istanbul, in 1942, to teach Byzantine history at the university, I was allotted a handsome young lady to be my translator and assistant. Her family, the Karaçalaris, had been old-established tobacco magnates in Kavala when it was Turkish. She was related, in the female line, to the founder of the line of the Egyptian khedives. Some generations before, a husband and wife – ancestors of those tobacco people in Kavala – had an only daughter, admirably well endowed financially but not physically, and when she was married off to the son of a neighboring tobacco king and he unveiled her he couldn't face it, so an Albanian adventurer, having heard the story, went to the father and said, "It's a good dowry, I'll take her on," and he did, and they were the parents of Muhammad Ali, the first khedive of Egypt. For a time, the Egyptian government kept up the house where he was born in Kavala. Kavala, as you must know, was transferred earlier from the Turks to the Greeks, and all the Turks had to leave. The Karaçalaris family in Kavala had always rather despised their relatives in Egypt. Muhammad Ali had assigned them large lands in Egypt, but they had never bothered to go to Egypt or do anything about the land. It was only at the exchange of populations between Turkey and Greece, in 1922, that the Kavala cousins remembered their rich cousins in Egypt. But it was too late. Everything had gone by default. They had to go to Istanbul.'

I tried to keep my mind fixed on Steven's words, which rose in pitch, so at sudden moments I heard only the rising pitch, and I must fix my mind on the words.

'My assistant's uncle was a great friend of Atatürk. Atatürk came to the house once while she was studying, and he asked her what she was studying, and she said, "Old Hittite." Atatürk wanted to prove the Turks Hittites. He said, "It's just like old Turkish, isn't it?" She said, "No, it's more like old Armenian." The family were aghast. Atatürk giggled and said, "You know, sometimes I think I'll have to prove the Armenians Turkish." She was a bright girl. She was married to His Highness the Çelebi Effendi. Of course, he wasn't allowed to use his title in Turkey, but he was the hereditary head of the whirling dervishes – the Mevlevi dervishes – descended in a direct male line from the founder, the great philosopher Jalal ad-Din ar-Rumi. Before the sultanate was abolished, in 1922, the whirling dervishes had a great many establishments all over Turkey, and, indeed, the hereditary head was one of the chief people in the Ottoman regime. He had to gird the Sultan with the sword of Islam, even though the Mevlevi dervishes were considered a little heretical, a little bit too tolerant, by strict Islamic standards. Then, with the revolution, Atatürk secularized and annexed all the Mevlevi establishments in Turkey and banned the use of titles. So the Çelebi Effendi moved to Syria and settled in Aleppo, where he still had his tekke, or monastery. Just before the Second World War, the Turks managed to force the French, who were then in charge of Syria, to yield the province around Antioch to Turkey. The Syrians were furious, and turned out all Turkish citizens living in Syria, including the Çelebi Effendi. He had to go back to Turkey and live there as a private citizen. He was out of touch with all his remaining establishments in Syria and Aleppo, and, of course, the war made him even more out of touch.'

Steven's voice reached such a pitch it became song, and he seemed, for all the dense interconnected detail of his account, to go into a trance, as if such dense interconnections always put him into a trance.

'As he was the husband of my assistant, I saw the Çelebi Effendi often. The first time I dined with them, he said that if I could smoke a hubble-bubble without being sick he'd give it to me. And there it is. Not a very beautiful one, as hubble-bubbles go. One day, he died, quite suddenly, leaving by an earlier marriage a son of sixteen, who was the heir. This was towards the end of the war, the beginning of 1944. The boy, in order to be accepted as head of the Mevlevi, had to go round the various establishments and have his knee kissed. That was the proper ceremony. But how could a boy of sixteen, in war conditions, get a visa to Syria? The Free French were in occupation, and I had a friend among them,

Count Stanislas Ostroróg, who was of a Polish family that, in the eighteen-forties, had fled Russia to settle in Istanbul. They had one of the most beautiful houses on the Bosporus, where Stanislas' elder brother lives, married to a daughter of Sir Basil Zaharoff, the arms magnate.'

Steven stopped, closed his eyes for a moment as though to contemplate the circumference of his trance, then, opening his eyes wide, said quietly, 'Sorry for all these details,' and closed his eyes to continue, with a slight swaying of his shoulders, within his ever widening trance. 'I had stayed with Stanislas in Damascus before the war, when he was Résident there, and I knew he would understand, because he was interested in such things as the whirling dervishes. I wrote to him. The immediate result: a huge envelope came back to the boy, addressed – never before had he been addressed like this – to "Son Altesse le Çelebi Effendi," with the visa and everything needed for his trip to have his knee kissed. So off he was able to go to Syria, blessing me. And when I followed, on leave, a month or so later, at every station a delegation of whirling dervishes came to greet me. They asked me if I would like them to dance for me, and I made them dance at Aleppo and Homs. I thought that perhaps twice was enough. Anyhow, they all said, "You see, you're one of us."'

Steven now looked at me and, back to a low, growling voice, said, 'In Istanbul, they were started up as a tourist attraction, which is really monstrous. We real ones consider this indecent. We don't approve. But we are in a very bad way, because the Syrians decided to close the tekke in Syria. One had a wonderful international situation – the Turkish government suing the Syrian for annexing the property of Turkish citizens, though they'd done it themselves several years before. Practically no tekke is dancing still. I'm not sure the one in Cyprus dances.'

I was, in my own way, in a trance, assuming as I did that Steven's ability to make connections could go on and on, connecting all the stars, making of them all one great story. He did tell a story, the suspense sustained not just because of the unexpected events but the unexpected connections. I had asked myself if the young Çelebi Effendi would be able to get out of Turkey to have his knee kissed and save the Mevlevi. The answer was yes, made possible by the unexpected connection in Istanbul between a Polish count from Russia and a Scottish historian. And all along there were unexpected connections made – Turkish, Greek, Egyptian, Albanian, Hittite, Armenian, French, Syrian, Polish, Russian – so I was drawn into the story with expectations of the even more unexpected, which was the interconnection of everything. I understood so little, but I thought that there was no way, ever, for me to understand everything, and that was the great mystery of history: to understand everything. I imagine Steven does.

A spoon, a button, a coin could be the center of world history, so complex, however, that the history could never for me be known.

And, in a sense, I imagine my diary as historical, recording what may appear to be incidentals, spoons, buttons, coins, arcane table manners, but about these incidentals expands more than I could ever possibly account for, expanding into history.

I think I am in one place at one time, but really I'm in many places and at many times, too many for me to make the connections that Steven is capable of making.

Steven Runciman on history:

'From my earliest childhood, I've liked history. I wasn't drawn to it by a scientific desire for knowledge. Oh, no. I was drawn by romantic imaginings. I've always liked stories. I've always liked people, and I've always liked trying to understand the great stories of the past. As romantic as my imaginings are, I have always wanted my stories to be based on truth. Because of this, I have never got much pleasure out of reading ghost stories that are fiction. I like my ghost stories, too, to be real. I prefer history to fiction – though, like all historians, I would like to write an historical novel. It would be so marvellous to be able to put down what you're quite sure did happen but you can't prove it. It's a wicked temptation, however, and I must stick to the sterner discipline.

'The Crusades was one of the big stories of history, and, as it hadn't been told recently, I wanted to tell it. I suppose I'm considered a rather old-fashioned historian. What the Namier historians of the new French style think of me I can only too easily imagine. They concentrate on details, and I – well, I know I'm terribly in disgrace with the Crusading historians because I'm not interested in things like the detailed legal arrangements, although I know roughly what they were. These historians are very recondite, I think, and have a snobbish and undemocratic view of history. I, in my old-fashioned way, am much more democratic. I want to know what made the whole story happen. They forget that the word history means story.'

I said I would like to know how he writes history.

He sat at the very edge of his armchair, with a pile of newspapers and magazines behind him.

'Well, one starts with the sources. Published sources proliferate. If Gibbon, who when he wrote the Decline and Fall had consulted practically all the printed sources available to him in his day, were to write the same book today, he'd have about three times as much to consult. Then, there are the unpublished sources – the material in archives, often ill catalogued, and sometimes not catalogued, or even arranged in any order. Then, there is always the possibility of something hitherto unknown being discovered – the life of a saint in a monastic library, or a batch of letters, or a forgotten character. But in classical and medieval history such finds are very rare, and most primary material has been published. Occasionally, one thinks as one goes through catalogues of collections, oh, this would be interesting. Then one finds it has been published in slightly different form or under a different heading elsewhere. I've never found, myself, any new manuscript of any value. In fact, I'm not very good at reading manuscripts. And I can't bear reading on microfilm. I've got a rather fitful memory. When I go into a library and don't happen to have a notebook on me and I see somewhere in a book something that is of great interest, I think that I shall certainly remember it. I remember exactly what it looked like on the page, but I can't remember which book it is in. In the end, I'll locate it.'

Steven was not looking at me but over my head.

'With so much to consult, a historian, not unnaturally, does tend to take refuge in details, a detailed discussion of some small point. What he produces is very useful, but he is not really writing history; he is providing another secondary source. To write history, he has to bring the details together into a significant whole.'

(How can I, in recording this talk, not stop on the words 'a significant whole,' which suddenly appeared to centre my whole life in a vision?)

'There are some historians who begin with the significant whole – before they have mastered the details. The trouble is that to explain the course of all history you should be acquainted with all history – and it would be hard to find such a polymath. I rather like the idea of writing a story. The idea is to find some well-rounded theme – without being afraid of the large theme – that makes a story of its own. But it must fit into the stream of history, and the historian must be conscious of its causes in the past and its influences in the future. All the reading takes time, but during that time you're thinking about the work, consciously and often subconsciously. Much of your best thinking is done, say, on a country walk or when you're working in the garden. It's helpful to have a garden.'

History to Steven is world history.

London

I don't know why, but when people insult me I take the insult as a joke.

I was invited to a conference at Assumption College in Worcester, Massachusetts, on Franco-American literature, I suppose because I have written in The Family about the Franco-American world, the world of my family.

At the conference, someone approached me and asked, 'Est-ce que vous connaissez Paul Theroux (the The- pronounced as Té-)?'

I answered that I had met him.

Why, I was asked, had Paul Theroux, a Franco, not written about us, Franco-Americans?

I didn't know.

Back in London, at a book-launch party, I saw Paul and went to him, and, hardly saying hello to me, he spoke about himself so rapidly it was as though he was stopping me from talking about myself. I tugged at the lapels of his jacket and said, 'Paul, it's about you that I came over to talk to you.' He waited, and I told him what I had been asked by someone at the conference: why doesn't he write about Francos, as he is one? He jabbed a finger at my chest and said, 'Because you do.'

Then I said, 'Il m'a demandé si je te connais.'

'Et tu as répondu?'

'Oui.'

He looked up and away and said, 'Si quelq'un me demanderait

si je connais David Plante, qu'est-ce que je lui dirais?' He looked down at me and said, 'Non.'

He turned away and I did laugh.

It is innate among Franco-Americans, our truly lost tribe, that not one of them wants to know, much less help, another one, and how very few we are.

I would never expect from Paul Theroux any recognition of any kind.

John Fleming has written that Patrick Kinross is dead. The illness that killed him was never diagnosed. He was reduced to a skeleton.

Thinking about him, I think of how, the more I live in London the more, yes, I am fascinated by connections that take me back into history, and, yes, people I have met in London have taken me far back into history, far back, linking me to history, which I think of as the most formative evolution of anyone's life; and the connection with one person in the past brings more than that person into the present, the connection brings into the present past époques.

So when I, turning the pages of a biography, came across a photograph taken in the 1920s of Patrick Kinross dressed for a fancy ball in eighteenth-century court dress complete with wig, he among others also in fancy dress, leaning over a pit in which roughly clothed navvies are digging, one of them with a pneumatic drill, Patrick and his company presumably in conversation with the navvies, I reacted with a mixture of revulsion at the class divide (as would Nikos) and fascination (as would I). The fascination is, I like to think, justified by my seeing the scene historically representative of past ages, for Patrick in his court dress does appear to have come directly from the eighteenth century and to have found himself in a London where, curiously, men were digging a pit with a strange, stuttering instrument that he must stop and ask about. But, yes, I am glad that the époque of Patrick in fancy court dress divided by class from the navvy in overalls with his pneumatic drill is past, however fascinating I find it, because, if I had been born and raised in working-class

England as I was in working-class America, I would have been the navvy in the pit looked down upon by the baron.

Still, Patrick did make even details historical, as when he said that, before attending the coronation of Queen Elizabeth in his robes, he was warned to pee, because the ceremony would be interminable, and I took this as a detail that was a warning to everyone in the deep past who attended royal ceremonies, a detail that gives historical particularity to the historically grand event. I do like details.

And no doubt the Queen sustains the details of history.

Roy Strong told me that he loves being High Bailiff and Searcher of the Sanctuary at Westminster Abbey, an honorary role which includes attendance at all great state occasions in the building, which duty allows him to wear a ruff.

———

An image often comes to me – as do many many many images – from when I first came to Europe in 1959, when I was nineteen and in Barcelona in a barber's chair from which I saw reflected in the mirror before me a door behind open and a man's hand appear holding the edge of the door, the nail of his little finger long and pointed, and a shudder passed through me at what I had never seen affected by a man, and what I later learned was his way of demonstrating that he was not a manual worker, and this made me wonder at the long history of keeping the nail of one's baby finger long and pointed. And so, over and over again, I find myself wondering about such small details for having long histories. And it was in Spain that I met a Spaniard who, shaking my hand, scratched my palm with his index finger, I wondering what this meant and only after realizing that it was a sexual message, a message, I imagined, that had its long history within Spanish sexual signaling. It is always a pleasure to me to try to decode these coded messages, which make me so aware of what I like to think of as an occult foreign world.

And so the occult world of London.

And, more, Nikos' occult Greek world.

———

More about Patrick Kinross.

After Oscar Wilde, whose trial and imprisonment did cause such contemporaries as Arthur Symons anguish by suppressing their sexuality, and did ruin the lives of such men as Simeon Solomon arrested for importuning –

(though I do wonder if, for queer men of this past generation, the law did not discriminate unless some more serious crime was committed to which sex was incidental, but which, in the process of the trial, became more and more the issue, for, surely, there must have been male brothels the police knew about as they also knew about those men who frequented the brothels, both tolerated by the police) –

but which trial and imprisonment of Oscar Wilde seems not to have caused queers of the generation of Patrick Kinross, not so far removed in time from the trial and imprisonment, to suppress knowledge of their sexuality, and not even to stop them from acting on their sexuality. The trial and imprisonment seem, instead of leaving a legacy of harsh suppression and harsher trial and imprisonment, to have brought out the sexuality of the generation of Patrick into common knowledge. They, the queer men of Patrick's world, must have assumed the law that condemned Wilde didn't apply to them, for why should any disposition as common as homosexuality be criminal? And all their friends, of whatever sexuality, assumed the same about them. Everyone must have known that when Patrick married he was queer, and that he divorced because he was queer, and I dare say he remained friends with those who knew he was queer, such as Charlotte Bonham Carter. All this, perhaps, among the upper-middle into the upper classes. But this is only guessing about a world I know nothing about, and dangerously near the speculation I avoid.

Still, it comes to me: we of course take an outstanding event from the past, as the trial and imprisonment of Oscar Wilde, to speak not only for the whole past but the whole present, and this is what causes are based on.

Chartres

Nikos and I went to Chartres to visit the cathedral.

I had been before, when I was a student at the Catholic University of Louvain, Belgium, where theology was a living discipline with essential problems to be discussed: how can the immutable and eternal God, the Uncaused Causer, change enough in time to have caused the universe and the world, to have created Adam and Eve, to have condemned them for their sin, then to have changed again in time from condemning them to forgiving them? As I no longer believe in God, these problems are mere curiosities. But I had believed when I first visited the cathedral.

From the car, we saw the spires of the cathedral rise from the flat, pale green fields of spring wheat. I pulled over to the side of the road, not far from a ditch along which were pollarded willow trees, and I stopped the car. This view couldn't have changed in twenty-five years.

There was heavy traffic in what was no longer the town I'd known, but a city. The buildings were new and had wide, stark windows, and the traffic was dense. Nikos and I had a row. With difficulty, we found in a hotel a room with a view of a darkening back yard.

As if our being late was my fault, Nikos said resentfully, 'We'll unpack later. We'd better get to the cathedral before it closes.'

He was always the one who was late and whom I had to hurry along.

With a map, we found our way to the vieille ville, which had been, I recalled, all the ville when I'd been there, and I thought I should be able to find my way in the vieille ville to the cathedral. Nikos asked, Was I sure? Yes, I was sure. But I lost the way. Finally there, a guard said the cathedral was closing.

I told Nikos I was sure I could find a restaurant from years before. I was sure it was on a street very near the cathedral. It had white curtains on a brass rod over the lower part of the many-paned window, and through the top you saw inside to the dark wood wainscoting. I walked up and down the streets.

'I guess it's gone,' I said.

He found a restaurant in the nouvelle ville.

While we were eating, I said, 'I really am sorry that restaurant is gone. It was run by an old woman, I remember. The floor was flagged with stone, and the restaurant smelled like a stone cellar. I remember the old woman, without being asked, bringing glasses and a carafe of wine, then soup bowls, those heavy, deep, white soup bowls, and a metal tureen of potage which she carried by its handles with a dish towel and placed on the table, where it steamed in the chilly air. We served ourselves. The big ladle was dented.'

'We should have looked more carefully,' he said.

'This place is fine.'

'But I want everything to be the way you remember it.'

'Maybe it's just as well it isn't.'

In our hotel room, we undressed silently.

We lay flat on our backs in bed, our heads on the long bolster.

We didn't sleep well.

In the morning, I got up before Nikos and sat in a chair before the window that looked out onto the back yard, where a young man was holding the front wheel of a bicycle off the ground and rotating it, so its small, rapid clicks became a whir. A woman came into the yard pushing a bicycle. By the time Nikos got up there were ten people with bicycles in the back yard; they spun their wheels and talked quietly.

I don't know why, but these details are important to me,

perhaps because our visit to Chartres was in every way important to me.

I said I'd go now to the cathedral, but he said he'd want breakfast first. Would he mind if I didn't join him, but went off to the cathedral? He looked hurt, but he said, 'Go, of course go,' and offered me the map as he knew I wouldn't be able to find my way on my own.

I didn't take the map, but after a few wrong turns I came to the cathedral. A great cloud was passing high above the spires, and, as though my senses were caught off balance, it appeared to me that the spires were moving, the cloud was still.

I hesitated before I pushed open the frayed, padded door, and blinked in the inside dimness. From what seemed to me far below, I saw high pillars, and I walked among them. I came upon an altar, before which, stuck on rows of spikes on wrought-iron racks, were hundreds of burning tapers leaning towards one another and melting in the heat. The wax dripped onto iron sheets below the racks. I looked at the burning tapers and the flames reflected in hundreds of golden hearts hanging around them.

I leaned my forehead against a pillar and wept, but turned when I felt a hand on my shoulder to see Nikos standing by me.

He said, 'Give in, give in.'

I asked, 'To what?'

Greece

Ifinally got my driving license, and in a car Nikos is allowed as director of Thames & Hudson, I drove us – I'm tempted to use the old British expression, 'we motored,' which doesn't indicate who drove, as if the motor car could motor itself – down through France and Italy on our way to Greece, and on the way stopped to stay with Elizabeth and Christopher Glenconner on Corfu.

As a car can't reach the house, Christopher met us in a little boat, and then a walk along a path through pines, he, perhaps not knowing quite who we were, but, as guests of Elizabeth, his guests, and he laughed with the pleasure of having to meet us in a boat and the walk through the pines.

We arrived in time for drinks, Christopher taking charge, though I noted that he stared at the bottles for a long while to figure out what was what, but, as always, he laughed lightly as with the pleasure of preparing drinks. And Elizabeth looks on him with what I can only think of as a slightly unfocused, but, for all that, total love.

He told us about his exploits in the navy during the war.

Nikos said later that Christopher is a hero in the cause of liberating Greece from the Nazis.

Christopher has taken to painting, his favourite view that of the small bay below their house, down a rocky cliff.

Stephen and Natasha have stayed, and so has Steven Runciman, who gave to Christopher and Elizabeth an icon to keep the house blessedly safe.

And now in Nikos' occult world, and I in it as if a Frank Kermode trying to find in it the occult meanings –

In Athens, where there are graffiti on walls from the years of the dictatorship, stenciled images of the phoenix rising from flames. Here and there, in scruffy plots of red earth, small playgrounds for children, I suppose to show off the concern the colonels had for the very young. And, given the colonels' lack of zoning – thinking there should be freedom to exploit wherever exploitation was feasible – apartment buildings encroaching on the holy hill of Lycabettus, the least of exploitations. On a long walk, we passed an abandoned building where, Nikos said, prisoners of the colonels were tortured. Once again, when I hear about torture I can't particularize any one person being tortured, and, much less, any one person applying the torture, as if this last can't be attributable to a human being.

The flat of Nikos' mother, in Tsoha Street, has green mottled marble floors in the entrance and parquet elsewhere, and there is a sense of white space in the rooms.

Here I am, where Nikos' world is most emblematic in objects that he tells me about, and that I am possessive of, as if possessive of his world.

The silver dish is from Constantinople, taken with whatever the family could take, at the time of the exchange of populations in the 1920s.

On the dining-room table is a green bowl on three pedestals, a great chip broken from it, the result of a bomb meant for the airport near where Nikos' family lived in Elliniko but exploding in and destroying the house next door, the shockwaves causing a fragment of the ceiling of the dining room in the family house to fall and break the bowl on the dining-room table. The shockwaves also caused the locks in the house to jam. This was when Nikos and his mother and aunt Fula were hiding under the dining-room table, the live-in maid with them, all crowded together.

In the living room, furniture designed by Nikos' father, an architect who designed the neo-classical Athens College, where Nikos spent ten years of his life as a boarder.

Also in the living room, small chairs with carved wood frames and string mesh for the seats, from, Nikos said, an island, though he wasn't sure what island, as his family do not come from an island about which they can say, 'Our island,' and return there for holidays. His mother has no interest in the Greek islands.

In fact, his mother had no interest in Athens, having lived in Constantinople, to her Athens a dusty provincial town, the Greeks there not Greeks but Albanians.

The rugs, which Fula identified, also brought from Constantinople.

Nikos told me that she still has her dowry, gold sovereigns, which she keeps in secret places but she forgets where. When she forgets, she blames the maid for stealing the coins. She came out of the kitchen with a tea caddy – only, Nikos said, for fascomilo tea, mountain tea, drunk only when not feeling well – and from it took out a little bag with a draw string and from the bag a gold sovereign which she gave to Nikos. He showed it to me: a small coin minted with the profile of EDWARDVS VII D: G: BRITT: OMN: REX F: D: IND: IMP. To read in Athens on a gold coin minted in Great Britain an honorific in Latin – to account for the history of these conjunctions would, I thought, require a study in Western history, and here it was in the palm of my hand. Nikos said that these gold sovereigns are still the basis of calculating, say, the price of a house in a contract. As for aunt Fula's dowry – her prika – it was never used, for her role was set for her to take care of her older sisters, she the cook, the over-looker of the maid, the factotum.

Once I said to her that Nikos is a complainer, which she took in with her jaw stuck out and her lips pressed tightly together. Nikos told me that she then went to him to inform him not to trust me, as I speak behind his back. So I am warned.

In the kitchen, even there I look for totems of a world that I want to be mine, and note the large tin of olive oil beneath the sink, the bottle of ouzo on the marble counter, and in a cup a thin gelatin made, as Nikos explained, by the seeds of quince – kidonia – in water, prepared by Fula for her to drink, Nikos wasn't sure for what reason.

And then, oh yes, there is the ceremony of the gliko koutaliou and cold water and coffee, all prepared by Fula for when Nikos and I wake up from our naps, those deep, deep naps that seem to come with an Oriental stupor in the afternoon, a stupor which needs the shock of the sweet and the cold water and the coffee to wake one from.

And the walks about Athens, Nikos' Athens, the Athens of his youth – such as the nineteenth-century apartment building behind the cathedral where his extended family lived during World War II, when, he said, family life was a circle of devotion. He pointed out to me the balcony where his family kept the turkey that flew down to the street and was grabbed by an amazed passer-by.

And in the entrance hall of the apartment building, the floor, Nikos showed me, is paved with white and black squares of marble, which often come into his dreams. And so, I am able to participate in his dream imagery.

We went to neo-classical Athens College, designed by his architect father. There, Nikos spent eight years of his youth, and, from outside, he pointed out the window of the dormitory room where he slept.

He showed me the cinema, Rex, where he was awakened to sex by a man sitting next to him who unzipped him and masturbated him, Nikos so amazed that he got up and left the cinema with his penis exposed.

And we stopped outside the basement garçonière (I noting the use of French) which he had rented to get away from home, acceptable among Greeks of his world, though assumed without it being said, for the sexual life of a young man that he cannot have at home; and I did have more than a twinge of jealousy for the past Athenian sexual life of Nikos, as I fantasized it, there in the basement of an apartment building, a sexual life that of course left me out, but in which I should have been the partner.

As we passed a low, abandoned building somewhere up the hill from the American Embassy, and not far from the American ambassador's residence, Nikos said that here people were tortured during the dictatorship, the building spiritually and morally and, I felt, physically contaminated, now left to decay.

Nikos' mother, Natalia, is a delicate woman, in no way the prototype of a Greek mother.

Sustaining a fashion that has long gone out of fashion where it originated in Paris and London, Nikos' mother has at-homes every Wednesday. When Nikos was living at home, he used to like to shock the friends his mother received by revealing family secrets, as he cannot abide by the secrecy that seems to be the way all of Greece works: don't tell, don't tell, keep it a secret. In Constantinople, an impoverished member of the extended family went to the opposite side of the city to work as a seamstress to keep the humiliation a deep secret, or, again in Constantinople, an impoverished family would take out their best china and silver and clink the silver against the empty china, the windows open, so that neighbours would think they were having a feast. Never mind, Nikos said, what the government ministers are keeping secret, to which his mother quietly demurred, but she then did say, 'You see, we were so long under the Ottoman Empire, and had to keep our secrets.'

Mrs Stangos – or I like to address her in the Greek Kiria Stangou, which seems to me to add a linguistic dimension to her name – speaks perfect English, with the soft accent Nikos has. She also speaks French and German and Russian, but only kitchen Turkish, though born and brought up in Istanbul. She winces at the Greek pronunciation tri-buison for the French tire-bouchon, and in English will use French expressions such as vernissage, which Nikos used to use until, in London, he changed to 'gallery opening.' I note that, in Athens, he uses English expressions that he has taken on, I think, intentionally, such as 'that's rich,' or 'that's rum,' or 'stuff and nonsense,' as if to claim his foreignness in a country where he has always felt a foreigner.

Fula, not the mother, answered the door when Nikos rang, I behind him, and Nikos and Fula embraced warmly. His mother, in granny shoes, came and held Nikos lightly. They spoke in English, I thought because of me, and she greeted me in English. She had been a teacher of English at Athens College. I noted that her most overt sign of affection towards Nikos is to tap him on the arm and smile at him, somewhat sadly, and he smiles back somewhat sadly. A refined woman, of a deep culture that evolved over more years than her age, she wears her hair in braids curled in spirals that cover her ears.

We went to visit his aunt Tato. He had talked to me of her, a formidable woman whose formidability was rounded out by history that made her presence historical. She is, as I learned to distinguish, from other Greeks, Cosmopoliti, those Greeks from Constantinople a class apart, in fact more cosmopolitan than Athenian Greeks.

She was dressed in black, her grey hair pulled back in a small chignon, and I immediately felt that I was in her good graces when Nikos introduced me as a young writer, which to her meant that I was of course a cultured person. Nikos had told me one of her novels was based on a very intense relationship, a loving relationship, between two girls, equal, he thinks, to anything written by

Colette. We spoke in French. A maid served us ouzakia – the glasses and bowl of pistachios served on a round tray covered in a cloth embroidered in gold, details that I am always attentive to – while Tato spoke with the kind of authority that can only come from having lived through what many others were defeated by, with no nonsense. There were piles of books everywhere, books with paper covers as is the way in Greece, and among them Nikos pointed out a collection of American Black poetry translated into Greek by Tato's husband, now dead. He and she had monumental rows, monumental. She told me she would very much like to go to America to see the Mississippi River.

As we walked about Athens, Nikos stopped at the bust on a plinth of Ersi Hadgimihali's aunt, which I remembered Nikos mentioning when Ersi visited us in London, Ersi now dead.

In Ermou Street, we saw a man goading a dancing bear to keep on dancing, stepping from side to side, the bear with an iron collar with a chain that the man held in one hand as he goaded the bear with the other. And we saw beggars exposing their stumps of legs and arms. And there was a barrel-organ player, turning the handle to play folk tunes.

From time to time in London, Nikos has severe migraines, so severe one of his eyes becomes bloodshot and weeps. Here in Athens, his migraines are frequent. Though it is not done to close a door – I closed the door to our room where I withdrew to lie down but Nikos' mother opened it, asking didn't I prefer to have the door open for the air to circulate? to which I demurred – when Nikos feels a migraine come on he asks me to come into our room with him and, he sitting on the edge of his bed and I standing before him, he presses his forehead into my abdomen. This fills me with feelings too strange to sort out, from an erotic charge to the greater charge of such love for him in his helplessness that I would like to stay forever with him there, he in unendurable pain pressing his forehead into my abdomen.

His mother does not open the door.

She treats me with delicate affection.

Nikos had warned me not, in Athens, to call him Agapi mou, allowed only between lovers.

Nikos has shown me photographs from his past:

Nikos orating before a class at Athens College.

Nikos with mates from Athens College in a taverna. He is on the extreme right.

Nikos with someone he said he would rather forget, on an
excursion to an island.

And then Nikos showed me documents from the German
Occupation:

On the back is written, in cursive Latin letters, 'Stangos', and in English, 'He will help you unload things give him a tip I will pay the five hundred,' signed illegibly, and also in English, 'Received with thanks,' and signed in cursive Latin, 'Adamantiadis,' Nikos' uncle.

And this, with stamps costing 2,000,000,000 drachmas each:

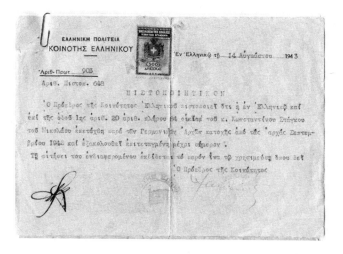

From a more remote past, this photograph, taken in 1913 by Nikos' mother of a friend in Constantinople, the friend dressed as an ancient Greek.

How can I get all of Nikos' past life in here, as I want to, as I am possessed to do?

I went with him and his mother to the cemetery, the Second Cemetery where refugees are buried, to wash the family tomb, where his father is buried, and stood to the side when Nikos asked a priest to come and say a prayer before the tomb, he in his long black robe and high black conical hat, rocking back and forth, chanting the prayer, for which Nikos gave him a coin. Nikos' mother appeared hardly able to endure being there, as if it was all Nikos' desire to be there, to wash the tomb, to have a prayer said, his desire a stubborn need for ritual.

This need in him occurred to me as if for the first time, for observing Christmas and the New Year and Easter, and, especially, birthday celebrations, he insists on, as a matter of principle that he – yes, stubbornly – must not give up on, as if against a fate that threatens to defeat all such rituals. He will say he doesn't want to socialize, but he will be the one to insist on having many friends round for a holiday celebration, for which we spend a lot of time preparing.

London

Nikos came home with a copy of Ezra Pound's Cantos, published by Faber & Faber in what Nikos complains of as a shoddy publication of a great work. This comes to me: Nikos' admiration of Pound goes beyond the amazing use of images, as amazing as any images in all of literature, but for an ideology that is in fact opposed to Nikos' ideology, as opposed as Communism is to Fascism; for, though Nikos is in his very instincts opposed to the imposition of any ideological dogma, he has a vital sense of the importance of ideology as inspiration, and has the deepest appreciation of someone whose vision is of 'un paradiso terreste,' as was Pound's. But, deeper than that appreciation of a vision of a 'paradiso terreste,' as different as they are in their visions, what they share, as I sense Nikos senses in Pound, is that in their visions of a 'paradiso terreste' both are defeated. I may think to myself, thank God both visions are defeated, but I can feel that the defeat of an ideology aspired to is tragic.

In the poetry of Pound, the following moves Nikos to a state in which he is speechless for what it expresses beyond words, so that he simply closes his eyes and shakes his head:

I have brought the great ball of crystal.

What daring to write that in all its sublimity.

Ah, to rise in a diary to the level of

> A little light, like a rushlight
> To lead back to splendour.

But something more comes to me thinking of Nikos and Ezra Pound: that in the way Pound was essentially intellectually and culturally and ideologically centered in the world of the ancient Mediterranean, so is Nikos, and so in Nikos am I.

Ηγάπησεν πολύ

And this comes to me: hang it all, Pound, your Sargasso or my Sargasso, your Sargasso your Cantos, my Sargasso my diary.

And in my diary to sustain the belief in the divination, in the faith: it coheres all right, even if my notes do not cohere –

———

Julian Jebb has killed himself. He was someone who could only have evolved in England, as, say, the Samuri evolved in Edo Japan. Julian was known to be elfin, with tight trousers and a polo-neck jersey, his gestures quick and fluid, his effeminacy such that if he had been an American no American would possibly have taken him seriously as an interviewer, critic, man of intelligence and culture. How far I have come from America to have appreciated Julian for what he was as English, for I was always aware that he was English. Even in his suicide, I think, he was English, in that I imagine him saying to himself as he swallowed pill after pill with water, as I suppose, 'Now don't be histrionic about this, just get on with it.' (Which makes me think of someone else whom I consider to have evolved in England and in no other country, the costume and set designer David Walker, elfin too, with tight trousers and a tightly fitting shirt often printed with little flowers and buttoned at the neck, his wig very carefully calculated to blend in with whatever hair he has, whom I see from time to time and who once told me that a friend of his, a young woman, had confided in him that she couldn't bear living any longer and longed to do herself in, to which David advised, 'Then do it, darling, but don't make a fuss of it.' I asked, 'Did she do it?' and David, extending his neck and thrusting out his jaw and looking at me expressionlessly, said starkly, 'Yes, she did.') I am incapable of that utter distancing of feeling from death, even from grief, which I think of as English (or whatever small enclave of the British I know), and will never be able to reconcile myself to it. So, what do I remember Julian for and hope to appreciate in him? For his own appreciation of intelligent wit, that appreciation so marked in his interview with Evelyn Waugh (in which Harold Acton is mentioned) for the Paris Review, as when he asked Waugh if he found any professional criticism of his work helpful and mentioned Edmund Wilson, about whom Waugh asked, 'Is he an American?' and went on, after Julian said yes, 'I don't think what they have to say is of much interest, do you?' And I can hear Julian's delight. What am I to feel about his suicide? Germaine Greer, who is not English, published a severe letter addressed to him in which she condemned him for the act.

———

In what other world than the world Nikos and I live in could this have been written by one man about another?

From 'Pure Reason', Nikos' additions from since we met:

> I pray for you in a way you never suspect except perhaps intuitively when we touch in sleep. I pray for you without knowing I pray, for when, asleep myself, I hold you at night something like prayer flows from me, surrounds you, enters you through your skin.

Perhaps, without our being aware at all of this in our love for each other, we are ourselves living a cause. I say this, because we in fact do not participate in the gay movement, would not, for example, go to a reading of gay poets because they are gay to support them for being gay. Our failing.

———

At dinner at Ann Stokes', one of the guests, a lively friend of Ann's, told me I was wrong to assume Edward VIII abdicated for political reasons: 'Not at all, I know exactly why he abdicated. My mother told me, and she was very much a part of that world, so would have known. He abdicated because he had no testicles. There was no way he could have had children. He had to step down.'

———

At times, Nikos will say something that strikes me as odd coming from someone I know to be intelligent and original but who seems not to be aware that what he says is a sentimental cliché – such as his describing someone having skin like jasmine petals and eyes like sapphire, or, to express regret, that we long for what we can no longer have, too late now – and then it comes to me that Nikos could be quoting from poems by Constantine Cavafy. In fact, such sentimental clichés are expressed in Cavafy's poems and are accepted by Nikos not only because within the poetry of Cavafy but within a tradition in which Cavafy wrote his poetry, a tradition in which Nikos, too, finds his expressions. If I were a social anthropologist – and living with Nikos makes me aware of culture as I never had been before – I would try to investigate the derivations of these sentiments, which I think refer to layers and layers of culture that make up Greek culture, and I would guess that one of these layers is, say, French literature of the Belle Epoque, and, of course, Baudelaire, all evident in the more recherché poems of Cavafy.

I'm reminded of Nikos talking, with amusement, of an uncle who in his youth was known as the Oscar Wilde of Constantinople, which suggests a quite dazzling layer of the culture of one country becoming the cultural history of another, very different country.

———

Steven Runciman has sent me this limerick:

> The stories I tell David Plante
> Soon acquire a curious slant.
> His fertile invention
> Twists all that I mention.
> I could tell him more,
> But I shan't.

Paris

I'm in Paris, on my own, to see Kitaj and Sandra, who have been living here for some months. They told me to meet them at a brasserie in rue des Ecoles for dinner, where they were sitting by the window at a table covered with a stiff white cloth, the napkins stiff and white, too. We embraced over the table.

They said they see few people and work, and I had the sense, all the more vivid for seeing them out of London context, of their exclusivity, which makes seeing them something of a privilege. And, looking at them, I had the momentary flash that they were strange, and I noticed things about them that I hadn't before, or had lost sight of. Sandra sits upright, looking right at you, smiling with her American red lips open, her eyes American bright, her long black American hair loose about her shoulders. It is as if to be attentive is to her to smile. Kitaj's deafness is worse, so he has to lean close, his elbows on the table, his left or right ear turned towards you as he tries to look at you at the same time, but as he can't quite manage this he keeps turning his head in different directions. His way of being attentive is to frown and press his lips together. His beard is almost all white.

We seemed to be reflected on all sides by mirrors.

We ordered. The waiter said something in French to Kitaj which he clearly didn't understand, but as he didn't want to let on that he doesn't know French, all he said was, 'Bien, très bien,' and with a gesture dismissed the waiter, who appeared puzzled.

Sandra defers to Kitaj. He said he first came to Paris when he was nineteen, in 1952. With the hesitant way he speaks, often clearing his throat and hitching up a shoulder as if to put a muscle back in place, he told me he had wanted to come to Europe because of the writers he'd read who had found Europe a revelation of creativity, and one of those writers was of course Hemingway. He knew that a great creative flowering, equal to that of fifth-century Greece or Renaissance Florence, had occurred in Paris over a period of, say, a hundred years, when so many of his American compatriots had gone and themselves produced amazing works. But when he got to Paris he found something different: Paris only seven years removed from German occupation. 'And imagine what it felt like,' he said, 'to walk down a street and know that people there had been pulled out by the Gestapo and sent off to concentration camps. It was, really, my first awareness of being a Jew. At home, I was brought up with little awareness of being Jewish. In my high school, before a game, I'd make the sign of the cross and say a prayer. Europe made me aware of something I hadn't expected.'

He spent only a few days in Paris, then he took the Orient Express to Vienna, and there it was as if the war had ended the day before he arrived. He saw American jeeps being driven around, and in the jeeps soldiers from each of the Four Powers. His grandmother, who was born in Vienna but went to America, had inherited a chemist's shop in Vienna that had been taken over by the Nazis; the reparation money Kitaj himself collected from a lawyer representing his grandmother, just enough money to live on while he studied at the academy in Vienna. The lawyer lived in a medieval courtyard. Once a week, Kitaj would go to his flat for the money. The flat was over a Soviet barracks, and after lights out the lawyer and Kitaj would go into the bathroom to listen to the soldiers singing in the darkness. People wore the same clothes they had worn during the war. He remembers people in the streets grovelling for food, and the great number of beggars.

I said that, when I first came to Paris in 1959, I came expecting the Paris of Gertrude Stein and Ernest Hemingway and Ezra Pound, came expecting that that world, which seemed to me a secret world within the larger secret of Paris, was there to be discovered, found that my attention walking down a street was not on the architecture but on the bullet-strafed walls. The real secret of Paris was the war.

Kitaj said, 'You talk about the secrets of Paris.' He put his hands behind his head and raised his elbows, and as he did he spoke from the side of his mouth, his eye narrowed. 'Perhaps there are no longer the secrets we fantasized were here, but I make it my business to invent a secret Paris, even if it doesn't exist, or only partially. I have two secret cities here.' He leaned forward and put his elbows on the table edge, and continued to speak from the side of his mouth, often stretching his neck as if he was wearing a tight collar, or hitching a shoulder as if to ease a suspender strap. The collar of his shirt was open, and his jacket was unbuttoned. 'The first secret,' he said, 'has to do with sex. I first visited the red-light district along the rue Saint Denis about thirty years ago, and it hasn't changed much, or at least I tell myself it hasn't. A few of the women there are beautiful.' He stretched his neck and laughed. 'They renew themselves like sperm all up and down the mile-long street. I find places where I can lose myself in forgetfulness. I usually go to bed early, but a couple of nights during the month I'll disappear into Saint Denis. Sandra knows about it. I have no secrets from her.' Sandra smiled. 'In Saint Denis I can create my own Paris, and savour the sexual flavour of the place. I go to restaurants, bars, among whores and pimps, and I write or sketch. One reason why I came to Paris is to enjoy the myths. Sex is a myth.

'And the other secret Paris,' he said, now sitting back in his chair, but with his hands on the table, 'is what is left of Jewish Paris. In the Marais, deep in the Marais, is the Pletzel, the area where the Jews still have their separate culture, and Sandra and I will have a meal, once a week, in a kosher restaurant there. What is it called?'

'Joe Goldenberg,' Sandra said.

'We don't have many friends here except for Avigdor Arika and his wife Anne, he a Jew who was in a concentration camp, she an American Jew who only heard about the camps. With Anne I went to Drancy, once a concentration camp for Jews outside of Paris where they were sent before being sent off to the death camps. Avigdor didn't want to go. Drancy is a Communist working-class area. The buildings of the camp, originally thirties buildings, are now council flats. There is a monument to the Jews, an eleventh-rate sculpture. That's all. There's no coincidence between good art and such—' He stopped, both his eyes blinking, not both together, but one after the other. He appeared to have suddenly forgotten what he was talking about. He looked out.

I asked Sandra when she first came to Europe.

'In 1969,' she said.

I asked, 'Why did you come?'

She clapped her hands together and then pressed them into her lap so her shoulders were raised, and she leaned her elongated body to the side. As if worried about what she would say, she smiled at me.

'I guess it's an impossible question,' I said.

She said, 'In Los Angeles, I painted in the morning before going to work. I dreamed of coming to Europe to become a painter.'

'Did you have an image of Paris before you came?'

'From pictures and from what I'd read. I don't feel sentimental about some lost European culture, but I sense that here there are so many references to the past that are still alive. A plate of oysters and a glass of white wine are reinforced by paintings, by literature.'

After dinner, Kitaj and Sandra and I walked to their apartment, near the Seine, in what Kitaj said is one of the oldest streets in Paris, the rue Galande. His studio is the largest room in the apartment, and has stone walls and a well, as in a medieval courtyard. By the well is an easel. Paved with lithograph stone, the floor has large sheets of paper strewn over it. Kitaj picked up the sheets, one at a time, to show me soft-ground etchings of people he knows, and drawings of himself with twisted expressions.

I asked him if there were any exhibitions of art that I should see. He said, 'Not that I know of. It pleases me that there's no noteworthy painting going on. There is only Avigdor. He's the greatest artist-scholar alive, and he is my mentor here. I see him every other day.'

Kitaj has a way of making such a statement, this about Avigdor, sound portentous.

I said, 'For myself, it isn't what is going on in the world of European writing that I live in Europe. My writing isn't at all connected to anything happening here. Not that I think it is connected to what is happening in America.'

'What's that?'

'Oh, what are called the Fabulists.'

Kitaj grunted.

He said, 'If what you're talking about is what's finished for you in Europe, what's finished for me is my affair with Mediterranean-centred European culture. That's all gone for me.'

'Ezra Pound.'

'My favourite anti-Semite.'

And yet, I said, European culture does exist. Living in Europe, have we just become so used to the culture that we don't see it any longer, in the way we saw it as Americans before we even came to Europe? We're no longer self-conscious about being Americans in Europe.

'Are we used to it?' Kitaj asked. 'No, I don't think so. I think it was never ours for the having. It was and is an alien culture in which I had and have no business. Were Hemingway and all kidding themselves in their love affair with Europe? I don't know.'

'Then why do you stay?'

'Habit,' Kitaj said. 'And habits are not simple. They're as complex as love affairs.'

As he was showing me out, Kitaj said, 'Did I tell you I discovered that we're living over a medieval Jewish cemetery? Right under our feet are Jewish bones.'

He smiled his large rectangular smile, his white clenched teeth showing in his white beard.

I'm writing this in my hotel room.

London

Lunch with Caroline Lowell. She appeared to age in the few hours we were together, she drinking vodka after vodka. We talked about the Falkland Islands crisis, about which she was witty, scathing, and utterly pessimistic. Britain in the person of Margaret Thatcher is trying to flex muscles, and in showing off is revealing just how flaccid the flexed biceps of the country are. In going to war to keep the tiny, insignificant Falkland Islands British, what Britain is demonstrating to the world is how tiny and insignificant the country is. Even if it recovers the islands from Argentinian occupation, the country has lost, and won't regain, what remained, in myth, of its prestige as a nation. Caroline rings up her friends in New York for the real news, as the British news fabricates in favour of a petty war. She can laugh and groan at the same time, a dry laugh and a dry groan. Her large green eyes are as they appear in the painting of her by Lucian Freud, and when I look into them I see the painting, not in terms of art, but of personal relationships that come before art.

———

Nikos' mother has died, and he went to Athens for the funeral and burial. In the cemetery, his mother in a coffin in a room where the coffins were kept for burial, he insisted on having the cover removed to see her. He said he touched her and felt she was still warm, and believed that she was alive, and was horrified that she would be buried alive.

Stephen has given me a copy of E. M. Forster's Commonplace Book, just published. He said he didn't want it in the house in case Natasha picked it up and read what Forster wrote about him, as it would upset her. How could it not upset Stephen? 'Stephen Spender loses honour constantly through an interminable diarrhoea composed not entirely of words.' Is this what Forster thought of Stephen when we visited him?

And there is an entry about Natasha and Stephen's former lover from before he married Natasha, Tony Hyndman, who visited Forster: 'Tony Hyndman has been in, recovering from shock also, administered electrically at the Fulbourne mental . . . Natasha Spender has come out well. I did not suspect such generosity and responsibility. I saw only the climber, who is always with the most interesting people.'

Forster was right about Natasha's generosity and responsibility, which Nikos and I have experienced in her inviting us into her life with Stephen.

Often I do think that I don't care at all about keeping a diary, have no interest at all in keeping a diary, so must stop.

Not less and less as time separates us from the past, but more and more, a photograph of bombed-out buildings in a magazine will make me aware that Nikos and I, he ominously, are of the after-war generation. I believe that we have inherited the consciousness of, even the conscience of, the total incomprehensibility of World War I and World War II, the history of those wars dumb-making, blind-making wars that leave one asking, What were they about? What? What? Was it something more primitive than the justification of war in defense of an ideology, so primitive it stands apart from any ideology, more powerful in its destructive domination of the world than any ideology, even an ideology intent on dominating the world, with its own overwhelming intentions far, far beyond the intentions of any ideology? What, what was the instinct that left churches bombed-out ruins? When looking at images of the devastation, the reaction is, with a helpless loosening of all one's mind, Unbelievable, unbelievable, unbelievable.

———

Ossie Clark was found dead in bed, murdered, it's reported, by a boy he picked up for sex.

———

Nikos has written a letter to Anthony Blunt to express his sympathy for the pain his having been exposed as a spy for the U.S.S.R. must have caused him. We have at times met Anthony – at the flat of John and James, or at the flat of the art historian John White and his Alexandrian wife Xenia, and once were invited for lunch in the flat he and his partner John Gaskill had in rooms above the Courtauld Institute in Portman Square, in an Adam-designed house. As Anthony was the Keeper of the Queen's Pictures, she would have lunch with them in their flat, and John, the cook, would simply set an extra place for her at the table. After the revelation, they moved to a high-rise off the Edgware Road. John and James asked Nikos and me if we would collect Anthony and John and drive them for lunch to their house – now in the curiously named Ashchurch Park Villas, where they've moved to, and where they had given Anthony refuge. I parked the car before the high-rise apartment block and Nikos went in to let Anthony and John know we were waiting, which, as he said once they were in the car, surprised John, as others would park blocks away and ring from a distance. I suppose I anticipated Anthony saying something extraordinary, as if to have him in the car, he now notorious, was to anticipate the extraordinary, but he said nothing. His face was gaunt and his lips very thin, the upper part of his body apparently twisted in one way at the waist and his head turned the other way, and his arms twisted in different ways. John looked old and worn, unshaven. Talk at lunch – which consisted of a pie made with boiled eggs and wild rice and wild mushrooms – had mainly to do with the world of art historians, as if Anthony were still an active part of that world. He said a young man had, a few weeks back, read to him a paper about Lukács, but Anthony didn't know who Lukács was. This was extraordinary, that Anthony Blunt hadn't heard of the greatest Marxist critic.

———

Steven Runciman, at supper, mentioned that in 1963, when King Paul and Queen Fredericka of Greece made a state visit to London, he was in Fredericka's entourage in the foyer of the Covent Garden Opera House when someone shouted an insult at her, 'Boo, bourgeois', so Steven stood up in her defence and retorted with, 'No, upper class'. I think Steven toned down the insult.

Then Nikos revealed that he had been in the large company of the King and Queen when they'd made that controversial state visit to London, their train met at Victoria Station by Queen Elizabeth and Prince Philip; he had even attended a reception at Buckingham Palace.

Did I think Nikos hypocritical for having been ancillary to that state visit? No, because Nikos has his own reasons, which I never judge.

What, I asked Steven, is to him bourgeois?

'I think Beethoven the beginning of the end. Beethoven is where the bourgeoisie come in. And, as for Wagner, that's the bourgeoisie pushed all the way to fascism. I detest Wagner, but I love Verdi.'

———

Richard Wollheim arranged for us to be invited to a drinks party given by friends of his, psychoanalysts, who have a flat on Primrose Hill overlooking the zoo, from which they can hear the cries of the animals at night. I'm sure we were both invited because of Nikos, who is publishing Richard's books, the last called Painting as an Art. In the crush of many people, I was introduced to Hanna

Segal, and I, with a sudden audacity and also thinking that she as an analyst would indulge my audacity, told her that my partner Nikos Stangos had gone to see her for possible analysis, and that she had told him that analysis would change our relationship in an unpredictable way, but that, when Nikos reported that to me, I was so sure of our relationship I was willing to accept the unpredictability of his analysis. I also said that Nikos was disappointed that she hadn't taken him on but had passed him onto a Miss Richards, who had left him to go to Australia. 'Where is Nikos?' Hanna Segal asked. 'I want to speak to him.' I went into the crowd to find him, but when I did and with him returned to find Hanna Segal, she was gone.

————

At lunch with Stephen and Natasha, Nikos proposed that he and I give Stephen a party for his birthday. I recall Stephen once saying that he has sacrificed his poetry to his friendships, which he considered much more important. He knows he is social, sees an amused and amusing right to drop names, and is excited by parties. But, at the lunch with him and Natasha, when we asked whom he'd like to have to his birthday party, he said, 'I have no friends.' Natasha said, 'Oh come now, you have so many friends.' He insisted, 'No, I don't. Who are my close friends?' Natasha went silent.

Nikos tells me I have no friends.

Nikos did most of the cooking for the party: lentils, rice, a chicken stew, salad. We bought a huge vulgar cake. And there were many bottles of wine.

Stephen had asked us to invite: Stephen and Stevie Buckley, Frank Kermode, Francis Bacon (who came with John), and, somehow, Caroline Lowell came. On our own, we invited Suzi Gablik and Germaine Greer. Then Matthew Spender and Maro Gorky, who were staying with Stephen and Natasha, came too.

I was, throughout, anxious that the people would not get on, that one of them might have said something that was not, say, in the spirit of the party. The fact is, I am not, basically, a social person, if to be social is to feel at ease among people. I kept filling glasses with wine and talking, talking, talking, and whenever there was a moment of silence I talked as though to talk for everyone all together. Nikos was at ease, but not I, and I wished, by 9:30, that everyone would go, but everyone stayed on till late, and I, drunk, had to let go of my attempt to keep all the connections vital and let whatever happened happen. And the connections did in themselves seem to sustain vitality without me straining to sustain them.

After everyone left and I hardly had enough energy to do the clearing and washing up, Nikos said, 'Well, that was a nice party.'

What people talked about, and which person to which other person, I can't at all recall. Did Suzi have anything to say to Germaine, Germaine to Maro? Did Frank and Francis speak to each other, and if so, about what? And whom did Stephen B. joke with apart from Stephen who likes Stephen B.'s quick wit? And Natasha, whom did she talk with? All I can recall of any talk was that of Caroline Lowell, who is finishing a book about the Duchess of Windsor that is so libelous it can't be published as it is, and who said, 'As a matter of fact, Edward abdicated for the reason everyone believes he did abdicate for: because he loved Wally and wanted to marry her, and he couldn't have as king. He really was in love with her.'

———

Do I have a vision? Yes, I do – and the more I consider it the more it rounds out simply in the vision of all things coming together to form a whole globe, but coming together somewhere beyond my intending the coming together, it all happening of itself and suddenly occurring, and I as suddenly recognizing that it has all come together, and thinking: the joy of it, the joy of it!

———

I think of Richard Hamilton as a political artist.

I once told him that I believe his painting of the Northern Irish H Block prisoner, The Citizen, is equal in its power to

Jacques-Louis David's The Death of Marat; he looked at me, I guess, with appreciation, but also as if I didn't quite understand.

He has long narrow teeth – teeth so long and narrow he seems to talk through them – and small eyes set high in his face, always wearing a denim jacket and a denim cap.

And it seems to me that the work of Rita Donagh, the partner and later wife of Richard Hamilton, that concentrates on the H Block makes her a political artist. Her subtle work of delicate lines and passages sensitizes that place of brutality, giving the brutality the sensitive dimensions of tragedy.

————

David Hockney rang from California, grumbling that no one in London was reacting against Margaret Thatcher's Clause 28, which makes it possible for anyone to object to an exhibition or drama or book that favours homosexuality and that is supported by local government funds. It's true that Nikos and I are not very active in promoting homosexual rights – not, say, in the way the artist Derek Jarman is – but we took up the cause and sent a letter to a number of people asking for them to sign a petition in protest. We asked R. B. Kitaj to be the recipient of the letters in response, thinking that he, unambiguously heterosexual, would make the claim more – what? – unbiased. A trick was to include in our letter the list of people to whom it was sent, so that each person would know what company he or she was signing up with it. Nikos was the one who was most responsible for the letter and the list.

I remember being with Kitaj and Sandra and Nikos in the basement of the Marlborough Gallery, waiting for a telephone call from the Sunday Times, a long time in coming, Kitaj, pacing, more and more impatient, his impatience rising to anger. Whoever the editor was should have known that R. B. Kitaj wanted to speak. The call came and Kitaj spoke in a severe tone. He was promised that our letter to the Sunday Times and the list of protestors would be published. It was, more or less as a footnote in the back pages.

As I think of my diary as a repository of what one day will be considered more than a personal diary, but an account of a certain time, I include the letter and the names of the people who signed, who in themselves represent much of what was happening during that certain time:

Fighting censorship tooth and clause.

Your editorial on clause 28 expressed the hope that the clause 28, now clause 29, 'will prove to be unworkable as its critics predicted . . . that having been put on the statute books it will now be forgotten'.

Though we appreciate the stand taken by those against the clause, we think it must not be forgotten. The House of Commons did confirm it, and anyone who wishes to invoke it may do so if she or he feels that a local council contravenes it. Contravention of the clause is open to interpretation, both arbitrary and subjective. The mere possibility that anyone may now initiate what are in effect procedures of censorship will also result in self-censorship by libraries, galleries, theatres, and so on funded by local councils. In a country without a declaration of human rights [I must say, I wanted this in], this clause is a real threat to civil liberties.

David Hockney is not alone in perceiving the pernicious implications of clause 29. Any person who is concerned about the erosion of civil liberties in this country must agree that clause 29 constitutes a grave danger, not just to arts, but to the future of our society.

Roger de Grey PRA, Sir Alan Bowness, Neil MacGregor, Sir Hugh Casson PPRA, Sir Michael Levey, Nicholas Serota, Sir Norman Reid, The Duke of Beaufort, Francis Bacon, Frank Auerbach, Howard Hodgkin, R. B. Kitaj, Leon Kossoff, Michael Andrews, Richard Hamilton, John Piper CH, Sir Laurence Gowing, Dame Elisabeth Frink RA, Dawn Ades, Eileen Agar, Craigie Aitchison RA, Gillian Ayres, Barry Barker, Nancy Balfour, Glen Baxter, Adrian Berg, Tony Bevan, Sandra Blow

RA, Lewis Biggs, Peter Blake RA, Stephen Buckley, Robert Buhler RA, H. T. Cadbury-Brown RA, Jeffery Camp RA, Fabian Carlsson, Richard Cork, Michael Craig-Martin, Trevor Dannatt RA, Richard Deacon, Jennifer Dixon RA, Anthony d'Offay, Rita Donagh, Peter de Francia, Robyn Denny, Joanna Drew, David Elliot, Anthony Eyton RA, William Feaver, Stephen Finer, Sandra Fisher, Angela Flowers, Barry Flanagan, Terry Frost, Hamish Fulton, Frederick Gore RA, Anthony Green RA, Janet Green, John Golding, Patrick George, Andy Goldsworthy, Alex Gregory-Hood, Nigel Greenwood, Tim Head, Maggi Hambling, Colin Hayes RA, Gerard Hemsworth, Patrick Heron, Paul Huxley, Timothy Hyman, Nicola Jacobs, Bernard Jacobson, Bill Jacklin, Tess Jaray, Derek Jarman, Allen Jones RA, Anish Kapoor, John Kasmin, Philip King, James Kirkman, Mark Lancaster, Catherine Lampert, Christopher LeBrun, Lillian Lijn, Kim Lim, Marco Livingstone, Gilbert Lloyd, Richard Long, Peter Logan, Leonard McComb, Bruce McLean, James Mayor, Dhruva Mistry, Robert Medley RA, Lisa Milroy, Richard Morphet, Julian Opie, Maureen Paley, Myfanwy Piper, Jacqui Poncelet, Nicholas Pope, Patrick Procktor, Deanna Petherbridge, Piers Rodgers, Norman Rosenthal, Leonard Rosoman RA, Vera Russell, John Russell Taylor, Michael Sandle, Richard Shone, Karsten Schubert, Anne Seymour, Yolanda Sonnabend, Frances Spalding, Julian Spalding, Ruskin Spear RA, Jenny Stein, David Sylvester, John Titchell, Joe Tilson, Peter Townsend, Julian Trevelyan, William Turnbull, Euan Uglow, Lady Vaizey, Hester van Royen, Leslie Waddington, Richard Wentworth, Bill Woodrow, Jack Wendler, Carel Weight RA, Richard Wollheim.

Some days later, at a gallery opening, I heard David Sylvester shout at Anthony Caro, 'Why didn't you sign that letter?' to which Caro replied, 'I only sign letters I've written.'

I met John Gaskill in a supermarket in the Edgware Road and asked him to come to tea. He looked as if he could hardly bear the weight of his short, square body. At tea, he told me that he had had no idea, none, about Anthony being a spy, which had shocked him. Shortly after the revelation, Anthony suggested they go to Florence, which John thought would be a relief, but wondered where they would stay in Florence. Anthony said, with the British consul. John replied that they couldn't. And Anthony asked, why not? 'He never took in what he had done,' John said, and shrugged and sighed. He regretted leaving after an hour, and I felt sorry to let him go.

John Golding, in charge of Anthony's memoir, which Anthony wrote while staying with John and James, said that he has given it to the British Library with an injunction of some years. Laughing, John said that the big secret of the memoir is how boring it is.

———

Francis rang and asked Nikos and me and Stephen to dinner in a restaurant. I drove us to Reece Mews, and, crossing the cobbles to where he lives over a garage, I saw him look out of a window. He met us at the top of the steep stairs and kissed us all on the cheeks.

He said, 'John wanted to come, too, but he's too drunk,' and he laughed his rough laugh that dismisses everything as: well, of course.

In his narrow sitting-room–bedroom, at one end with a large oval bed covered with a multi-coloured spread and a bookcase and a table by the bed piled with books, we sat at the near end on sofas and drank champagne, and we talked about drawing, and what really is drawing. While I wasn't talking myself – and Nikos tells me I talk too much – I told myself to pay attention to the conversation of the others, which was extraordinary, and remember it all, Nikos' incisive remarks, Stephen's impressionist remarks, and Francis' authoritative ones, but I've forgotten, but how alive the remarks were, and how alive I felt.

Stephen was very attentive to Francis, was, as I once noted he was with Auden, deferential to him. To whatever Francis said, Stephen responded with, 'Yes, you're right,' to which Francis responded with, 'Well, perhaps I'm not at all right. I don't know how to draw, really.'

Like a son who, at a certain age, sees a weakness in his father, I saw a weakness in Stephen, and I quite consciously decided that I would not defer to Francis, but disagree with him. I no doubt said some silly things about drawing, but I had said them and I wouldn't give them up when others – especially Francis – didn't agree, or didn't see my point. I thought Stephen became a little annoyed with me because I didn't defer to Francis but was expressing something that I presumed was of interest to him. I know that Stephen can't take seriously what I say, and is puzzled by my – what he himself would say about himself – near success as a writer. That I should take myself seriously talking to Francis (whom Stephen considers a genius) Stephen, I feel, takes as an impertinence. Maybe I'm imagining this – imagining his disapproval of me – but his look, his eyes half lidded and his jaw set, seemed meant to stop me from talking, and I wouldn't be stopped. Nikos didn't stop me. At times, Francis would say, 'David has made an interesting point,' and only then would Stephen nod and say, 'Yes.' Then I thought that Stephen resented that I was paying more attention to Francis than to him, so I tried to pay as much attention to him as I did to Francis, asking Stephen questions. This is all very silly. We drank three bottles of champagne.

Then, at the restaurant, more lively talk, now about intention in art. As this interests me a lot, I, again, said what I had to say, and Francis pushed what I said as far as it could be pushed by saying, 'I have no intentions. I don't know what I'm doing, not at all. I have a critical sense, developed over the years, and I rely on that, a purely instinctive critical sense, but beyond that I have no idea what I'm doing.' I said, 'Do you count on anyone – say, some really informed critic – to say what you might be doing?' 'No,' Francis said, 'I don't.'

I recalled seeing, on the big, plain table under the window of the sitting-room area, books by Michael Leiris, the French philosopher who has written extensively on Francis.

Francis talked about Van Gogh and intention or the opposite of intention, and once again I concentrated, thinking, I must remember this, but I've forgotten.

Stephen said, 'I like to think that if I'd been around when Van Gogh was painting, I'd have been one of the few to recognize his genius, but, in fact, I think that I, like most people, would have considered him an impossible mad man, and wouldn't have wanted to have anything to do with him.'

'I should think definitely not,' Francis said; 'he was mad.'

Then we talked about health, I don't know why. Stephen keeps going to doctors for tests, though he says he is in perfect health, really. He said, 'Somehow I'm not frightened of death. I think I was brought up not to be frightened of it, but to consider it as something that would inevitably come and not to be made a fuss over. I suppose I don't think myself important enough to make a fuss about dying.'

Francis said, 'I'm frightened of death. I'm very frightened of it.' He laughed. 'Of course, I may die tomorrow. I'm seventy-three – just your age, Stephen.'

Stephen said, 'How is it, then, that my hair is white and yours not?'

'Because I dye it,' Francis said. 'You should try it.' He named the dye and how to use it.

I asked Francis, 'Why are you frightened of dying?'

He said, 'Because I love life. It's all I have, and I don't want to lose it. I love it.'

'So do I,' Stephen said.

'David doesn't,' Nikos said.

'You don't?' Francis asked me.

'I love Nikos,' I said.

A waiter came to Francis and whispered something into his ear, then left. 'It's John,' Francis said to us. 'He's out in the street, drunk. I'd better go get him.' He left, and in a little while came back with John, who did not appear to be drunk.

He had not been able to get the fancier pub he'd been negotiating for, and we were sorry for him; but he didn't seem to mind, and said, 'It don't matter.' He told us about his trip to America, to Atlantic City, with his brother, with whom he's going into business buying and selling old furniture. Francis said, 'Really a load of old junk.' I wondered how much old furniture they could buy and sell in Atlantic City, the gambling capital of America, and thought that couldn't be their business.

Then he took out a photograph of himself and his boyfriend Philip, who had been allowed out of prison on a three-day pass. John wanted to give the photograph to Francis, and asked Nikos, sitting next to him, if Nikos would spell out his dictation, so that he, John, could write it, as he couldn't spell words but he could write letters. As Nikos dictated the letters, John wrote: FOR MY FRANCIS WITH MY LOVE JOHN.

John leaned over the table towards Francis and said, 'I want to tell you something,' and Francis leaned forward so John could whisper into his ear. Francis sat back suddenly and said, in a loud voice, 'That's ridiculous. I'm not going to listen to it. That you want to die is ridiculous. I'm not going to listen.' John smiled. He held out his hand to Francis and Francis took it. John said, 'I love you.' Francis said, 'And I love you, and because I do I'm not going to listen to you talk nonsense.' John turned to us. He said, 'I love Francis. I love my friend in prison, and I love Francis, though, you know, with Francis I have a non-sexual relationship.' And we all nodded.

John told us he has a new house, a big house in the country, with outbuildings and two acres of farmland, where he would live with his boyfriend. They've been together for fourteen years, and they make love every day, sometimes twice a day, except when Philip is in prison. 'I'm real horny,' John said. He'd decided to live in the country because if he and Philip continued to live in London they'd end up killing themselves with drink or get some terrible sexually transmitted disease. About the house, he said, 'Of course Francis helped me.' About the house in the country, John said he had had one of the outbuildings done up into a cottage for Francis to stay when he visited. Francis raised his shoulders and let them drop and said, 'I loathe the country.' John said, 'The cottage has a nice view.' 'I loathe views,' Francis said. They both laughed, John very amused by Francis. John invited Nikos and me to the house in the country for Easter Sunday lunch.

It was midnight, and Stephen said he had to go. Nikos and I left with him. I had drunk very little to be able to drive. On the way to his house, Stephen said, 'All night, whenever Francis said something extraordinary, I'd tell myself, this is something I'll never forget, and I've forgotten everything. I must try to remember it all for my diary.'

We talked about the relationship between Francis and John. Stephen said, 'Of course, anyone who has a relationship with a genius will end up wanting to kill himself out of a sheer sense of inadequacy.'

We left Stephen off a block away from his house. He said Natasha didn't know he was having dinner out with Francis and us, and might get upset if she saw us leave him off; she'd think we were conspiring to keep her out.

Back home, Nikos and I talked about Francis. 'He's wonderful,' Nikos said; 'he's totally without pretensions. Totally. I've never known a man to be so totally unpretentious.'

Often, over the evening, I'd look at Nikos and think: how beautiful he is. A great refinement has come to his face. I'd think, And he's my love! with surprise at the fact.

The next time Stephen came to us, I noted that he had brightened his hair with a blue rinse.

―――――

An observation — though there are multiple connections among people in London, there are, too, many intended disconnections, for Steven Runciman may know Stephen Spender, but does not like him, and does not connect with him.

An example of Steven's irony, this about the ritual of the ceremony of fire in the Church of the Holy Sepulcher in Jerusalem.

The sepulcher itself is held by the Greek Orthodox Church, and every Easter appoints a priest, frisked first so it is sure that he doesn't carry matches or anything that will ignite a fire, to enter into the sepulcher, which is then sealed until the priest knocks to be released, always, unfailingly, carrying a candle lit miraculously in the sepulcher, from which all the candles in the church are lit. Having told the story, Steven will stick out his lower lip and raise his chin as if in defiance of anyone contradicting him and his implied belief that of course the candle was lit miraculously. As amused as he is by telling such a story, the irony is that you are left thinking he may in fact believe in the entertaining miracle.

Stephen is incapable of such subtle irony, and would frown with disapproval that anyone should be so ridiculous. This is not to say that Stephen doesn't have any respect for belief, but, unlike Steven, he takes such belief seriously, for, as I've written before, Stephen is not good at irony.

Nor am I good at irony. I sometimes write prayers, one of which I gave to Stephen, who, I saw, was moved by it. I would never give a prayer to Steven, who, claiming as he does that he is a warlock and can cause someone to break his leg, would take the prayer to be at the same level of entertaining magic.

This comes to me as a little revelation, though I don't at all know what it means: that Nikos and I know people who may have met one another, but who would have no interest in, or would even withdraw from, knowing one another. So, I can't imagine Steven Runciman and Francis Bacon spending an evening together, or Stephen Spender and Patrick Kinross, or . . .

———

While Nikos was at work –

I rang Germaine Greer to ask her to lunch. I thought I'd invite Stephen too, and rang him, and then asked if Natasha would like to come, so they both came: game pie and salad and cheese and grapes, with wine.

Germaine was animated. At moments, she stopped talking, put

her hands across her bosom and made a moue of her lips as if in astonishment, then suddenly laughed as if at herself. She made the luncheon party.

Talk about the war in the Falklands, everyone horrified by Thatcher's grandstand gesture.

After lunch, Stephen asked me if I'd written in my diary about our dinner with Francis the other night, and I wanted to say, 'But you said I mustn't mention that in front of Natasha.' I said, 'Yes,' and offered to read out the entry, which, with coffee, I did – leaving out the reference to Natasha. Now, at least, Natasha and Germaine know I keep a diary, and what it is like. I could have said I've stopped keeping it, leaving it to be read after everyone, including myself, is dead; but then I thought that would be a lie, so why not let everyone know what I write while we're alive?

I said, 'In my diary, I never try to account for others' opinions, always too complicated, too subtle, for me to account for them in a sentence or two.'

Stephen said, 'You try to be descriptive.'

'I try,' I said. 'I would never try to account for Germaine's opinion about abortion.'

'No,' she said, 'you don't do that. But you sin by omission. You use the glass-pane technique, which is just to record what you see. You may think that's truthful, but it can be a total distortion of the truth. If you see someone washing his face in vodka, and record that, you give the impression that the man is a mad alcoholic; it may be that he's cut himself and is using the vodka as an antiseptic.'

Natasha said nothing.

I did think that if I saw a man washing his face in vodka, I would wonder if he was simply bonkers.

Nikos returned early from his office and I recounted the luncheon party to him, not sure he was interested.

———

Should I wonder that most of the people we see are that much older than we are – old enough to be of another generation? The

attraction is simple: we have so much to learn from them historically, as they do represent history. What they have to learn from us
I have no idea.

But then there are friends of our generation whom we see often:
Stephen Buckley, Keith Milow, Mark Lancaster when he's in
London, Richard and Sally Morphet, Julia and Howard Hodgkin,
Joe and Jos Tilson, Kitaj and Sandra, all in the art world. Do we
have any close friends among writers of our generation?

———

The Falkland Islands have been freed of Argentinian occupation,
and Britain shows off to the world that there is still a British Empire.

———

Nikos and I received invitations to the opening of Francis'
grand retrospective at the Tate Gallery. There were long tables
covered with white cloths and waiters standing behind the
tables serving champagne and cooks serving portions from
whole salmon.

John was as excited as if a party was being given for him. He was
wearing a beautiful suit. He told Nikos and me he was very angry,
as one of Francis' old cronies from the Colony Room had, on this
most important occasion, asked Francis for fifty pounds, and John
had insisted Francis not give the money. John said to me, 'I was
having a nice time until this happened. Francis has given him
hundreds of pounds, more than hundreds, and he never pays back.
If you borrow, you pay back. Fuck it.'

Francis' friend Dicky Chopping came to us and said, 'Francis is
going round to look at his pictures. Why don't you join us?' We
followed Francis from picture to picture – Study for Portrait of Van
Gogh II, Lying Figure with Hypodermic Syringe, Crucifixion
1965 – and standing for a moment at each one he would laugh and
say, 'Isn't it loathsome? I loathe it. I really loathe it.'

I went off on my own to study the great Triptych May–June
1973, the one depicting the death of George Dyer in the hotel in

Paris when Francis was having his grand retrospective show in the Grand Palais. George is doubled up on a toilet in the left-hand panel; in the right one he is vomiting into a washbasin; and in the central panel he is half dissolved in blackness that pours out through an open doorway. I saw how essentially, how passionately, how heartbreakingly this triptych depicted Francis' reaction to the horror of the death of someone he had loved.

From this I went to the pastel, almost sentimental portraits of John, filled with – what can I write? – tenderness.

Dawn Ades, who wrote an essay for the catalogue, said she thought the colours were 'breathed on to the canvas,' and she held her palm before her mouth and breathed onto it.

———

What would I most like to write? I would most like to write a short book called The Spiritual in Literature, something like Kandinsky's Concerning the Spiritual in Art.

———

To tea at Kitaj and Sandra's. I mentioned that Avigdor Arikha had given to Nikos an etching of himself, perhaps in recognition that Nikos had included him in the Dictionary of Art and Artists, which Nikos is editing and in which he does include Keith Milow and Stephen Buckley, but Kitaj looked away, and Sandra said, 'We don't see Avigdor any more,' and I was left wondering what had happened, but wouldn't ask.

Then, as if by looking in the distance is the dimension in which Kitaj thinks, he turned to me and said he had recently seen Francis Bacon in the street, Francis wearing red basketball shoes, and Francis asked him, 'Do you ever have days when everything goes wrong?' Now Kitaj laughed his shrugging, masculine laugh, his eyes bright. I wonder about Kitaj's obsession with being Jewish, for though his stepmother was Jewish, I think, from what I've heard him say, that his biological mother and father were not, and, if so, he was brought up so far removed from Jewishness that, and this he did once tell me, when he was in high school he used to pray a Hail Mary and make the sign of the cross before engaging in a baseball game. He is taking instruction from a rabbi before marrying Sandra, who is Jewish, but he baulks at the problem of how God could allow so much suffering to his people. Kitaj listened to me when I said I object to the word 'Holocaust' to define the horrors of Jewish suffering, as that means a burnt offering to God, and what God would accept such an offering, and to what end? I prefer to use 'Shoa,' which, incidentally, the Vatican uses, understanding the meaning of 'holocaust.' Kitaj said nothing, and I worried if I had offended him, so went on to say that I believe his painting If Not, Not, which has been made into a tapestry that hangs in the foyer of the British Library, is a masterpiece, no greater indictment of the horrors of the twentieth century, more potent than Eliot's The Waste Land, than that painting, with the façade of the entrance building of Auschwitz commanding the landscape of civilization in ruins.

———

Sylvia Guirey asked me to come to her studio to show me her latest paintings, all dots, and to talk to me about her relationship with Richard and Mary Day. Mary Day has accepted Richard back on the condition that he does not see Sylvia. Sylvia is bewildered by the whole situation and doesn't know what to do.

I listened, but didn't understand; when friends confide in me, which they seem to do, they confide generally, leaving the details out, so that when, later, another friend tells me the details, I'm amazed, even at times shocked. I had no idea why Sylvia wanted to talk to me.

I walked home through South Kensington, through Kensington Gardens and Hyde Park; the chestnut trees and hawthorn are in full bloom, and the grass is thick and fresh.

Nikos had some Greek friends for drinks. As I came in, he said, 'Your editor at the New Yorker, Dan Menaker, just rang to say they've taken your latest story.' I had drinks with his Greek friends, who stayed for supper.

———

Could it be that the images we witness of World War I and World War II have more power now than they would have had at the times of the wars, and form in us the consciousness, the conscience, of a world united in suffering – suffering, once seen as localized among certain people, now made global as the images expand beyond the local into the world, and, if it can be said that the wars had any positive legacy, expanding into the consciousness, the conscience, of a whole world that has, all together, to guard against such suffering?

The nuclear bombs, impelled by the wars, make us think of the whole round world.

Certainly, it is unthinkable that Germany and Britain could possibly be at war with each other, which occurred in my lifetime, and which I believe must now bring Britain and Germany, and all of Europe, close together, that consciousness, that conscience, formed by the suffering of the wars that divided the countries now uniting them.

And so I believe in and take joy in the possibility of a United States of Europe, and, with even more extended belief and joy, in a United States of the World.

This vision of the whole world has evolved; if in part as an intention, mostly unintentionally, historically.

———

Nikos and I to supper at John Golding and James Joll's, who have been painted as a couple by R. B. Kitaj. Mario Dubsky there, and, however much I should by now assume it as common, I was surprised by the appearance of someone in a social situation I know from another social situation, for I didn't know that John and James know Mario. Conversation about the art world.

I said I would like to write a frivolous novel about a young man who cannot see the causal relationship between work and money, and imagines they have nothing to do with each other. John said, 'No one has ever assumed for a minute that you imagine they have anything to do with each other.' Nikos smiled, and, I don't know why, I felt the attention paid me was in itself an affectionate compliment.

Florence

A fter the death of John Pope-Hennessy –
 Some years after he had retired from his curatorial positions
at the Victoria and Albert, the British Museum, and the Metropolitan Museum in New York, and moved to Florence, I would
visit him from Lucca, where Nikos and I have a small flat in a
duecento tenement building, up seventy-three steps. John did once
visit us there, and, looking about, again as if in all directions at
once, squealed, 'Very enviable.' In Florence, I climbed the wide
stone stairs within the courtyard of the palazzo to the doors of the
apartment on a landing and rang the bell at the side of the thick
glass doors with heavy metal grill, forged into decorative curves,
over the glass. The door was opened by a maid in a black dress and
white apron (as his maids were dressed in London and New York),
and I was shown into the sitting room to wait. There, in a corner,
stood a Venetian cabinet of curiosities, and I stopped to look
through the glass – the original glass, John later told me – which
made the objets de vertu inside appear to waver as I studied them,
and among them was my little carved wooden rhinoceros I had
given to him in London. (The meaning of objets de vertu intrigues
me – were precious objects seen as inspiring virtue?) When, moving
as always briskly, John entered, I thanked him for keeping that little
memento, but he didn't respond. He had just bought a painting of
the Assumption of the Holy Virgin Mother by Pietro de Francesco

degli Orioli, and together we looked at it.

After he died, the contents of this flat were auctioned by Christie's in New York, and I saw in the catalogue the furniture, the bronzes, the pictures I had seen in the flat. When I had visited him, the rooms, especially a round, rotunda-like dining room with a round cherrywood table in the center, the walls, as I recall, pale yellow, with vitrines on three sides filled with objects as in a museum, made the objects contained in them appear so carefully and knowledgeably chosen that I felt whatever small items of little worth I had were collected haphazardly and without any overriding historical knowledge to make them a coherent collection. In no way could I have identified a Giorgio d'Alemagna miniature, a red-chalk drawing by Ventura Salimbeni, a painting of the Baptism of Christ of Pier Francesco Mola and more, and all privileged by the knowledge of Pope-Hennessy. But, again, seeing them separated out in the catalogue, they lost that privilege. He had often said he had no money, and, studying the objects in reproduction, I realized that, of course, he had had money, but not enough that individual works, taken out of the context of the flat in Via de' Bardi, retained the uniqueness they appeared to have there. I was told that there was a blizzard at the time of the auction, and the sale was not as had been hoped. Among the items of furniture auctioned was the Venetian lacca povera corner cabinet, decorated with commedia dell'arte figures, in which my little carved rhinoceros had been displayed, but that object clearly not auctioned.

John liked, he said, to show friends off on trains, and from the other side of the Arno he would accompany me across the Ponte Vecchio, walking more vividly than I, past the Giotto Tower and Baptistry and the Duomo and all the tourists and to the train station at Santa Maria Novella. The whole of Florence seemed to be his privilege, his way through the city le droit du seigneur.

When with others, he went first through a doorway or up a flight of stairs; he took it for granted that his position in a car was next to the driver. A mutual friend said about him, 'It's not as though he has bad manners, it's that he has no manners at all.'

And yet, in his apparent total, authoritative self-confidence, he was a man without conceit, without pretensions.

I always felt totally intimidated by him, and never understood why we were friends.

One hot evening we arrived too late at the station for the train to Lucca, and he matter-of-factly announced, 'You'll have to spend the night.' Back in his apartment, he asked his assistant to show me to a bedroom, and I was given toiletries, pajamas and a change of underclothes for the morning by his assistant, Michael Mallon. I did not sleep well.

At breakfast, Michael Mallon, as if this needed a reminder, said that the day was Epiphany, and Pope-Hennessy (or, as he was called, the Pope) was almost operatically high-pitched when he exclaimed, 'Off to Mass!' and he and the assistant left me to go for their missals, I now at the front door waiting for them. They were off to Mass in a church, S.S. Annunziata of the Servite Friars, whose devotion was (is) to the Mother of God, especially as La Mater Dolorosa. By special dispensation from the Vatican Pope, the old Tridentine Mass of 1570 was celebrated, the Mass, I said, of my youth, long before the Second Vatican Council of the early 1960s changed the Latin Mass to the vernacular. I asked if I could join them, and was not refused.

But we were early, and went into the Ospedale degli Innocenti across the Piazza Annunziata to look specifically at a painting of The Adoration of the Magi by Domenico Ghirlandaio, a strange painting, for behind the scene of the Magi bringing gifts to the infant Jesus and his parents was the gory scene of the Massacre of the Innocents, perhaps an ironical reference to the Ospedale degli Innocenti which was established to save orphans from death. No one said a word, but simply studied the painting for a long while, long enough to take in all its details, especially the Massacre of the Innocents enacted in a bloody landscape behind the manger, which I so wondered at, but which I felt I must not ask about. No doubt my silence was guarding my ignorance, but I also sensed too great a reverence in the silence of Pope-Hennessy and his assistant to break it.

The Mass was very much the Mass of my youth. John and Michael followed the ceremony in their missals, which I vividly remembered doing when I was at Mass in my parish. The priest, in a green chasuble and carrying the chalice under a green veil, one hand flat on the square purse on top and the other holding the chalice beneath the veil, came down the aisle of the small white church. Two servers in surplices were with him, one carrying a smoking censer by its chains and the other a little silver boat of incense. The choir in the loft at the back of the church sang. The priest climbed the steps to the altar and placed the veiled chalice on it before the tabernacle and descended the steps, made the sign of the cross then turned to the congregation and held out his arms and intoned, 'Introibo ad altare Dei,' and the servers on either side of him responded, 'Ad Deum qui laetificat juventutem meam,' and I felt a strange movement in me at those words invoking God the joy of my youth.

In the church of S.S. Annunziata in Florence, memory brought back Sunday after Sunday in my parish church. I remembered the Latin. I remembered the times to stand, to kneel, to sit. I remembered the way the wide, stiff chasuble of the priest moved with the movement of his shoulders when, his back to the congregation, he moved his shoulders with the movements made in the ritual. I remembered the Bible on its stand being changed by the server from one side of the altar to the other.

I watched the priest lift the purse from the veil and remove from it the corporal, the white linen, handkerchief-like cloth, which he spread on the altar; watched him remove the veil from the chalice placed on the corporal, still covered by the pall and the purifier. I remembered all the names. And I remembered the moment of the elevation and consecration of the host, announced by the delicate chiming of bells rung by a server, and the bowing of the congregation in adoration of that high white host which was no longer a wafer but was transubstantiated into the body of Christ.

A feeling started up in me that I felt sway back and forth in me, like keening. John and his assistant went to the rail for communion, but I, more than ever, could not. The choir in the organ loft sang.

After the Mass, out on the pavement, Pope-Hennessy introduced me to a number of people, one of whom a countess who, in refined appreciation of the chant, commented that the Gloria was pre-Gregorian.

I left John Pope-Hennessy for the train station and on the train to Lucca I looked out at the grey and dun-brown Tuscan winter countryside, where, here and there, bare persimmon trees were hung heavily with bright orange fruit, and I calmed down.

A mutual friend who lived in Florence, Thekla Clark, rang me out of interest to tell me that John Pope-Hennessy had told her that I was praticante. I said, no, no, I was not praticante. She asked, 'You're an agnostic?' and I answered, 'I'm an atheist.' She repeated, 'Not an agnostic?' And I repeated, 'No, an atheist.'

Some time later, another mutual friend, John Fleming, with whom the Pope often stayed, rang me to inform me: my visit with the Pope had not been a 'success.' Oh? I had gone to Mass as a non-believer. This shocked me. The Pope objected to my going to Mass for the aesthetics of the ceremony. This shocked me more. I protested: I had gone because the Tridentine Mass was the Mass of my youth and as such had a very deep meaning to me, whatever that meaning was. Well, I might write a postcard to the Pope to explain. I was on the verge of being excommunicated. I did write a postcard, and I did see Pope-Hennessy again, this time as guests of John Fleming and Hugh Honour outside Lucca, and no mention was made of my heresy.

As if to get back into his good graces, I mentioned that I had been very impressed by an essay he had written on Michelangelo, which ended with something like: 'Michelangelo prayed for the angels to descend to help him, and the angels did.' On that high note that was always near a delicate screech, he turned away and said, 'I don't remember,' and my attempt to be blessed was dismissed. Michael Mallon was able to name the essay with which the lines concluded.

We were, with drinks before lunch, beneath a loggia by a lotus pool. John didn't refer to my postcard or his having objected to my going to Mass as a non-believer, and I knew not to refer to either myself. As he had dismissed my reference to angels in his essay on Michelangelo, I thought I would be clever by saying how marvelous the footnotes are in Gibbon's The Decline and Fall of the Roman Empire, in particular the footnote about the prophet Iamblichus who miraculously evoked two fountains to rise from the desert from which the gods of love, Eros and Anteros, emerged, fondly embraced him, and at his command stepped back into the fountains which would then sink back into the earth.

Self-consciously laughing, I said, 'If only that were possible.'

John did laugh, and I thought I had at least amused him. Then he asked, 'You don't believe in miracles, David?'

'No,' I said somewhat apologetically.

'You don't believe that the natural order can be suspended and what was thought to be impossible becomes possible?'

'I'd like very much to believe that,' I said, 'but I don't.'

He said, 'I believe all the miracles depicted in predelle.'

John laughed his high, abrupt laugh and turned away, but I felt that what he had said was not a joke. It was as though he, with the absoluteness of his self-confidence, had never questioned his belief in miracles, had not even considered that some people do not believe. I couldn't see John Pope-Hennessy as helpless in any way, couldn't see him giving in to longing, or, more, passion, but I saw him encircled by absolute belief, and this precluded any questions. Did he know theology as thoroughly as he knew the history of art? He would have thought it impudent of me to question not only his absolutism but the absolutism of Roman theology. I could no more have questioned him about his beliefs than I could have asked him why he had kept that little wooden rhinoceros in a cabinet in his sitting room.

And yet, the questions remain.

If he hated aesthetics, hated style, what was his vision of art?

What, I wonder, did he see in the Domenico Ghirlandaio painting of The Adoration of the Magi in the Ospedale degli Innocenti with the Massacre of the Innocents as background?

London

Dinner at Germaine's (individual soufflés, boiled mutton with a caper sauce, rhubarb sponge, all prepared on an enormous cooker with many ovens and hobs, and the wines very good, as if Germaine has all the time in the world and all the money in the world for such a meal) in honour of the writer David Malouf, an Australian compatriot of Germaine. She invited Stephen and Natasha, Stephen often laughing at her inventive use of expletives, Natasha wide-eyed with amazement so that, as she told me later, she kept thinking her eyebrows would fall off. Germaine, like an Italian peasant woman, never sat with us, but prepared the courses while we ate, and the food appeared and disappeared and appeared on the table.

She kept apologizing about the food, and treated it, in serving it, as if she was embarrassed that it wasn't good enough and shouldn't be given the attention it in fact deserved.

Feeling at home with her, Nikos carved the mutton joint; I helped with wine, coffee.

I had the vivid sense of a woman entertaining completely on her own who was frantic that she wasn't up to the entertainment. All the while we ate, the telephone kept ringing and other people, among them Melvyn Bragg, kept arriving.

An insight into Germaine, or so I like to think: she has a huge chest of drawers inlaid with mother of pearl, as extravagant as I imagine Germaine to be, but when I commented on it she told me she didn't like it, and if I wanted it to take it away. So I see in her an attraction to the extravagant and, at the same time, indifference to that extravagance, she herself as if between extravagant statements and at the same time willing to let the statements go.

Her palms pressed to her bosom to make the enthusiasm heartfelt, she so enthused over a poster by David Hockney he had given to us that we gave it to her.

She can be so intimate, taking one's chin in her hand and staring into one's eyes as if one were the only person in the world, and then she turns away and she sees something altogether unrelated to one that leaves one totally apart, leaving one to wonder what that intimacy was all about.

A memory: John Byrne – who, I must say, has all too meaning a name as he was severely burned when a boy, dancing in a hula skirt too close to an electric fire in his mother's sitting room – is a close friend of Germaine, and he invited her and Nikos and me to a fish and chip restaurant, which John, not the richest young man in the world as a dealer in rare books and manuscripts with Bertram Rota, could afford, and there, all of us in a booth, Germaine held John's chin tightly and kissed him on the lips, the expression on John's scarred face one of joy, an expression of unrestrained affection on Germaine's part that was for the moment, after which she looked with a frown at the menu, as if in Germaine there is no continuity between a moment of almost sexual affection and what to order on the fish and chip menu.

Nikos thinks Germaine amazing, as he says when he meets someone who is totally original – that is, she takes nothing for granted, but will, after having made a statement for which she in the public is known, overturn the statement and make a contradictory statement, such as her finding Muslim women in an Arab country perfectly content to be in purdah.

Steven Runciman sent me this limerick about Germaine, whom he met at supper at our flat:

> They told me to stay clear
> Of the formidable doctor Greer,
> But, in spite of her learning,
> For all my discerning,
> I find her rather a dear.

———

John Gaskill has killed himself.

The art historian Michael Jaffe told me that when he was showing the Queen round the Fitzwilliam Museum, she paused at the painting by Poussin she recognized from when she had had lunch with Anthony, and all she said was, 'Poor Anthony.'

———

Nikos, always enthusiastic about works he calls 'innovative,' took on at Thames & Hudson a book called Current Trends in British Art, among the young artists in the book Liam Gillick, Grenville Davey, Damien Hirst, Gary Hume, Michael Landy, Sarah Lucas, Lisa Milroy, Julian Opie, Rachel Whiteread. Many of these were students of Michael Craig-Martin at Goldsmiths' College. Looking through the book, it is very difficult to generalize about the works as representative of a generation, given that some seem to be contained within flat rectangles while others are as free of the containment as glass milk bottles and stacks of chairs, or the list of bids at the auction of a Stradivarius violin, or photographs of the artist in a morgue among the dead, the faces and bodies of the dead blocked out. I defer to Nikos, he who will say with excitement about Titian, Vermeer, Chardin, 'How innovative!'

———

To Loudoun Road, the blue and white house set among dark green bushes, for tea with Stephen, Natasha out. We sat in Stephen's study, the tall, glassed-in bookcase with a classical bust in plaster on top, all around loose papers, letters, books and paddy bags, crumpled newspapers, he in an armchair and I on a chair. I said never mind the tea, as Stephen, in his deep armchair, appeared so deep in it I thought it would be difficult to rise, and there he appeared to be settled deeply into his life.

He spoke of people whom I knew of from his autobiography, World within World: of the family cook and housekeeper, Bertha and Ella, who were called, together, Berthella. Berthella didn't approve of having bells rung for them by the family and served meals only when they were ready to. Stephen spoke lightly in a dry voice of his older brother Michael, a young man who insisted that even the beauty of the music he played so well on the piano could be explained scientifically; his sister Christine, who, receiving instruction to become a Catholic, refused to believe dead unbaptized children go to Limbo. He laughed lightly, as if he, in his advanced years, was seeing his early years with humor. But when he remembered his father saying, 'May God, for as long as possible, preserve my son in his innocence,' he became silent and I sensed him withdraw into himself in a way he almost never allows, and from which he suddenly sat up a little and said that perhaps we should have tea. I said I'd prepare the tea, and he thanked me and sat back into his armchair.

After our cups of tea, Stephen did heft himself up and out from the armchair to go out, and, alone, I stood and turned to the glass-fronted bookshelves in which the room was dimly reflected, so that, my back to the room, I saw the reflection as another room, and between the two rooms were shelves of books as if suspended in space. Leaning close, I saw some of my own novels were there on a shelf, and it came to me that years have passed since I first came to London and met Nikos, met Stephen, met so many people that do make up a world.

When Stephen returned, he suggested we listen to some of Tristan and Isolde, and again we sat in our deep armchairs, he so deeply that I rose to change the records. Hours later, during the Liebestod, Natasha appeared at the doorway and, seeing Stephen and me in a state of stupefying enthrallment, smiled and left us.

Nikos and I went to a recital at the Institute of Contemporary Arts of one of John Cage's chance pieces for piano. He had taken a blank score sheet and placed over it a map of the stars, and wherever there was a star he pushed a pin through to the blank score sheet below, which pin pricks became notes, notes played on a piano by an intense-looking woman with thin grey hair, each note, it sounded to me, a non-resounding plunk. After the recital a brief talk given by David Tudor, John Cage standing by, and after the lecture questions from the audience. I raised my hand and, standing, I asked, If there is, as there seems to be according to research into linguistics, a deep generative grammar that makes sounds into words and sentences, couldn't there possibly be a deep generative grammar to sounds that makes sounds comprehensible as music, so that random sounds aren't comprehensible as music is? David Tudor said something, but John Cage nothing.

Later, I talked about this with Nikos. He said, yes, I may be right about that deep generative sense of music, but perhaps what seems superficial chance in the music of Cage and Tudor is in tension with that essential sense, and, simply by our paying attention to their music, that essential sense makes sense of the superficial chance, and it may even be that the essential sense rises up and makes of the superficial chance a composition that is not intended by the composers but that occurs beyond their intentions.

Yes, I said, yes, of course, but I do sometimes want some intention to contain, to proportion and balance the unintended. I wonder if too much is left to chance in all the art forms and not enough is brought up of the essentials to the surface.

It is as though the essentials are not for us to determine, but must assert themselves against our inability to determine them, or, even, against our doubt that they exist, so we rely on chance with a strange faith that the essentials will determine themselves, or even show that they exist.

I would like to write an essay on how, in literature, the reliance on imagery, on description, has become the only way a writer – who cannot allow himself to determine the essentials because he doesn't know what the essentials are, or if there are any essentials – has of allowing the essentials to show themselves, as if faith in the image is for the writer the only chance he has for something more to occur in his writing than what he can make occur. More and more, I think this reliance on the image is limiting, and imposes itself on literature in a way that flattens out the deeper, generative grammar of essential human values in justice, in love, in grief, and, too, beauty, which values are as deep in us as language. I wonder if style has been subjected to the use of superficial imagery to the detriment of style, and so I read Jane Austen for a style that, not dependent on the image, brings the essentials somewhat closer to the surface with a greater depth of deep, generative grammar than the image can. But this is a huge subject.

John Edwards' house is in Suffolk. It is a brick house, and its outbuildings are behind a brick wall, in very flat green countryside over which the wind blew hard when Nikos and I were there. About twenty cars were parked in a field outside the brick wall. Within the gate we saw no one, and the place appeared deserted. It was only when we approached the house that I saw, through a window, Francis sitting at a table, talking to someone and smiling, not country people, but city people who preferred to stay inside.

Some sixty people were inside the house, most of them John's family and friends from the East End, and some queens from the Colony Room. I met John's mother and father, he a retired publican, and the rest of the family. They were all talkative and friendly and called me Dave. 'Whenever you'd like to come to my house in Portugal, Dave, you let me know,' one of John's brothers said, and I said I'd like that.

I wandered about the house, which is furnished with over-sized Victorian-Italian-Renaissance pieces, the mantelpieces elaborate. On the walls are many framed reproductions of Francis' paintings, among them paintings of John. In one room, Philip, sunk into an armchair, was smoking pot.

In yet another room, I found Nikos listening to Ian, the man who runs the Colony Room, shouting at Denis Wirth-Miller, 'You're a fake. A total fake. You're a terrible painter. The only person who would buy one of your paintings is the Queen Mother.' Denis, who at around seventy years old looks like a withered boy, simply smiled. His friend Dicky Chopping was also standing in the room, but looking away. I stood by Nikos and listened to Ian, who continued to shout at Denis, and Francis, wavering as he walked, came into the room and he, too, stood and listened with his head lowered, looking like a priest listening to a confession. When Ian paused, Francis raised his head and said calmly, 'It's absolutely true, Denis is a fake. That's what he is, a genuine fake.' Denis went on smirking, his teeth showing. I left.

I went to look at the outbuildings, one of them the cottage done up for Francis. The interior of one long outbuilding was converted into a snooker room with a fringed, green lamp hanging low over the snooker table. At the end of the room were floor-to-ceiling mirrors and a bar, and over a beam of what must have been a barn roof dangled a pair of boxing gloves. Some men were playing snooker.

I returned to the house to find Nikos, who said, 'You shouldn't have left. In a strange way, those men were showing affection for one another.'

We went to the snooker room, where Francis was watching the men playing. Francis said, 'I loathe parties. I simply loathe them.' Then John came into the room with friends and Francis said to him, with a wide smile, 'What a lovely party, John. Such a lovely party.'

Nikos and I had to leave. Francis walked us to our car. Outside the brick wall in the field, we stood in the wind and talked about John.

Nikos said, 'He's very special.'

'He's very special,' Francis said.

'He is,' I said.

'He can't read or write,' Francis said, 'but, you know, there really is something very special about him. You see, John is an innocent.'

In the car, Nikos and I waved at Francis who was still standing in the field. He was wearing a suit and tie. His thin dyed hair was blowing in the wind. He smiled and waved. The green field behind him was flat and gave way to equally flat green–gray countryside.

Why is it that the words I want to use, but which I am too intimidated to use because I'm told that they do not convince in the age I live in, are convincing in song, in, especially, Schubert, in Wolf, in Strauss? – in Wagner? I don't believe that such singing refers so much to the historical age in which the songs were composed that I can respond to them only as some residue of that past historical age, for when I hear the singing something rises in me, in this historical age I live in, that strains for an expression that I feel so passionately it has to be rising from deep within the age I live in. What is it that strains so for expression that I sense so deeply is in this age, but for which this age can't find the expression? The inner straining – yes, the longing – for the moment when everything does come together into a whole globe, and then the expression of it . . . ?

Nikos and I to Loudoun Road for lunch.

We talked about the bad reception I am getting for my book Difficult Women, about my relationships with Jean Rhys, Sonia Orwell, Germaine Greer, all taken from my diary.

I said, 'I don't understand what, in England, is private and what is public, what you can say "in the club," and what you can't say outside it.'

Nikos said, 'I don't know if I see the difference between what is known about me by a few people and by many people.'

'But there is an enormous difference, Nikos!' Natasha said.

Stephen sat back and looked worried, then he said, 'It shocked me when people objected so much to my portrait of Ottoline Morrell in my autobiography that they wouldn't speak to me – and all I'd said was that she dropped an earring in her cup of tea and, moving, disarranged her clothes so a breast was exposed – and yet these same people would, among themselves, say much more objectionable things about Ottoline.'

'I suppose I should worry that I have written objectionably about Jean and Sonia and Germaine,' I said.

'You perhaps should worry,' Natasha said.

'Nonsense,' Stephen exclaimed. 'You should write exactly what you want. For forty years I haven't written anything because I've been made to feel I'd offend if I wrote what I've wanted to write.'

'Oh,' Natasha exclaimed even more, 'that's not true!'

'It is,' he said.

'Well,' Nikos said, 'it is obviously a very complex moral problem.'

'Yes,' Natasha agreed; 'and I think writers shouldn't write auto-biography, but fiction, because, even though we may all know who's being written about, the public don't. Fiction is a mask.'

We talked on, Nikos often saying, 'It is a complex moral problem.'

After lunch, Nikos and I worked in the garden with Natasha for an hour while Stephen, in his study, worked on a book that Nikos had commissioned: a book about China, where Stephen had gone with David Hockney and Gregory Evans, Stephen to write the text, David to do the drawings, Gregory to organize them.

Perhaps Stephen is truly anti-class when he says, 'Write anything you want.' But, then, he doesn't do it. I do.

———

Vera R. to tea. She asked me, 'Tell me, David, are you, as I am, high-born?'

'No,' I said. 'I'm working class.'

'Oh, that doesn't matter. Henry –' I understood her to mean Henry Moore – 'is working class. I'm talking about something of the spirit. You've a high-born spirit.'

'Maybe that's my French-Canadian blood,' I said, and wondered if she knew I was joking.

She said, 'Yes, you have a high-born spirit, and, like me, are attracted, as high-born people are, to common people – you to common women, I to common men.'

'I never thought that,' I said. 'I'll have to give it a lot of thought.'
'Do think about it.'

I saw Stephen and Natasha, who had seen Germaine, I think at a reception. She had told them, as Stephen recounted, that I am a 'creepy crawler,' which made Stephen laugh his shaking laugh and made Natasha look at him with that somewhat suppressed delight she has in his being méchant.

A weekend with Frank and Anita K. in Cambridge, Nikos and I and Michael Craig-Martin. Michael helped Anita design the lay-out of her flowerbeds, which she can now consider works of art. While they worked, Frank and Nikos and I read the Sunday papers. Then lunch, and help laying the table while Anita cooked, she keen on using exotic spices. A sense among us of containment, yet, at the same time, of dimensions around us of the outer world of art and literature which we referred to as we ate. Stephen is right: we do live worlds within worlds. Also, extending in unknown dimensions all about us, were our different lives when we are not together. I know about Nikos' and my lives together, but of Frank's and Anita's only what they reveal by their easy reactions to each other on a charming weekend with friends, and Michael, who is wonder-fully knowledgeable and articulate about what is going on in the art world, reveals nothing about his life.

Then there are unexpected dimensions. Tony Tanner told me something that revealed, in the Kermodes' relationship, a passion and turbulence that I had not been aware of.

I sense none of that passion in Frank as he calmly smokes his pipe, which keeps going out and which he keeps relighting.

But some time later Anita told me this story from early on in her relationship with Frank:

She and Frank, having left their families and pasts to be together, were living in a rented flat across from the British Museum. There,

all of Anita's inherited jewelry was stolen, along with the food –
including a duck and the wine and cheese and even a cauliflower
– meant for a dinner she was going to prepare before she and Frank
were to leave for France. They did leave at the end of the rental
period, and had no place to return to. The idea was that they
would drive, in a rented car, to the South of France. In Angoulême
they quarreled. The reason for the quarrel was incidental to the
way Anita felt defeated by Frank's vicious use of words, leaving her
deprived of any language at all and helpless. The quarrel was so
fierce that they stopped at the first hotel in the town they came to
and Anita got out with her suitcase and Frank drove off to another
hotel. It was a Friday evening in the town, which was deserted, but
in the morning the square outside the hotel was filled with market
stalls, parked cars, a crowd of people. Anita waited but Frank did
not show up. She waited for hours, and he didn't appear. She felt
shocked and abandoned. After more hours, she thought that Frank
may have driven off to Stephen and Natasha's house, Saint-Jérôme,
in the Alpilles. She decided to chance taking a train to Maussane,
the nearest town to Saint-Jérôme, and there she found a hotel and
asked the proprietor to phone the Spenders, but no one was there.
Clearly, she had no idea where Frank had gone.

Several days went by. Then a dream she had about being alone
on a Russian seashore after World War III made her feel she was
alone in the universe, but that it was all right. On long walks in the
countryside she tried and failed to understand what had happened.
On the fifth day she thought to telephone a mutual friend in
London, and he told her that Frank was there, staying with him. In
Angoulême, market day, Frank hadn't been able to find the car he
had parked the day before in the town square; when he had found
the car, he couldn't remember what hotel he'd left Anita off at, and
went from hotel to hotel, but she was in none. He thought she
must have returned to London, so in his rented car drove back
there, where, with no other place to stay, he was staying with their
mutual friend. Though Frank had very little money, as did Anita,
he flew back to France and from the airport, rented a car and drove

to Maussane where he and Anita put their quarrel to bed. The mix-up in Angoulême, Frank tried to explain, was typical of the utterly absurd situations he tended to find himself in.

Hearing Anita tell this story, I, forgiving myself, laughed, but she laughed too. She said, 'It is all one with the passionate madness of our relationship.'

———

Do I dare put this in, which may smack of just what Nikos has told me I must not do, justify myself? I had from Philip Roth, living in London with Claire Bloom, a letter praising Difficult Women and asking if we could meet. Well, yes, we could, and we did, and we meet often for lunch in a restaurant in Notting Hill, where he has a studio. He told me he had had a long row with Harold Pinter about the book which may have ended their friendship.

As I was entering a drinks party, I saw, across the room, Vidia Naipaul, who with both arms raised beckoned me to him. On the way, I did stop to have a word with one or two friends and when I got to Vidia he said, with a smile, 'David, you have become so grand you didn't come immediately.' He put his hands on my shoulders and said that he had read my book about the women, his only criticism being that I was too kind, and that, because of the book, he had decided to stop writing fiction and from now on would write only non-fiction.

Philip said to me, 'You're a tough person. An enigmatic and tough person. Perhaps there's a note of masochistic self-exposure about the book, but you do stand out as tough.'

———

I collected John Lehmann in my car to take him to Stephen's for dinner. John is as feeble as he is big; he walked very slowly and unsteadily with a stick to the car and got into the seat with great difficulty; he smelled of whiskey and uncleanliness.

He said, 'I may have to leave Stephen's rather early, dear boy.'

John Golding and James Joll were also there, and the Australian poet Peter Porter. Natasha is in the South of France, and Nikos at the publishing house.

Stephen told me to sit at the opposite end of the table from him – he giggled – 'As the wife.'

He had prepared a huge roast, but the roast potatoes that went with the meat were inedible.

He seemed hardly to speak to John, on his right, and often Stephen got up to serve more beef, but not the potatoes.

From time to time, John would ask, 'How are your legs, Stephen?' or 'What did you think of the reviews of your last book, Stephen?'

After dinner we all went upstairs to the sitting room, the talk inconsequential, and shortly after John asked if I'd take him home.

In the car he was silent for a long while, then he said, 'I suppose I must accept the fact that Stephen and I, after all these years, can't be friends. I can't help but feel he's suspicious of me.'

'What do you mean?' I asked.

'I'm not sure what I mean, dear boy.'

'It's very interesting, and you should think about it.'

'It is interesting.'

'Oh yes.'

He said, 'I keep hoping that a true affection will flow between us but it never does.'

I let him off in front of his door.

The next morning I spoke to Stephen over the telephone, and recounted what John had told me, hoping that Stephen might be touched by John's wanting affection to flow between them.

Stephen said, 'Suspicious! Of course I am. Did you hear those catty questions he kept asking me? Still, perhaps I didn't pay him much attention during the evening –'

Stephen has said, with a laugh, that it's assumed he and John once had an affair because they are both so big; then Stephen frowned and, with sudden anger, insisted, 'We did not!'

———

Nikos is in Russia, commissioning books.

While he is away, Roxy and I went to Paddington Station to meet Joe and Jos Tilson, up from Wiltshire, to join a huge CND demonstration against the proliferation of nuclear bombs. Many special trains were arriving at the station, which was crowded with demonstrators who stood on the platform with their banners, waiting for the organizers with megaphones to tell them what to do. Some young punks, with red and blue hair and ☮ painted on their cheeks, were passing out placards on sticks; we each took a placard and by tube went to Notting Hill, where, at Ladbroke Grove, a third of the demonstration (the Western contingent) was forming into a long, wide march. On the pavements, West Indians were beating bongo drums. Young people wearing fall-out cover-ups, white with zippers up the front, passed along the crowd with plastic buckets, asking for donations, and people threw in loose change. We stood for a while on a pavement by the bongo players and watched the march go by, wanting to choose which banner, held by the leading representatives of each contingent, and when a beautiful purple banner with silver fringe approached we all said, 'That's lovely! That's the one!' but when we saw emblazoned on the banner FEMINIST LESBIANS AGAINST DEATH we decided to wait, given that we were not lesbians. There were banners for doctors, scientists, musicians, trades unions, and mostly for towns and cities from all over Great Britain. There came along a small wood of large, paper oak leaves carried on sticks, and on the leaves was SAVE NATURE, and Joe thought we should join this contingent, which reminded him of his art, and so we did, and behind the wood we marched down Ladbroke Grove, up Notting Hill, down Kensington Church Street.

At one point in Kensington Church Street we stepped out of the march to go into a pub for beers, and through the high windows of the pub we could see the banners go by. It was a bright, hot day.

We rejoined the march, which turned into Kensington Gardens and from there into Hyde Park, where we marched along curving paths, and at the curves were able to see, ahead and behind, the marchers with their banners, and the march appeared endless; it was as though we were looking at a distant march under the great green plane trees, and it was with a sense of wonderful unity that I realized that we were in a long, long march of demonstrators that reached so far ahead there was no seeing to the beginning and so far behind that there was no seeing to the end.

Demonstrators were also coming into the park from Hyde Park Corner and from Oxford Street. Our Western contingent along with the converging Northern and Southern contingents advanced towards a massive crowd in the middle of the park, all gathered about a platform and a number of huge megaphones high on a derrick. We didn't stay for the speeches.

A youth was arrested for igniting a smoke bomb, a harmless bomb that released a cloud of bright orange smoke. Five policemen took him away, two grasping his arms, all of them smiling. The boy, half the size of the smallest constable, looked down, frowning.

I thought, as we marched: this demonstration would not be allowed in Russia.

There were about a quarter of a million people.

Joe and Jos and Roxy came to the flat for lunch.

———

I drove Stephen and Natasha (just back from the South of France) to dinner at the Glenconners'. I sat between Natasha and Lord Esher, with whom I had a very interesting talk about 'half-truths' in writing and autobiography. He was wearing an ugly, green and red knit tie (a New Yorker, a stickler for what is and what is not done, once told me that one never wears a knitted tie in the evening, a fact of sartorial knowledge that the American would assume an Englishman must of course be fully aware of); and it came to me that he was not so much wearing that tie as wearing a tie, and it didn't matter what it looked like.

While he has been away, I've had disturbing dreams of Nikos abandoning me.

———

Stephen, laughing as he spoke, said he is very keen on hearing what Nikos has to say about Russia. 'We should devise a chart,' he said, 'with on one side the insights into Russia by Thatcher, Reagan, Brezhnev and on the other side Nikos' insights, and then calculate which side wins.'

———

Nikos has come back from Russia with many Communist badges on his lapels.

James Joll told him that he is the last of the Romantic Communists.

Nikos retorted: James did not understand what Communism meant in Greece after the defeat of the ideology in the Civil War, for Communism meant equality and justice for all people, meant the fulfillment of a promised Republic.

James nodded.

Nikos and I talked about the U.S.S.R. and the U.S., I complaining that, whereas he protests violently against the U.S. suppressions in the world he doesn't about the suppressions of the U.S.S.R.

He said, 'The two cases are utterly different.'

'They may be. I'm talking about what you feel towards Russia and America.'

He said, 'I loathe Russian suppression – of course I do – and you know that I love America. But I'll tell you: in my heart I believe that Russia is on the side of life and America is on the side of death.'

I sat back, silent, and I suddenly thought: is he right?

———

Getting into bed with Nikos, I said to him, 'You know, I don't believe I give you any joy.'

'Sachlamares!' he said, meaning, 'What rubbish!'

———

Both Stephen and I were surprised when, at supper, Nikos said about Russia: 'No one calls Leningrad Leningrad, but Saint Petersburg. The country is ready for another revolution.'

———

I always feel, in a social situation with Natasha, that she thinks my presence is a presumption on my part, as though I have somehow ingratiated myself into a world in which I do not belong. Stephen has told me that the only reason why Natasha has accepted us is because so many people she knows have accepted us. Elizabeth Glenconner, he says, particularly loves Nikos, doesn't stop talking of Nikos before Natasha, as if to let Natasha know that if she, Natasha, can't ever feel close to him, she, Elizabeth, does, and what else can Natasha do but sit at the same table with Nikos – and, by extension, with me? If I were a different kind of writer, I'd have presented to me the makings of a comedy of manners.

———

Stephen rang me to say he'd written a long account in his diary about a luncheon he'd recently had with John Lehmann; he wanted me to read it and invited me to lunch to do so. It is very funny and, I hope, indicative of the diary Stephen says he has been keeping religiously. What he wrote about John Lehmann has the quality of humor Stephen has in conversation but not in his writing, the quality in which resides, W. H. Auden said, Stephen's genius.

———

At the opening of an exhibition of Adrian Stokes' paintings at the Serpentine Gallery, I met Natasha, and together we walked to the Royal College of Art, where she teaches, I think, aspects of music. She said, 'Let's sit on a bench for a while and have a little gossip,' so we sat by a group of school children playing ball in Hyde Park, and chatted.

———

As we were standing together on a corner in Notting Hill Gate by a red postbox, Philip Roth and I were talking when an Englishman

I knew came towards us in the crowd, and I wanted him to see me talking with Philip Roth, but he didn't see us, and walked past.

When Philip is keen on whatever he is talking about, his nostrils contract. He stops talking, and his eyebrows, too, contract. I always take the first step to get us walking again. As we walk, he talks, and often stops, and he talks much more than I do, and much more intensely.

The last time we met at the restaurant, he talked of 'real stuff' in writing, and gave me this, written on a torn sheet of paper, to think about:

You must so change that in broad daylight you could crouch down in the middle of the street and, without embarrassment, undo your trousers, and evacuate.

I forget where the quotation comes from – I think from some nineteenth-century author.

Philip added: 'The emphasis is on the word could. Not that you would, because you wouldn't, but you should be capable of doing it.'

We went to his studio, a simple room in a white stucco town house, with a large electric typewriter on a desk and a huge waste-paper basket on the floor by the desk, the basket filled with discarded pages.

Philip said, 'Updike and Bellow hold their flashlights out into the world, reveal the real world as it is now. I dig a hole and shine my flashlight into the hole. You do the same.'

I said that I want to write about the moment I'm living in, as I do in my diary. In my fiction, I'm still an adolescent, learning about a world that's now no longer the world I live in.

We went on to a nearby restaurant, Monsieur Thompson's, with white tablecloths and white napkins peaked on white plates.

Philip asked me if I often think of death.

'For some reason,' I said, 'I'm reassured by death. I guess the reason is that death can't be faked.'

This startled him. 'Oh no,' he said, 'you can't be reassured by that.'

'I shouldn't be.'

His hand to his chin, he appeared to study me for a long while, then, with a quiet seriousness I have got used to in him, he said, 'Yet I'm sure of the final doom. The nuclear holocaust is well on its way.'

'And that reassures my dark soul.'

He dropped his hand from his chin as if with impatience with me, and brusquely asked, 'What is your dark soul?'

'Of course it must never happen, but that it could happen reassures me in my sense that what is true is that everything is fated for destruction and that there is nothing we can do about it all happening.'

Again, he stared at me. 'There is a devil, isn't there?' he said.

I laughed.

'Now I've become rather dark myself,' he said.

'I'm sorry.'

'Can you write when you're in a dark state?'

'Yes, I can.'

'I can't. I have to be in a lively state.'

We mixed up sexual obsession in our talk about doom. I said I am less and less obsessed, and this is a relief. He said, 'I'll be as obsessed when I'm eighty exactly as I was when I was eighteen.'

———

I visited Tony Tanner in his rooms at King's Cambridge. He asked me to attend a seminar he was to give on George Santayana. The Last Puritan meant a lot to me when I read it as a teenager, so I felt drawn to a seminar about his work, but, at the seminar table with the graduates, I realized that what I knew about Santayana (that he was homosexual, that he died cared for by Blue Nuns in Rome during the time of Mussolini, that he was Spanish but never repudiated Franco) would be irrelevant to the more elevated vision of the philosophy of Santayana that was the subject of the seminar. The moment I try to expound upon a philosophy, I'm lost, and in no coherent way can I articulate the vision. (Nikos can.) So I have to bring myself down from the high level of philosophy to the low level of sex, place, nationality, politics. I resent this deeply, because, oh, what I long to write is PHILOSOPHY. I said nothing during the seminar.

Back in Tony's room, he told me that he had tried to kill himself. He had made a terrible mistake leaving King's to go to Johns Hopkins in Baltimore and King's had him back. Drink ruined his nervous system so he walked with two sticks. But he always appears dapper, usually with a black polo shirt and a tweed jacket, and he was, as always, affable.

'Read this,' he said, and handed me, open to the page, Winnie-the-Pooh, and after I read about Eeyore's gratitude at being given a deflated balloon, Tony asked me, 'Whom does that remind you of?' and I said immediately, 'Frank!' and we doubled up with laughter. 'Of course,' he said, 'we love Frank,' and I said, 'Of course,' but we couldn't stop laughing.

Paris

We are in Paris, Hotel de Suède, with Julia. We've come to see the Chardin exhibition in the Grand Palais. The walls of the hotel room are pale grey, and the carpet is soft, pale grey. I am lying on one of the two single beds, the silky spread rumpled at the foot, and I am covered by a loose blanket and a sheet. When I lie back fully my head lolls on the bolster and the large, square pillow and I look through the net curtains of the double windows at the soft, grey rain falling. Lolling, I am attentive to all the most delicate details in the room.

From down a passage beyond the other bed comes the sound of splashing water. Those sounds of Nikos splashing water against himself in the bath fill me with great contentment.

Later –

Nikos came in from the bath and sat next to me on the edge of my bed, so I moved to let him lean back against the same pillow and bolster I rested on, and he looked with me out of the window where the rain was falling more fully.

I said, 'What a dreary morning.'

'Is it?' he asked.

'Isn't it?'

'You mean, outside?'

'I mean outside.'

'It's not so bad inside.'

And one of those times occurred as if different from anything else we'd ever known, together or apart.

Heavy rain was hitting the windows, and through it the light from outside became stippled with fine shadows in the room, and gently swaying vertical stripes appeared on the grey walls.

I ordered two cafés complets, and, each of us in a bathrobe, we sat on delicate chairs with rattan seats and backs at a delicate table with a marble top.

'Give me your cup,' he said. I did, and he poured into it steaming coffee from a tall white porcelain pot with a little bouquet of flowers on its side. The white cup, so fine the coffee showed through, was also decorated by a tiny bouquet of flowers. I took the cup back from him and added, from a heavy silvery jug, a dollop of milk that almost remained intact until, with a silvery spoon, he stirred it round and the black coffee turned dark brown. I said, 'I think I'll take sugar,' and Nikos handed me the two-handled basin, also heavy and silvery, from which I lifted a cube with the small tongs and dropped it, with a splash, into my cup, and then, saying, 'I'll take two,' I dropped in another cube and stirred the coffee and milk and dissolving sugar into a liquor that became rich enough to ripple thickly about the spoon, and, sipping it, I said, 'Oh yes,' and Nikos smiled.

There were croissants, warm and wrapped in a large, bright white napkin in a silver basket, and rolls of butter on crushed ice and little jars of jam, each one of which Nikos picked up to study – fraises, abricots, myrtilles – choosing, finally, the strawberry. I watched Nikos put the napkin, pleated and standing upright on his plate, to the side and pick up a croissant and pull it apart, the thin, flaky, tawny crust separating to reveal a pale, elastic interior, and, placing one-half of the croissant on his plate, he used the butter knife to take up a whole roll of butter, scored and dotted with water, to transfer it to the edge of the white plate, and then, with his shining knife, he spread the butter onto half the warm croissant, after which he used the tip of his knife to scoop up one whole but almost liquid strawberry to smear it into the melting butter. As he brought the confection to his open mouth, he looked up at me smiling at him.

When we met Julia in the foyer to go to the exhibition, she said that in the morning she had looked out of her window into the rain and seen a body in a body bag being taken out of the hotel into a waiting van, the back doors open.

———

Philip said to me, 'You're not taking care of yourself, David. You should join a club and go every morning for an hour's exercise. You're too young and good looking not to take care of yourself. And you should go to a hair clinic to get some treatment to keep your hair from falling out. It's too late for me, but not for you.' He went on and on. I said, 'All right, all right,' thinking that of course I wouldn't do anything of the sort.

———

Nikos' interest in aesthetics makes me interested, so I find myself wondering, Well, what does constitute a work of art? Self-containment, and within the self-containment proportion and balance?

We went to Paris for a grand exhibition of the paintings of Chardin. How beautiful the still lifes, in which the perspectives are all at different angles, and the whole so proportioned and balanced.

Even though John Golding claims Cubism to be a radical shift from Renaissance perspective, studying an Analytic Cubist painting by Picasso, I see it as self-contained, proportion and balance delicately, exquisitely sustained.

And then, at an exhibition of the works of Marcel Duchamp at the Tate, I stare at a miscellany of odd objects in a glass case, and I think, Well, out go self-containment, balance and proportion.

Michael Craig-Martin, teaching at Goldsmiths, told me that he had a Japanese student whose work consisted of his burning lumps of Styrofoam with a hot poker, and when Michael, not knowing what else to say, commented, 'It's very ugly,' the student responded, 'Yes, yes, very ugly,' and Michael went on to the next student.

He says there is no definition, none, to what is or is not art.

Perhaps there is an aesthetic for the unformed in art rather than the formed.

Karsten Schubert, gallery owner, says there is no way that one can relate the work of Andy Warhol to that of, say, Chardin, no way.

———

Lunch with Philip at Monsieur Thompson's. I had given him my story, 'Paris, 1959,' published in the New Yorker, to read and, if he wished, to comment on. He said it's the best writing I've done and he also said, 'You're an odd bird, Plante, a really odd bird. I'm not saying you write oddly, I'm saying you're odd, and that's why your writing is odd.'

I said, 'Your praising my writing terrifies me.'

'Why? Because you feel you've got to start taking yourself seriously as a writer?'

'If, five years ago, I fantasized about a respected writer praising my writing, I can't imagine I would have considered you as a possibility. Our writing is so essentially different from each other.'

'It is,' he said. 'But whereas you think you're a dreamy writer and I'm a realistic writer concerned with the hard facts of life, the opposite is true: I'm the dreamy writer who's always trying to invent a world in which all my dreams will be fulfilled. My writing doesn't come from my life. I make up everything.'

'And I'm a realist?'

'Yes, you are. Goddamn it, you are. You're tougher than I am.'

We talked about many subjects, always autobiographically.

He said, 'To be an American simply requires one to be obsessed with finding out what an American is,' and he described how he, from his childhood, felt he was a foreigner in America wondering what America was, and then he realized that this very condition made him an American.

I told him that Antonia Fraser once told me that she plays a game to herself whenever she is with you and her husband Harold

Pinter: she tries to guess which of the men will be the first to use the word 'Jew,' and within how many minutes of their meeting.

Philip asked me, 'How long do you give me?'

'Before you say anything else when we meet, even hello, you say, "Jew."'

He tilted his head back and laughed.

I said, 'You can question what it is to be an American Jew because there are enough American Jews to give you an American identity. Try questioning yourself as a Franco-American. We have no American identity at all. How many Franco-Americans do you know, and what do you imagine can be their identity in America?'

'I don't know any,' he said.

We walked together to a bookshop in Notting Hill, and he told me about Claire and how he loves her. He is quite sure he is keeping her from suicide. In the bookshop, he looked around for a short while as if generally, then left, and I stayed an hour.

———

At supper, Nikos told me that when he came to London from Athens, he was filled with ambitions. He had had a list of people he wanted to meet, and he has met them all. He said, 'I was going to take London by storm.'

'And do you feel you've fulfilled your ambitions?'

He smiled. 'Some,' he said.

'Which?' I asked.

'My biggest ambition was that I would meet someone and fall in love and live with him.'

'And was that ambition fulfilled?'

His smile deepened. 'Somewhat.'

Florence

In Florence, I rang Harold Acton. As there is only one telephone in the villa, I had to wait until he came to it, no doubt handed to him by the butler who had answered. He is well over eighty, and he seemed not to have changed since his sixties. He greeted me in the drawing room and made Oriental gestures of welcome, leaning forward a little and rolling his hands on his wrists. His skin appeared tight on his long face and bald head, his nose thin with high, arched nostrils. He started almost every sentence with 'Ooooh' and spoke with an accent that put the emphasis, often on one syllable of a word, at odd places in the sentences. 'Ooooh, you will tell me about people in London.'

He asked me, as he always did, if I would like to see the garden, and as we walked about the statues among the cypresses he told me, as he always did, how the cocks of the statues had been knocked off. Someone had suggested that Acton kept the statues as mutilated as they were to be able to talk about his 'problem' – should he replace the 'appendages,' or, instead, attach fig leaves which would, by the bulge in them, suggest 'something substantial underneath?' He retained his curious, lightly jerking walk.

His Tuscan kitchen would, he said as we walked back to the villa, produce a very modest meal, not up to the culinary delights he was sure I was used to. We had spaghetti to start, then slices of beef and peas served by the white-haired butler, Dino, in the high, vaulted dining room, among polychrome wooden statues of saints on chests.

Acton said he could hardly leave his house now – only for brief periods – for fear of its being broken into. It had already been broken into eight times. A painting by Daddi was taken off a wall and never recovered. He couldn't trust anyone, not even his staff. (About a new cameriere, he said, 'His room, into which I happened to step to enquire about some small matter, is a great mess, filled with cigarette butts –' he used the American expression – 'and reeking of cigarette smoke.') His staff didn't do their jobs properly, were in fact quite useless, but what was one to do today when help simply could not be found and no one was to be trusted? He delicately shrugged his broad shoulders and pressed his thin lips together. How he envied people who weren't dependent on staff, how he wished he weren't dependent, but what could one do? To give up his staff would be to give up La Pietra.

'How times have changed,' he said. 'When my parents were alive, they had a staff of thirty-five. I have only a staff of twelve, and I don't dare ask them for anything.'

When he started to talk about a recently published novel which he thought terrible, he became violently angry. He called the writer, a woman, a bitch, a slut, a third-rate whore – Barbara Skelton – and I had no idea why he should rage so against her, but thought it must be for personal reasons. He said, 'Yes, art excuses all. With art one can write about anything, anything. But that novel is too bad even to say about it that it was written.' He was raging.

To get him down to a subject that would make him less aggressive, I asked him what his favorite work of his own was. He raised his hands and said he always reread his work with great embarrassment.

I said, 'All writers do that. The fact is, we don't really know if what we write is good or bad.'

He bowed his head and said, 'Ooooh, that is true.'

And then he became light spirited, and began to gossip. He said, 'Count Morra, whom I used to visit in his peculiar villa outside

Cortona, used to be somewhat to the Left, you know, somewhat to the Left. I often wondered if this had something to do with his liking for Blacks.'

He became even more light spirited talking about sex, about, ooooh, lovely cocks.

After lunch, Acton asked me if I'd like a nap, as the train I was to take to London was to leave in the evening. He asked a maid to prepare the blue room, la camera blu, which I followed him upstairs to. It was a huge, high-ceilinged room, with a great bed and tapestries and paintings on the walls, and a view of the cypress avenue to the gates from the high windows. He left me with the maid, whom I helped put linen sheets on the bed. She also brought in an old electric heater because Acton said the room was cold. I undressed and got into bed and looked at the room beyond the gilded, spiraling columns at the corners of my bed, and I thought: Well, here I am.

He was waiting for me in the drawing room for tea before I left, and here he continued to gossip about people in London, mostly homosexual men, with lightness and charm.

He was as he had once been, when his talk was all lightness and charm, with pauses that suspended you in the wonder of what the point of a sentence was going to be.

He said, 'I am preparing for my departure –' he paused and smiled a little '– to Switzerland.'

After tea, I walked along the cypress avenue to the gate and got onto a crowded bus into the center of Florence.

London

Walking alone along Wigmore Street, I heard my dead mother call out my name.

———

Like Stephen (and he has noted this, joking that we are both Piscean, whereas Nikos is Scorpion), I do not have an analytical mind, and whenever I try to be 'philosophical,' whenever I try to 'intend' an explanation of a 'philosophical' vision, I make a mess of it. Still, I know that I am as if within the circle of a vision that is greater than myself.

It happens from time to time that I read something which sets off in me an illuminating awareness of the vision. (Nikos tells me that almost everything I read I read as if included in and expanding on the vision.) I think that what Frank wrote in The Genesis of Secrecy illuminates the vision. And recently I read in William James' lecture 'Philosophical Conceptions' this:

> A collection is one, though the things that compose it are many. Now, can we practically 'collect' the universe? Physically, of course we cannot. And mentally we cannot, if we take it concretely in its details. But if we take it summarily and abstractly, then we collect it mentally whenever we refer to it, even as I do now when I fling the term 'universe' at it, and so seem to leave a mental ring around it.

Oh, I think, yes, yes, that's the vision I have which is the mental ring about everything I think and feel, and certainly everything I write, even in this diary.

———

I'm at my desk in my study. Nikos just came in from his study, where, when we have a rare evening at home, he works on his poetry. He said, 'You're writing in your diary.' 'Yes,' I said. He said, 'I've stopped reading your diary.' 'I know,' I said, 'but why?' He said, 'You've been writing things against me, which I don't want to read.' I didn't think there was anything in my diary against him, though it is in him, as a Greek, to imagine even me writing things against him. He would never stop me from writing anything I want.

———

Stephen and Natasha came to dinner.

Stephen was very excited about the bitchy remarks about him in the latest volume of Virginia Woolf's diary to be published; he laughed a lot, quoting them.

Spender has the makings of a long-winded bore –

Natasha said, 'You'd think that Stephen would at least have been told by the editors, if not given the choice as to whether the remarks should be published or not.'

She spoke in an emphatically rotund way.

Stephen seemed to enjoy the notoriety of Woolf's remarks, if that's the word.

He went on to talk about Auden: 'He never wanted to drive a car. He always imagined himself, never a car, but a train, for which all the lights would automatically be changed to green.'

Someone is writing his biography, which Stephen is not enthusiastic about. As excited as he seems to be by Virginia Woolf mentioning him in her diary, he does not want a biography. This occurs to me: he is excited – excited and amused – by the Woolf comments because they're unsympathetic, because they don't take him seriously. Stephen can't bear to be taken seriously, not really, as he feels anyone taking him seriously would soon reveal the pretensions of the seriousness of, as Woolf wrote, 'his muddled theories.' He reads the Woolf comments as lively jokes, and he loves jokes, especially about himself. He told me that his favourite work of literature is The Importance of Being Earnest, and he adores reading parodies, especially Beerbohm's, which have become his preferred reading. As Auden once said, I recall, Stephen's genius is all in his sense of humour, and he has never used that in his writing.

Natasha has obviously read the first draft of the biography, because she said, 'I've got the writer to limit the use of "homoerotic" to once per page, so the second draft won't be as bad as the first.'

After dinner, we played Scrabble (Natasha of course won – she always wins – and there is among the other players a deference to her true intelligence) and then we listened to music. Again, within a private circle, Natasha is loving. Nikos and I knew that she and Stephen were both pleased to have spent the evening with us, and there were kisses all round with the goodnight.

Mind you, Stephen may be deeply hurt by the comments made about him by Virginia Woolf, whom I do not think of as a nice woman.

But many think of me as not a nice man.

Stephen said, 'I told Natasha that when I die I don't want any services of any kind, especially no memorial service. I made her promise that.'

Natasha appeared distracted, as she often does appear, and in her distraction a blankness comes to her face.

When this happens, Stephen tries to bring her into the conversation, which, however, she seems not to have heard.

She asks, 'Yes, darling?'

He presses his lips together.

Then he will tell another anecdote, slightly irreverent, laughing brightly. And Natasha, looking at him, smiles. She calls him 'méchant.'

The next day, Saturday, Nikos and I arranged books, went grocery shopping, had our usual afternoon nap, and in the evening went to a recital at the Wigmore Hall.

———

To dinner, Nikos and I, at Loudoun Road, the other guests Elizabeth and Christopher Glenconner and Anne Wollheim and Valerie Eliot.

It comes to me that dining tables are very often the settings of diary entries, and this is because dining tables are where people most often gather. Valerie Eliot was very amusing, her skin smooth and clear and bright. (Stephen says she has marzipan hair.) There were times when I thought she had all the gusto of a young working-class man in drag affecting seriousness and class, and then suddenly the seriousness and class would collapse and she'd laugh. I'd thought she'd be reserved about talking about her husband, but no, not at all – 'Tom did this, Tom did that.'

We were sitting together on a sofa before going down to the dining room to dinner. She told me how when she and Tom were in America newspapermen invaded their privacy all the time, even to hiding tape recorders behind sofas. I said, 'It's dreadful, the way they have no respect for privacy.' 'Yes,' she said, 'dreadful.' Then she asked what I do and pretended to have heard of me when I told her. She asked what my last book was, and I said, 'Oh, I think you'll disapprove of it. It's an invasion of the privacy of three friends.' 'Oh?' she asked, and her eyes widened. 'Yes,' I said, 'I've written of my rather personal relationships with Jean Rhys, Sonia Orwell, and Germaine Greer.' She rubbed her hands together, threw her shoulders back, and, her face bright red, she exclaimed, 'But that sounds like great fun!' and it was as though she was prepared for a good old gossip. But Natasha, hearing us, came over and changed the subject; Valerie Eliot, however, wouldn't change, and told me stories about the writer Djuna Barnes and what a difficult woman she was! Again, it was as though she had dropped all the affected disapproval of a middle-class woman to become suddenly a drag queen eager for a gossip and loving it, even parodying it with slight exaggerations of her hands and voice. I was sorry when we had to go down to eat, where we were separated. I sat between Natasha, who never sits at the other end of the table from Stephen, and Anne.

I heard Valerie Eliot talking with Christopher. She said something about 'Tom,' and he asked, 'Who's Tom?' She answered, 'Oh, my late husband, who was Tom Eliot.' 'And what did he do?' Christopher asked. 'He was a poet,' she said. 'Oh, isn't that lovely,' Christopher said; 'a poet! What fun to be a poet!'

Christopher never remembers who Nikos and I are, but is as gracious to us as if we just might be old friends. He never quite knows where he is, but acts as if wherever he is is familiar to him. He laughs and claps his hands and says, 'How lovely! How lovely!' He probably doesn't recognize Stephen and Natasha.

She prepared a wonderful meal: onion soufflé, then poached salmon with boiled potatoes and cooked cucumber and homemade mayonnaise, then a pudding of sliced apples cooked in butter. Champagne and very good wines.

As Nikos and I were leaving, Stephen, laughing, said, 'I know I'm getting old. You may be alarmed by it, but for a moment this evening, when you both came in, I didn't know who you were.' Nikos and I laughed with him.

———

Could T. S. Eliot have been a human being, married, in love with Valerie? Could he have been more than a disembodied spirit?

I did once see him. He came to Boston College, when I was a freshman, to give a reading of his poetry, and I sat marginally on the stage while he, centered at a podium, read in a low cadence, the cadence often the meaning of the poem whose meaning was higher than my understanding. And now I think the meaning was higher, too, than his own understanding.

I used to think he knew exactly what was meant by the lady and the three white leopards under a juniper tree, but I think now he wrote somewhere between intention and the unintentional, and often the unintentional rose higher than the intended, and he let this occur, let this occur especially in the music, so the music filled his low dry voice with the resonance of what his poetry tried to say but, on his own admission, could only fail saying.

I do go to Four Quartets for spiritual recourse.

But I think

> In the room the women come and go
> Talking of Michelangelo

the silliest couplet in the English language, 'go' and 'Michelangelo' occurring suddenly to Eliot, who liked silly rhymes, his only way of using it seriously in a serious poem, however, to condemn it as silly, so it is not he who is being silly but the women coming and going in the room. And the exegeses on such silliness.

In fact, I often go to Four Quartets for spiritual recourse, as this, written with such conviction:

> And all shall be well and
> All manner of thing shall be well
> By the purification of the motive
> In the ground of our beseeching.

– the word 'beseeching' stirring in me the residue of a religion in which to beseech was, perhaps still is, the impulse, though to whom it may still be the impulse I have no idea.

What a relief it would be to think and feel within the defining intentions of a religion, which I imagine T. S. Eliot finally did.

I recall from the church services of my youth: pray for the intention of . . .

The unintentional and the intentional – what Nikos would call the antinomies, arguments contradictory but equally reasonable.

Florence

Harold Acton is dead. I spoke at length about Acton and La Pietra with Giuseppe Chigiotti, a young, close friend of Acton, particularly in his last years.

He told me the funeral in the church of San Marco in Florence was very solemn, with carabinieri in full-dress uniform flanking the coffin. John Pope-Hennessy was the first to arrive, then Joan Haslip, the historian of European royalty, looking rather like a widow. (Joan Haslip had hoped to be left something by Acton, but she got nothing.) The butler, the cook, the head gardener (who, alone of all the domestics, was left five million lire, about three thousand dollars) were present, and a few people from the Florentine aristocracy. Florence was represented by many officials, and the British ambassador gave a reading. A young, distant kinsman of Acton appeared, wearing a hat with a feather, and was shown to the front of the church, the only self-proclaimed kinsman of Acton to attend. But there seemed to be no representatives of the royals, whom he had entertained at La Pietra, not even an equerry. The Mass was said by the Jesuit priest who had administered Extreme Unction to Acton.

Was, I asked, Acton religious? No, Chigiotti said, religion for him didn't exist. He was, however, superstitious, and kept chestnuts on his desk and medals in his pocket. Though he didn't have anything to do with religion, the formalities of the Catholic Church were very important to him. He was, to the world, a man of great formality, a formality he felt was in keeping with La Pietra.

After the Mass, people were invited to the villa for breakfast, during which Chigiotti saw that some objects were missing from the rooms. There was, he found, no proper inventory of the contents, and the disappearance of items went unexplained. Chigiotti wondered if the key to the La Pietra safe was still under the wooden Buddha in the library where it had been kept when Acton was alive.

The day after the funeral, New York University held a luncheon party at the villa to inaugurate its activities. La Pietra, Chigiotti said, was supplied with an avalanche of silverware, but the silver was gone. And never would Acton have had a marquee put up on the grounds, but there it was, huge. And never would he have walked with people about the garden with drinks (he always accompanied guests about the garden, didn't leave them to wander on their own), but there hundreds of people were wandering in the garden with glasses. And many of the people invited to this luncheon Acton, who was very open about inviting people, would never have invited to his home – people he didn't like, people who simply wanted to see where the royals had stayed, small functionaries from Florence.

Giuseppe Chigiotti, an attractive, clear-faced man with delicate eyelashes, held up his hands and shrugged.

Could he tell me why Acton left nothing to Florence, which had made him an honorary citizen shortly before he died? Chigiotti said that Acton's relationship with Florence was 'un po' complicato.' Certainly Florence had hoped to get something. The Uffizi was hoping they would get the Vasari, and the Bargello one or two statues.

But Acton knew that the Bardini collection, which had been given to the city, was destroyed by being dispersed, and he did not want La Pietra to be destroyed in the same way. It would be better to give La Pietra to an English or American university, with Harvard's commitment to Bernard Berenson's I Tatti as a good example of what an English or American university could do. La

Pietra was offered first to Acton's college at Oxford, Christ Church, who turned it down, then to New York University, who accepted.

However, there were other reasons why Acton didn't leave anything to Florence that went back to his parents and the way the Italian Fascists had treated his mother. Mrs Acton refused to have anything to do, not only with Florentines who had been Fascists, but with all Italians, and spent most of her time in the villa, dressed in Chinese Mandarin clothes, drinking. Acton's mother so repudiated Italy, she would go, once a month, all the way to Switzerland to have her hair done. And Joan Haslip said to me, 'Because of the way his mother had been treated by the Fascists, Harold would never have dreamed of turning La Pietra over to the Italians.'

But Florence had never taken much interest in the Actons, as it had never taken much real interest in Berenson and his circle. As provincial snobs, the Florentine aristocracy had few relations with foreigners, and most of these few were entirely sexual, not social. Acton's father had affairs with Florentines with whom he had illegitimate children, but there was the question of his own legitimacy (Arthur Acton, whose name does not appear in Burke's Peerage, may have been illegitimate, and all the information Harold Acton gives about his father's past in More Memoirs of an Aesthete is: 'as an orphan he had been brought up by priests . . .'), which itself would have made him not quite respectable.

Though Harold Acton, after his mother's death, did entertain Italians, including some members of the Florentine nobility such as the Frescobaldis, Florentines on the whole, if they thought of him at all, thought of him as too worldly for them. When he was knighted, Florentines were not impressed – they had thought Acton was a baron, which was in fact a title given to him by his domestics.

But by the time Acton did impress Florence by having the royals stay, particularly Prince Charles and Princess Diana, Acton lost interest in the city. He was invited everywhere, and, out of as much curiosity as a sense of duty, he went (though before he went to certain houses, where he knew he would be served only a scrawny battery chicken, he asked for sandwiches to be made at La Pietra for his return), and he was more and more disappointed. He had thought the city had something for him, had thought he would discover a Florence of interesting people, as interesting as Florence was in the twenties and thirties, when Orioli was publishing sexually explicit books that couldn't be published elsewhere and there was an Italian avant-garde. He didn't find it.

Florence, Chigiotti said, drained Acton. Even the British Institute, which his father had helped found and which he was for a while governor of, and where he was treated as a royal himself with an armchair in the first row for any lecture he attended, in the end disappointed him. It was for his services to the Institute – and not, he would say with a wry smile, for his writing – that he was knighted, but he argued with the director, his old friend Ian Greenlees, about Greenlees' boyfriend, who behaved badly and insulted people and was simply not sortable (passed the jug of cream, he would, after pouring some onto his pudding, lick the spout before passing it on) but who was made by Greenlees the Institute's librarian, and Acton distanced himself.

Though he didn't think his life's work was to be the custodian, the vestale, of La Pietra, what else was there for him to be? Because of La Pietra, Acton became worldly in a way he did not want to be. He became something of a tourist attraction in Florence, showing around strangers from England and America who had heard about La Pietra.

He became, Giuseppe Chigiotti said, a prisoner, not only of his duties toward La Pietra, but of his own illusions about his fame. Every time he walked down the main street of Florence, the Via Tornabuoni, he imagined people recognized him. Chigiotti would tell Acton about places he'd been to for a bit of amusement, and Acton, who was always very curious, especially about anything that had to do with sex, would say, Oooh, he wished he could go, but how could he, with La Pietra on his shoulders? Though he was not a puritan about sex, his grand sense of ufficialità would not allow him to be public about what he in private had no reservations about admitting, with a warble of pleasure. And he became especially concerned about his reputation when the royals began to visit, as he would have worried very much about his causing, as their host, any sexual scandal that might reflect on them as guests.

However, Acton learned to use La Pietra. The young friends of older friends were always welcome, and no doubt a handsome young man of twenty to twenty-five would be very impressed by Acton, as polite and deferential as a Chinese aristocrat, inviting him into his humble house.

In the end, he had lived in five rooms – his small study, the library, but only to pass through it to go to his study, the drawing room, the dining room, and his bedroom – and all the rest of the rooms were eternally closed.

Soon I will be in Lucca, in a flat Nikos and I bought for holidays, and here I find myself within yet another world among the many worlds I appear to live in.

Every year, for the past 1,168 years, a procession takes place in Lucca in honour of the Volto Santo, or Holy Face, a dark, wooden, Byzantine-like, life-sized figure of Christ which is supposed to have been carved by a disciple, Nicodemus, and which mysteriously reached the Ligurian shores in a boat pushed off from the coast of ancient Palestine, a long and circuitous way. Both the Pisans and the Lucchese claimed the Volto Santo, their dispute resolved when the statue was placed in a cart with two white oxen on a road that diverged at one point toward Lucca and at another point toward Pisa, and the oxen took the road to Lucca. The Volto Santo became one of the most revered icons of the Middle Ages, and it is seriously revered, as everything in Lucca is. It is a conservative town, and when it celebrates the festival of the Volto Santo, called La Luminara, it does so with a certain calm, even grim, devotion. There is something even a little severe about the procession, with drums beating a slow, heavy march, and long periods when it progresses in total silence.

I was invited by a Lucchese woman to view the procession from the open windows of her palace. Along the old stone sill, held by rusted iron rings long ago inserted into the stone, was a row of flickering white votive candles in clear glasses. Across the square the palaces were all outlined, along window sills, around the architraves of doorways, along the lengths of façades, with flickering candles, so that the buildings appeared to disappear and Lucca, all other illumination turned off, became a transparent town made up entirely of candle flames. And when I leaned out the window, I saw the long line of the procession, the people in it carrying candles, enter a cathedral of light, the bell tower illuminated at each arched Gothic level with fire. The last people of the procession to enter the cathedral were dressed as they would have been dressed centuries ago, the men in doublets and the women in gowns with long, loose sleeves, their waists cinched in tightly.

The party I was invited to was held in an apartment with high, high-beamed ceilings and dull red-tile floors without rugs, and large paintings of mythological figures and tarnished mirrors in Venetian frames tilting out from the walls, where a *cameriere*, wearing a white, high-collared jacket, circulated among the guests, the women wearing pearl necklaces and the men somber ties, the *cameriere* offering glasses of red or white wine or orange juice. And at the end of the procession, the *cameriere* came in with a large steaming tureen of pasta. I was not only in a different world, I was in a different age.

I spoke with a woman who is the minister of culture of the town. She is, she said, worried about mass tourism, bus loads of tourists who wander the narrow, traffic-free, medieval streets in large groups. Lucca doesn't need tourism, she said; Lucca is a rich place. Smiling a little, I suggested shutting the town gates, those enormous, wooden, spike-studded doors, some quite rotted, which perhaps haven't been shut since they were opened for Napoleon.

I left the party about eleven o'clock to go into the cathedral, all the high pillars draped in red damask, and to see, in a separate little temple behind a grill, the Volto Santo, wearing a golden crown, a golden apron and golden shoes which are for the rest of the year preserved in the cathedral museum.

And then I wandered, alone, around Lucca. Off the main streets – the principal one being the Fillungo, paved in endless semi-circles of small paving stones – I found myself completely alone, though the votive candles were still flickering along the outlines of the buildings. I felt, alone, not only safe, but secreted away in the town, and because secreted away in possession of the town. As I crossed a narrow side-street, I saw, where it ended at the town walls, fireworks exploding on the walls, and I stood and watched them, then walked on, and saw no one else, no one else at all, until I reached the medieval building where Nikos and I have an apartment. But I stood outside in the street for a while longer, amazed, I suppose, by the sense of everyone in the town behind locked doors and closed shutters, while their streets were still blazing with candles.

I heard, in the far distance, an odd sound. The sound became louder and louder until I saw, coming toward me, a woman on a bicycle. As she passed me, saying 'Buona sera,' I noticed the chain of her bicycle was hitting the mud guard and making the noise, that tiny noise echoing throughout the silent town. Then there was the deep, deep silence again.

I went to have a look around La Pietra, invited by Alexander Zielcke, a painter and photographer, and Acton's companion for some thirty years. It was raining. Inside the gates of the grounds, the taxi passed, on the right of the avenue up to the villa, an olive grove with high, uncut grass. In the wild-looking olive grove was a very well-maintained, small garden and in that garden well-restored buildings identified by a sign as offices of OLIVETTI, who had the buildings on a lease from the estate. Just as the taxi left the olive grove a statue on a pedestal appeared, its forearm broken off, a rusted iron rod sticking out from an elbow.

The taxi circled a great stone tub in the midst of clipped hedges and stopped at large, nail-studded, double doors, shut. A woman, in a pink and white striped smock and a blue and white striped apron, was standing at a smaller door to the left. As I got out of the taxi, she said that she was the cook, Vanna, and that all the other servants had gone, and, also, that there was no one guarding the villa. She spoke in a high voice, as if I were very far away, and she apologized that she couldn't show me in through the main entrance but must ask me to come in through this side entrance. This led into the chapel of the villa, grey and white, with tall candlesticks and two bottles of champagne on the altar. In the holy water font just to the side of the entrance were, I noted, some rags. The chapel looked dusty. When I asked if it had ever been used, Vanna said no, no, as if it had never occurred to her that it could have been used. It led into an anteroom with a telephone, and from this room I went into the main entrance hall of the villa.

The rotunda, built into what was originally the fifteenth-century central courtyard, had a fountain in the middle, a huge stone goblet with goldfish. A circular flight of stairs, with tapestries hanging on the curved walls, went up to the next floor.

The rotunda was where Harold Acton had been laid in state for three days.

Vanna took me beyond into the drawing room, il soggiorno, to show me the chair where il Barone always sat, a red, wing-back armchair among other armchairs and a red sofa. The upholstery of the chairs looked stained and threadbare.

From there, we went through a doorway at the side of a huge fireplace into the vaulted library, with medieval wooden polychrome statues of saints on top of the Renaissance shelves. Hanging over the long table in the center of the room from chains were three lights, the red, fringed shades shredded and decomposing. In a corner was a large Buddha.

The study, like the library, was vaulted and had Renaissance bookshelves, but as narrow as a passageway. The shelves were sagging under sets of books such as The World's Best Literature, The Encyclopaedia Britannica, La stirpe de' Medici di Cafaggiolo. Acton's desk was a big table, narrow like the room, on which were piles of papers that looked as if they had been there years and years, untouched, and in the midst of the papers a framed, black and white photograph of a thin, elegant woman which appeared to have been taken in the thirties.

I said to Vanna that must be Acton's mother.

Vanna sighed and said yes, a beautiful woman. He loved her very much.

On the desk was a silver pen holder which had in it, along with old pens and pencils and stamps and paperclips, chestnuts. Touching them, Vanna said il Barone thought they brought luck.

He was a Catholic, wasn't he? I asked.

Oh yes, Vanna said, il Barone was religious. He kept in the breast pocket of his jacket silver medals and crosses. No, he didn't go to church, but he believed. He received Extreme Unction and Communion before he died.

Vanna bit her lips, as if hesitant, then said that three days before il Barone died he called for her to come to his room. He was suffering so much. He asked her to put her hand on his back, and she did, and that helped him. He thanked her sincerely. Tears rose into Vanna's eyes. Il Barone was a very special person, she said, unique, a gentleman who even when he was in carpet slippers always wore a suit with a vest. She missed him very, very much. Would she stay on when the villa was taken over by the University? She looked around and more tears rose to her eyes, and wiping them away, said she didn't know, but she was very attached to the villa. 'Sono molto attaccata alla villa.'

At the rear of the study were closed double doors, and when I wondered what was behind them, Vanna opened them into what she thought was a sala d'attesa, a waiting room. On first view, the room, Venetian-like, with delicately painted walls and sconces with porcelain statuettes, gilded armchairs upholstered in yellow silk, a birdcage on a scagliola-topped table, appeared grand, but the more I looked the more I saw flaking, nicks, worn patches, a fine greyness over everything, and I thought no one had sat in one of the chairs for ninety years, which was since Acton's father, Arthur Acton, had bought the fifteenth-century villa and had it redone.

Vanna asked if I wanted anything to drink, and I said, yes please, a glass of mineral water. Because I wanted to see as much of the villa as I could, I followed her down a passage into a large, vaulted anteroom to the kitchen, with glass-fronted cupboards all round the walls filled with piles of plates and wine glasses, and silver salvers and silver platters with covers. On the walls over the cupboards were pock-marked frescos of landscapes in tromp l'oeil. Vanna took a glass from a cupboard and a silver salver from another and placed the glass on the tray, and I followed her into the kitchen proper where there were plastic bottles of mineral water on a table.

The kitchen was stark, with two large working tables in the middle, a stainless-steel sink, and a gas stove which Vanna said was getting too old to cook on, and was no longer good for the soufflés il Barone had liked so much.

She told me how every Monday the maggiordomo, the butler, came and told her he was in his armchair in the soggiorno ready to talk to her, and how il Barone would, gentilemente, tell her to sit by him, and they would go through the guest list of the week, arranging menus according to who was coming. When the Prince and Princess of Wales had stayed, they'd eaten her food, though they ate little.

Then, as if she couldn't not tell me and had been waiting for the moment, she told me, breathlessly, that she had seen il Barone, he had appeared to her, but, looking around to make sure we were alone, she said people would think her mad for saying this. 'Io sono molto sensibile,' she said. She sensed presences. She was sweating, and said there were presences around which were making her sweat. Then she began to weep more.

From another part of the villa, someone called, 'Vanna, Vanna,' and she, anxious, ran, I behind her, to the room with the telephone, where Alexander Zielcke, a large, pale, middle-aged German with grey, longish hair combed smoothly back and leaving his ears exposed, was waiting. In a slightly false voice, Vanna told him that she had been telling me how il Barone and she used to discuss the week's menu.

Zielcke, impatient with her, said, No, il Barone never was so concerned about the week's menu.

He was, Vanna insisted.

'No, no,' Zielcke said, turning away abruptly. Then he turned back and asked Vanna for coffee to be brought up to the office and she went back to the kitchen. Zielcke left me to wander alone, which I could not have done while Acton was alive.

I went up the circular stairs in the rotunda to the next floor. The shutters couldn't be opened because of the alarm system, so there was electric lighting in the corridors. I wandered down a long corridor, with double doors along it which I opened into dim, shuttered bedrooms, the bedclothes heaped up on the beds, and bathrooms with enormous tubs behind screens, and chaises longues and tables covered with objects.

I passed an internal window, and through it saw the pink-orange plaster falling away from a wall.

The master bedroom, called la camera della Baronessa, which had been the bedroom of Acton's mother and which had been used for royal visits by the Prince and Princess of Wales, by Princess Margaret, by the Queen Mother, had a large Renaissance bed, covered with a red silk counterpane, with gilded columns at its corners, and over the grand fireplace the most valuable painting in the villa, a Madonna and Child with Saint John the Baptist by Vasari, still in its original frame. The fringe hanging from the bottoms of the chairs was in places coming off, the gilt on the slightly tilting columns at the corners of the bed was worn, and the counterpane looked as if it had not been cleaned since the Renaissance.

From this bedroom I went into a bathroom, where a man in jeans and a tee-shirt was measuring a wall from a corner to the edge of the deep embrasure of a window. He was taking measurements of all the rooms. Beyond the bathroom was a low, very narrow room with a new toilet, perhaps put in especially for the royals.

When I came back along the corridor, I found Alexander Zielcke and the lawyer in charge of the will and the secretary in the office, all gathered about a sheaf of papers held by the lawyer. I nodded at them and continued down another corridor.

In a huge, dim room, many eighteenth-century chairs were

lined up along the walls. I was in the ballroom. From there, I opened double doors onto another room, so dark all I could see were points of dim light and shapes of furniture, and I didn't search for a light switch. I shut the doors and returned to the office.

Before I left, Zielcke said he would walk around the grounds with me. With an umbrella, we went into the walled-in garden to the side of the villa, where vegetables and flowers for the house were grown. There were many lemon trees in pots which would, during the winter, go into the immense limonaia, a vast building with a dirt floor and huge beams along one side of the garden. Then we wandered about the formal garden at the back of the villa.

Zielcke said he had been having some of the box hedges replanted. He couldn't have done this while Sir Harold, as Zielcke called Acton, was alive. Sir Harold, who didn't notice how the garden was going in places, would have been worried by someone replacing old, dying hedges with new ones. He had thought everything was in perfect order. The garden, designed in 1904 by Sir Harold's father after a Renaissance garden, was as old as Sir Harold himself. I noted, as we walked about the garden, that the statues were crumbling, as were the architectural follies. A stone bench in front of cypress trees was broken in two. The steps of pebbles imbedded in cement were covered with moss and the kerb stones cracked. Sections of hedge were missing, and sections so overgrown I could see through the dark green leaves to the grey twisted branches.

I am, I know, indulging somewhat in the decay of the villa, and, with the villa, the, to me, fantasy life lived there. Perhaps I am jealous, perhaps, and want it all to decay. I do realize, more than ever, just how much Harold Acton was a fantasy figure to me, and, yes, the fantasy does – no, did – hold me. Trying to be as sincere as I possibly can be, I also realize that the fantasy no longer does hold. Nikos is right to have derided me for my fantasy figures. The sense of possibility I had in knowing Acton – the possibility of entering a world that should have been the realization of a young man's most colorful vision of an artistic, a social, and, especially, a sexual world – seems to me exposed as having in fact little possibility in it, and, in fact, to be abandoned by the world for some other world that Nikos would approve of. The world of Harold Acton is in no way in my world to revive it in my memory, but I have the deep sense that it has little inner value in the memory of the outside world, which outside world Nikos has always been more aware of than I have.

If I were to tell Nikos this, he would simply smile, not quite believing me.

London

Of course, I think of writing novels and short stories, which require forms of art, as being superior to writing a diary.

Where else but in fiction can such moments occur as – ?

When, in Pride and Prejudice, Darcy lets go and admits to Elizabeth: 'I love you.'

When, at the end of Dostoyevsky's The Idiot, Prince Myshkin weeps over the body of the murderer Rogozhin, so his tears drip on the face of Rogozhin.

When, in Conrad's Heart of Darkness, we hear out of the darkness, 'Mr Kurtz, he dead.'

When, in Hardy's Jude the Obscure, we read the note, 'Done because we are too menny.'

When, in Waugh's Brideshead Revisited (and this is the only novel by Waugh that rises to the pitch), Lord Marchmain makes the sign of the cross before dying.

———

When I tell myself, everything is too much, I can't bear it, what, I ask myself further, is that everything that is too much and that I can't bear?

If too much, let go of everything, let go for –

What?

———

When I saw Nikos silently lower a book he had been reading –
Chekhov stories, and I knew in particular 'Ward Number 6'
– now in tears, this came to me: that Nikos feels he is a defeated
person.

In him the sense of the unbearable is not merely aesthetic, but
moral, spiritual, because it comes to him with such an acute awareness of all that is unbearable in the world.

This came to me: that I need him to give authority to an authentic moral and spiritual awareness of the world, he so much more a
witness than I.

Then this came to me: that as I do need him for the authenticity
of a feeling I have in me, the feeling has to be in me, has to be in
me and has to be crying out to him to make it relevant to a world
I hardly belong to, a world in whose history I have so little a part,
but a world that I feel is the world at its most authentic, which is
Nikos' world.

Does he know this about me, that I need this in him because it
is a need in me? A strange need. I think he does know, for, his book
lowered, he stares at me staring at him, and he smiles a little, and
what happens? – I feel roused in me an almost sexual desire to go
to him to be held by him.

About Chekhov: how can any reaction to his work be anything
but moral, spiritual?

———

As the birthdays of our neighbor Joseph Bromberg and of Frank
coincide, Nikos and I offered to give them a joint birthday party.
In the dining and sitting room, we arranged card tables covered
with white cloths, and bought folding chairs, enough places for
some fifteen or more people. Anita helped to serve the Kidonato
– lamb and quince – that Nikos had prepared. And there were
many bottles of wine. Most of the guests were friends of Frank and
Anita: Al and Anne Alvarez, Jonathan (writer and director of plays
and operas) and Rachel (medical doctor) Miller, Luigi (novelist)
and Katia Meneghello, and our mutual friends Richard and Mary

Day Wollheim, and Nikos' and my friend from Greece, Fani-Maria Tsigakou. And, Philip Roth being away from London, Claire Bloom on her own. The Brombergs supplied the dessert, a confection of ice-cream in a bowl made of ice.

It is very strange to meet someone who is as famous as Claire Bloom, so that when I am with her I am with Charlie Chaplin in Lime Light, with Laurence Olivier in Richard III (which I saw when the film was shown on black and white television in the living room of my family home when in 1955 I was fifteen, an event of very high culture), with Richard Burton in The Spy Who Came in from the Cold. Claire's refined beauty appears to be one with the refinement of a culture she represents as an actress, and even when we are talking about, say, the weather, I hear in her voice the voice I have heard declaiming Shakespeare. In person she seems shy, and often pulls back her hair as if suddenly not sure of herself, and then a look of sadness comes to her eyes.

About Chekhov, Claire Bloom made this remarkable connection – when she was in Hollywood preparing for her part in The Brothers Kavamazov with Yul Brynner to play Vronsky, he suggested they have a Russian coach, Michael Chekhov, the great-nephew of Anton Chekhov.

———

Fani-Maria is staying with us. She is a curator at the Benaki Museum in Athens. Thames & Hudson published her book The Rediscovery of Greece, which expands on what Nikos has told me about Europeans and Europeanized Greeks wanting in A.D. 1830 to reclaim 500 B.C. Greece from the defeated Ottoman Empire.

Fani-Maria explained how the myth of ancient Greece has been such an influence in Greek history.

During the four hundred years of Ottoman Occupation and continuing after Greek independence from the Occupation, the myth of Hellenic Greece – that is, the myth of a unified Greece that in reality hardly ever existed in ancient history – was kept alive as a way of 'determining the ideological and cultural identity of an independent nation in the collective memory of Greeks.'

This myth has had some bad consequences.

'Hellas' became the rallying cry in the early nineteenth century for Greece to invade Turkey to win back the Empire of the Hellenes, but Greece lost, and the result was the Catastrophe.

'Hellas' also became the rallying cry of the colonel dictators, who used the age of Pericles as their dictating mythological vision of Greece.

That myth of ancient Greece in Greek education is still seen as a source of enlightenment dating from the ancient illustrious ancestors, but also resented because it is a myth. The Greek political Right emphasize that ancestry, which the Greek political Left keep challenging as nationalistic.

And yet, the myth is there, informing Greeks that they have a past that dates back to Plato and Aristotle, Solon and Pericles, Aeschylus, Sophocles, Euripides, Aristophanes, Phidias and Praxiteles, Ictinus and Callicrates, for the reality of the myth is that the greatest philosophers to define all the philosophy of the Western world remain Plato and Aristotle, the statesmen who defined Western democracy were Solon and Pericles, the greatest playwrights ever are Aeschylus, Sophocles, Euripides, Aristophanes, the greatest artists are Phidias and Praxiteles, the greatest architects are Ictinus and Callicrates, and all were Greek. There is a degree of indulgence for a Greek in – and here Fani-Maria stopped for a moment as if not sure she should use the word, but then she did – 'narcissistic' feelings for being poised between the myth and the reality of Greece's classical past, with an emphasis on the myth.

Well, what is the reality? There is no doubt that there exists one unbroken and living bequest from the classical past: the Greek language.

Fani-Maria said she becomes both furious and sad that not just foreigners but Greeks are unaware that, however altered grammatically and syntactically, modern Greek is in an unbroken line from ancient Greek, the vocabulary of which can be traced back to Homer.

I said I recalled from when Nikos and I, on the island of Paros, were walking along a field where farmers were working, and a woman raised her arm at us and called, '*Xairete*,' and Nikos told me that that is an ancient Greek expression of welcome.

'There, you hear?' Fani–Maria exclaimed.

When I asked what remains in Greece of the four hundred years of Ottoman Empire, which most Greeks I know do not quite recognize as a determining part of the reality of Greek history, she listened but she didn't respond.

As I want to get world events into this diary, I should put in that, after a referendum in Greece, the young King Constantine, heir to the Greek throne, lost, and now lives as ex-King with his family in London.

Stephen told me that his daughter Lizzie, who had been on holiday in Greece where, with friends, she more or less lived and slept on a beach, back in London was invited to an event where she knew the ex-King Constantine would be, and she brought along photographs of Greece to show him, he filled with nostalgia for a country he cannot return to.

Nikos said that the ex-King has enough money in Switzerland that he doesn't have to be nostalgic for Greece, which, given his non-Greek ancestry, was never his native country.

———

Philip telephoned to say he is back in London after the funeral and burial of his mother. He said he couldn't look at her body. He didn't want that meaningful image to obliterate all the images that matter.

During the two weeks he spent with his father he took notes about the funeral and burial. He is still taking notes.

I asked, 'What kind of people are we that we don't even stop taking notes about the funeral of a mother?'

'Good enough,' he answered.

'Are we?'

———

At an Italian restaurant with John Lehmann and his young nephew or cousin. John moves with great difficulty because of his hip. He is hard of hearing. His hands shake badly, so when he pours out wine the bottle shakes against the glass and wine spills over. His false teeth keep falling out; he smiles a tight, sinister smile to keep them in. So few people like John. Do I like John? Like or dislike, such unimportant opinions; I neither like nor dislike John, for there he is, and I am interested in him for what he is. His nephew or cousin and I did most of the talking while John smiled at us.

His nephew or cousin is an historian. I said, 'I know so little history, but would you consider me justified to think that historians have tried for too long, and with too limited a vision, to identify nations and national politics and sciences and arts, whereas, really, they should pay much more attention to international politics, to the international influences on the sciences and the arts? I think history should refer outwardly to relating and integrating the whole world in every historical event. Steven Runciman, I believe, does this.' He said, 'Yes, you're right, history should do what you say, as expansive a task as that would be. But I don't like the history of Steven Runciman so very much; his writing is dull.'

As I do, and I'm ashamed that I do, I assumed to know better by knowing Steven Runciman, and I said, 'I once asked Steven if his style of writing was influenced by any other writer, and he answered, immediately, yes, Defoe.'

This made John's relative jut out his chin.

———

When I mentioned to Caro Hobhouse that Sybille Bedford was to me a mythological figure, a writer whose work I think of as itself having a mythological aura about it, especially The Legacy, Caro said, 'But Sybille Bedford is not at all a mythological figure,' and she arranged a dinner party for me to meet her. I arrived early, and Caro asked me to stir a special sauce she was cooking and not stop stirring until she told me to, and I felt at ease, as I felt at ease with Sybille Bedford, the talk about the table mostly about haute cuisine. Sybille Bedford appeared to me a dry but sharp woman, her face pale and her long thin hair pulled back severely except for strands. I knew that she knew Bruce Chatwin, and she said how much she did admire his writing and took it seriously, if – and here she smiled a tight smile – she found him in himself perhaps a little too glamorous to be taken with total seriousness, and, as circumlocutious as this was, I sensed it was a dry, sharp judgment. I felt I should be wary of her for her judgments on any form of pretension, but I wanted her to like me. I offered to drive her home, which she accepted, and outside where she lived we sat together in the car for a little while and she thanked me for admiring her work, which, however, was earning her so little she was not sure what she would do, and I felt she was making herself vulnerable to me, and, by making herself vulnerable to me, I thought that she must like me. I asked if I could see her again, and she said it would be a pleasure.

A week or so later I invited her to a restaurant not far from her in Kensington Church Street, collected her, and hoped the restaurant, though simple, would be to her liking, which it was as she asked for a card and even the number of the table we sat at so that she would be able to reserve it. I asked her to choose the wine, which she did carefully, clearly aware that I was being extravagant by inviting her. She said sharing a meal is a ceremony, and I did imagine we were engaged together in a ceremony of getting to know each other.

She talked about Brian Howard, whom she knew: a failed poet, an exquisite man who, having found his wallet and all his clothes stolen from him in a male brothel in Paris, borrowed an apron from a maid and went out into the street to hire a taxi to take him to his hotel; he was very courageous during World War II, acting in the resistance to save people's lives at the risk of his own life, a soldier at the landing of Dunkirk, an agent for MI5.

Now a connection occurs from outside: Keith Walker rang the day after he came to a supper party at our flat to say that he had had an adventure back at his flat during the night: wanting to pee, he, still drunk and stark naked, went out of his flat onto the landing looking for the loo, and the door shut behind him; he waited until dawn and rang the bell of his neighbour to ask for a blanket, and, wrapped in the blanket, he went out into the street to hail a taxi to bring him to his office at University College where he had extra keys to his flat and money.

Keith thinks that the recently discovered long poem by Byron about his love affair with a boy in Athens is genuine.

Back to Brian Howard, with another connection to the side: Stephen told me that Howard once complained to Auden that he, Auden, didn't have enough imagery in his poetry, so Auden wrote 'The Fall of Rome' (dedicated to Cyril Connolly, but I'm sure there is a poem by Auden dedicated to Howard), which has the most haunting last image of any imagery I know of:

> Herds of reindeer move across
> Miles and miles of golden moss,
> Silently and very vast.

Stephen – who, I think, is not within the world of Harold Acton, nor Christopher Isherwood nor W. H. Auden – told me that Blanche, of Brideshead Revisited, is partly based on Brian Howard, Stephen referring to a world that he seems to look at from a distance.

I know that whenever I mention Steven Runciman, Stephen frowns with disapproval.

Yet another aside: when referring to W. H. Auden to Nikos and me, Stephen never calls him Wystan, even when in his presence, but always as 'Auden,' as if Stephen is shy of presuming on familiarity with Auden.

My mind is always making connections, now so many that I do begin to think that they refer to one another more than they refer to me, so that I have begun to assume that everyone I meet knows everyone else, and all of them with their own interconnections too complicated for me to sort out.

Sybille Bedford had heard of Nikos, and asked about him – and how long had we been together, where did we live, did we have pets? Then, leaning towards me over the table, she said, 'You must always hope to outlive Nikos to save him the pain of grief,' and for a moment we looked steadily into each other's eyes. She did not talk of herself, and I knew I shouldn't ask her. When she stood to leave, she put her hands into the pockets of her trousers with something of a masculine gesture, and she appeared about to fall over but she righted herself and walked to the restaurant door, as if leaving alone.

––––––

Something I've been wanting to write about – I rang Claire to invite her and Philip to dinner, but they couldn't make it. I emphasized how much I want to see them, and sent her love, etc. After I hung up, Nikos admonished me, 'You were totally false. Utterly insincere.' I groaned. 'I know, I know,' I said. 'I thought you had outgrown your falseness, your insincerity. Your niceness towards Claire was completely unconvincing. I really thought you had reached a point in your development where you were no longer like that.' I groaned more. 'What shall I do?' I asked. He said, 'Be aware. The fact is, you're intimidated by Claire and Philip, that's why you are the way you are with them. I thought you were no longer intimidated by people you think grander than you are. I thought you'd even become bold.' 'You're right,' I said, 'I am intimidated by them. I've ceased to be intimidated by most people. But I am by them.' 'Why?' he asked. And I thought: He isn't intimidated, so can't understand being intimidated by people I believe to be on a level of having something I do not have.

Later, this occurred to me: that, yes, I have ceased to be intimidated by certain people because I do not want anything from them, whereas I remain intimidated by people from whom I want something they have, which, in the case of Claire and Philip, is their fame. This is difficult to admit.

––––––

When Nikos came home from work, he, cold, got into a hot bath and while he soaked I sat on the edge of the bathtub and we talked. I left him to go down to the kitchen to prepare hors d'oeuvres

– mussels and bits of lobster and spring onions and thin slices of toast – and drinks, for when he came down, and we talked more. For supper we had a gray mullet baked with dill and lemon, and we talked more. Nikos said, 'How lucky we are to have what we have,' and then he added, 'Spit three times because we may lose it all,' and I said, 'We won't lose it.'

———

A party at Claire and Philip's house in Fulham. At 10:30, I said to Philip, 'I must get home and write in my diary for an hour. I don't want to experience any more today, I've got all I can manage to get in. So no more stories from you.' He said, 'I'll write my stories down for you and you can simply paste them in.' Nikos and I came home and, very tired from seeing so many people, went to bed. I had had no intention of writing in my diary, and I wonder if I'm at the point of giving it up, as I so often want to do.

———

Stephen rang to say that he'd woken that morning at three o'clock and couldn't go back to sleep. I asked him why. 'I have so much work,' he said. He is working on publishing his journal, on a new Collected Poems, on his translation of the Oedipus plays. Stephen is the least self-indulgent person I know towards critical reception of his work – that is, outwardly – and he expects others to be the same. He was annoyed with me for being upset about the bad press I had for Difficult Women. I feel he is now upset by his bad press which has continued since the publication of his last book of poetry, The Generous Days, but he would never admit this. As Auden used to say, 'Mother wouldn't allow it,' I think Stephen says to himself, 'Wystan wouldn't allow it.' I wonder if the reason why he can't sleep is that he is in fact worried what the reaction will be to his journal, his Collected Poems, his translation – all of which he must feel his final work.

I've sensed in the past his hidden upset as a tremendous inability to concentrate on what I'd been saying to him, as if he couldn't help thinking of something he at the same time told himself he must not think about. He frowns. Perhaps because he is such a big person, all of this seems to happen on a massive scale. Then, suddenly, he does rise above his upset, and I tell him something that makes him giggle.

Because Nikos was too tired and needed to be alone for a while – he worries about losing his soul by socializing – I went alone to Loudoun Road for dinner with Stephen and Natasha and Lizzie, en famille. It was a deeply pleasant evening. 'Cozy,' Natasha called it. I left feeling I love them, their lives, their house, the objects in their house –

The next day Natasha was off to the South of France, to Saint Jérôme, to pick olives. Stephen rang. Often, speaking to one or the other of us, he'll say, if me, 'I'd like to ask David –' and if to Nikos, 'Would you and Nikos like to –' as though he displaces one of us for the other. He didn't have anything to do that evening, and wanted to invite Nikos and me to dine at the Savile Club with him. I told him to come have supper with us at home. Julia Hodgkin coming.

Nikos and I prepared risotto, mussels, salad and cheese, tangerines, marrons glacés and coffee, and of course wine. Stephen and Julia kept saying, 'A feast!'

Stephen said, 'Wystan always thought that if he got a bad review it was because the reviewer wanted to go to bed with him. He never cared about reviews. Now, what do we think about them?'

Quietly, Julia said, 'We don't think about them.'

Stephen said, 'Yes, quite,' and he sat back.

Julia then said, 'Of course I'm not the one to say, as I don't get reviewed.'

I wondered if Stephen was referring to the mixed reviews his latest volume of poems has had, The Generous Days.

He had given copies to Nikos and me, each one of us, a deluxe edition. In the one he gave Nikos he inscribed, 'see page 9,' on which page is his poem to Nikos, now a 'Fifteen Line Sonnet in Four Parts.' In the copy he gave me he inscribed, 'see page 16,' and there I found this poem:

PRESENT ABSENCE

You slept so quiet at your end of the room, you seemed
A memory, your absence.
I worked well, rising early, while you dreamed.
I thought your going would only make this difference –
A memory, your presence.
But now I am alone I know a silence
That howls. Here solitude begins.

This poem refers to that time when Stephen and I were at Saint
Jérôme, supposedly working in the garden planting trees but tour-
ing about with Francis and George. Stephen and I shared a large
room, he sleeping at one end and I at the other, I sleeping deeply
and, yes, dreaming. When I read the poem, I think: does he love
me so? Does he love Nikos so? In whatever way, he loves us, I feel,
as a couple, even more than he loves us individually, and his love is
a world about our world.

I also feel that London loves us as a couple more than we are
loved individually, and I owe London that love.

———

How often lines from Stephen's poems come to me, as:

My love and my pity shall not cease . . .

Or:

Was so much expenditure justified
On the death of one so young and so silly
Lying under the olive trees, O world, O death?

And I try to see these thoughts and feelings as having come from
Stephen when I see him. They move me as if distanced from him,
and often enough lines move me more than entire poems (which
happens to almost all poems I read), but do I read them as having

been written by Stephen, he at our dining-room table for a supper of cottage pie, which he likes? And yet, he wrote the lines, and I am aware that somewhere in his spirited talk is a deeper spirit, that of love, of pity, of grief, the deeper spirit which in love, in pity, in grief calls out, O world, O death!

And how beautiful and mysterious the lines:

> The outward figure of delight
> Creates your image that's no image
> Dark in my dark language.

Philip belongs to a club in Pall Mall, the Royal Automobile Club, where we from time to time have lunch, he always ordering chicken sandwiches without mayonnaise, as he is very conscious of his diet for reasons of health. His health is a big preoccupation. About the club, he of course joked about being a Jew who finagled to get in. The last time we met, he told me he has decided to move back to New York. Claire will go with him. He needs the vulgarity of New York against the politeness of London, the hypocritical politeness. He needs someone in a traffic jam to roll down his window and shout at him, 'Asshole,' which would make him relax and with a deep sigh of relief feel he was back at home.

He told me he had taught Claire to use the word FUCK, and had had printed as the headlines of a fake newspaper something like SHE HAS USED THE WORD! and presented it to Claire, who was amused and touched.

Of course, once again, I ask myself why I keep a diary, why I have kept it for years, day after day after day, trying to include everything that I can possibly include. Is it, as Nikos tells me, because I am so possessive that I must get everything in? The only other way, I think, is to leave everything out, and not account for anything.

I think that in the end, whatever the end may be, my diary will have nothing at all to do with me, but on its own bulge with such a vast roundness that it will go on turning of itself, and I will no longer command a diary but the diary will command me. My diary is in itself more possessive than I am, possessed by the concept of everything, and impelled by the possession. I have tried, over and over, to stop writing my diary, but my diary won't allow me to stop. My diary is a vast jealous One who will have everything, and won't listen to me insisting that that can't be, that my diary can have this or that or the other, but cannot have everything, which is impossible; no, the One will. This is a One beyond believing in One or not, a One with the One's own all-commanding will to have everything in one great round world.

———

I've lived long enough in London to have memories of my life here – as when Nikos and I were with Francis in the Colony Club, where the barman – not Ian, but a young man with tight black curly hair who was very very good looking – flirted with Nikos, who responded with a shy smile. I had never seen Nikos respond to someone flirting with him, nor would I have thought he would have responded by smiling a shy smile, because I don't think of Nikos as shy. My reaction was to wonder: why wasn't the barman flirting with me?

———

Evening after evening alone together at home, Nikos and I. We are very close – closer, I think, than ever before. He has come round to loving our flat here at 38 Montagu Square, as I do: our home.

We listen to music, Nikos and I, always his choosing, as he has much more understanding of music than I do, and I defer. My ear concentrates on the moment, on, say, a passage, while

Nikos hears the development of a passage into a whole, as in a fugue.

We were sitting side by side on the sofa, listening to Artur Schnabel play a Beethoven sonata, and it occurred to me to wonder again:

What is that too much when, listening to music, you feel that the music is too much, is beyond all my feeling and thinking too, and you tell yourself, I can't bear this?

Frowning as he listened, Nikos' eyes were closed.

Will whoever reads this indulge me for claiming that this is what I feel, this is what I think, when I look at Nikos and tell myself I can't bear my love for him?

He seems to me to be content.

As I write this, I hear him come in downstairs and call me –

————

Some time after Francis Bacon died, Nikos, looking through the catalogue of a posthumous exhibition, came upon a photograph and stopped and, calling me over to the desk, pointed to it and said, 'That's you!' Among the mess of rubbish left on the floor of his studio, piece by piece catalogued and sent to a reproduction of Francis' studio in a museum in Dublin, was this:

I recognized the photographs from when, in the train station at Avignon, Francis, George, Stephen and I had taken photographs of ourselves in an automatic photographing box. From the number Francis had taken away with him, he later pasted three strips on the back of an old cover of a book. In the caption under the reproduction in the catalogue I was not identified. I rang Miss Beston at Marlborough Gallery, who took care of Francis – if he wanted £10,000 in cash, she had it sent to him – and I identified myself, and she sent me the above. My wonder is: why did Francis paste me alongside himself and George?

————

Both Nikos (he at a weekend conference in the country) and Natasha (she in the South of France) away, Stephen invited me to dinner with Julian Trevelyan and his wife Mary Fedden. I did not know his paintings, but looked them up, and wondered if Surrealism was ever really possible in Britain, as Surrealism requires deep shadows and I have no sense of these deep shadows in the British, considered by the British as negatively unBritish as Logical Positivism is British. It seems to me axiomatic that for a Brit, if it can't be articulated, it is of no interest. Yet there is a primitive charm to his work. As there is to hers, based on, say, the simplicity of fruit and flowers.

Julian talked of having been the head of the Etching Department at the Royal College of Art, where one of his students was David Hockney, and he praised David's line.

Stephen had prepared, or bought, kipper pâté, then a risotto which I helped him with. His shirt tails were out and he was in his stocking feet.

During supper, he said, 'I sometimes think that the most important relationships are invisible relationships. Matthew is my son, but, really, I think of him as a brother, and our being brothers is an invisible relationship that is stronger than the visible. I think I have invisible relationships with David and Nikos in which they are my sons. All these relationships are so much more real than the visible.'

I was very moved by this, and, walking home, I thought of all my invisible relationships, invisible even to me but important to me, and I thought: they are your reason for being alive and loving life, those invisible relationships all around you right now, as you walk home.

I slept alone.

I'm reminded of the fragment from Sappho that Nikos used in 'Pure Reason': ἐγω δε μόνα κατεύδω . . . I sleep alone.

———

I often think of how I almost didn't meet Nikos. I was given his name and telephone number by a mutual friend in New York and I rang him on my arrival in London and he invited me to tea on a

Sunday afternoon, but when I at four o'clock rang his doorbell at 6 Wyndham Place he didn't answer. I thought he had meant five o'clock, so wandered about Hyde Park for an hour, among people lounging on the grass in the sunlight, then returned and rang his doorbell, and he answered, and I, oh yes, went into a trance that has lasted all these years since. He told me later that he, standing at the window of his flat, had seen me ring a bell but his bell inside hadn't rung. When he saw me leave he went out to test his bell and found it didn't work. He unscrewed it, attached some wires that had become detached, and thought, that was that, assuming I would not return, as he would not have returned if someone who had invited him wasn't there to welcome him. If he had not lived on the ground floor and had not been standing at the window to see me, and if he had not wondered if I was the one he had expected and, after my leaving, had not gone out to check his bell and repaired it, and if I had not returned, I would not have met him. But I did return.

———

Here are some photographs taken at a book launch given by Thames & Hudson, photographs I found in a drawer that bring back memories of the world Nikos and I have lived in:. Sonia and me, behind us Frank Auerbach:

Nikos:

The back of Big Suzi, on either side Francis Bacon and Stephen Spender:

Robert Medley and John Russell and Frank Auerbach, Francis in the left-hand corner:

Freda Berkeley and Lucian Freud in the distance (and next to him, I think, the head of Marlborough Gallery, Harry Fischer) and the eye surgeon Patrick Trevor-Roper:

And so we have lived long enough in London to look back at events fixed in photographs.

———

How little I account for in my diary, how very very little.

Some Thirty Years Later

I remain an American citizen, and I am also, officially, a British citizen, with my United Kingdom passport in which I am inscribed as a citizen, an anomaly, certainly, as the United Kingdom is not a republic.

So many of my early fantasies about living in England did come true. As writer in residence at King's College, Cambridge, I did sit at High Table wearing an academy gown. I sat across from the Lord Kahn who, I was told, had given to Maynard Keynes all his ideas about economics. I had pre-prandial sherry in the combination room with the Bloomsbury paintings hanging on red walls, and I went to the College Feasts when all the silver was brought out from the vault. I had drinks in the rooms of Dadie Rylands, there where, on a window seat, Virginia Woolf had thought of writing A Room of One's Own, Dadie's rooms decorated by Dora Carrington, and on the wall a portrait of Lytton Strachey. In a cupboard I found the pictures that had hung in E. M. Forster's set, the one I most remembered of a boy leading a horse by Picasso. I went every evening to Evensong, especially during Lent when the chapel was almost empty but for the dean, the lay dean, the choir and the choirmaster, the boys singing plainchant and the flames of the candles in their glass chimneys shaking in the cold drafts.

But so much of the London I knew in the first formative years of my life here has gone.

W. H. Auden is dead, Sonia Orwell is dead, Mary McCarthy is dead, Philippe and Pauline de Rothschild are dead, Francis Bacon is dead, Stephen Spender is dead, Natasha Spender is dead, John Lehmann is dead, Adrian Stokes is dead, Patrick Procktor is dead, Johnny Craxton is dead, Lucian Freud is dead, James Joll is dead, Frank Kermode is dead, Richard Wollheim is dead, Catharine Carver is dead, Patrick Kinross is dead, Christopher Glenconner is dead, Tony Tanner is dead, Anne Wollheim is dead, Sylvia Guirey is dead, David Sylvester is dead, Joe McCrindle is dead, Eva Neurath is dead, Robert Medley is dead, Anne Graham-Bell is dead, Keith Walker is dead, Bruce Chatwin is dead, Vera Russell is dead, Öçi Ullmann is dead, John Fleming is dead, Ben Nicolson is dead, John Russell is dead, Nikos Georgiadis is dead, A. J. and Dee Ayer are dead, R. B. Kitaj and Sandra are dead, John Edwards is dead, Barry and Sue Flanagan are dead, Francis King is dead, Olivia Manning is dead, Max Gordon is dead, Sybille Bedford is dead, Mario Dubsky is dead, Joseph and Ruth Bromberg are dead, Sebbie Walker is dead, John Golding is dead, Angelica Garnett is dead, Valerie Eliot is dead –

And, oh, my great love Nikos is dead.

Julia Hodgkin, our pal when Nikos was alive, the primary witness to our ups and downs and always reminding us of the ups, came to his burial in Athens and she held me as I sobbed in her arms.

I went with her to visit the cathedral at Durham, which I had for years wanted to do with Nikos, and which Julia proposed we do shortly after his death.

When we entered the great Norman cathedral, I had the vast sense, a sense held down by the grand pillars, of vast associations that I would not have felt had I not been British, a sense that I was now within my history. That the history of the cathedral is Norman, a history imposed on Anglo-Saxon history, made me aware of layers of history, layers and layers, and all together British history.

And, too, I had the more personal sense that I have my own British history. I came to London from New York in 1966 with a sense of total failure – failure in my vocation as a writer and failure in relationships. In London with Nikos I began a positive life, and to have lived for forty years in a relationship sustained by love, and, too, to have achieved some realization of a vision as a writer, can only be to have grown from the immaturity of previous years into years of maturity in London. Yes, that's it: I grew up in London, the most important years of my life those early years in that world – early years that developed into later and later years, all those forty years during which Nikos' and my inward world extended into an outer world. Nikos and I had – and I still have – our deep London past, and by extension beyond London into Wiltshire and Devon and Yorkshire and Cambridgeshire and Oxfordshire and Somerset and Cornwall and Cumbria and Wales and Scotland our British past, our past of friends and events, of worlds within worlds which I felt revolving around me in the cathedral.

Julia and I stayed in the cathedral for a long while, the sunlight through the high windows slowly fading. The hour for Evensong was approaching, and as if in inverse order to the central service of the cathedral tourists left rather than gathered. Julia and I sat at the very front row of chairs to watch the procession, the verger leading, carrying a great silver mace over a shoulder, followed by other members of the clergy and the choir into the choir stalls. A member took hold of the thick, multi-coloured pull attached to a rope that, beyond view, was attached to the bells, and the sound of the bells was so distant the resonance was all we heard. And the choir sang.

At the same time, in all the cathedral towns of the realm, choirs were singing, as they have for centuries.

Whatever 'British' means to me, at that moment the meaning was filled out, rounded out, with love.

Acknowledgements

Bloomsbury has opened up a world to me, and for that I thank Alexandra Pringle, Michael Fishwick, Anna Simpson, Phillip Beresford, Oliver Holden-Rea, David Mann, Paul Nash, Tess Viljoen and Ellen Williams; Nancy Miller and Sara Mercurio at Bloomsbury in New York; and Peter James, Sarah-Jane Forder and Geraldine Beare.

Index

A NOTE ON THE TYPE

The text of this book is set in Bembo. This type was first used in 1495 by the Venetian printer Aldus Manutius for Cardinal Bembo's *De Aetna*, and was cut for Manutius by Francesco Griffo. It was one of the types used by Claude Garamond (1480–1561) as a model for his Romain de L'Université, and so it was the forerunner of what became standard European type for the following two centuries. Its modern form follows the original types and was designed for Monotype in 1929.